VIA AUGUSTINI

STUDIES
IN MEDIEVAL AND
REFORMATION THOUGHT

EDITED BY

HEIKO A. OBERMAN, Tucson, Arizona

IN COOPERATION WITH

THOMAS A. BRADY, Jr., Eugene, Oregon
E. JANE DEMPSEY DOUGLASS, Princeton, New Jersey
GUILLAUME H.M. POSTHUMUS MEYJES, Leiden
DAVID C. STEINMETZ, DURHAM, North Carolina
ANTON G. WEILER, Nijmegen

VOLUME XLVIII

VIA AUGUSTINI

Damasus Trapp, O.S.A.
In honorem et cum gratitudine

VIA AUGUSTINI

AUGUSTINE IN THE LATER MIDDLE AGES, RENAISSANCE AND REFORMATION

Essays in Honor of Damasus Trapp, O.S.A.

EDITED BY
HEIKO A. OBERMAN AND FRANK A. JAMES, III

IN COOPERATION WITH
ERIC LELAND SAAK

E.J. BRILL
LEIDEN • NEW YORK • KOBENHAVN • KÖLN
1991

The paper in this book meets the guidelines for permanence and durability of the Committee on Production Guidelines for Book Longevity of the Council on Library Resources.

Library of Congress Cataloging-in-Publication Data

Via Augustini: Augustine in the later Middle Ages, Renaissance, and
  Reformation: essays in honor of Damasus Trapp / edited by Heiko A.
  Oberman and Frank A. James, III, in cooperation with Eric Leland
  Saak.
      p.   cm.—(Studies in medieval and Reformation thought, ISSN
  0585-6914; v. 48)
    Includes bibliographical references and index.
    ISBN 90-04-09364-8 (alk. paper)
    1. Augustine, Saint, Bishop of Hippo—Influence.   2. Theology,
  Doctrinal—History—Middle Ages, 600-1500.   3. Theology, Doctrinal—
  History—16th century.   I. Trapp, Damasus.   II. Oberman, Heiko
  Augustinus.   III. James, Frank A.   IV. Saak, Eric Leland.
  V. Series.
  BR1720.A9V53   1991
  270.2'092—dc20   91-6912
                                                              CIP

ISSN 0585–6914
ISBN 90 04 09364 8

PRINTED IN THE NETHERLANDS

CONTENTS

ABBREVIATIONS

CChr.SL	*Corpus Christianorum: Series Latina.* Turnhout, 1953ff.
Lectura	*Gregorii Ariminensis OESA Lectura Super Primum et Secundum Sententiarum*, ed. A. Damasus Trapp and Venicio Marcolino, vol. I: Super Primum Dist. 1–6 (1981); vol. II: Super Primum Dist. 7–17 (1982); vol. III: Super Primum Dist. 19–48 (1984); vol. IV: Super Secundum Dist. 1–5 (1979); vol. V: Super Secundum Dist. 6–18 (1979); vol. VI: Super Secundum Dist. 24–44 (1980); vol. VII: Indices (1987), Spätmittelalter und Reformation Texte und Untersuchungen 6–12, Berlin, 1979–1987.
PL	*Patrologiae cursus completus: Series Latina,* ed. J.P. Migne. Paris, 1844–1865.
WA	*D. Martin Luthers Werke. Kritische Gesamtausgabe.* Weimar, 1883ff.
WA BR	*D. Martin Luthers Werke. Kritische Gesamtausgabe: Briefwechsel.* Weimar, 1930–1985.
WA TR	*D. Martin Luthers Werke. Kritische Gesamtausgabe: Tischreden.* Weimar, 1912–1921.

VIA AUGUSTINI: INTRODUCTION

With a variant upon the sobering French insight, "Les hommes passent, les institutions subsistent," it can be said that "Les livres passent, les editions subsistent." As long as medieval studies will be pursued, the name of Damasus Trapp will be remembered and respected for the seven-volume critical edition of the Sentences Commentary of Gregory of Rimini (†1358).[1]

With a paleographical precision unequalled in our day, and with a photographic memory of the Vulgate Bible, the Latin Fathers, and the scholastic doctors, Damasus Trapp was able to constitute Gregory's text and identify a vast number of quotations and allusions to the preceding tradition already in his first draft. Further, as a wise, patient, and warm leader of a team of younger scholars, he not only guided this vast project through the arduous process, from first transcription to final printing, but also trained a new generation of editors who are now applying themselves to new undertakings, such as the Sentences Commentary of Hugolin of Orvieto (†1373) and Marsilius of Inghen (†1396).

The foundations for this truly *magnum opus* were laid in some thirty articles over thirty years. The reason why my original plan to celebrate and honor the 80th birthday of Pater Damasus Trapp—on September 3, 1987—by publishing his collected articles had to be abandoned is an indication of the significance of his work. The response of a broad phalanx of scholars was unanimous in asserting that they not only kept these articles on their library shelves, but also lived with them as daily companions.

This original plan was not rejected, but transformed when Professor Frank A. James, III offered to cooperate in the venture of preparing a thematic *Festschrift*. The chief disciples of Damasus Trapp—both in a direct and an indirect sense of the word—were asked to express their gratitude in the form of a contribution to the clarification of the late medieval *via Augustini*, elucidated in so many ways by Pater Damasus himself.

---

[1] *Gregorii Ariminensis OESA Lectura Super Primum et Secundum Sententiarum*, ed. A. Damasus Trapp and Venicio Marcolino, vol. I: Super Primum Dist. 1–6 (1981); vol. II: Super Primum Dist. 7–17 (1982); vol. III: Super Primum Dist. 19–48 (1984); vol. IV: Super Secundum Dist. 1–5 (1979); vol. V: Super Secundum Dist. 6–18 (1979); vol. VI: Super Secundum Dist. 24–44 (1980); vol. VII: Indices (1987), Spätmittelalter und Reformation Texte und Untersuchungen 6–12, (Berlin: Walter de Gruyter, 1979–1987).

The composite picture of Trapp's articles on John of Basel (†1392)[2], Peter Ceffons of Clairvaux (fl.c.1350)[3], Gregory of Rimini (†1358)[4], Dionysius de Burgo (†1342)[5], Angelus de Dobelin (†c.1420)[6], Simon de Cremona (†after 1390)[7], John Klenkok (†1374)[8], and Michael de Massa (†1337)[9], yields the common characteristic that all are based on a close reading of the manuscripts, enriched with extensive transcriptions and at times even with partial editions of text. As a good nominalist would note with approval, Trapp always stays close to the evidence of the particular text, while shying away from encompassing universal interpretations—a procedure which goes far to explain the continuous use and usefulness of his articles.

When the author on occasion does draw inferences with broader claims, one still discerns the wise fear of generalization: "What happened in the Early, in the High, and in the Late Middle Ages may, who knows, be pressed into the following, somewhat daring, formula: early scholasticism had both an Augustine and an Augustinianism of its own; Aristotelic Thomism had an Augustine but no Augustinianism; late scholasticism rediscovered Augustine within an Augustinianism of its own!"[10]

It is this suggestion, tentative in form but bold in content, that underlies the conception of this *Festschrift*, which intends to make a contribution to the ongoing pursuit of the reception of St. Augustine in the Later Middle Ages, Renaissance, and Reformation.

One would not do justice to the work of Damasus Trapp unless one also acknowledges his other contribution, namely, the clarification of what is—next to St. Augustine—the second component of Gregory's spiritual and intellectual world: late medieval nominalism. At the time

[2] "Hiltalinger's Augustinian Quotations," *Augustiniana* 4 (1954), pp. 412–449.

[3] "Peter Ceffons of Clairvaux," *Recherches de Théologie ancienne et médiévale* 24 (1957), pp. 101–154; see also, "A Round-Table Discussion of a Parisian OCist-Team and OESA-Team about AD1350," *Recherches de Théologie ancienne et médiévale* 51 (1984), pp. 206–222.

[4] "Gregory of Rimini's Manuscripts, Editions and Additions," *Augustiniana* 8 (1958), pp. 425–443; see also, "New Approaches to Gregory of Rimini," *Augustinianum* 2 (1962), pp. 115–130.

[5] "The Quaestiones of Dionysius de Burgo OSA," *Augustinianum* 3 (1963), pp. 63–78.

[6] "Angelus de Dobelin, Doctor Parisiensis, and His Lectura," *Augustinianum* 3 (1963), pp. 389–413.

[7] "Simonis de Cremona OESA, Lectura super 4 LL. Sententiarum MS Cremona 118, ff. 1r–136v," *Augustinianum* 4 (1964), pp. 123–146; see also, "The Portiuncula Discussion of Cremona (ca. 1380): New Light on 14th Century Disputations," *Recherches de Théologie ancienne et médiévale* 22 (1955), pp. 79–94.

[8] "Notes on John Klenkok OSA (d. 1374)," *Augustinianum* 4 (1964), pp. 358–404.

[9] "Notes on some Manuscripts of the Augustinian Michael de Massa (d. 1337)," *Augustinianum* 5 (1965), pp. 58–133.

[10] "'Adnotationes'", in *Augustinianum* 5 (1965) pp. 147–151; p. 150.

when Damasus Trapp started writing, nominalism was still widely associated with 'fideism' and 'skepticism', and was discredited as the disintegration of 'the great high scholastic synthesis' of Thomas Aquinas. As Trapp wrote in 1956: "... often the evaluation of the 14th century has been victimized by such an instinctive comparison to a falling curve descending from an apex somewhere in the 13th century ...".[11] The revision of this once accepted view is a red thread that can be followed through all his articles. Seldom articulated as abstract principles, his observations and perceptions are always based on a careful listening to the intention of the *moderni*.[12]

From decades of closely reading 14th and 15th century manuscripts, their marginals and additions, a new approach emerged which Damasus Trapp once formulated in a way that marks the transition from the 'old' scholarship to the 'new': "There is some common-sense quality about 'nominalistic' theology; it has great interest in casuistry, in experimenting for very positive ends. With the potentia-dei-absoluta idea, one can sound and probe into the foundations of theology, draw a circle around divine faith, and guarantee at the same time the God-given freedom of believing and discussing."[13] With an epistemological emphasis on the *cognitio rei particularis* went a new attitude toward citing sources, which Trapp labeled, "historico-critical".[14] This 'historical mindedness' of 14th-century theologians bore "traces of a new humanism"[15], and culminated in John of Basel, whose "theological legacy ... without exaggeration, might be called a 'Petit dictionnaire de la théologie du XIVe siècle'".[16] It is with great pleasure that we can reprint here Trapp's farsighted article on John of Basel. The vision and erudition evident in this article allow us to paraphrase Trapp's praise of John of Basel and attribute it to Pater Damasus himself; Trapp might be called a "Grand dictionnaire des théologiens du XIVe siècle".

To honor a scholar for the significance of his work and for the contribution he has made, it is not necessary to prove that his conclusions will stand until eternity. As Trapp himself observed: "Acceptance of Augustinianism should not be considered as the exclusive way of undergoing Augustine's influence. Rejecting may be just as formative ...".[17] Yet much of what Trapp has ventured to suggest has indeed

---

[11] "Augustinian Theology in the 14th Century: Notes on Editions, Marginalia, Opinions and Book-Lore," *Augustiniana* 6 (1956), pp. 146–274; p. 146.

[12] For Trapp's terminological distinction between "nominalists" and "moderni", see, "Hiltalinger's Augustinian Quotations," (as in note 2), p. 414, n. 10.

[13] "'Adnotationes'", (as in note 10), p. 151.

[14] "Augustinian Theology of the 14th Century," (as in note 11), p. 152.

[15] "Hiltalinger's Augustinian Quotations," (as in note 2), p. 419.

[16] "Hiltalinger's Augustinian Quotations," (as in note 2), p. 414.

[17] "A Round-table discussion," (as in note 3), p. 207.

become part of the scholarly consensus today. Although some of his readings and interpretations call for further testing, even in these cases the dictum that Trapp has called 'Gregory's massive formula' applies: "Concedendum vel saltem non negandum".[18]

The editors are grateful for the translators who allowed this volume to be published in one language and, hence, to be more accessible internationally. In particular they want to express their gratitude to their co-editor Eric Saak, who saw this volume through the press and carried on the complex correspondence with all the contributors. Finally, I owe a word of special gratitude to the associate director of E.J. Brill, Drs. M.G.E. Venekamp, who encouraged me to include this volume in the series *Studies in Medieval and Reformation Thought*.

Heiko A. Oberman
University of Arizona
Tucson, Arizona
May 15, 1990

---

[18] "A Round-Table Discussion," (as in note 3) p. 207: "... quia aliqua sunt naturaliter concedenda esse simpliciter possibilia vel saltem non neganda esse possibilia, quae non possunt poni et sciuntur etiam non posse poni in esse nisi per virtutem infinitam intensive. Igitur vel est concedendum esse aliquam talem virtutem vel saltem non est negandum." Gregory of Rimini, *Lectura*, I Sent. dist. 42–44, q. 3, art. 2 (III, 424, 6–9).

THE ARTICLES CONDEMNED AT
OXFORD AUSTIN FRIARS IN 1315

WILLIAM J. COURTENAY

Among the many contributions made by Damasus Trapp to the history of Augustinian thought and Austin Friar theologians in the fourteenth century, those dealing with Oxford hold a special place. Oxford was the seedbed for what Trapp characterized as Modernism and the "logico-critical attitude," and that university produced a series of theologians whom Trapp helped bring to prominence: Richard Kilvington, Monachus Niger, Nicholas Aston, Osbert Pickingham, Uthred of Boldon, and John Klenkok.[1] With unmatched codicological and biographical sluthing, Trappp added to our picture of what was then understood as the radical element of fourteenth-century thought, much of it English in origin, as well as to our knowledge of the conservative countermovement to which the Augustinian Hermits contributed so much.

It is surprising that many of the logico-critical methods, the provocatively-worded theological *sophismata*, and several of the most controversial fourteenth-century theologians came from England, specifically from Oxford, while the majority of recorded condemnations of unorthodox or radical opinions took place at Paris and Avignon.[2] Over against the long list of censured articles proclaimed at Avignon during the pontificates of John XXII and Benedict XII, or the many trials and censured opinions that were promulgated at Paris from the late thirteenth century on, there are few such lists or documented cases for England.[3]

---

[1] A. Damasus Trapp, "Augustinian Theology of the 14th Century: Notes on Editions, Marginalia, Opinions and Book-Lore," *Augustiniana* 6 (1956), 146–274; "Clm 27034: Unchristened Nominalism and Wycliffite Realism at Prague in 1381," *Recherches de théologie ancienne et médiévale* 24 (1957), 320–360; "'Moderns' and 'Modernists' in MS Fribourg Cordeliers 26," *Augustinianum* 5 (1965), 241–270; "Notes on John Klenkok, OSA, (d. 1374)," *Augustinianum* 4 (1964), 358–404.

[2] For the evidence and bibliography on this point, see William J. Courtenay, "Inquiry and Inquisition: Academic Freedom in Medieval Universities," *Church History* 58 (1989), 168–181.

[3] The few that are known include Archbishop Kilwardby's condemnation of grammatical and philosophical errors at Oxford in 1277, and Archbishop Pecham's censure of the Dominican Richard Knapwell for defending Thomistic theses after silence had been imposed. The most visible English case of the early fourteenth century, that of William of Ockham, was adjudicated at Avignon, not in England. And the Parisian condemnations

It is for this reason that a little-studied early fourteenth-century Oxford case is of interest. Several themes to which Trapp devoted his scholarly attention appear in the case: *potentia absoluta* speculation, the reaffirmation of Augustinian belief, and the condemnation of supposedly radical thinking.

In February 1315 a group of theological masters gathered at the Austin Friar convent in Oxford to pass judgment on the orthodoxy of a series of propositions that had recently been maintained at Oxford. Eight propositions, all dealing with the relation of the Trinity to creation, were condemned as heretical and not to be taught in the schools. No indication is given in the brief and only account of this event as to whether these eight propositions comprise the original list of suspect opinions or simply those extracted from a larger number. Nor does the document reveal any of the stages that led up to this event or what judicial sanctions were imposed as a result. In fact, no person (or persons) responsible for the propositions is identified in the document, although the names of the theological masters who condemned the propositions are given. The only surviving account is a summary of the final action taken, preserved in the opening folios of the *Liber cancellarii et procuratorum* for the University of Oxford.[4]

The account of this event, which has not attracted the scholarly attention it deserves, is important for several reasons. It is one of the few records of a condemnation of academic teaching we have from Oxford or from anywhere in England, in contrast to the many that have survived from Paris and Avignon during the thirteenth and fourteenth centuries.[5] It is the only one known to have occurred in England between archbishop Pecham's silencing of Richard Knapwell's Thomistic teaching in 1286 and the summoning of William of Ockham to Avignon in 1324. It thus has something to tell us about academic judicial procedures in England in the period before John XXII and Benedict XII called all such cases to Avignon for deliberation and judgment. Further, the content of the propositions, many of which employ the distinction of

---

of the 1340s, which resulted in the promulgation of the new Parisian articles, had no counterpart at either Oxford or Cambridge. It is primarily in the last half of the century that one again encounters official concern over heterodox or unpopular academic views in any way parallel to the period of Kilwardby and Pecham, namely the censured opinions of Uthred of Boldon, John Wyclif, and Henry Crump.

[4] H. Anstey, *Munimenta academica*, Rolls series 50.1 (London, 1868), 100–102.

[5] On academic condemnations see J. Koch, *Kleine Schriften* (Rome, 1973); M.M. McLaughlin, *Intellectual Freedom and its Limitations in the University of Paris in the Thirteenth and Fourteenth Centuries* (New York, 1977); J. Miethke, "Papst, Ortsbischof und Universität in den Pariser Theologenprozessen des 13. Jahrhunderts," in *Die Auseinandersetzungen an der Pariser Universität im XIII. Jahrhundert*, ed. A. Zimmermann (Berlin, 1976), 52–94; and Courtenay, "Inquiry and Inquisition."

absolute and ordained power, may inform us of theological concerns in England and the attitude or reaction of the Oxford magisterium some two years before Ockham began to read the *Sentences* at Oxford. Finally, the form of the account may reveal more about the composition of the Oxford theological magisterium than has been realized.

The Oxford Articles of 1315

The following articles were condemned as erroneous by masters of theology of the university of Oxford in the year of <our> Lord 1314 in the month of February:

1. That God the Father was able to have produced a creature before the Word in origin, nature or time.

2. That the Father was able by <his> absolute power to produce every creature without the Son producing, although not by <his> ordained power.

3. That although the Son would not produce or have produced, or have been able to produce a creature, since the Father in priority of origin would produce every creature able to be created, by the Word not produced, the Son nevertheless would be omnipotent, since he would have the same force and the same power as the Father, just as the Holy Spirit is omnipotent, although he is not able to produce the Son as the Father is able, because not withstanding this, he would have the same force and the same power with the Father.

4. That if a creature would be produced before the Word, it should be understood to be produced by the first person *in divinis*, not by the Father.

5. That the works of the Trinity with respect to creatures are not distinct, de facto; not, however, necessarily, since by the absolute power of God <a work> was able to be done in another way, just as the redemption of the human race was able to be done or to have been done without the death and incarnation of Christ.

6. That if the Father is able to produce the Word, which is greater than a creature, without an associate, by the same or greater reason the Father is able to produce a creature, which is less, without an associate, that is, without the Son producing.

7. That just as philosophers, who understood so distinctly and clearly, did not place the production of the Word *in divinis*, but rather asserted that all things emanate from one *suppositum*, which is perfect and sufficient, nor did they see in this any formal contradiction, so indeed I am able to posit that God the Father was able to produce creatures before the Word, without formal contradiction.

8. That if a creature was able to be produced before the Word, a formal repugnance of terms does not follow from this, neither on the part of the Father producing, nor on the part of the creature produced.

Be it known that these masters were then regents in theology, all of whom by unanimous consent decreed the aforesaid articles to be heretical, and they were also present at their condemnation at the place of the Austin Friars at Oxford, namely master Henry of Harclay, then chancellor, master Robert of Rithley <probably Kichley>, master John of Nottingham, master Antony Bek, master Simon of Mepham, master John of Selby, master Hervey, monk of Norwich, master Robert, monk of Margam of the

Cistercian order, master John of Wilton, Franciscan, master John of Chelveston, Carmelite, master William of Markeley, Augustinian.

Further, master Nicholas Trevet of the Order of Preachers, who resumed their lectures at that time, agreed with the aforesaid masters on the condemnation of each and every one of the aforesaid articles.[6]

We should not assume that the Austin Friars themselves played any special role in these deliberations. The Austin Friar convent at Oxford, in which the condemnation took place, was the traditional location where the theological faculty transacted its academic business before the

---

[6] As edited by Anstey, *Munimenta*, but with revisions, the text of the condemnation is as follows:

Isti articuli subscripti fuerunt reprobati tamquam erronei a magistris theologiae universitatis Oxoniae, anno Domini millesimo tercentesimo quartodecimo, mense Februarii:

1. Quod Deus Pater potuit produxisse creaturam ante Verbum origine, natura vel tempore.

2. Quod Pater potuit producere omnem creaturam sine Filio producente de potentia absoluta, etsi non de potentia ordinata.

3. Quod etsi Filius nullam creaturam produceret vel produxisset vel producere potuisset, cum Pater omnem creaturam creabilem in priori originis, Verbo non producto, produceret, Filius nihil minus esset omnipotens, quia haberet eamdem vim et eamdem potentiam cum Patre, sicut Spiritus Sanctus est omnipotens quamvis non possit producere Filium sicut Pater potest, quia non obstante hic tamen haberet eamdem vim et eamdem potentiam cum Patre.

4. Quod si creatura produceretur ante Verbum, debet intelligi produci a prima persona in divinis, non a Patre.

5. Quod opera Trinitatis respectu creaturarum sunt indistincta de facto, non tamen necessario, quia alio modo posset fieri de potentia Dei absoluta, sicut redemptio generis humani posset fieri vel potuisset fieri sine Christi morte et incarnatione.

6. Quod si Pater potest producere Verbum, quod majus est quam creatura, sine socio, eadem ratione vel majori Pater potest producere creaturam, quae minor est, sine socio, id est, sine Filio producente.

7. Quod ex quo philosophi, qui tam clare et limpide intellexerunt, non posuerunt cunctas re emanare ab uno supposito, quod est perfectum et sufficiens, nec videunt in hoc formalem contradictionem; ita et ego possem ponere quod Deus Pater potuit producere creaturas ante Verbum, sine formali contradictione.

8. Quod si potuit creatura produci ante Verbum, non propter hoc sequitur formalis repugnantia terminorum, nec parte Patris producentis nec ex parte creaturae productae.

Sciendum quod hi magistri erant tunc regentes in theologia, qui omnes unanimi consensu decreverunt articulos praedictos esse haereticos, et praesentes fuerunt similiter in reprobatione eorum, in loco fratrum S. Augustini Oxoniae, videlicet magister Henricus de Harkla, tunc cancellarius, magister Robertus de Rithley [or probably Kichley], magister Johannes de Nottingham, magister Antonius Bek, magister Symon de Mepham, magister Johannes de Selby, magister Herveus, monachus de Northwico, magister Robertus, monachus de Morgan ordinis Cistercii, magister Johannes de Wilton ordinis minorum, magister Johannes de Chelveston ordinis Carmelitarum, magister Willhelmus de Markely ordinis Augustinensis.

Item, magister Nicholaus Trivet de ordine Praedicatorum, qui tunc resumperant [resumpserat?] lectiones suas, consensit praedictis magistris, quantum comprobationem omnium et singulorum articulorum praedictorum.

Divinity School was constructed in the late fifteenth century. Moreover, the date indicated in the document, 1314, is according to the calendar then in use in England and elsewhere, in which the change of year fell on March 25. The February in question came in 1315 by modern calculation. The document, as has been stated, is not contemporary with the event described, but was drafted sometime later. The specific details of the account, however, suggest that the scribe drew from other documents then extant, probably the actual *cedula* of condemnation. Only two types of information interested the author of this summary: the propositions themselves and the names of the masters who condemned them. Yet contemporary procedures for academic condemnations, both in England and on the Continent, allow us to derive information on several fronts.

Process of Censure

By the opening years of the fourteenth century procedures for investigating and censuring erroneous or heretical opinions among university scholars was well established. As illustrated by continental examples, procedures differed between secular theological students and those in religious orders. Juridically, all cases were under the authority of the diocesan bishop or archbishop, but most aspects of each case were left in the hands of the theological masters who presumably had the technical knowledge required. Once questions about the orthodoxy of someone's teaching or writings had been raised, an investigative commission of theologians, invariably masters of theology, was appointed by the chancellor acting on behalf of the regent masters, or, if the student belonged to a religious order, the commission might be appointed by the leadership of the order and composed of theological masters from that order. Such was the case with Peter of Tarentaise around 1260, when a list of 108 suspect propositions extracted from his *Sentences* commentary was submitted for evaluation to Thomas Aquinas by the master general of the Dominicans, John of Vercelli. Procedures were similar for Peter Olivi in 1283, Durand of St. Pourçain beginning in 1314, and even William of Ockham, who was apparently called before a provincial chapter of the Franciscan order before he was summoned to Avignon in 1324.[7] But if the order did not initiate action or respond quickly enough, the chancellor and regent masters could exercise jurisdiction over a mendicant, as happened at Paris in the cases of brother Stephen (presu-

---

[7] J. Koch, "Philosophische und theologische Irrtumslisten von 1270–1329: Ein Beitrag zur Entwicklung der theologischen Zensuren," *Kleine Schriften* (Rome, 1973), II, 423–450. The discovery of a pre-Avignon investigation into Ockham's orthodoxy was made by Gerard Etzkorn.

mably the Dominican Stephen of Venizy)[8] in 1241 and the Franciscan, Denis de Foullechat[9] in the 1360s, and at Oxford in the case of a brother John in 1358.[10]

In all cases the suspect writings or a list of suspect opinions was submitted to the commission, which revised or substituted its own list of questionable theses. The accused was usually given a chance to respond to the charges, and this exchange between the commission or its representative and the accused might be repeated several times. When the theologians on the commission were in agreement on which articles if any should be censured and the degree or nature of the error in each instance, the action of the commission was officially ratified by a larger body of theological masters, sometimes simply those regent at the time, sometimes both regents and non-regents who were in residence at the time and place of final condemnation. Their action might or might not receive additional episcopal, archiepiscopal, or papal ratification, but it is unlikely that any judgment could be rendered or sanctions imposed without at least the acquiescence or indirect approval of ecclesiastical authority.

Between 1200 and 1318, when John XXII began to summon such cases to Avignon for adjudication, all known cases involved masters of arts and/or students of theology, almost never one who had already incepted as master of theology. The sole exception to that statement is the censure of Richard Knapwell by John Pecham in 1286, which was, properly speaking, not an investigation and censure of erroneous opinions but an excommunication by the archbishop for Knapwell's failure to observe the archiepiscopal moratorium on teaching certain Thomistic theses. In the other cases it was primarily opinions or propositions that were condemned, not the person who had mistakenly maintained them, and when it was a first offense, the career of the accused was only slightly delayed or altered.

Against this background, what hypotheses can be suggested for the missing stages or documentation of the Oxford Austin Friar case of 1315? Since the eight propositions are theological and were being judged at Oxford, the accused must have been in the theological faculty and at the stage in his career where teaching or writing would have been involved, i.e., at least a bachelor of theology. Moreover, since judgment was rendered by a group of masters of theology and not by a higher ecclesiastical authority, it seems almost certain that the accused was not yet a master of theology. Considering the nature of the propositions, the

---

[8] *Chartularium Universitatis Parisiensis*. ed. H. Denifle and E. Chatelain (Paris, 1889), I, 170–172.
[9] *Chartularium*, III, 114–124.
[10] Anstey, *Munimenta*, 208–211.

most likely text from which the propositions were taken would have been lectures on the *Sentences*, and the most likely status of the accused, a bachelor of theology. Considering the date of the condemnation and the time such deliberations normally required, the accused probably read the *Sentences* either in the academic year 1314–1315 or, more likely, in 1313–1314. It is difficult to conjecture much further. Had the accused been in a religious order, the investigation might have been conducted by theological masters from that order. But, as we have seen, that was not always the case, and we cannot rule out the possibility that the accused was a monk or mendicant.

At one time there would have been more documentation, at the very least the document of condemnation naming the accused and possibly specifying the nature and degree of censure. And unless the accused refused to abjure, there would also have been a record of his recantation.

Perhaps the most significant element in the document is that the condemnation was the action of the Oxford theological magisterium, not directly an action of the bishop of Lincoln or the archbishop of Canterbury. It suggests that Oxford had, for cases involving theological students, developed an inter-university procedure of control parallel to that which emerged at Paris in the opening decades of the thirteenth century. This authority to judge was not opposed to the authority of prelates or in place of it, but a delegated authority that controlled most aspects of the process of investigation and judgment.

Granted that judgment in this case was rendered by Oxford regents in theology, did they constitute a subcommission appointed by the chancellor, the total number of regents, or a group of regents and non-regents together? What does the document indicate, if anything, about the composition of the theological magisterium at Oxford in the early fourteenth century?

The Theological Masters

A.B. Emden assumed that the signers of the condemnation constituted a "commission of Oxford doctors," specifically appointed to this task.[11] That assumption seems unlikely for several reasons. First, twelve is an unusually large number for a commission, which would in any event have reported to the regent masters of the faculty whose role it was to pass final judgment. Secondly, we find each of the religious orders represented by one master, and only one, which again is not the way in which commissions were instituted.

---

[11] A.B. Emden, *A Biographical Register of the University of Oxford to 1500*, 3 vols. (Oxford, 1957–59), 1261 (hereafter cited as *BRUO*).

It is more likely, therefore, that we are looking at the complete or almost complete list of Oxford regent masters in theology in 1315. Twelve regents would make that body smaller than that of Paris in the early fourteenth century, which seems to have numbered around twenty. But keeping in mind the comparative size of the two universities, this should not surprise us.

As the document informs us, eleven regents were present at their meeting at the Austin Friar convent. Six of them were secular theologians, including the chancellor of the university in his capacity as regent and senior official. The five others were in religious orders: two of them monastic (a Benedictine and a Cistercian) and three of them mendicant (a Franciscan, a Carmelite, and an Augustinian). The missing mendicant, the Dominican regent, subsequently gave his full approval to the action of his colleagues.

We have in this document, therefore, a rare picture of the composition and individuals who comprised the regents at Oxford in the academic year 1314–15, just after the crisis between the university and the Dominicans had been resolved and the rights of regency restored to the Dominicans. The number of regent masters was evenly divided between secular theologians and those in religious orders. None of the secular chairs seems to have been connected to a college, and with one exception the secular regents were not college-affiliated. They were, as a group, highly successful in their subsequent careers, and one imagines that regency played a part in the achievement of that visibility.

Taking the regents in the order in which they occur in the document, Henry of Harclay had been chancellor for just over two years and was probably in his third year as regent master of theology.[12] He had begun his theological training at Paris, where he was closely associated with Duns Scotus and where he lectured, *secundum Scotum*, on at least the first book of the *Sentences*. After his return to England he had abandoned much of his Scotism and adopted positions on universals, relation, quantity, and epistemology that anticipated some of the thought of Richard of Campsall and William of Ockham.[13] This dramatic shift in thinking had already occurred by the winter of 1315, so that at the time of the investigation and condemnation the chancellor could not be characterized as a traditional, conservative theologian. He was at the forefront of critical thinking.

Quodlibetal questions and possibly disputed questions as well have

---

[12] *BRUO*, 874–875.

[13] See in particular the introduction in G. Gál, "Henricus de Harclay: Quaestio de Significato Conceptus Universalis (Fons Doctrinae Guillelmi de Ockham)," *Franciscan Studies* 31 (1971), 178–234, at 178–183.

survived from the second regent, Robert Kigheley, or Kykeley. He had incepted as regent master in theology by (and probably in) 1312, so that his seniority was roughly equivalent to that of Harclay. Kykeley's writings have not received sufficient study to allow characterization of his thought.

Among the other four secular regents, two had distinguished subsequent careers and two less so. During and after his theological education, John of Nottingham held a series of rectorships in Nottinghamshire and did not seek, or at least did not obtain, higher office in church or state.[14] Since he was still receiving licenses to study as late as 1313, he was probably in the first year of his regency at the time of the condemnation. Anthony Bek was also new to the magisterium, and in the previous year had served as one of the two proctors representing the university's interests in the resolution of the dispute with the Dominicans.[15] Soon after his regency Bek went to Avignon, where he served on several theological commissions for John XXII, became dean of Lincoln cathedral, and eventually ended his career as bishop of Norwich. Simon of Mepham had the most distinguished ecclesiastical career of the group, becoming archbishop of Canterbury in 1327.[16] At the time of our condemnation, however, Mepham was in the first year of his regency. John of Selby, the last secular master, may have been regent for several years by 1315, although evidence on his career is slight.[17] Like Bek, he soon left England for the papal court at Avignon and had abandoned his regency by 1318.

We know somewhat less about the theological regents among the religious orders. Hervey of Swaffham, the Benedictine from Norwich, incepted around 1314 and was probably in the first year of his regency.[18] We also know that he had left Oxford by 1317. Little outside this document is known of Robert, monk from the Cistercian house of Margam, and John of Wilton, OFM.[19] We know something more of the subsequent career of William of Markely, OESA, who was prior provincial in 1319, but as with Margam and Wilton, we do not know how long he had been regent in 1315.[20] The practice of brief regencies among the mendicants in order to allow the inception of younger coreligious means that Wilton and Markely had probably become regent masters in the

---

[14] *BRUO*, 1378.
[15] *BRUO*, 152–153.
[16] *BRUO*, 1261.
[17] *BRUO*, 1664.
[18] *BRUO*, 1827.
[19] On Robert see *BRUO*, 1578; on Wilton see *BRUO*, 2053.
[20] *BRUO*, 1222; F. Roth, *The English Austin Friars, 1249–1538* (New York, 1966), I, 49.

1314–1315 academic year. Fewer students among the Cistercians could mean that Robert of Margam may have been regent for a longer time.

The last two mendicant regents present us with a different career pattern. John of Chelveston, O.Carm., had spent much of his career on the Continent, as had his better-known coreligious, John Baconthorp.[21] Chelveston had been master of theology at least since 1290, had served as prior and regent master of the Brussels convent, and had lived and taught at Bruges. His appointment as regent master at Oxford was probably not long, since later in 1315 he was back at Bruges as prior. He was probably appointed by the Carmelites as an interim regent in the absence of any junior colleague ready for inception and regency. He was thus by far the oldest regent in our group and had produced numerous scholastic works, none of which have survived. Yet we do not know how "senior" his colleagues viewed him. He had not been in residence at Oxford during the preceding decade, and thus was as new to the Oxford magisterium as were they.

The situation with Nicholas Trevet is analogous.[22] He was the most distinguished theologian in the group, next to Harclay. Trevet had incepted as regent at Oxford in the opening years of the century, but was suspended from lecturing and was probably in exile on the Continent during the dispute between the University and the Dominicans. He had probably just returned to Oxford and to his regency at the beginning of the 1314–1315 academic year. He apparently was not present at the meeting that took final action on these propositions, and may not have taken part in their previous evaluation. But he fully concurred in the judgment of the regents. As to theological persuasion, Trevet can be characterized as a moderate Thomist and certainly possessed of a more traditional outlook than Harclay. Even without knowing the intellectual commitments of the majority of regent masters, the presence of Trevet and Harclay among the regents meant that a wide range of theological opinion was represented.

The Oxford theological regents in 1315 present us with a curious but probably not unusual mixture. Almost no one had been regent in theology at Oxford for very long, and most were in the first year of what may only have been a two-year regency. Four of the twelve were known to have produced numerous collections of quodlibetic or disputed questions, and they were already recognized as accomplished theologians by 1315. To what degree that influenced the younger or less accomplished masters, we do not know. The presence of Harclay, Kykeley, Chelveston, and Trevet did mean that the group of regents

---

[21] *BRUO*, 403.
[22] *BRUO*, 1902–1903.

was as learned in contemporary scholastic theology as they were diverse in their approaches.

The Trinity and Potentia Absoluta

The eight condemned articles in one way or another concern the issue of whether it was absolutely necessary for creation to have taken place after the generation of the Son, or whether God could have created the world before the establishment of the Trinity. There is no indication that the distinction of absolute and ordained power itself was under discussion and possible censure. The problem lay with the conclusions reached and perhaps, to a lesser degree, with the application of the distinction to this type of theological issue.

From one perspective, the anonymous bachelor was applying the distinction in the traditional way. He was not speaking about what God can now do or discussing a possibility for divine action. He was, instead, speaking about what God could have done. He was using the distinction to explore whether a hypothetical situation was entirely impossible, or whether it was a possibility initially open to God but rejected by him. Along lines similar to the Scotistic formal distinction between the decree of predestination (i.e., who is to be saved) that precedes the decree on the means of salvation (the possession of the habit of grace), the bachelor was conjecturing a moment in divinis that formally separates God in se from God as Trinity.[23] Moreover, if by "creature" was meant the divine ideas, then such issues had been discussed earlier. Scotus, for example, described God's knowledge of the rationes ideales in terms of two moments: a first moment in which God knows his own essence, and a second moment in which he knows creatures by means of his essence.[24] Inasmuch as the divine ideas for Scotus are substantially identical with the divine essence, although not formally so, they are in some sense necessary and eternal. Although Scotus maintained that the Persons of the Trinity were "produced" before a creature "in its intelligible being" as divine idea, it is easy to see how the necessary, eternal, and substantial identity of the divine ideas and the divine essence, along with the formal distinction of moments in divinis, could lead to a discussion of priority in divinis, de potentia absoluta and de potentia ordinata.

---

[23] For a discussion of Scotus's teaching on the decrees of predestination, see W. Pannenberg, Die Prädestinationslehre des Duns Skotus (Göttingen, 1954); H.A. Oberman, The Harvest of Medieval Theology (Cambridge, Mass., 1963), 212–215.

[24] Scotus, Reportatio Parisiensis, I, d. 36, 2, no. 33; I, d. 36, 3, no. 27; Collationes, 31 no. 5; Ordinatio, I, d. 2, pt. 2, qq. 3–4, in Opera omnia, vol. 2 (Vatican, 1950), 251–378. See the discussion in F. Copleston, A History of Philosophy (London, 1959), 2, 530; E. Gilson, History of Christian Philosophy in the Middle Ages (New York, 1955), 461.

From another perspective, however, the matter looks different. The distinction of absolute and ordained power was traditionally applied to causal and ontological relationships in the created order and in time. The distinction allowed one to express which parts of the divine plan were absolutely necessary and which parts were contingently necessary. Even the Scotistic division between the decrees on salvation concerned elements in the divine plan. By subjecting the Godhead to the dialectic of *potentia absoluta/ordinata*, the bachelor was implying that there was a "moment" before the generation of the Son and the procession of the Holy Spirit and that in some sense the Trinity was part of the divine plan. To grant such a position, even *de potentia absoluta*, was to reintroduce the Arian heresy, which would have been sufficient grounds for the regent masters to condemn this position as heretical.

However one reads these articles, they presuppose Scotistic formulations even if the conclusions reached depart from Scotus. Similar issues were under discussion at Paris in 1320–1321, which suggests that it may have been the conclusions of the Oxford bachelor rather than the topic or approach that worried the regent masters and brought about the censure.[25] It seems likely that a controlling concept in the Parisian discussion had probably played a part at Oxford as well, namely Scotus's theory that the first person of the Trinity possesses a *prioritas originis in quo* that allows certain statements about the divine essence or God the Father to be maintained that do not include the Son or Holy Spirit. The idea of a *prioritas in quo* was the conceptual foundation for Scotus's belief that in the beatific vision it was possible, *de potentia absoluta*, to see and enjoy the divine essence without seeing and enjoying the divine persons, or to see and enjoy one person without the others.[26] Although Scotus's position was rejected by Peter Aureol and William of Ockham, it was defended by Scotists, such as Francis Meyronnes at Paris in 1320.[27] His principal opponent, Pierre Roger, the future Clement VI, rejected the *potentia absoluta* argument on the beatific vision and rejected the notion of a *prioritas in quo in divinis* as well.[28] If this

---

[25] François de Meyronnes-Pierre Roger, *Disputatio (1320–1321)*, ed. J. Barbet (Paris, 1961).

[26] Scotus, *Ordinatio*, I, d. 1, pt. 1, q. 2, in *Opera omnia*, II, 17–45.

[27] *Disputatio*, 127: "Quarta conclusio, quod in divinis secundum istum ordinem est prius et posterius." Ibid., 129: "oportet ponere in divinis prius in quo et non solum a quo;" 133: "Quintus punctus est quod iuxta istam disceptationem stat quod in persona Patris est aliqua operatio prior actu generandi;" Ibid., 142: "Decimus punctus est quod ... potest quis de potentia Dei absoluta videre divinam essentiam non videndo personam ...."

[28] *Disputatio*, 53–54: "Prima conclusio erit ista, quod inter divinas personas non est aliqua prioritas originis in quo." Ibid., 70–71: "Prima conclusio est ista, quod obiectum beatitudinis quod est ipsa Trinitas beata, ita quod essentia non potest actum visionis beatae terminare sine personis."

Scotistic teaching was the conceptual presupposition on which the Oxford bachelor argued that the decision to create could have, *de potentia absoluta*, preceded the generation of the Son, it is likely that he was a Scotist in method if not conclusions, and, possibly, a Franciscan.

Was the Scotistic theory of a *prioritas in quo* under review at Oxford in 1315, just as Scotus's theory that the habit of grace was not necessary for salvation, *de potentia absoluta*, was under review at Avignon in 1324–1328 in the process against Ockham? Scotism was not a particularly significant element at Oxford, even among the Franciscans, before the return of William of Alnwick (c. 1316) and the *Sentences* commentary of John of Reading (c. 1316).[29] It might well be that the regent masters, including the ex-Scotist Harclay and the moderate Thomist Trevet, were not sympathetic to Scotistic views and could condemn positions that, because of the strength of Scotism at Paris, could not be condemned there. On the other hand, the Oxford regents were probably more concerned about the orthodoxy of the bachelor's conclusions on the relation of creation to the Trinity, not the formal distinction through which he arrived at them.

Conclusions

The Oxford Articles of 1315 are an important document in the history of academic censure in England as well as for the history of Augustinianism and of late medieval theology. Almost all our evidence for academic censures before 1315 comes from the Continent, specifically Paris. The two thirteenth-century English cases, Robert Kilwardby's condemnation of certain Oxford theses in grammar and logic and John Pecham's silencing of Richard Knapwell, were archiepiscopal and, on the surface, did not involve the bishop of Lincoln and only slightly involved the Oxford regents and non-regents in theology. But neither of those cases are typical. The unusual nature of the Pecham/Knapwell case has already been noted, and that of Kilwardby in 1277 concerned a series of propositions probably extracted from many different sources. In procedure (but not in content) the latter paralleled the Parisian articles condemned earlier in that year at Paris by bishop Tempier and was not an investigation of the teaching and writings of a particular person.

Does the paucity of recorded academic censures in England before 1350 mean that such cases were rare, and that when they arose, they were handled at the archiepiscopal level? The case at hand proves that Oxford had the same mechanisms for internal control as did Paris.

---

[29] Courtenay, *Schools and Scholars in Fourteenth-Century England* (Princeton, 1987), 185–190.

Moreover, the record of this case was preserved in the same way as most of those at Paris, namely in the book of the chancellor or, at Paris, the registers of the faculties. From this we can surmise that although there may have been additional cases at Oxford for which documentation has not survived, the larger number of known cases at Paris and the parallel means of record keeping suggest that there was more concern over orthodox teaching at Paris than at Oxford, at least before 1350. In any event, the surviving account of the Oxford condemnation of 1315 is a window through which we can glimpse the composition and working of the theological magisterium in the early fourteenth century.

When we turn from procedures to content, the results are no less significant. The concerns of the Oxford regent masters in 1315 were to reassert the Augustinian division between God and creation, and to protect the full divinity of the persons of the Trinity. The Oxford bachelor's application of the Scotistic *prioritas in quo* to the issue of creation posed the dual threat of inserting the possibility of creation, albeit *de potentia absoluta*, between the first and second persons of the Trinity, and placing the generation of the Son and the procession of the Holy Spirit potentially after a first moment of creation. For the regents, the act of creation and the generation of the Son were not choices that God could have arranged in some different sequence, *de potentia absoluta*. Generation and procession belong to the Godhead. Creation, on the other hand, was never absolutely necessary but was a contingent act of the Trinity.

If the condemnation of 1315 is evidence for the early presence of Scotism at Oxford, before the return of William of Alnwick and the lectures of John of Reading, it is also important evidence for a reaffirmation of Augustinian belief a generation before Thomas Bradwardine.

THE *FIGURAE BIBLIORUM* OF ANTONIUS RAMPEGOLUS O.E.S.A. (ca. 1360–ca. 1422): MS UPPSALA C 162

ERIC LELAND SAAK

Manuscript Uppsala C 162 contains the *Figurae Bibliorum* of the virtually unknown and heretofore unresearched Augustinian, Antonius Rampegolus de Janua. Rampegolus was a popular preacher and in 1390 succeeded Simon of Cremona as lector in the Order's *studium* in Genoa.[1] He has escaped the attention of scholars of St. Augustine's heritage in the later Middle Ages, Renaissance, and Reformation, largely because much of the work that has been done in this area has focused on the members of the OESA at the universities. The debate over the possible *Lehrrichtung* of what Johannes Hiltalingen of Basel referred to as the *schola nostra*[2] does not include the contributions of our friar to the shaping of the Augustinian tradition, and Rampegolus' voice has been silent in the historical research although it was clearly heard from the later fourteenth, to the end of the sixteenth century according to the historical record.

In order to approach the recovery of St. Augustine historically, we cannot overlook the heritage of Augustinian monasticism. The foundation of the Augustinian's life was not Gregory of Rimini's *complexe significabile*, but the *cor unum et anima una* of the Order's Rule. Our perspective must, therefore, also encompass what may be termed the "other side" of the Augustinian School—the experience of the *Ordensbrüder*. A precious source that may act as our window into the world of the "common Augustinian" is the *Figurae Bibliorum* of Antonius Rampegolus.

---

[1] David Perini OESA, *Bibliographia Augustiniana*, 4 vols. (Florence, 1929–1938), III, 111.

[2] At least four distinct characterizations of late medieval Augustinianism have been employed, based largely on the works of Augustinian *magistri*. In his article "Augustinian Theology of the 14th Century, Notes on Editions, Marginalia, Opinions and Book-Lore", *Augustiniana* 6 (1956), 146–274, Damasus Trapp argued that the *Schola Augustiniana Moderna* was characterized by a historico-critical attitude toward the citation of sources, combined with a source erudition regarding the entire corpus of St. Augustine's works. Trapp's major concern was the scholarly reception of St. Augustine's writings. Heiko A. Oberman paints late medieval Augustinianism with broader strokes which encompass Thomas Bradwardine as well as Gregory of Rimini, and he sees the culmination of the

I. *The Author*

Very little is known about the life and thought of Antonius Rampegolus. What we do know of his biography is based largely on the 17th and
18th-century Augustinian bibliographers, namely Elssius, Herrera, and
Ossinger.[3] With minor variations these authors claim that Rampegolus
was born c. 1360, entered the Order in Genoa, and taught in Naples,
Bologna, and Padua before returning to Genoa in 1390 to teach in the
Augustinian *studium*. They report that he was the leading preacher of
his age[4] and that he represented Genoa at the Council of Constance.[5]
He is said to have died c. 1422. David Gutierrez OSA and Adolar
Zumkeller OSA follow this basic account in their articles on Rampego-

---

movement in the *via Gregorii* at Wittenberg. See H.A. Oberman, *Masters of the Reformation. The Emergence of a New Intellectual Climate in Europe*, trans. Denis Martin
(Cambridge University Press 1981), chapter 6, "The Augustinian Renaissance in the Later
Middle Ages," 64–112; see also, Oberman, "Headwaters of the Reformation: *Initia
Lutheri—Initia Reformationis*," in *The Dawn of the Reformation. Essays in Late Medieval
and Early Reformation Thought*, (Edinburgh 1986), 39–83, 65–80. This essay was originally published in *Luther and the Dawn of the Modern Era: Papers for the Fourth
International Congress for Luther Research*, Studies in the History of Christian Thought,
ed. H.A. Oberman, v. 8, (Leiden: 1974), 40–88. Adolar Zumkeller OSA, also adopts a
broader perspective, focusing on the self-perception of the Order's theologians, claiming
that the *schola nostra* of the *Augustinerschule* spans the fourteenth and fifteenth centuries.
See, Adolar Zumkeller OSA, "Die Augustinerschule des Mittelalters: Vertreter und
Philosophisch-Theologische Lehre", *Analecta Augustiniana* 27 (1964), 167–262; see also
Zumkeller, *Erbsünde, Gnade, Rechtfertigung und Verdienst nach der Lehre der Erfurter
Augustinertheologen des Spätmittelalters*, Würzburg, 1984). William Courtenay focuses on
the influence of the OESA and St. Augustine's thought at the University of Oxford,
making the distinction between *Ordensbrüder* and *Lehrrichtung*. See, William J. Courte-
nay, "Augustinianism at Oxford in the Fourteenth Century," *Augustiniana* 30 (1980),
58–70; see also, Courtenay, *Schools and Scholars in Fourteenth Century England*,
(Princeton, 1987). Although these are four basic approaches to late medieval Augustinianism, David Steinmetz has detected a five-fold use of the term 'Augustinian'. See
D. Steinmetz, *Luther and Staupitz: An Essay in the Intellectual Origins of the Protestant
Reformation*, Duke Monographs in Medieval and Renaissance Studies 4 (Durham, North
Carolina, 1980), 13–15.

[3] P. Elssius, *Encomiasticon Augustinianum*, (Bruxellis, 1654; reprint ed., 1970), 77; Th.
de Herrera, *Alphabetum Augustinianum*, 2 vols. (Madrid 1644), I. 53; J.F. Ossinger,
Bibliotheca Augustiniana, (Ingolstadt-Augsburg 1768), 732–733.

[4] "... inter Concionatores sui saeculi Princeps." Elssius, *Encomiasticon Augustinianum*, 77.

[5] "... magnamque et sibi et Religioni nostrae in Concilio Constantiensi, cui nomine
Reipublicae Genuensis interfuit, perperit laudem, strenue enim contra Hussitas decerta-
vit." Ossinger, *Bibliotheca Augustiniana*, 732. However, there is no mention of Rampegolus in Giorgio Stella's *Annales Genuenses* nor in Mansi's *Collectio Conciliorum*. See
Stella, *Annales Genuenses*, ed. Giovanna Petti Balbi, in Muratori, *Rerum Italicarum
Sriptores* N.S. (Bologna: 1975), XVII/2, 317, 323; and Mansi, *Collectio Conciliorum*,
vol. 27 (Graz, reprint ed., 1961). See also, A. Zumkeller, "Die Augustinereremiten in der
Auseinandersetzung mit Wyclif und Hus. Ihre Beteiligung an den Konsilien von Konstanz
und Basel," *Analecta Augustiniana* 28 (1965), 5–56, esp. 24, and David Gutierrez, *The
Augustinians in the Middle Ages 1357–1517*, trans. Thomas Martin OSA, History of the
Order of St. Augustine (Vilanova, Pennsylvania, 1983), I/2, 150–151.

lus in the *Enciclopaedia Cattolica* and *Lexikon für Theologie und Kirche* respectively.[6]

Internal evidence from the MSS of Rampegolus' *Figurae Bibliorum* sheds only minimal light on his biography. The oldest MS of the work attributed to Rampegolus is MS Uppsala C 162, dated 1384. This is the same date given by Gutierrez for Rampegolus' ordination,[7] which raises the question of when in his career Rampegolus composed *Figurae Bibliorum*.[8] The MS begins with a *Prologus* addressed to *dilectis studentibus Neapolitani conventus fratrum heremitarum sancti Augustini*,[9] suggesting that Rampegolus was teaching in Naples before 1384. In the *Prologus* we read that our author is offering his work to the students at their request.[10] The *studium* at Naples indeed seems to be the context of the writing since Rampegolus, perhaps somewhat facetiously, acknowledges that his "laziness" and "imperfections" were not hidden to the students.[11] Thus, if we can say that Rampegolus was still in Naples in 1384, during the following six years he made his way to Bologna and Padua before being appointed lector of the Augustinian *studium* in his home town of Genoa in 1390.

Additional information is found in the *Liber Figurae* contained in MS Uppsala C 121, and dated 1373. Stegmüller lists this MS under Rampegolus' name, but notes that it is anonymous.[12] However, in the catalogue of MSS in Uppsala's Universitätsbibliothek, MS Uppsala C 121 is definitely attributed to Rampegolus and the editors have noted: *Der Titelzettel gibt Magister Anthonius als Verfasser an*, (an attribution which I have not found in my microfilm.).[13] From a comparison of the incipits and explicits of the individual sections of the work, it is certain

---

[6] "Rampegolo," in *Enciclopedia Cattolica* (Roma, 1953), X, col. 517; "Antonius Rampegolus," in *Lexikon für Theologie und Kirche*, I, 675.

[7] "Ordinata sacerdote nel 1384." *Enciclopedia Cattolica*, X, col. 517.

[8] Ossinger notes that according to Johannes Trithemius, Rampegolus was a Professor of Canon Law: "Teste Johannes Trithemio, fuit vir in Divinis Scripturis eruditus, et Juris Canonici Professor, et celeberrimus interpres, ingenio praestans, et clarus eloquio," *Bibliotheca Augustiniana*, pp. 732–733. Ossinger gives his source as Trithemius' *De Scriptoribus Ecclesiasticis*, (Cologne, 1546) 298. I, however, have found no evidence that Rampegolus held a law degree. For a listing of the known manuscripts of *Figurae Bibliorum*, see Adolar Zumkeller, O.S.A., *Manuskripte von Werken der Autoren des Augustiner-Eremitenordens in mitteleuropäischen Bibliotheken*, (Würzburg 1966), 65, nr. 117.

[9] MS Uppsala C 162, f. 1^r.

[10] "Dilectionis vestre conferens postulata metuo non incongrue ne lictus inanis araverim." MS Uppsala C 162, f. 1^r.

[11] "... quoniam novi vos meam inertiam non latere, cum imperfectum meum viderint oculi vestri." MS Uppsala C 162, f. 1^r.

[12] Fridericus Stegmüller, *Repertorium Biblicum Medii Aevi*, (Barcelona, 1950, reprinted ed., 1981), II, 126.

[13] Margarete Andersson-Schmitt and Monica Hedlund, ed. *Mittelalterliche Handschriften der Universitätsbibliothek Uppsala. Katalog über die C-Sammlung*, (Stockholm,

that the *Liber Figurae* in MS Uppsala C 121 is the same work as the *Figurae Bibliorum* of MS Uppsala C 162 dated 1384 and specifically attributed to Rampegolus. The 1373 work does not contain the *Prologus*. On the basis of this evidence we can suggest that the 1373 MS was Rampegolus' own copy—which perhaps had been composed when he was himself a student—and served as the basis for his teaching in the Augustinian *studium*. Desiring more of their master's knowledge of the Bible than they could collect in their notes, the students asked for a "text-book", so to speak, which Rampegolus somewhat reluctantly provided in the 1384 MS.

When we turn to the evidence from the registers of the priors general in the Order's archives in Rome, we find that the attempt to reconstruct Rampegolus' *curriculum vitae* on the basis of the manuscript evidence alone is not without problems.[14] This documentation apparently confirms Gutierrez's date of 1384 for Rampegolus' ordination.[15] It is only in 1388, however, that Rampegolus *began* his cursoriate,[16] and not until 1389 that we find him—together with Paul of Venice—charged with the responsibility for two public lectures to the students in the convent at Padua.[17] On November 4, 1389, Rampegolus was given permission to take his examinations for the degree of lector under the regent master at Bologna,[18] and only in 1390 does he finally appear as a lector, presumably at Genoa.[19] Thus, the *Figurae Bibliorum* was composed before Rampegolus began his official teaching career.

1988) Volume I of the work was published in 1988 and treats MSS C 1–50. Volume II, which is forthcoming, will complete the descriptions of MSS C 51–200. Monica Hedlund, the Assistant Librarian at the Uppsala Universitätsbibliotek, graciously sent me copies of the page proofs of the articles on Rampegolus in addition to rushing microfilms of Rampegolus' manuscripts in the C-Sammlung to Tucson in record time. Her accommadations are most appreciated!

[14] I would like to thank Fr. Dr. Adolar Zumkeller, OSA for sending me the passages he culled from the Order's archives dealing with Rampegolus and for his comments on an earlier version of this paper!

[15] Confirmamus gratiam factam fratri Antonio de Janua per nostrum predecessorem M.N. de eundo Januam Cantatum [ad cantandum?] missam apud suos progenitores.", dated April 28, 1384, Dd 2, f. 14ᵛ. [Dd = Archivum Generale O.S.A., Rome (Via S. Uffizio 25), codex Dd].

[16] "Concessimus licentiam fratri Antonio de Janua, ut suos cursus incipere et perficere possit in conventu Paduano, secundum quod sue discretioni videbitur expedire.", dated May 24, 1388, Dd 3, f. 65ʳ.

[17] "Ordinamus in conventu Paduano, ut frater Antonius de Janua et Paulus Francischus de Venetiis duas publice legant studentibus lectiones ...", dated August 29, 1389, Dd 3, f. 116ᵛ.

[18] "Concessimus fratri Antonio de Janua, ut communi examine previo possit sub suo magistro regente Bononie gradu lectorie insigniri." Dd 3, f. 119ᵛ.

[19] The registers do not explicitly state that Rampegolus was lector at Genoa. An entry dated August 11, 1390 states:"Precepimus Magistro Simoni de Cremona sub pena nostre inobedientie, quod si frater Michael de Albengana renuntiavit lectorie conventus de Janua et ibidem posuit pro lectore fratrem Antonium de Janua, ut dictas videlicet renuntia-

The question remains how to understand the *Prologus* of *Figurae Bibliorum* in MS Uppsala C 162 given the documentation of the registers of the priors general. Rampegolus explicity addressed his work to *dilectis studentibus*, not to *dilectis fratribus* or *dilectis sociis*, which indeed seems to indicate that he had been teaching in Naples. This argument is strengthened by the incipit which refers to Rampegolus as *magister*.[20]

The *Liber Figurae* in MS Uppsala C 121 merely complicates matters further. It is the only MS of the work not containing the *Prologus*, which suggests that it preceded the 1384 MS. The scribal errors existing between this MS and the one of 1384 also indicate an earlier date of composition. The given date of 1373 is called into question, however, if we accept 1384 as the date of Rampegolus' ordination. It is unlikely that Rampegolus composed such a work as *Figurae Bibliorum* eleven years before his ordination and sixteen years before his lector examinations. I have not, however, found any evidence that conclusively establishes 1384 as the date of Rampegolus' ordination. The prior General Bartholomew of Venice confers on Rampegolus the privilege of celebrating Mass—at Genoa!—and seems to indicate that he is reaffirming a pre-existing privilege.[21] If we take 1384 as the *terminus ante quem* of Rampegolus' ordination, then the 1373 dating of MS Uppsala C 121, though seemingly unlikely, cannot be categorically rejected on the basis of his *curriculum vitae*.

Until further research uncovers additional clues to Rampegolus' life and works, we must accept what evidence we do have without attempting to create a harmony for what may prove to be two distinct melodies, namely, the period before he obtained his degree and the time after he

---

tionem et institutionem per suas litteras et hanc nostram in conventu de Janua ratas et firmas fore nostra auctoritate debeat publicare. Et quod quidquid in predictis veritas contineat, nobis per suam litteram studeat intimare. Et sic eas approbavimus et rectificavimus." Dd 3, f. 131[v]. In 1393, Rampegolus is referred to as the lector at Bologna, although absent: "Concessimus licentiam fratri Antonio de Janua lectori conventus Bononiensis eundi cum uno socio ad suam provinciam et conventum in eisdemque manendum, quantum sue videbitur discretioni. Nolentes ut propter suam diuturnam absentiam a dicto conventu de Bononia privationem lectorie, celle vel gratiarum quarumcumque incurrere debeat quovis modo. Idem volentes de suo socio, si studens fuerit, ut nec studio nec cella privari debeat propter similem absentiam de nostra gratia speciali." dated April 12, 1393, Dd 3, f. 182[r]. It is reasonable to assume that Rampegolus' own province and convent was Genoa. We are still, however, left with the problem of where Naples fits. For the degree of Lector in the OESA, see E. Ypma, "La promotion au lectorat chez les Augustins et le 'De lectorie gradu' d'Ambroise de Cora", *Augustiniana* XIII (1963), 391–417.

[20] "Incipit liber figura, editus per magistrum Antonium ordinis fratrum heremitarum Sancti Augustini ut infra patet." MS Uppsala C 162, f. 1[r].

[21] "Confirmamus gratiam factam fratri Antonio de Janua per nostrum predecessores M.N. de eundo Januam Cantatum [ad cantandum?] missam apud suo progenitores." Dd 2, f. 14[v].

was appointed lector. What remains indisputable is the testimony of the MS of *Figurae Bibliorum*, a work completed before Rampegolus assumed his lectorship and one that is a rich source for obtaining a glimpse into the religious life of the "common Augustinian". The difficulty of reconstructing Rampegolus' biography precisely does not lessen the value of *Figurae Bibliorum* as such a source; not only the manuscript tradition, but the printing history as well testifies to its influence.

Figurae Bibliorum went through numerous printed editions.[22] The earliest edition listed in Hain's *Repertorium Bibliographicum* is Ulm 1475 by Johannes Zemer de Rutlingen, although the Newberry Library in Chicago possesses an Augsburg edition and gives 1473 as a possible date.[23] The work was reprinted in Ulm in 1476, in Nürnberg by Frideric Crusner in 1481, in Milan by Uldericus Seinzenzler in 1494, in Venice by George de Arrivabenis Mantuanus in 1496 and 1500, and in Paris by Andreas Bocard in 1497.[24] Ossinger notes that there were Parisian editions as well in 1503, 1510, 1513, and 1515.[25] According to Miriam Usher Chrisman, J. Knobloch published *Figurae Bibliorum* in Strasbourg in 1516.[26] Ossinger further lists Venetian editions in 1549, 1550 and 1587, a Lyon edition of 1570, and one in Argentorati in 1579.[27] Stegmüller notes that the work was placed on the Index *Librorum Expurgatorum* in 1584 and on the Roman Index in 1590 *donec corrigatur, prohibitus*.[28] The first expurgated edition was completed in Cologne in 1609 with a second appearing in 1617, and a third corrected edition was published in Antwerp in 1667.[29] The last printing was done in Naples in 1848.[30] Both the printing history and the extant manuscripts suggest that *Figurae Bibliorum* was a late medieval "best seller", meriting the attention of scholars.

---

[22] For the distinction between edition, issue, and printing, see Ronald B. McKerrow, *An Introduction to Bibliography For Literary Students*, Oxford, 1927, 175f. I am here listing all editions and printings known to me.

[23] Ludovici Hain, *Repertorium Bibliographicum*, (Stuttgart 1837, reprint ed. Milan 1966), n. 13681.

[24] See Hain, *Repertorium*, n. 13681–13690.

[25] Ossinger, *Bibliotheca Augustiniana*, p. 732.

[26] Miriam Usher Chrisman, *Bibliography of Strasbourg Imprints 1480–1599*, (New Haven, Connecticut 1982), 19. The *Compendium Bibliae* or *Aureum Bibliae Repertorium* was printed in Strasbourg in 1486 by the printer of the *Vitaspatrum*. Chrisman, *Bibliography*, 93.

[27] Ossinger, *Bibliotheca Augustiniana*, 732.

[28] Stegmüller, *Repertorium Biblicum*, II, 125.

[29] Stegmüller, *Repertorium Biblicum*, II, 125.

[30] Zumkeller, *Manuskripte*, 65, n. 117. It should also be noted that Rampegolus' *Biblia Aurea*, which may be the same work as *Figurae Bibliorum*, (see note 31 below) exists in an undated German translation, *Die Guldin Bibel*, although the British Museum's *Short Title Catalogue* suggests the date 1477. *Short-Title Catalogue of Books Printed in the German-Speaking Countries and German Books Printed in other Countries From 1455 to 1600 Now in the British Museum*, London, 1962, 724; Hain, *Repertorium*, n. 13690.

Figurae Bibliorum is not the only extant work of Rampegolus. His other writings include a *Compendium Bibliae*, (also referred to as *Biblia Aurea*)[31] and perhaps a collection of sermons.[32] In addition, of the six extant MSS of the treatise *De pugna spirituali*, in MS Bordeaux 267 Rampegolus is named as author. E. Ypma has argued that the author of the work was Augustine of Urbino, as three MSS attest. However, because of the similarity in content between this treatise and *Figurae Bibliorum*, further investigation is called for especially since Ypma's argument against Rampegolus' authorship is not completely convincing.[33]

Another treatise that may prove to be Rampegolus' bears the title *De Potestate Remittendi Peccata*. This writing is found in MS Uppsala C 121 directly below the *Tabula* of Rampegolus' *Figurae Bibliorum*, on folios 148ʳ through 149ᵛ, and is listed with Rampegolus' work in this MS by the editors of the Uppsala catalog. While giving an anonymous attribution, Morton Bloomfield lists this treatise in his *Incipits of Latin Works on the Virtues and Vices, 1100–1500 A.D.*, referring to MS Oxford, Bodl. Laud. misc. 277 f. 196f.[34] The title ascribed to this work, however, is misleading because most of the treatise is a discussion of Hugh of St. Victor's *De Sacramentis*. Bearing no introduction, the *opusculum* begins: *Hugo in libro de sacramentis parte 14, c. 8 sic dicit, potestatem remittendi peccata quidam soli Deo ita ascribere ....*[35] It is only at the bottom of the penultimate column of the work that we find *hec Hugo*.[36]

---

[31] Referring to Rampegolus' *Biblia Aurea*, n. 115 in his catalogue of Augustinian MSS, Zumkeller notes: "Das Werk zeigt nach Aufbau und Inhalt eine gewisse Aehnlichkeit mit dem unter nr.117 genannten *Compendium Morale* [alternate title of *Figurae Bibliorum*]. Bei der Unvollständigkeit der Initienangaben der Handschriftenkataloge lässt sich deshalb nicht immer mit Sicherheit entscheiden, ob es sich um das eine oder andere Werk handelt." *Manuskripte*, 62–63.

[32] Under his listing the MSS of *Figurae Bibliorum* (nr. 117), Zumkeller cites MS München BstB Cgm. 688 a. 1466 f. 1ʳ–20ʳ: "Exzerpt: Theumata sermonum collecte (!) ex libro fr. Anthonii de ord. S. Aug.", *Manuskripte*, 65. Ossinger lists as one of Rampegolus' works: "*Volumina aliqua Sermonum*. Testibus Cherubino Ghirardaccio, et Philippo Jacobo Foresto.", *Bibliotheca Augustiniana*, 733, and Elssius lists an *Opuscula Sermonum, Encomiasticon Augustinianum*, 77.

[33] "Le 'De pugna spirituali' n'est pas un ouvrage bien équilibré et souffre d'un certain manque de maturite. Cependant, on ne peut en vouloir à l'auteur. Il avoue lui-même qu'il n'a pas l'expérience du prédicateur lorsqu'il compose ce cycle de schémas. Encore étudiant, il le composa 'ad animi recreationem' et il s'excusa d'avance de ses lacunes.

"Il est donc peu probable que cet ouvrage ait été rédigé par un prédicateur renomme comme Antoine Rampazoli de Gênes ou par un savant comme Robert Holcot." E. Ypma, "Le 'De pugna Spirituali' est-il l'Oeuvre d'Augustin de 'Urbin?", *Augustiniana* 10 (1960), 235–244; 238–239. For Rampegolus' emphasis on spiritual battle, see note 92 below.

[34] *Incipits of Latin Works on the Virtues and Vices, 1100–1500 A.D.*, ed. Morton W. Bloomfield, Bertrand-Georges Guyot O.P., Donald R. Howard, and Thyra B. Kabealo, The Mediaeval Academy of American Publication n. 88 (Cambridge, Mass. 1979), 339, n. 4008.

[35] MS Uppsala C 121 f. 148ʳ.

[36] MS Uppsala C 121 f. 149ʳ.

Further checking will need to be done before this treatise is identified, and before we can ascertain whether it is the work of Rampegolus.

Additional research in Rampegolus' works will assuredly prove helpful for establishing his biography, but now we return to our manuscript.

II. *The Manuscript*

MS Uppsala C 162 consists of 117 folia of text and 10 additional folia comprising the *tabula*. The colophon reads: *Explicit tabula. sit altissimo laus, honor et gloria in secula seculorum amen, et cum spiritu tuo. Scriptus anno domini MCCCLXXXquarto.*[37] The scribe gives his name as Michaelis Pauli.[38]

The text is written in a German *bastarda*, with the section headings in gothic *textura formalis*. These section headings appear at the top of the folio for the first section, *Abstinencia* [f. 1ʳ–2ᵛ, col. A6], but then do not reappear in this place until the section *Residuum* [f. 106ʳ col. H9] and occur here for the rest of the work. Often the headings appear within the text at the beginning of a section and occasionally are found blocked in the right hand side of the text (but not in the margin).[39] New sections are also noted at the bottom of the sheet in cursive, and this sometimes is the only indication that a new section has begun.

Beginning on f. 113ʳ col. H36 with the section *Sanctus Spiritus*, we find much enlarged formal letters used not only for the major section headings but for the headings of the subdivisions as well. No where previously in the MS did the scribe employ such formality. At times, and not infrequently for an entire subsection of text, the hand tends far more to the *formata* and away from the *currens*.

Finishing strokes are often elaborate and not infrequently we find over extended ascenders and descenders. There are many heavily ornamented capitals in German fashion and the scribe has even gone so far as to illustrate the text with faces, including an entire figure of a praying nun(?) on f. 11ᵛ. col. A43. These, however, do not appear frequently. Spaces in scriptural references for the exact citation to be filled in later are frequent.[40] This indicates an interest in precise quotation—not apparent in the non-Biblical citations—which brings us from the manuscript itself, to its contents.

---

[37] MS Uppsala C 162 f. 127ʳ.

[38] MS Uppsala C 162 f. 127ʳ. There is no listing of Michaelis Pauli in Elssius' *Encomiasticon Augustinianum* and whether he was an Augustinian Friar is yet to be determined. The editors of the Uppsala catalogue, however, state that he was Swedish, *Mittelalterliche Handschriften der Universitätsbibliotek Uppsala*, II, 305.

[39] See for example the section *Conscientia* f. 24ʳ, col. B39.

[40] For additional description of the MS, see *Mittelalterliche Handschriften der Universitätsbibliothek Uppsala*, II, 305.

III. *The Text*

Figurae Bibliorum presents us with the problem of determining its place within the tradition of Biblical scholarship. This is due perhaps most of all to our lack of knowledge concerning the study of the Bible in the fourteenth and fifteenth centuries.[41] The work is arranged topically *secundum ordinem alphabeti* which is indicative both of biblical *distinctiones* and *exempla* collections.[42] *Figurae Bibliorum* is not a collection of *distinctiones* and was composed after the time when Richard and Mary Rouse claim that "... the distinction collection as a genre disappeared, by the simple process of turning into something else."[43]

There is perhaps a closer relationship between the material in our treatise and the diverse genre of *exempla*.[44] Welter has noted that certain types of *exempla* became joined to 'moralities' such as Robert Holcot's *Moralitates* (1323–1335) and the *Gesta Romanorum*.[45] Although the

---

[41] We do not have a work for the fourteenth and fifteenth centuries such as Beryl Smalley has given us for the twelfth and thriteenth centuries in her *The Study of the Bible in the Middle Ages*, (Oxford 1952; paperback ed. Indiana, 1964; 3rd ed. 1978). G.R. Evans, however, has made an attempt in her work *The Language and Logic of the Bible: The Road to Reformation*, (Cambridge, 1985). Although this is not the place for a full review, Evans' book leaves much to be desired. It is arranged topically and thus takes no account of chronological developments. For example, she deals with Wycliff, Bellarmine, and Melanchthon in a single paragraph—and in that order (p. 54). The book is a series of vignettes, and thus lacks a sense of "wholeness". Evans shows a marked lack of sophistication regarding fourteenth and fifteenth century theological debate when she writes: "In 1277 a dispute over the doctrines of Aquinas at Paris led to a row with echoes in Oxford and beyond." (p. 108), and traces the *via moderna* to the *logica modernorum*, naming its leaders—albeit adorned with a question mark—as Henry of Ghent, Duns Scotus, and William of Ockham. (p. 108). William J. Courtenay, however, has provided a point of departure for further research in his article "The Bible in the Fourteenth Century: Some Observations", *Church History* 54 (1985), 176–187.

[42] See, R. and M. Rouse, *Preachers, Florilegia and Sermons: Studies on the 'Manipulus Florum' of Thomas of Ireland*, Pontifical Institute of Mediaeval Studies, Studies and Texts 47 (Toronto 1979), 34–36; Ibidem, "Biblical *Distinctiones* in the Thirteenth Century", *Archives d'Histoire Doctrinale et Littéraire du Moyen Âge* 41 (1974), 27–37; Louis-Jacques Bataillon, "Intermédiaires entre les Traités de Morale Pratique et les Sermons: les *Distinctiones* Bibliques Alphabétiques", in *Les Genres Littéraires dans les Sources Théologiques et Philosophiques Médiévales*, Actes du Colloque International de Louvain-la-Neuve, 25–27 Mai 1981, Publications de l'Institut d'Études Médiévales, 2nd ser., Textes, Études, Congrès v. 5 (Louvain-la-Neuve, 1982), 213–226; J.-Th. Welter, *L'Exemplum dans la Littérature Religieuse et Didactique du Moyen Âge* (Paris-Toulouse 1927, reprint ed. Geneva 1973), 290–334.

[43] R. and M. Rouse, "Biblical *Distinctiones*", 34. Unfortunately the Rouses do not discuss this "something else" beyond the vague label of *compendia* of preaching material.

[44] See Welter, *L'Exemplum*, 83–108. Welter groups *exempla* into two principle categories—literary and personal—although he notes many subdivisions within each. Cf. Claude Bremond and Jacques Le Goff, *L'"Exemplum"*, Typologie des Sources du Moyen Âge Occidental 40 (Brepols and Turnhout 1982), 39–42. D.L. d'Avary has cautioned against seeing overly defined divisions between types of *exempla* and preaching aids in general. *The Preaching of the Friars. Sermons Diffused from Paris before 1300* (Oxford 1985), 68–69.

[45] See, Welter, *L'Exemplum*, part 2, sec. III, chpt. 3 "Les recueils d'exempla

contents of *Figurae Bibliorum* could possibly fall within the classification of *exempla* given by Claude Bremond and Jacques Le Goff,[46] on closer examination they do not so easily do so. The relationship between *exempla* collections and *Figurae Bibliorum* lies in Rampegolus' use of typology. His typological, or 'figurative' interpretation, however, is not concerned with extracting the moral from a story, but rather focuses on the proper meaning of scripture.[47] Rampegolus' "moralizing" is not so much in the *exempla* tradition as it is in that of one of his favorite sources, Gregory the Great's *Moralia in Iob*.[48]

Even though *Figurae Bibliorum* is arranged *secundum ordinem alphabeti* and treats such traditional topics as the seven deadly sins, it also includes other material which gives evidence that it is not simply a collection of *exempla*. For example, it contains a long section on the Virgin Mary which can be viewed almost as an independent mariological treatise rather than a "moralization" of Mary as an ideal to be emulated. Mary was crucified in heart and mind with the physical crucifixion of her Son.[49] She is the advocate of sinners, sanctified before her birth and free from all sin.[50] No one is saved without the active participation of Mary who is *omnibus omnia*.[51] Reading *Figurae Bibliorum* one receives the impression that its author is writing a work of biblical scholarship, focusing on *exegesis* for preachers, rather than gathering ready-made *exempla* to be inserted into sermons.

This impression is deepened when we note the resemblance between *Figurae Bibliorum* and the anonymous *Moralities on the Gospels* tradi-

---

moralisés", 335–375. For Holcot see 360–366 and 366–375 for the *Gesta Romanorum*.

[46] See, C. Bremond and J. Le Goff, *L'"Exemplum'*, 41–42.

[47] Bremond and Le Goff have made this same point regarding fourteenth century developments but their discussion is in the context of preaching rather than exegesis. *L'Exemplum*, 63–64.

[48] In his epistle to Leandrus prefacing his *Moralia in Iob* Gregory wrote: "... ut non solum verba historiae per allegoriarum sensus excuterem, sed allegoriarum sensus protinus in excercitium moralitatis inclinarem ...". CChr.SL 143.2, 47–50.

[49] "... quia omnes discipuli recesserunt, sed sola virgo mente et corde latebat in cruce cum filio suspensa." MS Uppsala C 162 f. 75v, col. F5.

[50] "... ut tam ab originali quam omni actuali peccato esset purissima et mundissima." MS Uppsala C 162 f. 71^r, col. E47.

"Omnis creatura pure humana fuit peccato subdita, et per consequens dyabolo tributaria, excepta virgine benedicta que in privilegio eterni regis fuit ante sanctificata quam nata." MS Uppsala C 162 f. 72^r, col. E51–E52.

"... que singulari prerogativa dicitur advocata peccatorum et mater." MS Uppsala C 162 f. 74^r, col. E60.

[51] "Videns divina iustitia peccatores dissimiles Christo in operibus suis, odit eos querens illos perdere, sed peccatorum pia mater et illorum advocata, scilicet beata virgo, ipsos sub alius sue misericordie protegit et abscondit quousque eos revocet a peccatis faciatque Christo similes creatori suo in virtutibus et bonis operibus quantum fragilitas permittit humana." MS Uppsala C 162 f. 77^r, col. F12.

"Unde Bernardus in Sermone: Maria omnibus facta est omnia." MS Uppsala C 162 f. 76^r, col. F8.

tionally ascribed to Robert Grosseteste.[52] This treatise was provided with two indices, one topical and the other alphabetical, and, as the Rouses have noted, "... appears to have originated as classroom lectures."[53] Rampegolus dedicated his work to his beloved students at the Augustinian cloister in Naples upon their request. It is not unlikely that *Figurae Bibliorum*, in a similar fashion to the *Moralities on the Gospels*, reflects Rampegolus' classroom teaching. Its primary use was to teach the proper exegesis of Scripture to students studying to become preachers, and only subsequently as a tool for preachers studiously composing sermons. Rampegolus went one step beyond the *Moralities on the Gospels* and not only provided a *Tabula*, but arranged his entire work topically and alphabetically. In this light, *Figurae Bibliorum* offers us insight into the study of the Bible in the Augustinian *studia*, and it is to Rampegolus' exegesis and view of preaching that we now turn.

Figurae Bibliorum is not a formal biblical commentary, and yet Rampegolus offers his own exegesis of biblical figures rather than merely gathering extant material. In the section *De Apostolis*, Rampegolus enunciates his view of figural interpretation.

> In the dining room of the Holy Scriptures are three tables, that is, three ways of understanding—namely, the historical, the mystical, and the moral. The first table is for the man on the streets, the second, for the learned, and the third table is common to both. The food on the first table is rather coarse, on the second, gourmet, and on the third, sweet. The first table offers the savor of *exempla*, the second, the power of divine mysteries, and the third, the sweetness of moral conduct. At the first table one is fed with miracles, at the second, with *figurae*, and at the third, with proverbs.[54]

Here we see a distinction between *exempla* and *figurae*. Both *exempla* and *figurae* can be given a moral interpretation, but whereas *exempla* primarily concern historical interpretation, directed to the simple,

---

[52] E.J. Dobson, *Moralities on the Gospels. A New Source of "Ancrene Wisse"* (Oxford 1975), 22–34. Dobson attributes the work to Alexander of Bath (86–122). For a different attribution, see R. and M. Rouse, *Preachers, Florilegia and Sermons*, 17–18. The Rouses dispute Dobson's dating of the work due to the presence of subject indexes—referring the reader to the review of Dobson's book by R. Rouse and S. Wenzel, in *Speculum* 52 (1977), 648–652—and hence prefer to give an anonymous attribution.

[53] R. and M. Rouse, *Preachers, Florilegia and Sermons*, 17. Dobson also notes that the *Moralia* could have originated from a series of lectures, but convincingly argues that the collection was a later compilation rather than a single course of 301 lectures, (Dobson, *Moralities on the Gospels*, 22–27) and writes: "The *Moralia* as published is very far from being lectures as delivered.", 25.

[54] "In refectorio sacre scripture sunt tres mense, id est, tres intellectus, videlicet hystorialis, mysticus, et moralis. Prima mensa simplicibus; secunda, doctoribus; tertia, communis est utrisque. In prima est cibus grossior; in secunda, subtilior; in tertia dulcior. Prima, continet saporem exemplorum; secunda, vim misteriorum; tertia, dulcedinem morum. Prima, pascit miraculis; secunda, figuris; tertia verbis [MS Uppsala C 121 reads: tertia proverbis, f. 6^r, col. A21]." MS Uppsala C 162 f. 6^r, col. A21.

figurae—the focus of Rampegolus' work—are *subtilior*. They concern the mystical sense and are directed to the learned.

The exegesis of *figurae* for Rampegolus is typological. The exegetical dichotomy, however, is not so much between *umbra* and *veritas*, as between the *figura*—which portrays the *rem temporalem*—and the *res ipsa*, which points the way to eternal life. Quoting St. Augustine, Rampegolus writes:

> ... Augustine in his twelfth sermon on the Gospel of John wrote: ... So that they might have eternal life. For this concerns the distinction between the *figura*, the image, and the true reality. The *figura* shows the temporal presence. The true reality of the *figura*, points to eternal life.[55]

For Rampegolus the *sensus verus* is the mystical interpretation of historical *figurae* which can only be gained by divine illumination.[56] In his section *Predicatores*, Rampegolus writes:

> When any man, however eloquent he might be. must speak the words of Holy Scripture, he is rendered mute unless he is first illumined by the grace of the Holy Spirit.[57]

Rampegolus' emphasis on divine illumination places his work within the tradition described by Jordan of Saxony in his *Liber Vitasfratrum* (completed by 1357).[58] In addition to the "book knowledge" of the Order's *doctores*,[59] for Jordan there is also the *scientia spiritualis*, the

---

[55] "... Augustinus super Iohannem, Homile 12: ... Ut habeant vitam eternam. Hoc enim interest inter figuram, ymaginem, et rem ipsam. Figura prestabat rem temporalem. Res ipsa cuius figura erat, prestabat vitam eternam." MS Uppsala C 162 f. 94ᵛ, col. G22. This is an exact quotation from Augustine, *Tractatus In Evangelium Iohannis*, XII, 11 (*CChr.SL* 36, 127). For an excellent discussion of the meaning of *Figura*, see Erich Auerbach, '*Figura*', in Erich Auerbach, *Scenes from the Drama of European Literature*, trans. Ralph Manheim, Theory and History of Literature 9 (New York, 1959; reprint ed., Minneapolis 1984), 11–76. Auerbach writes: "Figural interpretation establishes a connection between two events or persons, the first of which signifies not only itself but also the second, while the second encompasses or fulfills the first. The two poles of the figure are separate in time, but both, being real events or figures, are within time, within the stream of historical life. Only the understanding of the two persons or events is a spiritual act, but this spiritual act deals with concrete events whether past, present, or future, and not with concepts or abstractions; these are quite secondary, since promise and fulfillment are real historical events, which have either happened in the incarnation of the Word, or will happen in the second coming." (53). For a discussion of the distinction between figural interpretation and allegorical, see, 54–56.

[56] "... verum sacre scripture sensum, lumine spiritus sancti fidelibus datum. Hoc est enim sagina, qua populus fidelium vescitur in mensa fidei." "Incarnatio", MS Uppsala C 162 f. 60ʳ, col. E3.

[57] "Omnis homo quantumcumque eloquens sit, cum debet loqui verba sacre scripture, mutus dicitur nisi prius Sancti Spiritus gracia illustretur." MS Uppsala C 162 f. 105ʳ, col. H4.

[58] *Jordani de Saxonia, Liber Vitasfratrum*, ed. Rudolphus Arbesmann OSA and Winfridus Hümpfner OSA, Cassiciacum 1 (New York 1943). (hereafter cited as VF)

[59] Jordan indeed asserts the importance of what in his mind is the *schola nostra* when in

prerequisites for which are: 1) *cordis puritas*, 2) *mentis humilitas*, 3) *orationis pietas*, 4) *operum fructuositas*.[60] However, *scientia spiritualis* is only obtained by divine illumination,[61] and it is this ideal that characterizes the "other-side" of the Augustinian School by comprising the goal of the teaching in the local *studia* and the basis for the preaching in the cloister and community, as our Antonius bears witness.

Rampegolus' asserting the necessity of divine illumination for apprehending the *sensus verus* does not imply that his hermeneutics is based on the *veritas* of the New Testament illuminating the *umbra* of the Old Testament. Although the advent of Christ indeed revealed the proper interpretation of Scripture,[62] Rampegolus always keeps the Old and New Testaments together. Indeed, many *figurae* he treats are drawn from New Testament passages. Both testaments lead to heaven, as Rampegolus states in the section *Ecclesia*.

> In the Church is heavenly bread, namely, the bread of Christ's body, containing all the sweetness of grace. And two Tables are there as well, namely, the Tables of the Old and of the New Testaments, by which we are educated and instructed in divine matters, which lead to heaven.[63]

Every *figura*, whether an Old or a New Testament passage, is completed with an interpretation *spiritualiter*. The entire Bible lies in *umbra* until illumined by Christ, which is received by faith.

In the section *Sacra Scriptura*, Rampegolus echoes Jordan of Saxony's *scientia spiritualis* by writing that in the interpretation of Holy Scripture

---

the section *De Lectione seu studio Sacrae Scripturae* he gives a chronological account of the most important doctors in the Order and includes a list of their works, beginning with Aegidius Romanus extending to Herman Schildesche, VF II, 22, 235–242. In the Roman MS, however, there is a marginal addition that continues the list through Thomas of Strasbourg, Gregory of Rimini, Hugolinus of Orvieto, Bonsemblans and Bonaventure of Padua. This note must have been added after 1587 since the note makes reference to the *editio princeps* of the *Liber Vitasfratrum* which was completed in Rome in 1587, (the editors do not give the foliation). VF II, 22, 241. Jordan also notes: "Praeter praefatos venerandos fuerunt quam plures alii in Religione magistri et alii viri scientia preclari, de quibus longum esset enarrare. Et adhuc per Dei gratiam supersunt quam plurimi in Ordine viri doctissimi, vita et scientia famosi, de quorum laudum singulari descriptione stilum subduxi, ne viderer palpanistae officium usurpasse.", VF II, 23, 242.

[60] VF II, 22, 242–245.

[61] "Sed praeter has scientias, quae docentium verbis et studio lectionis acquiruntur, est alia scientia, scilicet spiritualis, quae non nisi per illuminationem divinam attingitur." VF II, 22, 242.

[62] "... quia Christus evangelium produxit, in quo ostendit atque exposuit veteris testamenti scripturam et nomen huius putei est latitudo, quia per Evangelium fides dilatata est super terram, tanta enim fuit evangelice doctrine suavitas ac dulcedo et tam magnam gustantibus bonitatis copiam tribuit ut omnes ab ea inveniantur refecti, magni et parvi, iusti et peccatores." *Sacra Scriptura*, MS Uppsala 162 f. 111ᵛ, col. H29.

[63] "In ecclesia est celestis panis, scilicet corporis Christi, continens omnem suavitatem gratie. Sunt et ibi tabule, scilicet veteris testamenti et novi, quibus informamur et instruimur divina que ducunt ad celum." MS Uppsala C 162 f. 42ʳ, col. C52.

St. Peter, as the symbol of faith, must precede St. John, who signifies understanding. For Rampegolus, repeating the dictum: *Nisi credideritis, non intelligetis*,[64] the key to understanding both the Old Testament and the New Testament is the mystical interpretation of the *sensus verus*, which, yielding *scientia spiritualis*, is received by divine illumination and is directed towards a tropological exhortation in the context of anagogical expectation.

Figurae Bibliorum is a "text book" of biblical exegesis for the Augustinian friar studying for the priesthood, and thus it sheds light on the "other side" of the Augustinian School. The study of the Bible, for Rampegolus, is inseparable from the office of preacher. Jordan of Saxony defended the existence of the Augustinian Hermits in the cities by pointing to the necessity of preaching and hearing confessions so that the friars might not live only for themselves, but would also serve the Church.[65] This same attitude is seen in *Figurae Bibliorum*, where Rampegolus calls preachers the dispensers and distributors of the spiritual food contained in the Bible.[66] If we can claim that *Figurae Bibliorum* represents Rampegolus' teaching in the *studium* at Naples—even acknowledging the problems of establishing Rampegolus' *curriculum vitae*—then what he taught was not an academic theology derived from lectures on Peter Lombard's *Sentences*, nor academic biblical scholarship as in the monumental biblical commentaries,[67] but rather exegesis necessary for practical theology. God entrusted His word to the preachers so that they might feed the people by expounding to them the Holy Scripture.[68]

There are two qualifications of the preacher, according to

---

[64] "Nos omnes fideles in stadio currimus per spatium vite praesentis, ut comprehendamus bravium eterne beatitudinis. Sed notandum, quod duplici gressu currimus, scilicet fide et intellectu: et licet per intellectum citius curramus, nihilominus oportet in hoc cursu fidem necessario precedere intellectum. Unde scriptum est. Nisi credideritis etc." MS Uppsala C 162 f. 111ᵛ, col. H30–f. 112ʳ, col. H31.

"Petrus siquidem est fidei symbolum, Ioannes significavit intellectum, ac per hoc—quoniam scriptum est: nisi credideritis, non intelligetis—necessario precedit fides in monumentum sacre scripture, deinde sequens intrat intellectus cui per fidem preparatur aditus." MS Uppsala C 162 f. 112ʳ, col. H31.

[65] "qui vero ex eis ad fructificandum in populo essent idonei, illi deberent in civitatibus habitare et populo praedicare ac confessiones fidelium eis confiteri voluntium audire et sic fructum salutiferum in Dei Ecclesia germinare ... non enim per hoc a statu suae primariae perfectionis degenerasse putandi sunt, sed potius maioris perfectionis statum acquisisse, utpote qui non solum sibi ipsis vivunt [Romans 14:7], sed etiam Ecclesiae Dei proficiunt." VF I, 16, 58.

[66] "Predicator est dispensor et distributor spiritualis cibi, id est, sacre scripture." MS Uppsala C 162 f. 104ᵛ, col. H2–f. 105r, col. H3.

[67] See Courtenay, "The Bible in the Fourteenth Century", 187: "Finally, the commentaries produced [in the later fourteenth century] were of monumental scope, ranging from hundreds to thousands of folios on a single work."

[68] "Nam verbi Dei predicatoribus precepit Dominus, ut cibum sacre scripture exponen-

Rampegolus—knowledge and leading a good life.[69] An exemplary life is necessary for effective preaching,[70] and yet learning is no less important.[71] Only the learned can be preachers, but they must accommodate their words to instruct and edify their audience.[72]

Given Rampegolus' view of the qualifications for the preacher, it becomes evident that the only men capable of fulfilling such an office, in Rampelogus' eyes, were the mendicants. To the *veri religiosi* who lead the pure life of poverty, chastity, and obedience—namely, the Dominicans, Franciscans, and Augustinians—God gave the *donum intellectus sacre scripture* so that they might know how to harmonize the Old and the New Testaments. They are the chosen instruments of God to teach people the way to salvation.[73] Such instruction, for Rampegolus, is based on a 'hermeneutical divide' that runs not between the Testaments, but between this life and the next.[74] The *sensus verus* is the harmony of both testaments and points to eternal life.

This approach to exegesis, and its translation into preaching, was imperative for Rampegolus because life in this world was so transitory

---

tes, et velud panem frangentes apponant populo Dei esurienti et indigenti." MS Uppsala C 162 f. 105^r, col. H3.

[69] "Candidus enim debet esse predicator, tam per splendorem scientie, quam per lucem bone vite ... Per has duas tubas argenteas, subaudi, verbi Dei predicatores, qui debent refulgere lucida scientia, vita bona, conversatione honesta, ceterarumque exercitiis virtutum ..." MS Uppsala C 162 f. 105^r, col. H3–f. 105^v, col. H5.

[70] "Gregorius in Moralium: lex ipsis predicatoribus posita est ut ipsi vivendo illuminent qui suadere loquendo festinant." MS Uppsala C 162 f. 105^r, col. H3.

[71] "... quod ut a prudentibus viris de verbo indiscipulinato notaretur. Ideo dicit quidam, ne doceas priusquam doctus fueris." MS Uppsala C 162 f. 105^r, col. H4.

[72] "... sed debet unusquisque attendere cuius conditionis auditores existant et secundum facultatem audientium ministrare cibum, ut sic reficiantur sapientes subtilibus verbis quod simplices fame non pereant, non putentes inconformem sumere cibum ... [iumentis et rudibus] expositiones eorum capacitati congruas, scilicet lucidas et grossas, illis conformes ut capere possint, et illi refecti sustinere ac proficere. Hominibus vero debet dare panem qui cibus est subtilior, quia provectus et acute intelligentibus debet subtilia predicare, et sic solvet debitum quod sapientibus et insipientibus tenetur si vero indistincte hunc cibum subtilem omnibus uniformiter apponeret cum non omnes sint eiusdem facultates, quosdam infunderet [MS Uppsala C 121 reads: confunderet. f. 122^r, col. N5] potius quam instrueret." MS Uppsala C 162 f. 105^r, col. H3.

[73] "Ex filiis Israel, id est, ex populo Christiano prepositus Christi, id est spiritus sanctus, elegit tres pueros, id est tres ordines, scilicet predicatorum, minorum et heremitarum sancti Augustini, qui puri et sine macula viventes, non sunt contaminati a cibis babilonicis, qui sunt concupiscencia carnis, concupiscencia occulorum, et superbia vite. Loquor enim de perfectis et bonis, qui profecerunt in Religione, non autem de hiis qui fecerunt [MS Uppsala C 121 reads: defecerunt. f. 126^v, col. N23]. Ideo Dominus dedit illis donum intellectus sacre scripture, didicerunt enim linguam chaldaicam, id est, sensum prophetarum et legis ut sciant optime concordare antiqua novis, et populum viam docere salutis." MS Uppsala C 162 f. 108^r, col. H16–f. 108^v, col. H17.

[74] The term 'hermeneutical divide' is that of James Preus who used it to describe the various views of the relationship between the Old and the New Testaments in medieval exegesis. J. Preus, *From Shadow to Promise. Old Testament Interpretation from Augustine to the Young Luther* (Cambridge, Mass.), 1969.

and short. The christian, being ever aware of the fleeting nature of earthly existence, should shun worldly goods and seek eternal blessedness.[75] It is in this light that Rampegolus' mystical exegesis takes on its tropological and anagogical characteristics.

The *veri religiosi*, however, were not comprised of all the mendicants uniformly. In his section *Religiosus*, Rampegolus makes it clear that he is speaking only about the perfect and the good, who live the religious life thoroughly.[76] Echoing Jordan of Saxony and Canon Law, Rampegolus reminds his students that it is not the habit that makes the monk, but the internal disposition.[77] Intensifying the necessity of true religious observance, Rampegolus associates those who fall away from their religious vocation with Judas[78]—they are the betrayers of Christ, and for this reason, they must be kept separate from the true *religiosi*.[79]

It is here, in his emphasis on separation, that Rampegolus' *Figurae Bibliorum* assumes additional importance. It is not only as a late medieval "best seller" that Rampegolus' work merits our attention—as a window into the religiosity of the Augustinian preacher—but *Figurae Bibliorum* is also a window into the "grass-roots" of the Augustinian Observant movement.[80]

Historians of the Order date the emergence of the observance to 1387 when the Prior General Bartholomew of Venice placed friar Nicholas of Ceretanis under his immediate jurisdiction as prior of the congregation

---

[75] "Nos habemus iter brevissimum presentis quod paucis diebus finiendum est ... Filii Christi exeuntes de peccato, et volentes ad celum per huius vite desertum tendere, non debent de farina egypti, id est, de divitiis huius mundi magnam gerere sollicitudinem, eo quod via brevis sit ... Non debent ergo fideles curare de corporali substancia quando in brevi expectant eternam beatitudinem." MS Uppsala C 162 f. 38^r, col. C35–f. 38^r, col. C36.

[76] "... loquor enim de perfectis et bonis, qui profecerunt in Religione, non autem de hiis qui fecerunt." MS Uppsala C 162 f. 108^r, col. H16–f. 108^v, col. H17. See also note 73 above.

[77] "... quia quidam portant religionis habitum, religiosi vero non sunt secundum cor et affectum ..." MS Uppsala C 162 f. 108^v, col. H18. Cf. Jordan of Saxony: "... quia habitus non facit monachum, sed professio et observantia regularis ..." VF I, 20, p. 72; and Gregory IX: "... quod quum monachum non faciat habitus, sed professio regularis ...", *Corpus Iuris Canonici* (ed. A. Friedberg, Leipzig 1879; reprint ed. Graz, 1959) pars secunda, col. 573.

[78] "Isti vero tales non sunt, quia nec Deo vacant contemplando ut Maria, nec procurant ut Martha, [MS Uppsala C 121 reads: nec proximum procurant ut Martha. f. 127^r, col. N25.] sed solum sibi ipsis ut Iudas." MS Uppsala C 162 f. 108^v, col. H18.

[79] "... sed nota quod animalia munda ab immundis segregantur quia in religione debent pravi et discoli a pacificis et devotis fratribus separari ..." MS Uppsala C 162 f. 109^r, col. H20.

[80] See, Katherine Walsh, "The Observant Congregations of the Augustinian Friars in Italy" (Ph.D. Dissertation, Oxford 1972); Gutierrez, *The Augustinians in the Middle Ages, 1357–1517*, pp. 73–98. I would like to thank Prof. Walsh for graciously sending me copies of the pages from her dissertation that deal with Genoa when I was first beginning research on Rampegolus!

at Lecceto.[81] This administrative separation of the observant houses from the established hierarchy of the order became the hall-mark of the movement. As Katherine Walsh has noted, for our knowledge of the early observance we are dependent upon administrative sources.

> Much of the material for the history of individual convents during the early years of the observant movement is of an administrative nature. The types of sources which would probably tell us most about the observance in practice and its effect on the quality of spiritual life in any religious community are lacking for the formative period.[82]

Rampegolus' *Figurae Bibliorum* is precisely the type of source that does offer us insight into the "quality of spiritual life ... for the formative period" of the obervance. In his emphasis on the necessity for the separation of the *veri religiosi*, Rampegolus offers us a glimpse of what would become administratively sanctioned as the *observantia regularis*. In his exaltation of the truly religious, Rampegolus reveals the experienced reality of the observant friar. It is only the *veri religiosi* who know how to interpret scripture properly. It is only the *veri religiosi* who, appearing as men, live their lives as angels. It is only the *veri religiosi* to whom God gave all wisdom and all knowledge.

> Human understanding is led into no modest admiration, because among all the adversity of the world, in speaking about the good and the holy, they

---

[81] Gutierrez, *The History of the Order, 1357–1517*, 76. See also the two-part study by Katherine Walsh, "Papal Policy and Local Reform, a) The Beginnings of the Augustinian Observance in Tuscany, b) *Congregatio Ilicetana*: The Augustinian Observant Movement in Tuscany and the Humanist Ideal", *Römische Historische Mitteilungen* 21 (1979), 35–57; 22 (1980), 105–145.

[82] K. Walsh, "The Observance: Sources for a History of the Observant Reform Movement in the Order of Augustinian Friars in the Fourteenth and Fifteenth Centuries", *Rivista Di Storia Della Chiesa in Italia* 31 (1977), 40–67; 53.

If Genoa was Rampegolus' residence until his death (c. 1422), then there is close temporal proximity between his teaching career and the official recognition of the observance. Although the observance did not become securely established in Genoa until 1442, when it was "re-established" by Giovanni Rocco, (see Walsh, "The Observant Congregations ...", 270) there had been an earlier attempt in 1422 to introduce the observance in Genoa, when Paul of Vivaldi "... was appointed to Sta. Tecla with all the usual prerogatives of a visitor—he was to correct, punish and imprison, to provide to the convent in head and members and take whatever steps might seem necessary for its reform." (267) It is important to note that this reform was instigated not by the Prior General, Augustine Favaroni, but rather by the citizens of Genoa: "Concessimus fri. Paulo de Vivaldis de ianua, provincie Lombardie, ut auctoritate et vice nostra possit recipere et acceptare quandam ecclesiam sub titulo Ste. Marie de Cellis, sitam extra Ianuam, in villa Sti. Petri de Arena, quam quidam cives Ianuenses volunt donare nostro Ordini, ut in ipsa stent fratres.", from Dd IV, P.S. Lopez, "Notitiae circa observantiam in genere contentae in regestis ordinis," *Analecta Augustiniana* XIX, 113. Walsh notes that according to Herrera's *Alphabetum Augustinianum* II, 280, Sta. Maria della Cella previously belonged to the Canons Regular. Walsh, "The Observant Congregations", 266, n. 4. For an account of this early attempt to establish the observance in Genoa, and its failure, see Walsh, "The Observant Congregations", 265–270.

lead an angelic life, although they are men. For since all the world is cast into evil (*maligno*), that is, into evil fire (*malo igne*), nevertheless, the *religiosi* are not burned. And although this world is full of the lust of the eyes through avarice, the *religiosi*, however, continue to live a life of poverty. And even though the world is overflowing with the lust of the flesh through filth, the *religiosi* remain in chastity. And although the world is poisoned by pride, the *religiosi* retain the humility of obedience. Therefore, God gave them all wisdom and all knowledge.[83]

Whereas for Jordan of Saxony *scientia spiritualis* was a particular type of knowledge in addition to the knowledge derived from academic studies, for Rampegolus, not only has it become the primary source of divine knowledge, but also the unique possession of the *veri religiosi*.

The *veri religiosi*, however, were not to keep such knowledge to themselves, but through their preaching were to dispense the spiritual food contained in the scriptures to the people.[84] It is in this context that Rampegolus sets forth a four-fold purpose of the mendicant preacher. His words should: 1) call the people from their sins, leading them to penance; 2) move the camp of the *milites Christi* from this transitory world to the heavenly land of promise; 3) arouse the faithful to war against the devil; and 4) lead to the desire for the rest of heavenly glory.[85]

Preaching is the call to action, leading Christians out of the darkness of sin,[86] and it is in this sense that Rampegolus' *Figurae Bibliorum* assumes the nature of a *Compendium Morale*, the title given the work in one fifteenth-century manuscript.[87] This exhortation is based on the mystical exegesis of scriptural *figurae*, resulting in a practical theology, and furthermore, a practical theology that is imperative, because for

---

[83] "In non modicam admirationem potest induci humana cognicio quod inter tot mundi adversa, loquendo de bonis et sanctis, ducant vitam angelicam, cum sint homines. Cum enim totus mundus sit in maligno positus. (I John 5.19) id est in malo igne, ipsi tamen non igniuntur. Cum autem mundus iste plenus est concupiscencia occulorum per avariciam, ipsi nichilominus servant paupertatem. Cum eciam mundus repletus sit concupiscentia carnis per immundiam, ipsi vero servant castitatem. Et cum mundus infectus sit per superbiam, ipsi servant obedientie humilitatem. (Cf. I John 2:16) Ideo deus dedit illis omnem sapientiam et scientiam." MS Uppsala C 162 f. 108ʳ, col. H16.

[84] See note 66 above.

[85] "Debet igitur hec tuba ad quatuor deservire quia vox predicantium debet vocare multitudinem de peccatis ad penitentiam ... Secundo debet tuba predicationis clangere ad excitandum populum ut moveant castra, id est affectus delicationum temporalium ab huius caduci mundi tentoriis ad terram promissionis per contemplationem eternitatis in regno Dei ... Tertio debent hec tube inducere fideles ad bella contra dyabolum iuxta illam scripturam. (space left for reference – cf. II Sm. 10:2): Estote fortes in bello et pugnate etc. Quatuor debent pulsare ad festa sabbatorum, id est ad requiem glorie celestis." MS Uppsala C 162 f. 105ᵛ, col. H5.

[86] "Filli Israel in egypto sunt Christiani morantes in peccato, sed Moyses, id est divina inspiratio vel divina predicatio, seu conscientie investigatio, volens eos de tenebris peccata educere." MS Uppsala C 162 f. 17ᵛ, col. B14.

[87] Vienna Nat. 1594 f. 1–61. Stegmüller, *Repertorium Biblicum*, 126.

Rampegolus, this life is a continuous fight against the devil and sin.

The devil, the *inimicus crudelissimus*[88], attacks christians who live the virtuous life night and day without cease.[89] Although mankind is freed from the devil by grace alone,[90] hope and works of charity are necessary to reach eternal life.[91] We are in constant battle armed with our works and the articles of faith:

> Our life is a certain military service. Therefore, in the art of spiritual battle, we must conduct constant exercises in spiritual arms. These arms are the articles of the Catholic faith, by true adherence to which our understanding ought to be protected, and not by speculation. And these arms must be brought forth in war through works of charity, by which our understanding and emotion must be defended. And then, the entire man is armed against the raging lion.[92]

With this ever present in mind, in keeping with Jordan's fourth prerequisite for the attainment of *scientia spiritualis, operum fructuositas*, Rampegolus taught the mystical exegesis of biblical figures and composed his *Figurae Bibliorum* for the Augustinian students studying to become preachers in Naples.

---

[88] "Dyabolus est inimicus crudelissimus et pessimus dominus, et pessime servos suos tractans." MS Uppsala C 162 f. 31^r, col. C7.

[89] "Nos habemus hostem proditorem, scilicet dyabolum, qui videns nos proficere in virtutibus, die noctuque nos impugnare non cessat." MS Uppsala C 162 f. 31^r, col. C8.

[90] "Sola gratia divina liberat hominem." MS Uppsala C 162 f. 33r, col. C16. In his section "Ecclesia" Rampegolus writes: "... Christus plus restituit in gratia quam perierat in natura ..." MS Uppsala C 162 f. 43^v, col. C58. Although he makes this statement in the context of the comparison between what was lost in paradise and what will be gained in heaven, this position is very close to that of the fifteenth-century preacher Stephanus Thegliatius (d. 1515) who, as John W. O'Malley has discussed, in his sermons *coram papa* expressed the position that human beings are "... in a *better* state now than if Adam had not sinned. With the Redemption, all that was lost in the Fall was restored—and more besides," O'Malley, *Praise and Blame in Renaissance Rome. Rhetoric, Doctrine and Reform in the Sacred Orators of the Papal Court, c. 1450–1521.* Duke Monographs in Medieval and Renaissance Studies 3 (Durham, North Carolina 1979), 139.

[91] "Cum Dominus voluit nos educere de servitute dyaboli cui eramus obligati peccata primorum parentum: ipse primo mare rubrum in passione sua apperuit, quia effundens aquam et sanguinem sanctificavit baptismum. In quo nos per fidem catholicam intrantes a diaboli tyrannide liberamur, et intramus iter terre promissionis. Sed quia sola fides non sufficit, nisi illi spes et caritas commiscentur, prebuit illis ignem per caritatem et spem per sacram eius doctrinam, et sic affectantis observatis hiis omnis securi possumus accedere ad primam claritatis eterne." MS Uppsala C 162 f. 46^r, col. D7. For the late medieval Augustinians' emphasis on the insufficiency of works, see, Adolar Zumkeller OSA, "Das Ungenügen der menschlichen Werke bei den deutschen Predigern des Spätmittelalters", *Zeitschrift für Katholische Theologie* 81 (1959), 265–305.

[92] "Vita nostra quedam milicia est. Ideo in arte spiritualis pugne nos oportet assiduum in armis spiritualibus exercitium gerere. Hec arma sunt articuli fidei catholice quibus debet intellectus muniri per veram adhesionem et non per investigationem. Et arma producenda sunt in bello per opera caritatis, quibus debet muniri intellectus et affectus, et tunc homo totus est armatus contra leonem rugientem." MS Uppsala C 162 f. 45^v, col. D5–D6. Cf. the section "Ecclesia" in which Rampegolus, referring to the synagogue, writes: "...

IV. *Conclusion*

In the past thirty years our knowledge of late medieval Augustinianism has been greatly enhanced. We are not, however, so fortunate as to have attained a scholarly consensus. Every new manuscript brought to light, every new interpretation advanced leads us to re-evaluate our view of St. Augustine's heritage. If our goal is to acquire a deeper understanding of this heritage than we now possess, then we cannot limit ourselves to particular philosophical and theological doctrines culled from *Sentences* commentaries, but must strive also to embrace sources that open to us the self-perception and experiences of St. Augustine's heirs. The "other side" of the Augustinian School cannot be ignored, as this study of Antonius Rampegolus has argued.

Further research may affect what I have said about the life and works of Rampegolus. One element, however, that I believe will stand is Rampegolus' emphasis on the importance of biblical scholarship. Rampegolus' approach to the Bible was indeed different from that of his fellow Augustinians who taught in the universities. Rather than give a scholarly commentary on individual books, as did Peter Gracillis OESA on Luke at Paris in 1381,[93] Rampegolus directs his work to the student training to become a preacher in the field of combat. For this purpose he arranged his work topically while emphasizing throughout the *sensus verus* of mystical interpretation, designed to withstand the attacks of the devil and lead to eternal life. The Bible—properly understood—was the source of our defence in the trenches. In this context Antonius Rampegolus is a voice worthy of being heard and occupies a place of importance in the *via Augustini*.

In *Figurae Bibliorum* there is little sign of a historico-critical attitude, a source erudition regarding St. Augustine's *corpus*, or a strong anti-pelagian element that have been seen to characterize much of late medieval Augustinianism.[94] Rampegolus' citations of St. Augustine are drawn mostly from the *Soliloquies* and sermons, and he does not quote a single contemporary author. Rather, his favorite sources in addition to St. Augustine are Gregory the Great and Chrysostom among the fathers, then primarily twelfth-century scholars—Bernard, Hugh of St. Victor, Peter Comestor and the *Glossa Ordinaria*. There are no references to mid-thirteenth or fourteenth-century writers. While making use of thirteenth-century developments, such as alphabetization, Rampegolus' *Figurae Bibliorum* harkens back to an earlier period of biblical studies.

---

furens contra redemptorem suum facta illi sicut leo in silva, Jer. 12. Et non solum in caput, sed etiam in membris deseviebat." MS Uppsala C 162 f. 43ʳ, col. C46.

[93] Courtenay, "The Bible in the Fourteenth Century," 185.

[94] See note 2 above.

Trying to place Rampegolus within the Augustinian tradition is problematic because he does not fit the characterizations of such a tradition given to date. Although he succeeded the *Recollector Hugolini*, Simon of Cremona, as Lector in the Augustinian *studium* in Genoa, he shows no evidence of a self-perception of belonging to the *schola nostra*. Even though he was an *Ordensbruder*, he in no way contributed to or even participated in the *Lehrrichtung* of late medieval Augustinianism.

Nevertheless, there are more extant manuscripts and printed editions of his *Figurae Bibliorum* than of either Gregory of Rimini's or Hugolinus of Orvieto's commentary on the *Sentences*. Rampegolus offers us insight into the religious world of the "common" Augustinian, and may very well present us with our first glimpse—from below—of the early Augustinian observance. It is thus that he merits a place—and our attention—within the *via Augustini* in the Later Middle Ages, Renaissance, and Reformation.

APPENDIX

Here follows a listing of the sections of *Figurae Bibliorum* as specified in MS Uppsala C 162, with foliation.

Prologus	f. 1r.
Abstinencia	f. 1r–f. 2v, col. A6
Adulatio	f. 2v, col. A6–f. 4v, col. A15
De Apostolis	f. 4v, col. A15–f. 6v, col. A23
Ascensio	f. 6v, col. A23–f. 11v, col. A43
Beatitudo	f. 11v, col. A43–f. 13r, col. A48
Caritas	f. 13r, col. A48–f. 15r, col. B3
Caro	f. 15r, col. B3–f. 20r, col. B23
Confessio	f. 20r, col. B23–f. 24r, col. B39
Conscientia	f. 24r, col. B39–f. 26r, col. B48
Compuntio	f. 26r, col. B48–f. 29v, col. C1
De Detractione	f. 29v, col. C1–f. 30v, col. C6
Dyabolus	f. 30v, col. C6–f. 35v, col. C26
Divitie	f. 35v, col. C26–f. 38v, col. C38
Eleemosyna	f. 38v, col. C38–f. 41v, col. C49
Ecclesia	f. 41v, col. C49–f. 45v, col. D5
Fides	f. 45v, col. D5–f. 48v, col. D18
Vana Gloria	f. 48v, col. D18–f. 53r, col. D35
Gratia	f. 53r, col. D35–f. 55r, col. D44
De Gula	f. 55r, col. D44–f. 56r, col. D48
Humilitas	f. 56r, col. D48–f. 57v, col. D54
Incarnatio	f. 57v, col. D54–f. 61v, col. E10
Patris Mandatus	f. 61v, col. E10–f. 62v, col. E13
De Iudicio	f. 62v, col. E13–f. 64r, col. E20
De Iudicio Prefatorum	f. 64r, col. E20–f. 65v, col. E25
Ira	f. 65v, col. E25–f. 66r, col. E28
Invidia	f. 66r, col. E28–f. 67r, col. E32
De Ypocritis	f. 67r, col. E32–f. 68v, col. E37
Lacrima	f. 68v, col. E37–f. 69r, col. E40
Luxuria	f. 69r, col. E40–f. 70v, col. E45
Maria	f. 70v, col. E45–f. 78r, col. F15
Malignitas	f. 78r, col. F15–f. 78v, col. F17
Misericordia	f. 78v, col. F17–f. 79r, col. F22
Mors	f. 79r, col. F22–f. 82v, col. F33
Mundus	f. 82v, col. F33–f. 85r, col. F44
Oratio	f. 85r, col. F44–f. 95r, col. G24
Patiencia Christi	f. 95r, col. G24–f. 99r, col. G39
Penitentia	f. 99r, col. G39–f. 104r, col. G59
Perseverantia	f. 104r, col. G59–f. 104v, col. H2
Predicator	f. 104v, col. H2–f. 105v, col. H6
Prelatum	f. 105v, col. H6–f. 106v, col. H9

Residuum	f. 106^v, col. H9–f. 107^v, col. H13
Religiosus	f. 107^v, col. H13–f. 109^v, col. H21
Resurrectio	f. 109^v, col. H21–f. 111^r, col. H28
Sacra Scriptura	f. 111^r, col. H28–f. 112^r, col. H31
Satisfactio	f. 112^r, col. H31–f. 113^r, col. H36
Spiritus Sanctus	f. 113^r, col. H36–f. 114^r, col. H39
Superbia	f. 114^r, col. H39–f. 115^r, col. H43
Temptatio	f. 115^r, col. H43–f. 116^r, col. H48
Xristus	f. 116^r, col. H48–f. 117^v, col. H49

INCERTI AUCTORIS
SERMO DE ANTICHRISTO

EDITIONEM AD FIDEM CODICIS CURAVIT
WALTER SIMON

Cuiusdam 'Sermo de Antichristo' adhuc ineditus et a nemine prius laudatus exstat in codice 2064/2252. Bibliothecae publicae civitatis Trevirensis foliis 57v–59r. Codex, quem praefecto Gunthero Franz permittente in re praesenti inspeximus, est chartaneus ex saeculo XV., ut satis apparet ex litterarum formis. Brevem et interdum perangustam descriptionem totius voluminis exposuit Gottfridus Kentenich ante annos abhinc fere octoginta in catalogo qui inscribitur 'Die Ascetischen Handschriften der Stadtbibliothek zu Trier' paginis 166–167, ubi singula, quae in hocce volumine continentur, ordine enumerat. Attamen liceat lectori in memoriam revocare, quod paulo post 'Sermonem' sequitur 'Quaestio de tertio statu mundi' eximii doctoris Iohannis de Dorsten, quam anno domini 1465 sive 1466 in universitate Erfordensi determinavit contra errores abbatis Ioachim de Floris, cuius opinionem et Iohannes de Paltz aliquot annis post in 'Quaestione determinata contra triplicem errorem', ubi agitur de Antichristo per totum, paucis quidem sed bene refutavit.

Quamquam nos posteri nescimus nomen auctoris nec occasionem, qua 'Sermo' sit habitus, satis edocti sumus, ex quibus fontibus hauserit qui conscripsit. Nominat enim ipse nonnullas auctoritates — ac si impleturus sit illud Erasmi: "pulcherrimum est, si suos quisque principes et auctores referat" —, nominat, inquam, Haymonem Halberstatensem († 853), compluries Hugonem de Argentina OP[1] († ca. 1270)

---

[1] Editiones 'Compendii theologicae veritatis', quas adhibuimus, sunt hae: Argentina apud Iohannem Prüss (1489), Coloniensis apud Henricum Quentell (1503), Veneta apud Christophorum Zanettum (1570) et Parisiensis a viro docto Peltier curata (1866). Notandum, quod codex Trevirensis 961/1866. 4° foliis 126ra–129vb nobis servavit fragmentum non levioris momenti eiusdem 'Compendii', scilicet ex libro septimo, ubi de ultimis temporibus et de Antichristi adventu disseritur. Rem Kentenich vix satis idonee his verbis describere conatur: "Bruchstücke aus dem 7. Buch eines unbekannten Werks". Est re vera textus continuus a capitulo VI. incipiens "alii autem, sicut episcopi ..." usque ad capitulum XXII., media in sententia sic resistens: "Ipsum etiam esse ...". Folia 126–129 ergo alterius codicis olim integri nunc deperditi esse suspicamur. — Si quis desiderat novam Germanicam translationem capitulorum VI.–XIII. libri septimi memorati, legat commentariolum a Christophoro Petro Burger conscriptum et in aedibus Friderici Wittig Hamburgensis anno MCMLXXIX. editum. Denique memoratu dignum est, quod illius

et Nicolaum Gorranum OP († ca. 1295); Adsonem Dervensem OSB
(† 992), quem adfert, silentio praeterit; capitulum primum 'Legendae
aureae' eum cognovisse verisimile est. Inde fit, ut 'Sermo' — si probe
recteque iudicare nobis licitum est — sit opus hominis multae variaeque
lectionis, in quo non aliquid videas artis aut proprii ingenii; quin immo
cento quidam aestimandus est, id est dicta et collectanea ex diversis locis
exscripta. Tamen dignus est, qui attento animo legatur — haec opinio
nostra nequaquam repugnat nostrae priori —, quia quasi tesserula una
inter multas Antichristi imaginem, qualem antea finxerunt, supplere
potest.

In hac ornanda editione id negotii credidimus nobis solum dari, ut
codicem accurate transscriberemus, librarii menda tolleremus, auctoritates allatas quoad fieri potest inquireremus variantesque earum lectiones in apparatum criticum referremus. Ad hoc propositum etiam
spectant adnotationes, quibus textum illustrare studuimus: ut imprimis
litterae firmarentur, tum demum loci intellectu difficiliores sive obscur-
iores explanarentur. Qua ratione ducti aliquot fructus, quos ex libris
virorum doctorum — unum nominamus plurimorum vice Alexandrum
Patschovsky — quasi de 'ligno scientiae' carpsimus, lectori porrigere
noluimus, ne deterreatur a nimia nostrarum notarum abundantia.

His satis commode, ut speramus, expositis, restat, ut nec nos laboris,
ne te, reverende Pater, paeniteat lectionis. Nos non omnino paenitebit,
si laudem tuam merebimus et quam plurimos exstimulabimus ad studium medii, ut aiunt, aevi. Vale.

---

divulgatoris Adami Walasser libellus 'Von dem Antichrist', qui anno MDLX. apud
Sebaldum Meyer Dillingae in lucem prodiit, pro maiori parte nihil aliud est quam Hugonis
verba Germanicè conversa, quae res non omnibus satis nota esse videtur.

SERMO DE ANTICHRISTO

Revelabitur ille iniquus, cuius adventus erit *secundum operationem Sathanae*, 2ª Ad Thessalonicenses[1] 2°. Ex quo de adventu Christi plura in isto et in aliis libris habentur annotata, restat etiam notare aliquid de
5 adventu Antichristi: Et p r i m o, ubi nascetur et a qua matre; s e c u n- d o, quomodo in mundo conversabitur; t e r t i o, de eius persecutione; q u a r t o, de eius occisione et eius poena.

Quantum ad p r i m u m, sciendum, quod Antichristus nascetur in Babilone ex Iudaeis de tribu Dan iuxta illam prophetiam Genesis[2] 49:
10 *Fiat Dan coluber in via.* Unde etiam Apocalypsis[3] 13 descendet *de mari*, id est de Babilone, quod iacet secus mare.

Sed quaeritur, a qua matre. Respondeo secundum Damascenum,[4] quod nascetur ex dampnato coytu, qui vocat eum bastardum. Hic Antichristus in *utero matris* adhuc positus *replebitur spiritu*[5] dyaboli
15 iuxta illud Apostoli, *cuius adventus est secundum operationem Sathanae.* Unde etiam de hoc loquitur Magister[6] in Compendio theologicae verita-

---

1 Antichristo] Anticristo *cod*

---

[1] 2 Thess. 2.8, 9.
[2] Gen. 49.17: *Fiat Dan coluber in via, cerastes in semita.* — Cf. Haymo Halberstatensis, *Expositio in Epp. S. Pauli*, 2 Thess. 2 (PL 117.780A): "Nascetur Antichristus in Babylone de tribu Dan, iuxta quod Iacob dicit: *Fiat Dan coluber in via, cerastes in semita*" = Glossa ordinaria ad locum. — Nicolaus Gorranus, *Postilla super epistolas Pauli*, ad 2 Thess. 2.4: "Nascetur autem de tribu Dan iuxta prophetiam illiam, Genesis xlix: *Fiat Dan coluber in via*, etc."
[3] Cf. Apoc. 13.1: *Et vidi de mari bestiam ascendentem, habentem capita septem et cornua decem.* — Vide etiam Hugonem de Argentina, *Compendium theologicae veritatis*, lib. 7 cap. 10: "Habebit secum magos et maleficos, reges quoque et principes. Unde Apocalypsis 13: *Vidi de mari bestiam ascendentem*, etc. Glossa: Id est 'Antichristum.'"
[4] Iohannes Damascenus in *De fide orthodoxa* 4.26 etsi de Antichristi generatione tractat, non tamen talia dicit. Sed vide Michaelis Francisci de Insulis determinationem *De tempore adventus Antichristi*, quae anno 1478 Coloniae pronuntiata est (fol. A3v): "Dicendum, quod multi tenent, quod erit bastardus, sicut Damascenus et Isidorus, Remigius et Haymo."
[5] Cf. Luc. 1.15: *et spiritu sancto replebitur* (scilicet Iohannes) *adhuc ex utero matris suae.*
[6] Hugo, *Compendium*, cap. 7: "Hic ex parentum seminibus concipietur. Sed post conceptum descendet spiritus malignus in matris uterum, cuius virtute et operatione deinceps puer nascetur, aletur, adolescet; propter quod et *filius perditionis* vocabitur. 'Nascetur autem in Babylonia de tribu Dan', sicut dicit Glossa super Apocalypsim capitulo 11. Post hoc veniet in Ierusalem et circumcidet se, dicens Iudaeis se esse Christum illis promissum, unde 'plebs Iudaea specialiter ei adhaerebit', sicut dicit Haymo super Apocalypsim ...". — Vide etiam adnotationes 10 et 14.

tis: "Post conceptum descendet malignus spiritus in uterum matris, cuius virtute et operatione puer aletur et nascetur. Propter hoc[7] *filius perditionis*" dicitur, "quia de aliorum perditione" erit "sollicitus"[8].

    Quantum ad s e c u n d u m, quomodo in mundo conversabitur et ubi
5 nutrietur, sciendum, quod Antichristus nutrietur in civitatibus Corozain et Bethsaida, quae quasi ad hoc praescitae ad mortem, quia olim in Christi praedicatione credere noluerunt. Unde Matthaei[9] 12: *Vae tibi Corozain, vae tibi Bethsaida*, etc. "Postmodum" Antichristus secundum Gorram[10] "veniet in Ierusalem in templum tunc temporis a Iudaeis
10 reaedificatum, et" circumcidens se dicet Iudaeis: 'Ego sum Christus vobis promissus'. Tunc Iudaei suscipient eum tamquam Messiam suum et[11] *credent in eum*, et tunc[12] *sed*ebit *in templo*, dicens mendaciter se esse deum, quia deceptus a dyabolo credit se esse deum, hoc quod Christus Iudaeis praedixit, Iohannes[13]: *Ego veni in nomine patris mei, et non*
15 *accepistis me; alius* autem veniet *in nomine suo*, illi credetis. Unde Haymo[14] super Apocalypsim dicit, quod "plebs Iudaica specialiter adhaerebit" ipsi "Antichristo".

    Item Antichristus dicitur[15] quasi 'contra Christum', quia sicut

---

5 Corozain et Bethsaida] *iuxta orthographiam Vulgatae,* Corrosaim et Betsayda *et* corrosaym – bethsaida *cod hoc loco et paulo inferius* ‖ 6 quia] quasi *cod* ‖ 15 accepistis] recepistis *Glossa ordinaria ad Iob 34, 30*

---

[7] Ioan. 17.12; 2 Thess. 2.3.

[8] Nicolaus Gorranus, ad 2 Thess. 2.3: "*Filius perditionis*: Et hoc tripliciter: Primo hyperbolice ... Secundo modo passive ... Tertio modo active, quia de aliorum perditione sollicitus."

[9] Matt. 11.21: *Vae tibi Corozain, vae tibi Bethsaida: quia si in Tyro et Sidone factae essent virtutes quae factae sunt in vobis, olim in cilicio et cinere poenitentiam egissent.*

[10] Nicolaus Gorranus, ad 2 Thess. 2.4: "Postmodum veniet in Hierusalem in templum tunc temporis a Iudaeis reaedificatum et circumcidet se, dicens se esse Messiam eis promissum. Et credent ei Iudaei et adhaerebunt ei." — Verba sequentia non sunt solius Gorrani, sed Hugonis (vide, quaeso, adnotationem 6) et, si diligentius exquisiveris, potissime Haymonis, qui dixit ad locum (PL 117.780B): "Et cum venerit Hierosolymam, circumcidet se, dicens Iudaeis, '*Ego sum Christus* vobis promissus.' Tunc confluent ad eum omnes Iudaei, et reaedificabunt templum, quod est destructum a Romanis, sedebitque ibi, dicens se esse Christum" = Glossa ordinaria ad locum. — Omnium fons est Adso: "... Hierosolymam veniens circumcidet se, dicens Iudaeis: '*Ego sum Christus* vobis repromissus, qui ad salutem vestram veni, ut vos, *qui dispersi estis, congregem* et defendam.' Tunc confluent ad eum omnes Iudaei."

[11] Cf. Acta 10.43; Rom. 3.22.

[12] 2 Thess. 2.4; vide adnotationem 16.

[13] Ioan. 5.43.

[14] Haymo Halberstatensis, *Expositio in Apocalypsim*, 3.11 (PL 117.1073D): "... ibi mortuorum corpora multipliciter pereant; ubi etiam intelligitur, quia Iudaica plebs specialiter adhaerebit Antichristo, quousque Enoch et Elia praedicantibus, qui ex ea salvandi fuerint, revertantur ad Christum." — Vide etiam adnotationem 6.

[15] Cf. Gorranus, ad 2 Thess. 2.3: "Unde et Antichristus dicitur quasi 'contrarius Christo.'" — Haymo ad locum (PL 117.780B): "Antichristus appellatur, eo quod sit

Christus est vas omnium virtutum, sic Antichristus erit vas omnium viciorum. Nam Christus venit humilis, ipse autem superbus; nam Antichristus erit superbissimus. Unde Apostolus[16]: *Extollitur* super *omne quod dicitur deus, aut quod colitur, ita* quod *in templo dei sedeat,*
5 *ostendens se tamquam* ipse *sit deus.* Unde dicit Gorra[17]: "Ecce maior superbia" Antichristi "quam Luciferi. Lucifer voluit deo se assimilari, sed iste super deum exaltari". "Ad maiorem igitur contumeliam" facient homines "*ymaginem* suam *adora*re, et omnes charactere suo signare"[18]; propterea destruet signa crucifixi et ymaginem suam statuet
10 adorari, sicut legitur Iudith[19] 3 de Nabuchodonosor, qui *praeceperat exterminá*ri *omnes deos terrae, ut ipse solus deus diceretur*; et faciet Antichristus.

    Item Antichristus erit super modum luxuriosus. Unde dicitur Danielis[20] 12, quod *erit in concupiscentiis feminarum.* Tunc idem erit
15 periculosum tempus. Unde Apostolus[21]: *In novissimis diebus instabunt tempora periculosa.* Glossa[22]: Ante adventum Antichristi ita manifeste peccabunt homines, "ut non erubescant adulterari, sicut iam loqui vel" comedere. Nam aliqui | [fol 58r] iam gloriantur in suis malitiis. Et isti sunt praecursores Antichristi. Item sicut Christus habuit Iohannem baptistam, qui fuit praecursor suus in omni humilitate et castitate, sic

---

3 super] *cod, Adso et Gorranus,* supra *Vulgata* ‖ 4 quod] *cod,* ut *Vulgata* ‖ 7 igitur] dei *Hugo* ‖ 14 idem] *cod, malim* item

---

'contrarius Christo.'" Adso: "... Christo in cunctis contrarius erit et Christo *contraria faciet*: Christus venit humilis, ille venturus est superbus ...".
  [16] 2 Thess. 2.4; vide adnotationem 12.
  [17] Gorranus, ad 2 Thess. 2.4: "Ecce maior superbia quam Luciferi. Lucifer enim voluit deo assimilari, sed iste super deum exaltari. *Extollitur*, inquam ..." Cf. Michael Francisci de Insulis, *De tempore*, fol. C1r: "Quidam dicunt hic, quod superbia eius erit maior quam superbia Luciferi, sed hoc non puto ...".
  [18] Verba sunt Hugonis, *Compendium*, cap. 8: "Item ad maiorem dei contumeliam faciet *imaginem* suam *adorari*, et omnes suo charactere signari *in manu dextera* et *frontibus suis*, sicut habetur in Apocalypsi 13." — Cf. Nicolaus de Lyra, ad Dan. 11.36: "quia Antichristus contumeliam loquetur contra *deum coeli*, quia ostendet se tamquam sit deus, ut dicit Apostolus, et (ut *varia lectio*) iam allegatum est"; quoad praecedentia Hugonis vide adnotationem 24.
  [19] Iudith 3.13.
  [20] Dan. 11.37. Cf. Hugo, *Compendium*, cap. 8: "Antichristus erit luxuriosus, et *in concupiscentiis feminarum*, ut habetur Danielis 11. In aperto tamen per hypocrisim simulabit sanctitatem, ut facilius decipere possit"; Nicolaus de Lyra ad Dan. 11.37: "Licet Antichristus finget castitatem exterius, ut facilius decipiat, tamen non erit vere castus, ut dicunt aliqui, quia erit plenus omni malitia et per consequens erit luxuriosus ... In bestia autem significatur carnalis lascivia." Glossa ordinaria ad Apoc. 17.1: "id est, quae (scilicet meretrix = Antichristus) regnat super multos populos, quos attrahit ad se luxuria." Cf. Michael Francisci de Insulis, *De tempore*, fol. C1r: "Item erit luxuriosissimus, nam ...".
  [21] 2 Tim. 3.1.
  [22] Cf. Glossa ordinaria ad 2 Thess. 2.8 = Walafridus Strabo ad locum (PL 114.622D): "id est, quasi de communibus, ut non erubescat homo adulerari vel furari, sicut nec ambulare vel loqui."

luxuriosi adulteri sunt praecursores Antichristi. Item erit avarus et
dives. Sicut Christus fuit pauper in nativitate et vita, item Antichristus[23]
*dominabitur thesaurorum auri et argenti, et ⟨in⟩ omnibus pretiosis
Egipti.* Item deum et sanctos blasphemabit. Unde dicitur Danielis[24] 11:
5 *Adversus deum deorum loquetur* blasphemiam; ergo blasphemi sunt
praecursores Antichristi.

Quantum ad t e r t i u m, sciendum, quod ipse Antichristus excitabit
persecutionem sub omni coelo, super christianos terrae autem subito et
ex improvisu Antichristus veniens totum humanum genus perdet et suo
10 errore decipiet. Duo magni prophetae in mundum mittentur, quos
misericors deus ad succurrendum mundo servavit,[25] scilicet Enoch et
Heliam, qui praedicabunt et convertent Iudaeos. Et tunc erit[26] *unum
ovile et unus pastor.* Apocalypsis[27] 11: *Dabo duobus testibus meis,*
Enoch et Heliae, *spiritum veritatis, et prophetabunt mille* lxvj *diebus.*
15 Glossa[28]: "Id est tribus annis et dimidio". Tunc Antichristus *faciet*
contra *eos bellum,* scilicet in disputationibus, in quibus eos non vincet,
quoniam ipsi veri testes erunt. Ideo postmodum *eos occidet, et corpora*
eorum insepulta *iacebunt in plateis* in Ierusalem *per tres dies et dimidium,*
nec *sinen*tur *poni in monumentis.* Tandem *post tres dies et dimidium,* ut

---

7–8 excitabit – christianos] Excitabit autem persecutionem sub omni coelo super christianos et omnes electos *Adso* ‖ 9 ex improvisu] *Quoad formam in -u desinentem vide ThesLL*
VII/1, 701, 51 ‖ 9 perdet – decipiet] perdat – decipiat *cod; Adso, longe post medium:* Sed
ne subito et improvise Antichristus veniat et totum humanum genus suo errore decipiat et
perdat. ‖ 14 Heliae] Helyae *cod* ‖

---

[23] Dan. 11.43.
[24] Dan. 11.36. Vide etiam Hugonem, *Compendium,* cap. 8: "Erit etiam blasphemus,
sicut Apocalypsis 12 dicitur. Unde Danielis 11: *Adversus deum deorum loquetur mag-*
nifica. Item ad maiorem dei contumeliam ...". — Glossa interlinearis: "*magnifica*:
Blasphemia."
[25] Cf. Glossa ordinaria ad Iob 18.20: "... priores patres Eliam et Enoch, qui in eius
expugnationem servati sunt, ... transfigat." — Hugo Cardinalis ad locum: "*et primos*
invadet: id est, Eliam et Henoch, qui in eius expugnationem reservati sunt."
[26] Ioan. 10.16.
[27] Apoc. 11.3. Cf. Ioan. 14.17, 15.26; 1 Ioan. 4.6 *spiritum veritatis.* — Quoad sequentia
vide Hugonem, *Compendium,* cap. 12: "De eorum praedicatione et sancta conversatione
dicitur Apocalypsis 11: *Dabo duobus testibus meis,* scilicet Heliae et Enoch, *et propheta-*
bunt, 'id est praedicabunt', *diebus 1260,* 'id est tribus annis', sicut ipse Christus praedicavit, *amicti saccis.* Glossa: 'Praedicantes poenitentiam et exemplum ostendentes' ...
Tandem Antichristus *occidet eos* in Ierusalem, *et iacebunt corpora eorum in plateis* 'tribus
diebus et tribus noctibus cum dimidio', quia nullus audebit corpora eorum sepelire propter
metum Antichristi. Occisores autem eorum erunt valde laeti propter mortem eorum. *Post*
dies tres autem *et dimidium* resurgent, et eorum occisores audient *vocem* talem: Helias et
Enoch, *ascendite huc,* et *ascendent in coelum in nube.* Antichristus vero ...".
[28] Glossa interlinearis ad Apoc. 11.3: "Id est tribus annis et dimidio, sicut ipse Christus
praedicavit." — Adso: "Postquam ergo per tres annos et dimidium praedicationem suam
compleverint, mox incipiet excandescere Antichristi persecutio et contra eos primum
Antichristus sua arma corripiet eosque interficiet...".

habetur[29] Apocalypsis xj, *spiritus vitae*, id est eorum animae, *intra*bunt *in eos, et st*abunt *super pedes* viventes et impassibiles. *Et audi*ent *vocem de coelo*, loquentem illis: *Ascendite huc* ad consortium angelorum, et *ascend*ent *in nube ad coelum* sicut Christus, ut habetur Actuum[30] 1. Et

5 iustum est, ut qui imitati sunt eum in tribulatione, praedicatione et passione, conformentur illi in ascensione.

Et tunc gravissima persecutio christianorum sequetur. Et hoc Antichristus faciet quattuor[31] modis: P r i m o per callidam eius persuasionem et praedicationem; "praedicabit enim novam legem" et ad

10 praedicandum cunctos licentiabit. Dicit enim Magister[32] in Compendio theologicae veritatis, quod Antichristus praedicabit et affirmabit falsis probationibus ante se nullum fuisse, qui talia praedicabat; propter quod discipuli sui "discurrent per universas mundi partes" eandem doctrinam

---

5 et] ad *cod*

---

[29] Apoc. 11.7–9, 11.

[30] Cf. Acta 1.9.

[31] De variis modis seducendi atque vexandi edocet nos Hans Preuss, *Die Vorstellungen vom Antichrist im späten Mittelalter* (Leipzig, 1906), 18. — Q u a t t u o r modos subvertendi homines enumerat Hugo de Argentina capitulo IX. Compendii supra memorati. Praeterea facit imperare Antichristum divitiis, terrore, sapientia et signis Honorius Augustodunensis in *Elucidario*, 3.10 (PL 172.1163B); item Antoninus Pierozzi Florentinus in *Summa theologica* (Veronae, 1740), 4.13.4 col. 722D–726E, per longum disserit de Antichristi quadruplici modo tentandi homines, scilicet doctrina fallaci, donatione divitiarum, pressura et miraculis; item Iacobus a Voragine in *Legenda aurea*, capitulo 1: "Ipse enim omnes decipere conabitur quattuor modis"; huius loci est denique Anonymi Pataviensis *Tractatus de Antichristo* (Clm 2714, fol. 48rb): "... quasi iiij cornibus armabitur, scilicet callida persuasione, miraculorum operatione, beneficiorum sive donorum largitione et minarum terrore", quae verba in libello *Vom Antichrist* (editio Gerhardi Völker; Monachi, 1970), 83, 126, qui falso Henrico de Mügeln ab aliquibus adscribitur, invenies in hunc modum Germanice transversa: "Die selb nauter cerastes haut vier horn ... Das ain sind sein valsch vnd böss rätt, das ander seine zaichen, die er tuot, das dritte die gross gaub vnd ere, die er git, daz vierd drawe vnd schricke vnd marter," — T r e s tantum modos praebent Alcuinus in *De fide sanctae et individuae trinitatis* 3.19 (PL 101.51C): "Alios adulationibus, alios terroribus, alios signis illicitans, ut se colant pro deo ..." et Adso: "Eriget itaque se contra fideles tribus modis, id est terrore, muneribus et miraculis" et Bonaventura, *Expositio in Ecclesiasten*, 12.6: "Et iste modus erit triplici via, scilicet per miracula, per donaria, per tormenta"; item Petrus Comestor, *Historia scholastica*, ad Dan. 7.8 (PL 198.1454D): "convertet ad se homines terrore, muneribus, miraculis"; Frater Fridericus Sareburgus in *Von dem Endchrist*, versibus 221–230, Antichristum facit alloquentem praedicatores suos (secundum conceptionem B, quae ante 1393 facta est): "Die ier aber dar zu / nicht müget pringen nu, / die sült ir betwingen / mit disen drein dingen: / gebt in schatz unde gut; / wer durh daz nicht tüt, / dem tüt grozze zaichen; / den ir nicht mügt waichen / also, den sült ir erslahn, / und wellent si nicht glawben vahn." — Q u i n q u e modos seu vias "ad seducendum mundum" offert nobis Michael Francisci de Insulis, *De tempore*, fol. C1v.

[32] Hugo, *Compendium*, cap. 9: "Primus ergo modus subvertendi homines erit callida persuasio. Praedicabit enim legem novam pravam esse, et legem Christi pro posse destruet. Praedicatores enim illius discurrent per universas partes mundi. Impedient quoque apostoli Antichristi, ut scriptura secundum veritatem exponatur a catholicis doctoribus ...". — Adso, post initium: "Deinde per universum orbem nuntios mittet et praedicatores suos."

praedicantes. Tunc, ut habetur in Psalmo,[33] *diminutae sunt*, id est
diminuentur, *veritates a filiis hominum.* Tunc, ut habetur Ysaiae[34] 59,
*corru*et *veritas in plateis.* Unde, sicut Christus Matthaei[35] 7 dicit, *arta est
via*; sed ipse Antichristus oppositum praedicabit, scilicet[36] *mollia* et
5 *lenia*; ideo multos audientes habebit. Unde Apostolus[37]: *Erit tempus,
cum sanam doctrinam non sustinebunt.*

   S e c u n d o decipiet bonos per miraculorum ostensionem, unde
Apostolus: *Cuius adventus est secundum operationem Sathanae in omni
virtute et signis et prodigiis*; nam Antichristus faciet signa magna[38]:
10 "Faciet enim arbores florere subito et arescere". Item faciet ymagines
loqui et futura praedicare. Item faciet "mare turbare" et subito tran-
quillare. Item aquarum cursus pervertet retrorsum. Item faciet tonitrua
et fulgura corruscare. Item mortuos | [fol 58v] fallaciter faciet resurgere,
quia maligni spiritus *corpora mortuorum*[39] intrabunt vel assument sibi
15 corpora in specie hominum, qui aliquando vixerunt. Item[40] *ignem faciet
descendere de coelo.* Glossa[41]: "Id est, malignum spiritum faciet super

---

1 Psalmo] p̄ᵗᵃ *cod* ‖ 3 7] 17 *cod* ‖ 3 arta] *cod*, arcta *varia lectio Vulgatae* ‖ 7 ostensionem]
operationem *Iacobus a Voragine* ‖ 11 et] *cod in mg* ‖ 11 praedicare] *cod*, praedicere *Hugo
de Argentina et Walafridus Strabo ad Apoc 13. 15 (PL 114, 734A):* Hic magica arte faciet
statuam loqui et futura praedicere = *Glossa ordinaria ad locum (vide adnotationem 41)* ‖
13 Item] In *cod*, *negligentiae scribae crimini dandum* ‖ 13 corruscare] *De r littera geminata
vide ThesLL IV, 1074, 19*

---

[33] Ps. 11.2. — Lyranus saepius modum praeteriti vel praesentis accipit pro futuro
"propter certitudinem prophetiae", ut declarat exempli gratia ad 2 Thess. 2.4 et ad Ps.
9B.1. Haymo Halberstatensis, *Expositio in Apocalypsim,* 3.11 (PL 117.1075D): "praeteri-
tum tempus est positum hic pro futuro."
   [34] Isa. 59.14.
   [35] Matt. 7.14.
   [36] Cf. Job 40.22: *aut loquetur tibi mollia*; 3 Reg. 12.7: *locutusque fueris ad eos verba
lenia.*
   [37] 2 Tim. 4.3.
   [38] Hugo, *Compendium,* cap. 9: "Faciet arbores cito florere et arescere, mare turbari,
naturas in diversas figuras mutari; mortuos etiam *in conspectu hominum* suscitabit. Tertio
..." — Hugonem hic ex Adsone hausisse perspicuum est cuilibet diligentius legenti:
"*Faciet quoque signa* multa, miracula *magna* et inaudita. *Faciet ignem de coelo* terribili-
ter *venire,* arbores subito florere et arescere, mare turbari et subito tranquillari, naturas in
diversis figuris mutari ..., mortuos etiam *in conspectu hominum* suscitari ...". In secundo
miraculo Antichristus imitatur miraculum virgae Aaron, ut explicat Bonaventura in sua
Expositione in Ecclesiasten, 12.3: "... ita etiam in aemulationem Antichristus faciet florere
et deflorere et alia miracula multa, per quae stulti convertentur ad ipsum."
   [39] 4 Reg. 19.35.
   [40] Apoc. 13.13.
   [41] Glossa ordinaria ad Apoc. 13.13. — Vide etiam Hugonem, *Compendium,* cap. 9:
"Secundus modus subvertendi erit per fallacia miracula, quia per artem magicam illa
faciet. Unde Glossa super Apocalypsim 13: 'Magica arte statuam faciet loqui et futura
praedicere.' *Faciet* — sicut dicitur Apocalypsis 13 — *ignem de coelo descendere in terram.*
Glossa: 'Id est, malignum spiritum faciet super suos descendere, ut loquantur *variis
linguis.*' Spiritus enim malignus descendet in eos *in conspectu hominum,* sicut spiritus
sanctus descendit in apostolos Christi."

suos descendere, et loquentur *variis linguis*". Quicquid enim Antichristus et sui praedicabunt scripturam male interpretando, per miracula confirment, sicut de apostolis dicitur Marci[42] ultimo: *Illi autem profecti*, etc.

5 "T e r t i o[43] decipiet" homines "per munera". Nam dyabolus ostendet Antichristo "thesauros" multos iam in terra "absconditos"; nam primo attrahit sibi magnatos et potentes, et postmodum consequenter alios homines. Hoc ostenditur Danielis[44] xj: *Dividet terram gratuite*. Unde Psalmo[45]: *Sedet cum divitibus in occultis, ut* etc. Glossa[46]:

10 Cum divitibus "huius saeculi", quos ditabit et cum muneribus sibi adunabit. Timeo, si hodie aliquis vellet praedicare haeresim, tantum admitteretur a dominis terrae, si daret eis aurum et argentum. Nam malitia Antichristi praevalebit propter ipsa munera tam in maiores quam in minores, Ieremiae[47] 8: *A minimo usque ad maximum, omnes*

15 *avaritiam secuntur*, etc. Psalmo[48]: *Regnum ipsius omnibus dominabitur*.

"Q u a r t o conpellet" homines per tormentorum fatigationem, quia quos praedictis tribus modis pervertere "non poterit", illos diversis suppliciis puniet. Nam Antichristus multa tormentorum genera excogitabit, Danielis[49] 13: Erit *tempus quale non fuit ex quo gentes esse*

---

1 et loquentur] ut loquantur *Glossa ordinaria et Hugo* ‖ 1 linguis] ligwis *cod* ‖ 9 gratuite] gratuito, gratuitu, gratis *variae lectiones Vulgatae* ‖ 11 tantum] tm̄ *cod*, tamen *malim* ‖ 14 8] 7 *cod in textu, correxit manus secunda in mg* 8 ‖ 14 minimo] *correxit manus secunda in mg iuxta Ier 8.10 pro* minore *in textu iuxta Ier 6.13* ‖ 16 fatigationem] illationem *Iacobus a Voragine*

---

[42] Mar. 16.20: *Illi autem profecti praedicaverunt ubique ... sequentibus signis.*

[43] Hugo, *Compendium*, cap. 9: "Tertio decipiet per munera. Ipse namque Antichristus inveniet thesauros absconditos, per quos ad sequendum se inclinabit plurimos. Ditabit enim divites huius saeculi, et tunc eorum falsam felicitatem ad decipiendum alios ostendet. Quarto ... ". — Adso: "Reges autem et principes primum ad se convertet, deinde per illos ceteros populos." Vide adnotationem 3.

[44] Dan. 11.39.

[45] Ps. 9B.8: *Sedet in insidiis cum divitibus in occultis, ut interficiat innocentem.*

[46] Glossa interlinearis ad Ps. 9B.8: "*cum divitibus*: Quos ditabit quorum felicitatem ad alios decipiendos ostentabit." — Nicolaus de Lyra ad locum: "*Cum divitibus* huius saeculi in hoc sibi adhaerentibus." Item Hugo Cardinalis ad locum: "*cum divitibus*: quos ipse ditabit, ut cupidos divitiarum ad se convertat." — Eandemque glossam citat Michael Francisci de Insulis, *De tempore*, fol. C3r: "Glossa: *Cum divitibus* huius saeculi quos ditabit."

[47] Ier. 8.10; cf. 6.13!

[48] Ps. 102.19.

[49] Dan. 12.1: *et veniet tempus quale non fuit ab eo ex quo gentes esse coeperunt usque ad tempus illud.* — E diverso argumentum proposuit Hieronymus in *De Antichristo*, in Dan. 39, dicens: "quoscumque terrore non quiverit, subiugabit avaritia"; hanc sententiam sine dubio accepit Anonymus Pataviensis (Clm. 2714, fol. 48vb): "Quos enim suo terrore subiugare non poterit, avaritia subiugabit." Ps-Henricus de Mügeln rem suis verbis capitulo XIV. sic reddit: "... wann die lut, die er mit ler vnd mit zaichen oder mit marter an sich nicht pringen mag, die pringet er mit gaub an sich."

coeperunt usque ad tempus illud. Item sciendum, quod tempore Antichristi erit persecutio gravior quam unquam fuit tempore martyrum.
Quamvis enim martyres multi passi sunt, tamen tempore Antichristi
boni maiores persecutiones habebunt, unde Magister[50] in Compendio
5   theologicae veritatis. Et maxime religiosos impugnat. Et omnes persecutores cleri sunt praecursores Antichristi, quod tunc temporis nec
emetur nec vendetur ab eis, *"nisi habe*ant *characterem"* Antichristi,
"scilicet signum adhaerentes" Antichristo.

O quam stulti sunt, qui optant, quod possent vivere *usque ad illud*
10   *tempus,* dicentes, si tunc viverent, quod pro deo multa pati vellent, qui
forte ad minimam persecutionem Christum desererent! Sane fateor,
quotiens de illo tempore cogito, corde contremisco. Considera, quid
evenerit Petro, et in persecutione semper timebis. Petrus enim Christo
se commoriturum promisit, sed adveniente persecutione Christum ter
15   negavit.[51] Quis enim poterit esse securus, quando erit tanta tribulatio
quanta umquam fuit in mundo?

Quantum ad q u a r t u m,[52] sciendum, quod Antichristus finget se
mortuum, ut habetur Apocalypsis[53] 13: *Vidi unum de capitibus suis,*
scilicet Antichristum, *quasi occisum* et fingentem se quasi mortuum et
20   "latens per triduum"; postea "apparebit, dicens se suscitatum". Et tunc
dilecti eius resurrectionem praedicabunt, in quos et ipse missurus est
spiritum malignum in specie ignis. Et tunc voce dyaboli loquentur[54]

---

3 multi] *cod*, multa *malim* ‖ 5 impugnat] impūgnat *cod* ‖ 6 praecursores] *correctum ex*
persecutores *et in mg iteratum*: praecursores ‖ 9 ad [hoc] illud *cod* ‖ 10 viverent] *addidit sed*
delevit vellent *cod* ‖ 16 umquam] ūquam *cod*, numquam *malim*

---

[50] Hugo, *Compendium,* cap. 9: "Quarto compellet per minas et tormenta, quos aliter
vincere non poterit ... Exhibebit enim cuncta, quae in praecedentibus martyribus impleta
sunt genera tormentorum, sed in illis regionibus tunc fideles maxime sunt vexandi et
vehementius, 'ubi dominus fuit crucifixus' ... Fideles quoque illo tempore non praedicabunt, quia tamquam excommunicati habebuntur tunc boni. Nihil vendetur eis, nec emetur
ab eis, *nisi habe*ant *characterem* (Apoc. 13.17), id est 'signum aliquod ad litteram, ut
adhaerentes sibi cognoscantur et alii interficiantur' ... Antichristus autem sicut erit
crudelior omnibus persecutoribus, ita sancti tunc temporis fortiores erunt omnibus retro
martyribus."
[51] Cf. Mar. 14.31: *Et si oportuerit me simul commori tibi, non te negabo.* Matt.
26.34–35, 75.
[52] Quoad quartum vide Hugonem, *Compendium,* cap. 9: "Item per artem magicam
simulabit se mortuum, et feretur a daemonibus in aera, quasi ascendat in coelum ... Sicut
enim Antichristus finget se a mortuis resurgere, ita etiam finget se ad coelum ascendere,
Apocalypsis 13: *Et plaga mortis eius curata est.* Glossa: 'Arte magica ascendet' Antichristus in aera, ferentibus eum daemonibus.' Faciet arbores ..." — Hugo equidem dependet a
Glossa ordinaria, quod non absconditum est intuenti adnotationes 53 et 56.
[53] Apoc. 13.3: *Et vidi unum de capitibus suis quasi occisum in mortem; et plaga mortis*
eius curata est. — Glossa ordinaria ad locum: "*Quasi occisum:* Simulabit se Antichristus
mortuum, et per triduum latens post apparebit, dicens se suscitatum."
[54] Acts 2.3–4: *Et apparuerunt illis dispertitae linguae tanquam ignis, seditque supra*

variis linguis, sicut apostoli ex *spiritu sancto*. Tunc, ut habetur Danielis[55]
xj, *veniet* Antichristus *in multitudine magna et figet tabernaculum*, id est
thronum solii sui in *monte Oliveti*. Qui de tali monte, ut dicit Glossa[56]
super Apocalypsim, "arte magica" et virtute dyabolica "ascendet in

5   aera" ut Symon magus, "ferentibus eum daemonibus". *Tunc secundum
Apostolum* | [fol 59r] *revelabitur ille iniquus* — Glossa[57]: id est, nequitia
et falsitas eius detegetur —, *quem dominus Ihesus interficiet spiritu oris
sui* — Glossa[58]: "id est, virtute spiritus sancti" — et hoc in loco illo,
intra quem dominus ascendit. Notandum, quod morietur mala morte,

10 primo quod morietur in *plaga* subitaneae *mortis*; secundo, quod morietur in peccatis mortalibus, Psalmo[59]: *In operibus manuum suarum
comprehensus est peccator.*

Quo[60] "interfecto *dominus* non statim *veniet ad iudicium*, sed secundum Glossam[61] Apocalypsis 14 conceduntur xl dies 'ad refrigerium

---

1 linguis] liguis *cod* ‖ 7 detegetur] *an legendum sit* detegentur, *diiudicare non ausim* ‖ 7 oris
sui] oris eius sui *cod* ‖ 8 spiritus sancti] sp^e spiritus sancti *cod* ‖ 14 Apocalypsis 14] *cod, iuxta
Hugonem legendum est* super Danielem ‖

---

singulos eorum; et repleti sunt omnes spiritu sancto, et coeperunt loqui variis linguis. —
Nicolaus de Lyra ad 1 Tim. 4.1: "*daemoniorum*: in falsis prophetis loquentium. Sicut enim
salvator praemisit discipulos in omnem civitatem et locum, quo ipse erat venturus, ut
habetur Lucae 10 et illi loquebantur in spiritu sancto, sic et Antichristus praemittet
prophetas suos loquentes spiritu diabolico."
    [55] Dan. 11.44–45. — Glossa interlinearis ad locum: "*tabernaculum*: Id est solii sui,
scilicet et thronum." — Videsis adnotationem 60, ubi Glossa ordinaria ad 2 Thess. 2.8 ab
Hugone citatur fere ad verbum: "Occidetur autem in *monte Oliveti* ... non statim *veniet*."
    [56] Glossa ordinaria ad Apoc. 13.3: "*Et plaga mortis*: Arte magica ascendet in aera,
ferentibus eum daemonibus; et sic curabitur *plaga mortis eius*, quia prius mortuus
credebatur, post vivens reputabitur." — Glossa interlinearis ad 2 Thess. 2.9: "*prodigiis
mendacibus*: Quia per magicam artem non veram, sed per phantasiam deludet homines,
sicut Simon magus quendam qui se eum occidere putans, arietem decollavit."
    [57] Locus incertus. — Recte quidem et expedite vox nequitiae explicatur in Glossa
ordinaria ad Ps. 52.1 additio 1: "... agitur de Antichristo, cuius principalis et propria
nequitia consistit in negando Christum esse deum."
    [58] Glossa ordinaria ad 2 Thess. 2.8: "*spiritu oris*: id est virtute spiritus sancti, qui dicitur
'spiritus oris', quia ab eo procedit."
    [59] Ps. 9.17.
    [60] Verba sequentia sunt Hugonis ex capitulo 14 *Compendii*; ex sua parte commixuit
Glossam ordinariam ad 2 Thess. 2.8 cum glossa interlineari ad Dan. 12.12 (quam in
adnotatione 61 integram iteramus), dicens: "Occidetur autem in *monte Oliveti*, in papil-
ione et solio suo, in loco, circa quem dominus ascendit in coelum. Interfecto autem
Antichristo non statim *veniet dominus ad iudicium*, sed secundum Glossam super Danielem concedentur quadragintaquinque dies ad refrigerium sanctorum, et ad conver-
sionem et poenitentiam subversorum. Quantum autem spatium sit inter illos
quadragintaquinque dies et finem mundi, nemo scit." — Cf. Petrus Lombardus, *Collectanea in Epist. D. Pauli*, 2 Thess. 2.3 (PL 192.320BC): "Occidetur autem, ut doctores
tradunt, in *monte Oliveti* ... penitus ignoratur", qui dependet ab Adsone sub fine dicente:
"Tradunt autem doctores, quod in *monte Oliveti* Antichristus occidetur ... nullus est qui
sciat, sed in dispositione dei manet, qui ea hora saeculum iudicabit, qua ante saecula
iudicandum esse praefixit." Adsonem imitatur — liceat velut obiter adnotare — Haymo
Halberstatensis (PL 117.781C).

⟨sanctorum⟩ et ad poenitentiam subversorum'", qui cognoscunt se deceptos ab Antichristo. Sed post hos dies spatium usque ad finem "nemo scit" nisi solus deus, qui ea hora et tempore saeculum iudicabit, quae ante saecula iudicandum esse praevidit.

5   *Rogamus vos per adventum domini nostri Iesu, ut non cito moveamini neque terreamini, quasi instet dies domini*, scilicet iudicii. *Ne quis vos seducat ullo modo; quoniam nisi venerit discessio primum, et revelatus fuerit filius perditionis*[62]. Glossa[63] semper: *Dominus non veniet ad iudicium*. Ubi Gorra[64] super isto verbo 'discessio' ponit tria, quae fient ante
10   adventum Antichristi: P r i m u m discessio "gentium a Romano imperio, quia ante idem tempus dividetur Romanum imperium in decem regna, sicut habetur Danielis[65] 7 in figura ⟨quartae⟩ bestiae habentis decem capita". S e c u n d u m discessio "ecclesiarum particularium ab oboedientia Romanae ecclesiae, quae diem domini praecedet". T e r t i-

---

4 quae] qua *Adso* ‖ 4 praevidit] prafixit *varia lectio apud Adsonem* ‖ 7 discessio] dissessio *cod, et sic semper deinceps perperam scriptum pro* discessio, *id quod 'apostasia'; Glossa interlinearis ad 2 Thess 2.3*: "discessio primum: alias dissencio"; *Ps-Henricus de Mügeln*: missehellung ‖ 8 semper] sp̄ *cod* ‖

---

[61] Immo Glossa interlinearis ad Dan. 12.12: "Dies quietis et pacis post mortem Antichristi, quadragintaquinque superioribus adduntur ad refrigerium sanctorum et ad poenitentiam subversorum."
[62] 2 Thess. 2.1, 3.
[63] Locus incertus et textus lubricus, sed vide Adsonem, Isaiam 3.14 afferentem: "nec statim *veniet dominus ad iudicium*."
[64] Gorranus, ad 2 Thess. 2.3: "Hoc potest intelligi tripliciter: Primo modo de discessione gentium a Romano imperio, quia ante illa tempora dividetur Romanum imperium in decem regna, sicut habetur Danielis vij in figura quartae bestiae habentis *decem cornua*. Secundo modo potest intelligi de discessione ecclesiarum particularium ab oboedientia Romanae ecclesiae, quae diem domini praecedet. Tertio modo de discessione quorundam christianorum a fide catholica, quae similiter circa illa tempora erit, j Timothei iiij: *Spiritus* enim *manifeste dicit, quia in novissimis temporibus discedent quidam a fide*. Nec dicit, quod post discessionem hanc statim futurum sit iudicium, sed quod haec discessio praecedet iudicium." — Triplicem discessionem annuntiat etiam Petrus Lombardus in suis *Collectaneis in Epist. D. Pauli*, 2 Thess. 2.3 (PL 192.317A), qui sequitur hanc opinionem Haymonis: "... id est, nisi prius gens a Romano discedat imperio ... Vel hoc dicit de spirituali imperio Romanae ecclesiae, vel de discessione a fide." — Taliter denique Anonymus Pataviensis imitatur Petrum Lombardum (Clm. 2714, fol. 45va): "... *discessio, id est, nisi prius gentes a Romano discedant imperio, vel discessio ecclesiarum a spirituali oboedientia Romanae ecclesiae, vel hominum <discessio> a fide, vel *nisi prius revelatus, id est manifestatus, *fuerit homo peccati ...*".
[65] Cf. Dan. 7.7: ... *et habebat cornua decem*. — Gorranus, ad 2 Thess. 2.7: "Ante adventum enim Antichristi Romanum imperium cessabit et dividetur in decem regna, sicut habetur Danielis vij." Glossa interlinearis ad Dan. 7.7: "Dicunt in adventu Antichristi decem reges orbem Romanorum esse divisuros." Hugo Cardinalis ad eundem locum: "'Hoc respicit ad finem mundi' dicit Hieronymus, sicut omnes doctores ecclesiastici tradunt, quia tunc Romanum regnum dividetur in decem regna, quod significatum est per decem soles in vaticinio Sibyllae, quos in fine mundi praedixit venturos." — Glossa ordinaria ad Apoc. 17.3: "*Et cornua decem*: id est, decem regna, quae erunt tempore Antichristi, per quae alia intelliguntur."

u m discessio "quorundam christianorum a fide catholica, quae similiter eo tempore erit, 1ª Timothei[66] 4: *In novissimis* diebus *discedent quidam a fide*". Et q u a r t u m signum superaddit quidam alius doctor,[67] quod ipse "Antichristus veniet in tempore peccatorum habundantiae". De
5 quo Daniel[68]: *Cum* veniant *iniquitates, consurget rex inpu*dicus. Glossa[69]: omnium iniquitatum plenus, etc. Et dignum est, ut iniquus veniens in mundum inveniet iniquitates, et non unam, sed plures[70]: homicidia, mendacia, adulteria, furta. Et unum peccatum aliud impellat.[71] Tunc veniet Antichristus, iniquus rex super malos subditos,
10 quia dicitur in Decretis[72]: "Praelatus malus quandoque datur pro peccato populi, 6 q. 1".

Quis dubitat iam facere proximum, cum iam ex mala consuetudine quasi infinita mala fiunt, quae parentum nostrorum in tempore non modici fuissent dedecoris, quae nunc inter finita computantur honoris,
15 etc?

---

9 impellat] *cod, idem quod* impellit

---

[66] 1 Tim. 4.1, ut in adnotatione 64 recitutum est.

[67] Locus minus certus. Sed afferre licet *Tractatum de Antichristo* Anonymi Pataviensis sic incipientem: "'De Antichristo venturo.' Antichristus veniet in tempore habundantiae peccatorum, sicut dicitur Danielis viij: *Cum creverint iniquitates*, id est habundaverint, *consurget rex impudens facie*" (Clm 2714, fol. 45va). Ps-Henricus de Mügeln, capitulo IV. hanc sententiam imitatur, dicens: "Der anticrist kumbt, wenne die welt mit vngerechtikait erfullet wirt." — Animum intende etiam ad Michaelem Francisci de Insulis, qui in *Determinatione* sua dicit (fol. A7r): "Et breviter ex omnibus istis sequitur finale signum, scilicet habundantia peccatorum secundum illud: *Quoniam habundabit iniquitas, refrigescet caritas multorum*."

[68] Dan. 8.23: *cum creverint iniquitates, consurget rex impudens facie*.

[69] Locus incertus.

[70] Cf. Matt. 15.19: *homicidia, adulteria, fornicationes, furta*.

[71] Proverbialiter dictum esse videtur, ut apparet ex *Thesauro proverbiorum* a K.F.W. Wander condito sub voce 'Sünde' 60, 66 et 68: "Ex peccato peccatum nascitur", haud immemor sis illius Terentii: "Aliud ex alio malo" (Otto Nr. 1019). Martinus Luther dixisse fertur: "una calamitas trudit aliam" WA 43.164, 34.

[72] Glossa ad *Decretum Gratiani* (Lugduni, 1506), C. 8 q. 1 c. 18 fol. CLXXXv/b: "Audacter] Haec est quarta pars quaestionis. In qua dicitur, quod quandoque dat deus malos praelatos propter peccata populi ...". — Auctor sermonis in mente habuit illam potius sententiam, quae in 'Margarita Decreti seu tabula Martiniana', id est in Appendice euisdem editionis Lugdunensis, legitur folio XXXIIIv: "Quod malus praelatus quandoque datur propter peccata populi vj q. j."

CONTRA RECTAM RATIONEM:
GABRIEL BIEL'S READING OF
GREGORY OF RIMINI, VERSUS GREGORY

MANFRED SCHULZE

Reason and Morality

The first critical edition of the *Lectura Sententiarum* of Gregory of Rimini, the Parisian Augustinian *magister* (died 1358), is a welcome means by which to reach out past two-dimensional representations and beyond general attempts at imposing order on intellectual history and to penetrate more deeply into the individual themes of his theology. The Gregory edition, which has been achieved through hard work and completed under the aegis of the man this commemorative publication honors, has created the sort of readability of the texts that makes it possible to pursue details within the whole and assess their significance.

For some time it has aroused amazement and attracted the attention of researchers that the seemingly typically modern hope for a rational secular morality, accessible to every human being of whatever faith or caste he might be, can make claim to a heritage that has reached modern times from the late Middle Ages. Gregory of Rimini, so it is said, was the one who lastingly posited and legitimated a worldly reason that could arrive at a valid moral judgment even without any tie to God. Hans Welzel, who came upon Gregory of Rimini while researching the history of natural law, discovers in Gregory's work not only the past, but also a turning toward the future, that he "made the validity of moral values hypothetically independent of the existence of God—and not only of His will, but also of His reason, at least as divine reason."[1]

In examining this interpretation in the context of the general history of natural law and the concept of reason it is, however, easy to lose sight of the grounds for Gregory's formulation of a theory which apparently points the way to the future. If one goes back to the texts, one comes upon a soberingly limited and, at least in the first place, disappointingly old-fashioned intent. There is no mention of the secularization of reason or the rationalization of moral values apart from the existence of God, but ample mention of sin and that which makes sinners of human

---

[1] Hans Welzel, *Naturrecht und materiale Gerechtigkeit*, 4th ed. (Göttingen, 1962), 94.

beings. What first strikes one is how unequivocally the Augustinian distances himself from voluntaristic descriptions of sin. He appears to trust in right reason, which is able to judge good and evil properly. He constantly imparts the same information in many variations: sin is humankind's offense against the 'recta ratio.' Gregory's rationally aligned understanding of sin was not able during the late Middle Ages to attract the sort of attention[2] it was to gain at the beginning of the modern era, starting among the Spanish late scholastics.[3] Only about 145 years after the first appearance of Gregory's commentary did the history of critical analysis of his definition of sin, as opposed to others of his ideas, begin. It was the Tübingen Magister Gabriel Biel (died 1495) who recognized the importance of this concept and even made it his own—in a way, however, that could only turn Gregory's intent on its head.

Thus it is first to be asked what Gregory himself meant by his definition of sin and what he achieved theologically with it. And then it is to be made known what Gabriel Biel, in this case the first significant analyst, discovered in the concept transmitted to him and how he made his own use of it.[4]

---

[2] One would have to designate Hugolin of Orvieto (d. 1373) as Gregory's closest disciple. He presented Gregory's definition of sin in his commentary on the *Sentences* and shared his interpretation. But where Gregory's argumentation about the *recta ratio* aims at its culmination he was unable to follow it and let it die. It was "non ... bene digesta," he objected. *Hugolini de Urbe Veteri OESA: Commentarius in quattuor libros Sententiarum*, ed. W. Eckermann OSA (Würzburg, 1986), III, 509, 217f. The commentary of Marsilius of Inghen (d. 1396) is among the significant anthologies of the literature of the *Sentences*. He too, the theologian of the *via moderna* was very familiar with Gregory's theology but entirely left aside his teaching on sin. In the comprehensive anthology of the *via antiqua* put together by Johannes Capreolus (d. 1444), one finds, according to expectation, thematically relevant Gregory texts concerning his teaching on sin, but not the crucial one as pertains to the theory of the *recta ratio*. Capreolus was interested in a critical confrontation with Gregory's view that sin was not a *res* but a *complexe significabile*. See *Johannis Capreoli Tholosani ... Defensiones Theologiae Divi Thomae Aquinatis*, ed. C. Paban and T. Pègues (Tours, 1903; reprinted, Frankfurt, 1967), IV, 409a.

[3] The following authors of Spanish late scholasticism have concerned themselves with Gregory, criticized him or analyzed him: Francisco de Vitoria (d. 1546), Luis de Molina (d. 1600), Gabriel Vázquez (d. 1604), and Francisco de Suárez (d. 1619). See Manuel Santos. "Die Sünden-und Gnadenlehre des Gregor von Rimini," (Dr. theol. dissertation, Tübingen, 1988), 26f.

[4] John L. Farthing is of the opinion that Biel's method of working is "notoriously eclectic." Such an evaluation leads one astray because it overlooks Biel's concern with demonstrating the concensus of doctrine within theology. Farthing is, however, right in that one must comprehend the way Biel deals with the traditions in the interest of a proper understanding of his theology. Then it also becomes apparent that Biel does not act in a "notoriously" but in a "deliberately" selective manner. See John L. Farthing, *Thomas Aquinas and Gabriel Biel: Interpretations of St. Thomas Aquinas in German Nominalism on the Eve of the Reformation* (Durham, North Carolina, 1988), ix.

Gregory of Rimini: The Irrationality of Sin

It was Gregory of Rimini's intention to set forth the description of what was to be understood as sin with definitive unequivocality: "Actual sin occurs out of the willful intention to do or to leave undone something which runs counter to the 'recta ratio.'"[5] This definition is completely sufficient and requires no supplementation. He who does not wish to sin, he assures his reader, should hold to staying in harmony with the 'recta ratio.'[6] He finds the interpretation that a sinner acts contrary to the 'recta ratio' to be set down in Augustine, although it will become apparent that interpretative efforts are required before the Church Father can be found to speak in the desired manner for Gregory's position.

The deciding Augustinian evidence was not found by Gregory himself, but has been a part of the compendium of authorities drawn upon concerning this issue since Petrus Lombardus.[7] In the Church Father's work *Contra Faustum* one finds the much-cited key sentence: "Peccatum est factum vel dictum vel concupitum aliquid contra aeternam legem."[8] This definition, so Gregory claims, is "convertibilis" and "consona" with his own, for Augustine meant none other than the 'ratio divina' with his 'lex aeterna,' and the 'ratio divina' in turn is identical with the will of God, who orders that the 'ordo naturalis' be preserved. Thus Augustine himself carried out the equation of 'eternal law' with 'divine reason,' or so Gregory holds.[9] The voluntative element in the pronouncement of the Church Father, however—"... voluntas dei ... iubens ..."[10]—is passed over without comment. Therefore since the divine 'ratio' is always and everywhere the right 'ratio,' Gregory can reformulate Augustine's definition of sin into his own: "... secundum Augustinum recte dicatur peccatum esse factum vel dictum vel concupitum aliquid contra rectam rationem ..."[11]

---

[5] *Lectura*, 2 Sent. dist. 34–37 q. 1 art. 2 (VI, 234): "... peccatum actuale non est aliud quam voluntarie committere aliquid vel omittere contra rectam rationem."

[6] *Lectura*, 2 Sent. dist. 34–37 q. 1 art. 2 (VI, 234): "Si enim quis agat secundum quod recta ratio iudicat esse ab illo agendum, agit sicut agere debet; et si sic, non peccat."

[7] This quotation from Augustine already functions as the *locus classicus*, which the chapter on definition opens in Petrus Lombardus: "Quid sit peccatum." *Magistri Petri Lombardi Sententiae in IV libris distinctae*, ed. PP. Collegii S. Bonaventurae, 3rd ed. (Grottaferrata, 1971), I, part 2, 529.

[8] Augustine, *Contra Faustum Manichaeum*, 22.27 (*PL*, XLII, 418); *Lectura*, 2 Sent. dist. 34–37 q. 1 art. 2 (VI, 235).

[9] *Lectura*, 2 Sent. dist. 34–37 q. 1 art. 2 (VI, 235): "Tantum ergo valet quod ait (scil. Augustinus) 'contra aeternam legem' quantum si dicatur 'contra divinam rationem etc.'"

[10] *Lectura*, 2 Sent. dist. 34–37 q. 1 art. 2 (VI, 235): "Lex vero aeterna est ratio divina vel voluntas dei ordinem naturalem conservari iubens, perturbari vetans." Cf. Augustine, *Contra Faustum Manichaeum*, 22.27;

[11] *Lectura*, 2 Sent. dist. 34–37 q. 1 art. 2 (VI, 235).

The dovetailing with Augustine fits exactly into the Augustinian's plan and yet one may not say that the rationally conceived definition of sin is simply the result of his analysis of Augustine. For this agreement does not in fact rise naturally to the fore, it must rather first be deliberately set up.

The Practical Principles of Action

Since it is sin to transgress against the 'recta ratio,' human beings should also be in a position to recognize what is sin and what is not. After all it is reason that sets the measure and not a hidden, obscure law, unfathomable to humans, that forbids one thing and allows another. Gregory appears to uphold this assumption, for according to his interpretation it is not necessary in every case to first create a law that makes a sin of naive action without consciousness of guilt, since even without a law the 'recta ratio' condemns the evil deed as wickedness.[12] This points to the conclusion that it would be consonant with his theological system to believe man to possess the power to recognize sin. If he has reason, then he also knows what is right and good. In fact one finds statements in Gregory's work that could support such a supposition: Although God's help is necessary for us to arrive at the understanding that God is to be loved above all things and not hated,[13] yet there are on the other hand also areas of action about which a human being can judge entirely from his own rationality, without Gregory's making a claim to God's help for the purpose. 'To honor one's parents' or 'not to persecute virtuous men with hatred' he characterizes as 'veritates practicae,' which are also in the gift of heathen philosophers although no law of God had been written for them.[14] Every man can conform his actions to such practical maxims, because does not every man know that he may not do anyone wrong, not return evil for good or envy anyone what is his. And even the prohibition against hating God[15] is counted by Gregory as one of the rationally discernible rules of action.[16]

---

[12] *Lectura*, 2 Sent. dist. 34–37 q. 1 art. 2 (VI, 237): "... multa ex se sunt peccata et non praecise quia prohibita. Quinimmo posito quod non forent prohibita, adhuc taliter agens peccaret."

[13] *Lectura*, 2 Sent. dist. 34–37 q. 1 art. 2 (VI, 237): "... esto quod nullum praeceptum datum fuisset aut foret homini dandum, adhuc auxiliante deo posset cognoscere et iudicare deum non esse odiendum sed diligendum super omnia, utpote summum bonum et omnium bonorum nostrorum auctorem."

[14] *Lectura*, 2 Sent. dist. 34–37 q. 1 art. 2 (VI, 237–238): "Posset (scil. homo) etiam cognoscere parentes et praesertim virtuosos ... esse honorandos a filiis, virum virtuosum inquantum huiusmodi non esse odiendum ... et multas alias veritates practicas, quas etiam mundi philosophi non habentes ulla praecepta vel legem prohibentem cognoverunt."

[15] *Lectura*, 2 Sent. dist. 34–37 q. 1 art. 2 (VI, 244, 242).

[16] If one does not want to find an inconsistency, one can assume that the contrariness to reason of hatred for God is counted by Gregory among natural principles, while he

The specified 'practical truths' are to be understood as principles in the strict sense.[17] Gregory designates them as "prima," as the foundations of knowledge without further presuppositions and they are not only "vera," but also "per se nota" and thereby as immediately intelligible as principles of geometry.[18] Since Gregory also defends the existence of such principles of action by invoking Augustine's authority,[19] there can be no doubt that he counts on a certain decisionmaking power of practical reason. He knows rules of action that are plain to every reasonable human being even without specific enlightenment.

Inconsistency in Gregory?

The assumptions described thrust upon us the conclusion that man is capable of knowing what is sin and what is morality. Principles of action are known to even the fallen human being, and the ability to think has not been lost to him in spite of sin. Neither fallen human beings nor fallen angels are so dazzled or so blinded. They all know the 'principia practica' and can draw practical conclusions from them. That was the interpretation as John Duns Scotus (died 1308) had presented it.[20] It would fit beautifully into Gregory's system. For if one recognizes the moral quality of action by its conformity to the 'recta ratio' and if reason is even able to name 'principia' of action, then it is only logical to concede man knowledge about good and evil, sin and morality. Whether he can then also transform this knowledge into practical

---

presupposes the help of God's grace for the gaining of the insight into the necessity of 'loving God above all else.' See above, footnote 13, and below, footnote 37.

[17] On the concept of principles in Gregory see my examination of the subject in "Von der Via Gregorii zur Via Reformationis: Der Streit um Augustin im späten Mittelalter," (Dr. Theol. dissertation, Tübingen, 1980), 38f.

[18] *Lectura*, 2 Sent. dist. 34–37 q. 1 art. 2 (VI, 244): "... nemini esse iniuriandum, nulli pro bono malum esse reddendum, nulli esse invidendum, et multa alia quae circa agibilia ita sunt prima principia et per se nota et vera, sicut quod, si 'eidem aliqua sint aequalia, sibi invicem sunt aequalia' (Euclid) ... aut quaecumque alia prima principia in speculabilibus."

[19] As Gregory reports, Augustine describes such principles as *lumina virtutum* and *regulae sapientiae*. *Lectura*, 2 Sent. dist. 34-37 q. 1 art. 2 (VI, 244). See also Augustine, *De libero arbitrio*, 2.10.29 (*PL*, XXXII, 1257).

[20] The problem is treated by Scotus as by Gregory with the framework of the doctrine of Angels. It does not concern a tangential problem of angelology, but a basic problem of theology. For Gregory's theology in particular, the question is: what fallen creation, human being or angel, is capable of achieving with its natural powers. Gregory renders Duns Scotus's answer correctly: "... intellectus angeli non est ita excaecatus, quod erret circa principia practica ... Ex illo autem principio potest (scil. angelus lapsus) deducere conclusionem practicam necessariam ... Igitur sicut voluntas nostra de tali conclusione deducta ex tali principio potest habere volitionem rectam, ita angelus sequendo dictamen intellectus sui potest habere volitionem bene circumstantiatam." *Lectura*, 2 Sent. dist. 7 q. 1 art. 1 (V, 58). See also John Duns Scotus, *Opera omnia*, ed. Wadding (Lyon, 1639; reprinted Hildesheim, 1969), XI, 1, 296f.

action, would be a second—although not secondary—question.

Now one comes upon a confusing state of affairs, however: the same Gregory who speaks of natural 'principia practica' accessible to reason had disputed these principles of action in Scotus. He saw in the concept that man is equipped with moral knowledge only the revival and even magnification of the old Pelagian heresy.[21] Such 'principia practica,' upon which moral action can be founded, do not exist, Gregory contends. It is rather God alone who makes possible the knowledge of and desire for the good. He must first create the foundations of morality because moral knowledge in man has been destroyed as punishment for the Fall.[22] Accordingly this must be the case: "The beginning of goodly desiring and knowing does not proceed from man himself. This is prepared and given by God, as becomes clear when one thinks upon the fate of the devil and his angels. These cannot find the way back to the good will." To his and his contemporaries' knowledge it had been Augustine who in 'his' work *De fide ad Petrum* had held the conviction that the 'condition humaine' becomes clear in the devil's fall:[23] without God's intervention the fallen remain irretrievably sunk in evil. Just those 'principia practica' which according to Scotus remain even to the sinner, are no longer present. If he is conscious of them nevertheless, then it is not because they have survived the Fall, but because God has given him them anew.[24]

With this Gregory appears to clearly contradict himself: on the one side he speaks of 'principia agendi' which are known to every one of themselves ('per se nota'),[25] on the other, however, he contests their natural existence. One cannot resolve the contradiction by always reading the recognizance of principles of action as if there were a previous indication of 'auxiliante deo'.[26] For principles cannot be known directly of themselves if one must lay claim to God's help to make it possible to recognize them.

---

[21] *Lectura*, 2 Sent. dist. 26–28 q. 1 art. 2 (VI, 58–59): "... ipsi (scil. Pelagiani moderni) absolute dicunt hominem posse sine adiutorio dei recte velle et agere, non ponentes ipsum indigere iuvari ad notitiam habendam de volendis et agendis; Pelagius vero ponit hominem tali dei auxilio indigere."

[22] *Lectura*, 2 Sent. dist. 7 q. 2 art. 1 (V, 93–94): "... poena peccati est quod mens aliquando perspicuas ratiocinationes formidet et de inventione veritatis desperet; aliquando etiam conetur in lucem intelligendi, et rursus decidat fatigata."

[23] *Lectura*, 2 Sent. dist. 7 q. art. 1 (V, 60): "... quod 'bonae voluntatis initium et cogitationis non homini ex se ipso nasci, sed divinitus et praeparari et tribui, in eo deus evidenter ostendit, quod neque diabolus neque aliquis angelorum eius ... bonam potuit aut poterit resumere voluntatem.'" Cf. Augustine (actually Fulgentius of Ruspe {d. 533}), *De fide ad Petrum*, 3.33 (*PL*, XL, 763).

[24] *Lectura*, 2 Sent. dist. 7 q. 1 art. 1 (V, 65): "... quod tale principium sibi (scil. diabolo) veniat in mentem ... non est in eius potestate sicut nec hominis, sicut docet Apostolus ..."

[25] See above, footnote 18.

[26] See above, footnote 13.

One of the possible interpretations would consist of letting the redundancy 'both ... and' stand for a sign of uncertainty. Gregory would then wish to speak both of the capabilities of man and of his incapabilities. That would accord with the vague sort of language he makes use of in one of his conclusions: '... no human being in his present sinful condition is able without God's special help to *sufficiently* ("sufficienter") recognize what he should desire or refuse, do or refrain from doing in moral matters.[27] Thus he can recognize, yet however not 'sufficiently.' That is perhaps the irresolution of someone undecided who is not sure of the realization in detail of his program.

The most probable thing, however, in the case of so circumspect an author as Gregory of Rimini should be to assume that he took this two-sided position on purpose. He would then proceed from the standpoint that a natural fundamental knowledge that has survived the Fall into sin does indeed exist. And yet this knowledge does not extend to insight into the essence of morality. For that the special help of God is fundamentally necessary.[28]

The Immortality of the Heathen

This two-sided position becomes understandable when we consider a practical example. For Christian ethics in Antiquity and the Middle Ages a challenging problem came into being in view of heathens and unbelievers, a problem with which Gregory too had dealt extensively: Does one not find virtue and morality among heathens as well, even 'shining stars with regard to virtues,' as one might say?[29] One can see in the example of the heathens that man exists as a moral being without God as well. He can honor his parents, help the poor, fight bravely and steadfastly for the fatherland—all this and much else happens without God's direct intervention and yet "iuxta iudicium rectae rationis." No-one would be permitted to claim that doing such were sin. On the contrary, this is good and praiseworthy.[30] That is the objection that Gregory formulates to his own arguments.

Gregory can now grant that every human being, thus the unbeliever

---

[27] *Lectura*, 2 Sent. dist. 26–28 q. 1 art. 1 (VI, 24): "... nullus homo etc. (scil. in statu praesenti, dei etiam generali influentia stante) potest absque speciali auxilio dei in his quae ad moralem vitam pertinent *sufficienter* cognoscere quid volendum vel nolendum, agendum vel vitandum sit." See also the analogous formulation in *Lectura*, 2 Sent. dist. 26–28 q. 1 art. 1 (VI, 52): *probatio secundae conclusionis* "Si homo potest absque speciali auxilio dei *sufficienter* cognoscere ..."

[28] *Lectura*, 2 Sent. dist. 26–28 q. 1 art. 1 (VI, 53f.).

[29] *Lectura*, 2 Sent. dist. 26–28 q. 1 art. 1 (VI, 46): "... splendidae stellae virtutum ...," according to a formulation of Robert Grosseteste (d. 1253), whom Gregory cites as sharing his interpretation.

[30] *Lectura*, 2 Sent. dist. 26–28 q. 1 art. 3 (VI, 66).

as well, has the principles and rules of a moral way of life at his disposal.[31] It should thus be kept in mind that he does not disavow the decent action of the heathen. He does not, from some superior, 'enlightened' Christian standpoint, try to reveal an apparent good deed as a shameful deed. Yet, the knowledge and application of principles of good conduct he grants do not suffice for someone to be able to think and act morally as well. The human being should be concerned rather with God,[32] that is, only with God, not with God's reward.[33]

Morality arises from the love of God[34] and not out of the feeling for decency that healthy human reason can undoubtedly muster up. What the heathens are able to achieve of good does not arise from the love of God and therefore not from virtue.[35] Because neutral action that is of no account before God does not exist for Gregory, such decency is nothing other than sin.[36] This is the meaning of the two-sided position taken by Gregory and at the same time what is objectionable in the strict

---

[31] *Lectura*, 2 Sent. dist. 29 q. 1 art. 2 (VI, 141): "... dico quod, esto quod concederem gentilem infidelem aut alium aliquem hominem naturaliter et sine speciali dei auxilio cognoscere nemini esse iniuriandum, nihil alienum praeripiendum, et similes veritates quae sunt principia et regulae moralis vitae, cognosceret etiam quid sit bonum ex genere et quid ex genere malum ... adhuc nihil habetur contra me." For Gregory's traditional distinction between actions that are of a good or bad sort, see Anton Meinrad Meier, *Das peccatum mortale ex toto genere suo*: *Entstehung und Interpretation des Begriffes* (Regensburg, 1966), 266–268.

[32] Out of the wealth of possible references let two be singled out. *Lectura*, 2 Sent. dist. 29 q. 1 art. 2 (VI, 144): "... numquam actus est moraliter rectus nisi immediate vel mediate ordinetur ultimate in deum," and *Lectura*, 2 Sent. dist. 38–41 q. 1 art. 2 (VI, 310): "... numquam fit aliquid ab homine virtuose seu bene moraliter, nisi fiat ex dei dilectione actuali vel habituali ..."

[33] *Lectura*, 1 Sent. dist. 1 q. 3 art. 2 (I, 261): "... deus est propter se gratis et non mercenarie seu propter aliquid aliud diligendus."

[34] The interpretation of Manuel Santos is concentrated on this one guiding moral principle: "The centering of one's entire existence on God is to him (Gregory) no lofty ideal of an unusual perfection, but the strict moral duty of every Christian and every human being. The love of God must shape all of life so that all that the human being desires and does must be exclusively in regard to God and out of love of Him." Santos, "Sünden und Gnadenlehre," 1. As the author rightly remarks, Gregory places himself outside the scholastic consensus with theology of love of God as a practical moral duty.

[35] *Lectura*, 2 Sent. dist. 29 q. 1 art. 2 (VI, 141): "Unde, esto quod quis verbi gratia cognoscat bonum esse subvenire indigenti et non iniuriari proximo nec rapere alienum, nisi cognoscat cum hoc, propter quid et quemadmodum sit subveniendum et ab iniuria et rapina abstinendum, non habet notitiam sufficientem ad bonitatem actus moralem, de qua loquimur. Quod patet, quia si quis subveniat indigenti et non propter finem debitum, non agit bene moraliter."

[36] *Lectura*, 1 Sent. dist. 1 q. 1 art. 1 (I, 193–194): "Unde, quamvis talia (scil. bona) sint propter se diligibilia, non tamen sunt propter se diligenda, et qui ea propter se diligit, peccat, sicut per Augustinum patet 19 *De civitate dei* capitulo 25, ubi ait: 'Licet a quibusdam tunc verae, honestae putentur esse virtutes, cum referuntur ad se ipsas nec propter aliud expetuntur, etiam tunc inflatae atque superbae sunt, et ideo non virtutes sed vitia iudicanda sunt.'" See also Gregory's statement which follows, (I, 194): "... actus dandi eleemosynam, si non referatur in deum nec actu nec habitu, est peccatum."

anti-Pelagian theology he embraces, that even the doer of unquestionable good is rejected as an acute sinner if he does not love God.

Doing the good alone is not yet the principle of morality, but only acting out of love of God. But only God can cause one to recognize this, for nature 'in statu praesenti' knows nothing of it.[37] To say that Gregory makes "the validity of the moral values hypothetically ... independent ... of the existence of God," as Hans Welzel puts it, is therefore an aggravating misrepresentation of the Augustinian scholar's point. In order to act morally human beings have need not primarily of the 'principia per se nota,' but above all of the 'principium per deum notum,' that all action should occur out of love of God. To the contrary assertion that reason has long been aware of this principle of a duty to love,[38] Gregory has only one lapidary answer: This assertion is simply wrong, "simpliciter falsa"—as wrong as the assumption which goes even further, that the will would be able to bend to this supposedly reasonable insight due to its predisposition.[39] For what must happen for God's sake can only come from God.

The Aim of Gregory's Rational Definition of Sin

In conclusion there is one more important question to be asked of Gregory: Does not the need to differentiate exist even according to his own points of argument? If the nature of the human being is furnished with insight into certain principles of action, then it would appear to suggest itself to concede him at least the ability to act 'secundum rectam rationem,' and thus not to claim he acts contrary to reason. Even if the deciding 'principium agendi' by which God makes his judgments is not in his grasp, yet there remains to him the plane of action governed by his own reason, to which he knows very well how to pin himself. That it is a sin to act against the 'recta ratio' would then be recognized and at the

---

[37] Here too Gregory's judgement concerning the heathens is illuminating: Do they know that they are to honor God above all else? It can be seen from the Epistle to the Romans that the heathens too have knowledge of this. Gregory's answer to this is, *Lectura*, 2 Sent. dist. 29 q. 1 art. 2 (VI, 148–149): "Dico quod homo non potest illud cognoscere sine speciali auxilio. Et cum infertur quod tunc 'habebit ignorantiam invincibilem de isto bono morali' (that is the objection of his opponent), si intelligatur quod ignorantia sit invincibilis sine speciali adiutorio dei, concedo istam partem consequentis." If one however claims that this ignorance excuses the human being from guilt, then Gregory points out that this ignorance is a punishment, a punishment for original sin.

[38] In William of Ockham Gregory finds the statement of the modern Pelagian, that the *ratio* can doubtless reveal the correct object of his love to the human being. The human being, so he summarizes Ockham's position, is in possession of the *rectum dictamen* that he should love God above all. *Lectura*, 2 Sent. dist. 26–28 q. 1 art. 3 (VI, 65). Compare Ockham, 1 Sent. dist. 1 q. 2 concl. 1, *Venerabilis Inceptoris Guillelmi de Ockham Scriptum librum primum Sententiarum*, ed. G. Gál (St. Bonaventure, 1967), I, 397–398.

[39] *Lectura*, 2 Sent. dist. 26–28 q. 1 art. 3 (VI, 72).

same time differentiated, in one instance measured against God's 'ratio,' in the other against that of humankind. Such a differentiation would create the possibility of recognizing the legitimacy of a naturally rational morality at the same time as one admits one's sinfulness before God: thus the rational creature would be a sinner before God and at the same time a moral being before humankind.

One will at first want to see Gregory's intention to measure the action of human beings by its agreement with the 'recta ratio' as his attempt to counter the dangers of 'moral positivism.' Whether the theology of the late Middle Ages, inasfar as it followed Ockham's doctrine, actually dangerously relativized moral law can remain outside the terms of the discussion here.[40] It must however be stated that Gregory of Rimini saw dangers, and that the assumption that he set himslf against an "unbounded moral relativism"[41] has its rightness. The Augustinian very energetically denies that God, the sovereign Majesty, is or ever could be a tyrant God who makes His caprice law for humankind.[42]

What is certainly passed over within these confines of interpretation is the immediately obvious question of what Gregory is trying to say specifically about sin with his rationalistic theory. On the search for an answer one first comes upon his polished sentences on the unity of right reason: what offends against the 'recta ratio' offends against every 'recta ratio,' regardless of who thinks them. That different, even contradictory right 'rationes' and truths can arise concerning one matter, is ruled out by Gregory. Truth and truth do not oppose each other.[43]

With this the question posed is already answered: Gregory rules out the possibility of differentiation. One and the same action can always only be measured against one and the same 'ratio.'[44] This principle is

---

[40] A summary of this discussion can be found in Helmar Junghans, *Ockham im Lichte der neueren Forschung* (Berlin, 1968), 243–254.

[41] See Santos, "Sünden und Gnadenlehre," 28.

[42] See for example, *Lectura*, 1 Sent. dist. 42–44 q. 2 (Utrum deus possit dicere falsum) art. 1 (III, 401): "... si deus posset falsum dicere, posset et falsum iurare et falsum promittere, et per consequens etiam posset periurare et fallere et se ipsum negare; quae omnia sunt plena blasphemiae et contra sacram scripturam ..."

[43] *Lectura*, 2 Sent. dist. 34–37 q. 1 art. 2 (VI, 235) "Et quicquid est contra aliquam rectam rationem, est et contra quamlibet rectam rationem de eodem, nam circa idem quaelibet ratio recta cuilibet rationi rectae consonat et nulla alicui adversatur sicut nec veritas veritati."

[44] A clarification is of course necessary. Not everything that appears the same is in fact the same and thus to be measured by the same *ratio*. Gregory gives an example for it. He who sires a child adulterously acts *contra rectam rationem*. But God, who forms and sustains this adulterously sired child, acts *secundum rectam rationem. Lectura*, 2 Sent. dist. 34–37 q. 2 art. 3 (VI, 272): "Et quia illum actum, quem homo contra rectam rationem et ideo male facit, deus secundum rectam rationem ac per hoc bene facit, ideo homo illum (scil. actum) faciendo peccat, non deus." The observation that the same thing yet is not the same can often be made where different persons act together. 'The one acts according to reason, the other, although he is involved in the same network of actions, acts against reason.' cf. *Lectura*, 2 Sent. dist. 34–37 q. 2 art. 3 (VI, 272):

defended in the following way with the help of that classical train of thought that was meant to secure the late medieval Augustinian a place among the theoreticians of natural law of early modern times. Gregory insists on describing sin as a transgression against the 'recta ratio,' 'so that no-one will get the idea that sin, strictly speaking, transgresses only against God's thinking concerning a matter, but not against every sort of rational thinking concerning the same matter. Furthermore: so that no-one can assume that a certain act might be sin, but not because it transgresses against God's reason, insofar as that reason is right reason, but only because it transgresses against that type of reason that is God's own.

'For: given the impossible, that there were no divine reason, that is that God did not exist, or God's reason erred, then he who offended against that right reason that an angel, or a human being, or any other creature—if such existed—was able to conceive, would yet sin. And if practically no-one would bring the voice of right reason to bear any longer, then he who acted contrary to a directive that put forth any form of right reason whatever, if it existed, would yet sin.'[45] These are Gregory's own words in loose translation.

This text full of assumptions in the Irrealis programmatically formulates the universal validity of the 'recta ratio,' independent of who represents it in any given instance. Reason, if its rightness then is truly certain, is without exception the one and the same, valid everywhere and generally binding, on whatever level of being it may make itself known. The binding nature of the 'recta ratio' is thus independent of the hierarchy of its spheres of influence and application. It is not valid because it is divine, but it is valid because it is right, wherever and by whomever it may have been conceived aright. That God's being is one with the 'recta ratio' does not confer upon its rightness any advantage over that 'recta ratio' conceived by a human being, if he conceives it 'aright.'

To make clear what this conception of the general validity of right reason means to the understanding of sin one must be reminded of the fundamental structure of Gregory's theology: it is anti-Pelagian theology which wants to prevent the encroachment of the 'natural theology'

---

[45] *Lectura*, 2 Sent. dist. 34–37 q. 1 art. 2 (VI, 235): "Si quaeratur, cur potius dico (scil. ego, Gregorius) absolute 'contra rectam rationem' quam contracte 'contra rationem divinam,' respondeo: Ne putetur peccatum esse praecise contra rationem divinam et non contra quamlibet rectam rationem de eodem; aut aestimetur aliquid esse peccatum, non quia est contra rationem divinam inquantum est recta, sed quia est contra eam inquantum est divina. Nam, si per impossibile ratio divina sive deus ipse non esset aut ratio illa esset errans, adhuc, si quis ageret contra rectam rationem angelicam vel humanam aut aliam aliquam, si qua esset, peccaret. Et si nulla penitus esset ratio recta, adhuc, si quis ageret contra illud quod agendum esse dictaret ratio aliqua recta, si aliqua esset, peccaret."

of the power of human beings to heal themselves.[46] In the service of this goal the concept of 'ratio' has the effect of guarding against the sort of differentiations that Gregory suspects of Pelagianism. Accordance with right reason can never coexist with a transgression against divine reason. He refuses to subscribe to the attempt to justify an independent moral 'ratio naturalis.' If reason judges rightly on the plane of human nature, then its rightness is identical to every right reason,[47] and particularly to God's reason. If this identity does not exist, however, then the human being has made a wrong judgment, for the general validity of the 'recta ratio' forbids one to call good on the created plane what must count as sin before God.

If Gregory on the other hand let stand those graduated measures by which wrong behavior can yet be justified as indifferent or even as a morally good deed, he would have himself deprived the thrust of his anti-Pelagian theology of its power to convince. He would then have put in force the measure of the natural, which opened to man the possibility of showing his action to be reasonable and thereby lauding it as moral.

Gabriel Biel as Analyst of Gregory

As long as one is moving within the framework of Gregory's work, one can proceed from the assumption that he succeeded in closing off all avenues for the justification of a legitimate natural morality. What this achievement actually adduces in the case of teaching on sin, however, is made clear by casting an eye on the analyst of Gregory, Gabriel Biel. In his Tübingen *Collectorium* he takes up Gregory's description of sin in such a way that he deals with Gregory's definition as a fundamental text[48] and mixes it with others of the Augustinian's texts as he finds opportunity. In this way the analyst puts together his own Gregory text.

Biel constructed his Gregory text in the following manner:

1. The fundamental definition of sin—according to the Gregory text:

"... peccare actualiter nihil aliud est quam voluntarie aliquid agere vel committere contra rectam rationem."[49]

---

[46] Concerning Gregory's anti-Pelagian theology, besides the work of Santos, see Christoph Peter Burger, "Der Augustinschüler gegen die modernen Pelagianer: Das 'auxilium speciale dei' in der Gnadenlehre Gregors von Rimini," in *Gregor von Rimini: Werk und Wirkung bis zur Reformation*, ed. Heiko A. Oberman (Berlin, 1981), 195–240. A dense but informative summary of Gregory's program is offered in *Lectura*, VI, the introduction.

[47] *Lectura*, 2 Sent. dist. 42–44 q. 1 (VI, 323): "Nam quomodocumque capiatur 'ratio naturalis,' dummodo sit ratio recta, quicquid est ei conforme, est conforme cuilibet rationi rectae de eodem, et quicquid alicui rationi rectae, sive naturali sive non naturali, est conforme, est illi et cuilibet rationi rectae circa idem obiectum conforme."

[48] It concerns the following excerpt from the text: *Lectura*, 2 Sent. dist. 34–37 q. 1 art. 2 (VI, 234–235).

[49] *Gabrielis Biel Collectorium circa quattuor libros Sententiarum*, ed. W. Werbeck, 5

2. Augustine's fundamental definition—according to the Gregory text:

"Peccatum est dictum vel factum vel concupitum contra legem Dei." (Gregory, according to the Augustine text: "... contra aeternam legem.")[50]

3. The matter of sin:

Biel interrupts the Gregory text and interpolates the question: "Quid ergo est peccatum ..."? Terminologically he largely goes his own way, but practically he remains in Gregory's footsteps: sin is not to be understood as 'res' but as 'actio.'[51]

4. Explanation of Augustine's fundamental definition—according to the Gregory text:

Biel takes up Gregory's interpretation literally and also concludes it with the reformulation of the Augustine quote: "... secundum Augustinum recte dicatur peccatum esse dictum vel factum vel concupitum contra rectam rationem."[52]

5. Eternal law and the natural order:

Biel interrupts the progress of the text and inserts two longer Augustine texts quoted by Gregory which are meant to make clear that the human being is to rule over his baser instincts by means of his spiritual powers.[53]

6. The various functions of the law:

The interruption of the fundamental text continues. Biel busies himself at length with the various functions of the law: it indicates, for one, and forbids, for the other, what is evil. Long passages from Gregory on this subject are quoted verbatim.[54]

7. 'Even if God's ratio did not exist ...':

The thread of discourse of the text has been lost after the two long interpolations. Biel therefore repeats his and Gregory's fundamental definition.[55] Immediately thereafter follows the rendering of Gregory's famous explanation: "It is 'contra rectam rationem' and not 'contra

---

vols. (Tübingen, 1973–1984), 2 Sent. dist. 35 q. un art. 1 (II, 608). Cf. *Lectura*, 2 Sent. dist. 34–37 q. 1 art. 2 (VI, 234).

[50] *Gabrielis Biel*, 2 Sent. dist. 35 q. un art. 1 (II, 608). Cf. *Lectura*, 2 Sent. dist. 34–37 q. 1 art. 2 (VI, 235).

[51] *Gabrielis Biel*, 2 Sent. dist. 35 q. un art. 1 (II, 608–609). Cf. *Lectura*, 2 Sent. dist. 34–37 q. 1 art. 2 (VI, 235–237).

[52] *Gabrielis Biel*, 2 Sent. dist. 35 q. un art. 1 (II, 610). Cf. *Lectura*, 2 Sent. dist. 34–37 q. 1 art. 2 (VI, 235).

[53] *Gabrielis Biel*, 2 Sent. dist. 35 q. un art. 1 (II, 610). Cf. *Lectura*, 2 Sent. dist. 34–37 q. 1 art. 2 (VI, 238).

[54] *Gabrielis Biel*, 2 Sent. dist. 35 q. un art. 1 (II, 611–612). Cf. *Lectura*, 2 Sent. dist. 34–37 q. 1 art. 2 (VI, 241–243).

[55] *Gabrielis Biel*, 2 Sent. dist. 35 q. un art. 1 (II, 612). Cf. *Lectura*, 2 Sent. dist. 34–37 q. 1 art. 2 (VI, 237).

divinam rationem,' so that no-one can assume ... ."[56] With this culminating point, which puts the finish to Gregory's definition, Biel too was
able to conclude his comments on the matter. What he had to say he
said using Gregory's words.

With this arrangement of the text Biel went in tandem with Gregory's
expounded rationalistic understanding of sin. Georg Ott, who has taken
up the problem area "justice and law" in Biel, accuses the Tübingen
scholar of succumbing to the secularization of justice and having broken
off the "bridges to God" as a follower of Ockham. That Biel however
did not refer back to Ockham but to Gregory of Rimini for this
supposed breaking off may have caught the attention of Ott,[57] but he
drew no conclusions from it. It remained hidden from him how fully the
Tübingen scholar expounded the unfamiliar doctrine and how carefully
he prepared his Gregory text for his use. Biel condenses the material
and orders it in a new way and yet, despite all the changes he makes, he
reproduces Gregory's statements correctly. Even if the original has
turned out to be more accessible due to the tighter clustering of the
exposition of problems, one would yet find a reliable substitute in Biel's
reproduction if Gregory's text had become lost for some reason.

It is clear that Biel explicitly did not want to follow his teacher
Ockham in his doctrine on sin. The 'Inceptor Venerabilis' went entirely
different ways than those Gregory had chosen. Sin, he makes clear, is
not the offense against the 'recta ratio' in and of itself, but the breach of
the divine will as it is expressed in the law. If the action follows the law,
it finds itself as well in accordance with God as—de potentia ordinata—
with right reason. The precedent and deciding measure of action in
conformity with God is not however the 'recta ratio,' but God's will.
The fulfillment or non-fulfillment of what God commands decides the
situation of man in relation to God.

Two of the Quodlibeta in which Ockham presents his doctrine on
sin[58] were known to Gabriel Biel. He mentions them but only concerns
himself briefly with their contents.[59] It was Gregory whom Biel wanted.
He did not simply break off the dialogue with him despite the incompati-

---

[56] *Gabrielis Biel*, 2 Sent. dist. 35 q. un art. 1 (II, 612). Cf. *Lectura*, 2 Sent. dist. 34–37
q. 1 art. 2 (VI, 235).

[57] See Georg Ott, "Recht und Gesetz bei Gabriel Biel: Ein Beitrag zur
spätmittelalterlichen Rechtslehre," *Zeitschrift der Savigny-Stiftung für Rechtsgeschichte*,
kan. Abt. 38 (1952), 251–296, 279, 295.

[58] See Ockham, *Quotlibeta septem una cum tractatu de sacramento altaris* (Strasbourg,
1491; reprinted Louvain, 1962), Quodlibetum IV, q. 6 art. 4 especially fol. g6va. (Edited
as Quaestio VII 'De connexione virtutum' art. 4 in *Opera theologica*, VIII, 390, 332–341).
This Quodlibet is identical with Quaestio 12 of the third book of the *Sentences*. See also
Quodlibet III q. 14 ad dub. 2, Strasbourg, 1491, fol. e4vb–e5ra. (Edited as Quodlibet III
q. 15 in *Opera theologica*, IX, 261).

[59] See *Gabrielis Biel*, 2 Sent. dist. 35 q. un art. 2 (II, 616).

bility in their doctrine on grace, as was assumed,[60] but demonstratively established the connection with him in the doctrine on sin which followed.

Biel's Theological Framework for Gregory's Text

If William of Ockham, the first authority mentioned in the *Collectorium*, is so evidently made to step aside, then one is at first inclined to want to discover an antivoluntaristic element in Biel—as in Gregory. It is known that the Tübingen scholar rejects the possibility of a meritorious hatred of God affirmed by Ockham.[61] Yet it would go considerably too far to already classify him as a rationalist for that reason.[62]

A more specific formulation of the question might produce more of a result: What does the taking up of Gregory's 'ratio' theory do for Biel's doctrine of sin and for his ethics? Is Wilhelm Ernst perhaps right after all in his thesis that one may not simply brand the Tübingen teacher a semi-Pelagian,[63] the more so when one discovers how faithfully he takes up Gregory's model of thought? However it must be tested whether the correspondence in the words also led to a correspondence in intent. One must bear in mind that Biel's entire theological concept still remains keyed to Ockham despite intensive analysis of Gregory. The point of the *Collectorium* is to create a space for a legitimate natural morality for man, entirely in opposition to Gregory. Biel wants to show that human beings can act morally precisely because the 'recta ratio' is at their disposal, and namely, not only on a solely low, earthbound level. By virtue of their 'ratio' they also partake of eternal law and are thereby enabled to direct their practical action far beyond the earthly toward God and his 'aeterna.' Biel's well-known doctrine of the 'portiones animae rationalis'[64] culminates accordingly in the concept that it is given constitutionally to the 'recta ratio' to instruct the will to love God above

---

[60] Compare Leif Grane, *Contra Gabrielem: Luthers Auseinandersetzung mit Gabriel Biel in der Disputatio Contra Scholasticam Theologiam 1517* (Gyldendal, 1962), 178.

[61] See Heiko A. Oberman, *The Harvest of Medieval Theology: Gabriel Biel and Late Medieval Nominalism*, 3rd ed. (Durham, NC, 1983), 93–96.

[62] Concerning this see Karl-Heinz zur Mühlen, *Reformatorische Vernunftkritik und neuzeitliches Denken* (Tübingen, 1980), 26. Biel presents his interpretation in the following manner: "Deus non potest contra rectam rationem, verum est. Sed recta ratio quantum ad exteriora est voluntas sua. Non enim habet aliam regulam, cui teneatur se conformare, sed ipsa divina voluntas est regula omnium contingentium. Nec enim, quia aliquid rectum est aut iustum, ideo Deus vult; sed quia Deus vult, ideo iustum est et rectum," *Gabrielis Biel*, 1 Sent. dist. 17 q. 1 art. 3 (I, 422–423).

[63] See Wilhelm Ernst, *Gott und Mensch am Vorabend der Reformation* (Leipzig, 1972), 412. See the critical appreciation of this attempt to relieve Biel of the suspicion of Pelagianism by Denis Janz, "A Reinterpretation of Gabriel Biel on Nature and Grace," *Sixteenth Century Journal* 8 (1977), 104–108.

[64] The basic text concerning this is *Gabrielis Biel*, 2 Sent. dist. 24 q. un art. 1 (II, 472). See also zur Mühlen, 29ff.

all things. The will—fundamentally a "potentia libera"[65]—is then also able to realize reason's commandment to love.[66] At this point an abyss opens up between Gabriel Biel and Gregory of Rimini.

Morality According to Reason

It must be said concerning Biel that he like Gregory holds fast to the keying of morality to God. The supposed "breaking off of the bridges to God" did not occur. But, very differently from Gregory, he believes reason capable of knowing what is the right goal of action and thus of leading the will to God. At the same time—and that is the other decisive contrast to the anti-Pelagian—Biel widens the sphere of morality when he characterizes the natural civility of practical reason too as morally good. Both motives for action, be it for God's sake, be it out of natural civility, are to be rated as morally good. They differ only in terms of their perfection.[67] Each of these manifestations of morality is accessible to human beings, according to the level that their 'recta ratio' has reached. Unbelievers follow their right reason when they strive with all their hearts after it and ask for enlightenment in order to be able to recognize the truth, the right and the good. Thereby heathens act according to that 'ratio' which is given especially to them, and this is precisely the 'recta ratio' on their level. Christians on the other hand, who know of the faith, obey a more developed reason when they curse sin and resolve to obey God.[68] Reason is present in both cases, and, namely, right reason, which is in the nature of every human being.[69]

---

[65] *Gabrielis Biel*, 1 Sent. dist. 1 q. 2 art. 2 (I, 95): "Omnis potentia libera potest habere aliquem actum circa obiectum sibi ostensum; sed voluntas est potentia libera; ergo potest habere actum circa tale obiectum ostensum. Et non necessario inordinatum, ergo ordinatum, etiam ex naturalibus suis, licet non meritorium ..."

[66] *Gabrielis Biel*, 3 Sent. dist. 27 q. un art. 3 (III, 504): "Viatoris voluntas humana ex suis naturalibus potest diligere Deum super omnia. Probatio: Omni dictamini rationis rectae voluntas ex suis naturalibus se potest conformare; sed diligere Deum super omnia est dictamen rationis rectae ..." Since among the *diligibilia* too no *processus in infinitum* is to be assumed, the *ratio* must needs come to know that God is the *summe diligendum*.

[67] *Gabrielis Biel*, 2 Sent. dist. 28 q. un art. 1 (II, 534–535): "... actum aliquem contingit tripliciter exerceri, sicut 'pascere pauperem,' 'dicere veritatem': Vel propter Deum; vel quia dictatur a ratione recta; vel propter aliquod bonum utile vel delectabile consequendum ... Actus vero primis duobus modis eliciti sunt vere virtuosi et habitus eis correspondentes sunt verae virtutes, sed primi perfecti, secundi imperfecti ...; uterque tamen finis honestus est et bonus."

[68] *Gabrielis Biel*, 2 Sent. dist. 27 q. un art. 2 (II, 518): "Potest brevius dici quod infidelis facit quod in se est, dum arbitrium suum conformat rationi ac toto corde petit ac quaerit illuminari ad cognoscendum veritatem, iustitiam et bonum. Fidelis vero facit, quod in se est, si secundum regulam fidei detestatur peccatum, proponens in omnibus oboedire Deo et eius praecepta servare."

[69] Biel draws approvingly on Alexander of Hales, *Gabrielis Biel*, 2 Sent. dist. 27 q. un art. 2 (II, 518): "... 'in quolibet homine est ratio recta per naturam, qua quilibet potest cognoscere suum principium, scilicet Deum.' "

And freedom is also present, as much to do evil as "pari ratione" also to do good.[70]

In comparison to Gregory the Tübingen theology seems to come from a different world. The human being Biel describes is not locked up in that inescapable prison of disaster which original sin along with its punitive consequences created and which the God of mercy must always break open anew, as Gregory of Rimini would have it. Biel's human being is the rational and free one who can let himself be led, and can change himself as reason commands. He has his will under his rational-moral control.[71]

Within such a framework Gregory's definition of sin acquires a meaning completely different from its original one; its intent is even turned into its opposite. The Augustinian teacher is now made to corroborate the anthropology and moral theology he fought against as Pelagian: that sin is action against the 'recta ratio'—this is the 'text,' including its illustrations, that Gregory supplies. But the intention that is coupled with this text is entirely Biel's own in the case of Biel's work: man can—at least partially and always anew—make himself free from sin and act in a morally good way. For right reason is doubtless present, even if, assuming the impossible, God did not exist. And every right reason, as differentiatedly as it may judge at each level of being, is the same in that it shows forth the right action.

It speaks for the perspicacity of the Tübingen Magister that he discovered what the unfamiliar concept could accomplish within his own system. The anti-Pelagian doctrine of sin becomes the promise of reason and morality. Gregory's text now conveys that right reason reigns among men. Sin therefore is not destiny, for morality is possible by virtue of reason.

---

[70] *Gabrielis Biel*, 3 Sent. dist. 27 q. un art. 3 (III, 505): "Homo errans potest diligere creaturam super omnia et frui ea ex puris naturalibus; ergo pari ratione potest diligere deum ex suis naturalibus super omnia et frui eo." The entire paragraph is a mixture from *opiniones* by Scotus, Ockham and d'Ailly. It is probably the consensus of doctrine encompassing all schools which Biel wishes to document here. The *par ratio* to which Biel refers arises from the argument that the human will is provided with the *libertas contradictionis*. See also *Gabrielis Biel*, 1 Sent. dist. 1 q. 6 art. 3 (I, 125).

[71] Biel does not neglect to cite the classical authority for his doctrine of freedom, *Gabrielis Biel*, 3 Sent. dist. 27 q. un art. 3 (III, 504): "Nihil est magis in potestate voluntatis quam voluntas." See Augustine, *De libero arbitrio*, 3.3.7 (*PL*, XXXII, 1274).

STAUPITZ AUGUSTINIANUS:
AN ACCOUNT OF THE RECEPTION OF AUGUSTINE
IN HIS TÜBINGEN SERMONS

RICHARD WETZEL

1. Staupitz's abounding use of Augustine for his Tübingen Sermons (around 1497–8)[1] is so obvious, furthermore he admits and substantiates it so clearly himself, that it seems superfluous to discuss it explicitly. The rather casually[2] formulated confession "De verbo ad verbum magis placet Aurelii sancti Augustini uti verbis quam propria speculatione, nec iniuste, quia pater et doctor meus est, immo et sanctae ecclesiae, intellectu profundissimus, sermone lepidus atque allegatione authenticus" (*TS* 7, 92–96), describes and justifies a practice which can be found generally. That this is the case and how it is accomplished will be the subject of this article.

1.1. The reason wherefore such a discussion is nevertheless not superfluous does not lie with Staupitz but with those who have done research on him. In a carelessness which needs to be explained interpreters have hurried past the signposts which Staupitz had set out on the comfortable road to Augustine he chose himself and instead followed the thorny path searching for traces of the possible influence of the late medieval Augustianism, especially of Gregory of Rimini's so-called *schola Augustiniana moderna*.[3] This can be explained by the fact that modern research on Staupitz, the first to make the Tübingen sermons[4] available in an edition prepared by Georg Buchwald and completed by

---

[1] Johann von Staupitz, *Sämtliche Schriften. Abhandlungen, Predigten, Zeugnisse*, eds. Lothar Graf zu Dohna and Richard Wetzel, vol. 1: *Tübinger Predigten*, ed. Richard Wetzel, Spätmittelalter und Reformation 13 (Berlin, 1987).

Hereafter this volume will be cited as *JvS* 1. The individual sermon will be cited as *TS* followed by a sermon and line number; D = dedication (Widmung to Johannes Brüheim) and P = prologue. The editorial comments are cited "annot." as distinguished from "footnote" for the notes of this article and simply "n." for all other notes.

[2] That Staupitz characterizes his own way of working in Sermon 7, was perhaps not merely coincidental, after all, cf. 6.1.1.

[3] Damasus Trapp OSA—who is to be honoured by this contribution—has introduced and infused this term with life in "Augustinian Theology of the 14th Century: Notes on Editions, Marginalia, Opinions and Book-Lore", *Augustiniana* 6 (1956), 147–265.

[4] Nikolaus Paulus had been the first to hint at them as lying unidentified in the Bayerische Staatsbibliothek at Munich (Codex clm 18760), see his "Johann von Staupitz: Seine vorgeblich protestantischen Gesinnungen," *Historisches Jahrbuch* 12 (1891), 310 n. 3.

Ernst Wolf (1927),[5] from its very beginnings is a by-product of research on Luther. This is plainly the case in Ernst Wolf's *Staupitz und Luther* (1927);[6] and although intended as a corrective complement to Wolf, David C. Steinmetz's *Misericordia Dei* (1968)[7] in this respect still adheres to an approach originally matched to Luther who is well known to have qualified Gregory of Rimini as Augustine's *fidelissimus interpres*.

This is not the place to delineate the history of the question about the continuity between a possibly exceptional cultivation of Augustinianism in the Order of Augustinian Eremites and that of the early Reformation, all the more since this has already been done several times.[8] Here, it will suffice to mention the two researchers who had again taken up this question seemingly fruitfully with a view to Staupitz, Steinmetz (1968),[9] guided by Heiko A. Oberman, and Oberman himself (1974).[10] In order to show a certain change of mind since then, I will quote one recent sentence from each of them. Steinmetz in 1973 and 1980: "The strongest Augustinian opinions which Staupitz cites are those of Augustine himself."[11] And Oberman in 1975 and 1977: "Ihre Augustinkenntnisse brauchte die nun" (around 1515) "antretende Generation nicht mehr auf diese nunmehr als Umweg empfundene Weise zu sammeln, nachdem die Amerbachedition zu kaufen war."[12] [13]

---

[5] Staupitz. *Tübinger Predigten*, eds. Georg Buchwald and Ernst Wolf, Quellen und Forschungen zur Reformationsgeschichte 8 (Leipzig, 1927; reprint ed. 1971).

[6] Ernst Wolf, *Staupitz und Luther: Ein Beitrag zur Theologie des Johannes von Staupitz und deren Bedeutung für Luthers theologischen Werdegang*, Quellen und Forschungen zur Reformationsgeschichte 9 (Leipzig, 1927; reprint ed. 1971).
Staupitz und Luther will be abbreviated *SuL* when repeated within the footnote.

[7] David C. Steinmetz, *Misericordia Dei: The Theology of Johannes von Staupitz in its Late Medieval Setting*, Studies in Medieval and Reformation Thought 4 (Leiden, 1968).
Misericordia Dei will be abbreviated *MD* when repeated within the footnote.

[8] 1968, 1973, and 1980 by Steinmetz, 1981 by Schulze. See Steinmetz, *Misericordia Dei*, 30–33, then his "Luther and the Late Medieval Augustinians: Another Look," *Concordia Theological Monthly* 44 (1973) (abbr. *AL*), 245–260, esp. 248–254, finally his *Luther and Staupitz: An Essay in the Intellectual Origins of the Protestant Reformation*, Duke Monographs 4 (Durham, North Carolina, 1980) (abbr. *LaS*), 16–27. See Manfred Schulze "*Via Gregorii* in Forschung und Quellen," in *Gregor von Rimini: Werk und Wirkung bis zur Reformation*, ed. Heiko A. Oberman (Berlin-New York, 1981), 1–126.

[9] Already cautious when formulating his theses in *Misericordia Dei*, 30, 33–4, he was even more retentive in his assessment p. 131: "… without conscious dependence upon Gregory of Rimini."

[10] "Headwaters of the Reformation: Initia Lutheri—Initia Reformationis," in *Luther and the Dawn of the Modern Era*, ed. Heiko A. Oberman (Leiden, 1974) (abbr. *Headwaters*), 40–88, esp. 73 (commercium admirabile: Augustinus Favaroni) and 77 (gratia gratum faciens, non deo hominem, sed homini deum: Jordan of Saxony.)

[11] *Another Look*, 256 (= *Luther and Staupitz*, 27). Concerning the scholastic sources of the Tübingen sermons he also states correctly: "Staupitz appears to be more a representative of the older Augustinian school" (Giles of Rome and Thomas of Strassburg) "than of the school of Gregory of Rimini," *AL* 257 (= *LaS* 28).

[12] I.e., "Now, that the Amerbach edition could be bought, the new generation" (around 1515) "did not need to collect their knowledge about Augustine via what was now

1.2. The Tübingen sermons themselves have profited very little from the discernment expressed in these two sentences.[14] But in the second volume (published prior to the first) of the complete edition of Staupitz's writings with his *De exsecutione aeternae praedestinationis*, 1517 (1979),[15] the remarks both on the history of the research on Staupitz[16]

---

being considered as a detour." Oberman, "Tuus sum, salvum me fac: Augustinréveil zwischen Renaissance und Reformation," in *Scientia Augustiniana: Studien über Augustin, den Augustinismus und den Augustinerorden*. Festschrift for Adolar Zumkeller on his 60th birthday, eds. Cornelius Mayer and Willigis Eckermann, Cassiciacum 30 (Würzburg, 1975) (abbr. *Tuus sum*), 350–394, esp. 358 = *Werden und Wertung der Reformation* (Tübingen, 1977), 91.

[13] Dealing with Staupitz's *De exsecutione*, 1517 (see footnote 15), *Nachfolgung*, 1515 (see footnote 37) and some passages from the *Salzburg sermons of 1512* (cf. footnote 136), Oberman refers to the great Amerbach edition of Augustine's complete writings which appeared in 1503–1506 in 11 volumes. For a bibliographical description see *Verzeichnis der im deutschen Sprachraum erschienenen Drucke des 16. Jahrhunderts.—VD 16 —*, sec. I, vol. 1 (München, 1983), A 4147.

The fact that Staupitz already made the most ample use of the preceding separate edition of Augustine's *De civitate* (see *Gesamtkatalog der Wiegendrucke*, vol. 3, Leipzig, 1928, n. 2887), which was published by Amerbach in 1489, has only been proved by the textcritical work on Sermon 28, see my annot. 19 and 30 and the textcritical apparatus to lines 164ff: *JvS* 1, 407–8, 410. See also my *Staupitz antibarbarus* (as cited in fn. 53), p. 119 along with n. 36, and 124 with nn. 38, 39.

Though without mentioning the Amerbach edition and without giving any evidence, Steinmetz maintains that Staupitz "reads" (Augustine) "in the best texts which are available to him," *Luther and Staupitz*, 28.

[14] Steinmetz's characterization of Staupitz's "direct reliance on Augustine," even as "obvious from the very beginning" (*Luther and Staupitz*, 28), unfortunately remains without any proof from the Tübingen sermons. Further, when he states: "His sermons breathe the theological atmosphere of the Augustinian homiletical literature" (*Another Look*, 257 = *LaS* 28), this right statement in the relevant chapter "Hermeneutic and Old Testament Interpretation" (*LaS* 35–50) is not only not exemplified, as one might have expected, but is rather, esp. p. 42 and 48, disproved (see below footnote 74) and on p. 49 merely varied. The promising equally true sentence: "It is the Augustinian exegesis of the Old Testament which is the door for Staupitz into the New Testament, especially the writings of St. Paul" (*AL* 260), in *LaS* 49 along with nn. 74, 75 is answered at the most by a hint of illustration: "interesting interplay."

The real examples Steinmetz mentions in *AL* 257–8 (= *LaS* 28–30), taken from *De exsecutione*, depend upon the interaction with Oberman's *Headwaters* (as cited in footnote 10). Cf. Schulze, *Via Gregorii* (as in fn. 8), 124–126.

In Oberman, *Tuus sum* (as cited in footnote 12) the Tübingen sermons are mentioned only once, 372 n. 90 = *Werden und Wertung* (as in fn. 12), 105 n. 90.

[15] Johann von Staupitz, *Sämtliche Schriften* ... (as in fn. 1), vol. 2: *Libellus De exsecutione aeternae praedestinationis, mit der Übertragung von Christoph Scheurl "Ein nutzbarliches büchlein von der entlichen volziehung ewiger fürsehung"*, eds. Lothar Graf zu Dohna, Richard Wetzel und Albrecht Endriss, Spätmittelalter und Reformation 14 (Berlin, 1979).

Hereafter this volume will be cited as *JvS* 2. Besides a "Geleit" by Heiko A. Oberman, the volume comprises an "Einführung in die Staupitz—Gesamtausgabe" by Dohna and Wetzel, in which they consider Staupitz's works, the history of research on them, their present accessibility in various editions, and the forthcoming complete edition, and, of course, an "Einleitung" by all three editors.

[16] *JvS* 2, "Einführung," 15 along with nn. 65, 66, and "Einleitung" 34 along with nn. 65–68.

and on the way the sources were to be presented in the notes of the commentary[17] have been drafted from this progressed state of scholarship.[18]

2. What, however, has the exploitation of Staupitz's Tübingen sermons by Wolf's and Steinmetz's variously interested monographs yielded about the author's reception of Augustine? It is worthwhile to gather these findings here, even though—or just because—the attention which Staupitz himself gave to this Father is far from being fully described in such an indirect account.

2.1. Wolf thought "Augustin wie den Lombarden, als für eine" (scholastic) "Schulzugehörigkeit nicht bezeichnend, vorläufig zurückstellen zu dürfen."[19] However, while he was working on the restricted field of the two topics, Staupitz's view of grace and predestination and the pious life according to him,[20] Wolf nevertheless regularly noted Staupitz's recourse to Augustine[21] and finally conceeded "daß seine maßgebenden Anschauungen" (along with Giles of Rome) "auch unmittelbar auf Augustin zurückweisen."[22] Reception as such is not a topic for Wolf, and hence, Staupitz's interest in Augustine does not coincide with Wolf's interest in Staupitz.

2.2. Unlike Wolf, who thus treated Augustine in a consequently

---

[17] *JvS* 2, "Einführung," 20–1 and "Einleitung" 37–8.

[18] So much the less I can understand Markus Wriedt (as cited at the end of this footnote). He ascribes to the editors' historical commentary on Staupitz's *De exsecutione* the intention of seeing Gregory of Rimini quoted there in several passages ("zitiert sehen", Wriedt 124–5). He does so, although the editors proceed from the result stated in the two sentences mentioned above and expressly refuse that their commentary be understood as a "genetical" one (*JvS* 2, "Einleitung" p. 38).

Furthermore, Wriedt does so, although while disproving that intention imputed to the editors, he can and (though without saying it clearly enough) also does take from their commentary the very instances which make any singular dependence disappear into a range of witnesses Staupitz actually quoted in his Tübingen sermons, i.e. Giles of Rome, Thomas of Strassburg, authorities of the older Augustinian school, but not Gregory of Rimini *et sequaces*.

Throughout the commentary on *De exsecutione* the term "zitiert" (in its abbreviated form "zit") is carefully used only when Staupitz himself marks a quotation. Among all his writings he only does so in the Tübingen sermons and, in a far smaller magnitude, in his *Nachfolgung* (see footnote 37); later on he hardly does it at all. For *De exsecutione* see *JvS* 2, "Einleitung", p. 37 and nn. 91, 92.

Markus Wriedt, "Via Guilelmi—Via Gregorii: Zur Frage einer Augustinerschule im Gefolge Gregors von Rimini unter besonderer Berücksichtigung Johannes von Staupitz," in *Deutschland und Europa in der Neuzeit*, Festschrift für Karl Otmar Freiherr von Aretin on his 65th birthday, eds., Ralph Melville, Claus Scharf, Martin Vogt und Ulrich Wengenroth (Wiesbaden, 1988), 111–131.

[19] I.e., that "neither Augustine" nor "Lombard" were "representative of a" (scholastic) "school and thus did not need to be dealt with for the present." Wolf, *Staupitz und Luther*, 27.

[20] Wolf, *Staupitz und Luther*, 36ff, 87ff.

[21] In the following, I will present Wolf's findings in parallel to those by Steinmetz.

[22] I.e., "that his major views" (along with Giles of Rome) "point immediately back to Augustine, too." Wolf, *Staupitz und Luther*, 122.

peripherical way, Steinmetz, in his work *Misericordia Dei* which includes theology, christology, and mariology, pointed out and even emphasized some of Augustine's views and influences as they appear in the Tübingen sermons. However, criteria for both the choice to be taken and the instances by which to verify it are not evident.[23] The following examples bear witness.

The Augustinian *uti–frui*.[24] This is not mentioned by Wolf. Steinmetz shows its reception in the Tübingen sermons by citing *TS* 6, 101–2.[25] As this is a sentence apparently formed by Staupitz himself, it seems to be a good indication for an appropriation of Augustine which, however, does not necessarily have to have been direct. This can be confirmed by taking *TS* 15, 88–90 (= Gregory the Great) as well as *TS* 5, 63ff (= Lombard) and *TS* 18, 291ff (= Lombard) into account.[26]

Moving on to the Augustinian acception of sin as a perversion of this structural relationship[27] adopted by Staupitz, Steinmetz gives no quotation at all. This lacuna can be closed in the best conceivable manner: "Tota perversitas hominis sumitur ex eo quod male utitur et male fruitur. Diligenter ideo agendum est, ne utamur deo et fruamur bono creato", *TS* 25, 59–60 (second half of the first sentence from Augustine via Giles).[28] In addition, this underscores his appropriation of the basic idea (58).

Confessio laudis. Wolf only touches it in connection with the *confessio peccati*.[29] Steinmetz has sufficiently proved that the Augustinian idea of the *confessio laudis* as the purpose of and reason for the creation of man is well established in the Tübingen sermons by his findings in *TS* 18, 291

---

[23] While Wolf point for point first separately examines the Tübingen sermons and then the more recent writings by Staupitz, Steinmetz draws on all the works by Staupitz simultaneously (for this see his justification, *Misericordia Dei*, 34), however preferring *De exsecutione* as a guideline. Strictly speaking, it is only then possible to trace a concept found in Staupitz back to Augustine if Staupitz quotes it directly or indirectly (cf. footnote 18). Steinmetz's instances from the Tübingen sermons, though the only ones to give full intelligence, often appear as merely additional reference numbers and it is rarely made clear which are Staupitz's words and which are quotations.

Wolf and Steinmetz refer to the Tübingen sermons noting pages and lines of the edition by Buchwald/Wolf (as cited in footnote 3), as we also still did in the commentary to *De exsecutione*. In the present article, all references are made to the new edition except in those cases where it is helpful to note both editions.

[24] Steinmetz, *Misericordia Dei*, 35–38. All Augustinian instances he gives there derive from *De doctrina christiana*, which, however, is cited only once by Staupitz via Lombard: *TS* 18, 289–90 along with annot. 37, 38: *JvS* 1, 300.

[25] Steinmetz, *Misericordia Dei*, 37 along with n. 6. It is likely that Lombard is the intermediary here also, see annot. 24 to *TS* 6: *JvS* 1, 104.

[26] See also *TS* 7, 161 and, without explicit antithesis, *TS* 16, 99, 105.

[27] Steinmetz, *Misericordia Dei*, 36.

[28] Cf. annot. 11–13 to *TS* 25: *JvS* 1, 377. Wolf has failed to reject Buchwald's illogical interpolation *male* after *ne* (see annot. 12).

[29] Wolf, *Staupitz und Luther*, 166 n. 1 with reference to *TS* 2, 216–7. (= Augustine).

(= Augustine via Lombard) and *TS* 30, 71 (= Lombard from Augustine).[30]

Mali causa non efficiens sed deficiens. Nothing can be found in Wolf on this idea. Although Steinmetz correctly names Augustine as the inventor of this formula, which is found in *TS* 5, 41–2 and *TS* 11, 206, he maintains that it only works via Giles.[31] In fact, Staupitz cites Augustine himself in *TS* 5, 86–7 and, even more clearly, in 90–107. This passage is a good example also indicating how a mediator such as Giles led Staupitz to the source itself of which he then makes ample use.

The Augustinian definition of evil: *malum non est nisi boni privatio* can be better shown from *TS* 31, 77–8 (= Augustine via Giles) than from *TS* 5, 181 (= Pseudo-Dionysius and Damascenus via Giles).[32]

The Augustinian definition of sin as voluntary: *peccatum adeo est voluntarium, quod, si non est voluntarium, non est peccatum*, *TS* 25, 44–5, is not to be found in *De diversis quaestionibus*, as Steinmetz claims, but in *De vera religione* (via Giles). For the excellent paraphrase of sin's "parasite existence" which he gives to the quasi-definition *peccatum nihil est* (*TS* 23, 58) Steinmetz cites no source at all in Augustine.[33]

2.3. In *Misericordia Dei*, surely, Steinmetz did not have to consider it his task to always exactly determine the degree of Staupitz's direct or indirect "indebtedness" to Augustine (even though the Tübingen sermons are so valuable for the very reason that the explicitness with which they refer to their sources allows this with a high degree of precision). For his topic was after all Staupitz's theology "in its late medieval setting." But as to some of Staupitz's basic ideas which can be traced to Augustine, Steinmetz refers to this source, even if there is no explicit recourse to Augustine by Staupitz. At other equally important points he omits references, for instance at such terms as *rectitudo* through *conformatio voluntatis*,[34] or the distinction between *timor filialis* and *timor*

---

[30] Steinmetz, *Misericordia Dei*, 58–9, esp. 58 n. 4 and 59 n. 3., cf. also 34 along with n. 2.

[31] Steinmetz, *Misericordia Dei*, 47 along with n. 5.

[32] Steinmetz, *Misericordia Dei*, 47 along with n. 6.

[33] Steinmetz, *Misericordia Dei*, 67 along with nn. 1, 5. For the first passage, in Buchwald/Wolf 199, 16–19 Giles had not been recognized as the source quoting *De vera religione*; cf. annot. 6 and 7 to *TS* 25: *JvS* 1, 376. For the second passage cf. annot. 11 to *TS* 23: *JvS* 1, 350.

[34] Wolf, *Staupitz und Luther*, 73 at the end of n. 1 as well as 90 nn. 1, 2 at least briefly mentions Augustine's example of Christ in Gethsemane which Staupitz quotes in *TS* 3, 23ff (= *Enarratio* 32); cf. already annot. 4 and 6 to *De exsecutione* chap. 9: *JvS* 2, 142–3. Wolf p. 91 along with n. 5 also mentions *TS* 3, 238ff (= *Enarratio* 31).

From the references by Steinmetz, *Misericordia Dei*, 156 n. 3, namely *TS* 3, 41–52 (of which 41–48 = *Enarratio* 32), *TS* 3, 142–3, and—I can not see why—Buchwald/Wolf 15.29–31 = *TS* 3, 173–175 (possibly meant 170ff?), Augustine does not emerge clearly as the source of this concept, although he is previously formally quoted in *TS* 3, 23ff.

servilis,[35] even though Staupitz explicitly recurs to Augustine.

With all the understandable and legitimate interest a modern researcher may take in the late medieval shades of Staupitz's theology, the
original interest of the author Staupitz, (i.e. to learn his theology
with the best teacher: *doctor meus, immo et ecclesiae*, and to then pass
on by teaching: *in aedificationem ecclesiae*), is thus disproportionally
neglected. Indeed, since Staupitz's direct recourse to Augustine merges
with the *Augustinus receptus* (via Lombard, Giles or others) and thus a
quasi-humanist new experience emerges in which this ancient authority
becomes quite contemporaneous, it is then our task to perceive Augustine not only as the distant authority who was in one way or another
involved in nearly all the questions of medieval theology, but also as the
near, new and fresh one. To bring it to a point: without considering
Staupitz's own direct reception of Augustine, a description of his theology in its late medieval setting will remain incomplete as well. For
around 1497–8 the former already is a constitutive part of the latter.

This dominance of the researcher's own interest over that of the
author can be seen especially well in the discussion of the *bonitas dei*.
Bonitas, bonus, adjective and noun, *boni, bonum, bona, bene* are the
words most often employed in the Tübingen sermons.[36] *Bonitas* is the
divine characteristic like no other.[37] Numerous passages may be found

---

Steinmetz sees *TS* 3, 202–206 as a parallel to a Gerson passage where, however,
Staupitz's explicit antithesis between *voluntatis conformatio* and *substantiae identitas* can
not be found (as, e.g., in those from Bernhard of Clairvaux and Jordan of Saxony, noted
in annot. 69: *JvS* 1, 72). There is certainly a passage by Gerson that would be more to the
point.

Buchwald/Wolf 196.14–22 (= *TS* 24, 264–272) and Buchwald/Wolf 196.38–197.6 (= *TS*
24, 290–300), also referred to by Steinmetz, had not yet been identified as quotations from
Gerson; see annot. 76 and 81: *JvS* 1, 371–2. Steinmetz does not take notice of Gerson's
report of Augustine's psychological interpretation of his boyish apple theft as "imitatio
quaedam omnipotentiae et libertatis divinae," found just between the two passages in *TS*
24, 272–281 along with annot. 74.

[35] Whereas Wolf (*Staupitz und Luther*, 111 n. 1, on p. 112, and 112 along with n. 1)
presents *TS* 4, 23ff correctly (although too briefly in that he does not distinguish Staupitz's
own part in citing Augustine from Lombard's), Steinmetz (*Misericordia Dei*, 38) neither
mentions the Tübingen sermons nor Augustine.

[36] *JvS* 1, index 537a–541a.

[37] God is "omnis boni bonum," *TS* 1, 101 (= Giles from Augustine); "bonitas per
essentiam," *TS* 2, 34–5 (= Giles from Proclus); "solus bonus," *TS* 3, 79; "ipsum bonum
summum," *TS* 4, 85; "summe bonus," *TS* 12, 91 (from Augustine). A creature is good
"per participationem," *TS* 2, 33 (= Giles from Proclus) and *TS* 5, 53 (= Giles) in so far as
it exists and only in so far as it exists, i.e., not automatically in so far as it wants and acts,
too: "inquantum sumus, boni sumus," *TS* 18, 290 (= Augustine via Lombard), in
opposition to "bene esse" in line 273. (This form of predication is called *reduplicatio* by
Staupitz in *De exsecutione*, para. 88.)

The *bene esse* is an additional gift to the creature: "quod sumus et boni sumus, a deo
est," *TS* 1, 3; "nec esse nec bene esse a creatura," *TS* 18, 273. In his *Von der nachfolgung
des willigen sterbens Christi* (Leipzig, 1515), chap. 1, Staupitz tells us what it consists of:
"... nicht allain sei, sunder recht sei (cit. Eccles. 7.30), einen guten willen hab, von

which prove Staupitz's teaching of God as *summum bonum*,[38] "doctrine of God within the framework established by Augustine," as Steinmetz tells us.[39] From among these[40] *TS* 12, 395 fulfills the criterion of being a direct reference to Augustine. Steinmetz's only citation from the Tübingen sermons is *TS* 6, 25,[41] which apparently does the same. But, in fact, it does not mean God as the *summum bonum ipsum* (= God), as it is the case in *TS* 4, 85, but the *summum bonum* on the scale of *fines bonorum et malorum* (*TS* 6, 33), i.e. man's highest purpose in life.[42]

In a further section entitled "Relation of Intellect and Will: Problem of Divine Bonitas" within his chapter on Staupitz's doctrine of God,[43] Steinmetz does not give any indication of Staupitz's indebtedness to Augustine as to the context of *bonitas dei*.[44] In a long and substantial footnote,[45] however, he criticizes Wolf's limiting of *bonitas dei* as the ontologically good being[46] and with good reason maintains that Staupitz's understanding of *bonitas dei/divina* as a motive for *restauratio* and *reparatio* shows the affinity between *bonitas* and *misericordia*. By examining his proofs more closely, one can easily demonstrate the Augustinian background of this idea: *TS* 12, 179, 299–304, esp. 302–304

---

welchem man allaine recht ist." *Johann von Staupitzens sämmtliche Werke*, ed. Joachim Karl Friedrich Knaake (Potsdam, 1867), 52. 17–8 Cf. Steinmetz, *Misericordia Dei*, 68 along with n. 7, 71–2; to this cf. below near footnote 48 and fn. itself.

[38] Steinmetz, *Misericordia Dei*, 35–38.

[39] Steinmetz, *Misericordia Dei*, 36.

[40] In addition to those referred to already in footnote 37, see also *TS* 4, 269; *TS* 13, 267, 359, 375; *TS* 24, 210–1; *TS* 30, 363–4.

Steinmetz, *Misericordia Dei*, 36 n. 4 finds evidence for the formula *summum bonum* in Staupitz's booklet, *Von der lieb gots*. The phrasing of this concept in *De exsecutione*, para. 3, to which Steinmetz (*MD* 36–7, along with 37 n. 1) reminds us of Anselm's well known definition, however, also has models in Augustine himself some of which Staupitz assuredly knew, cf. annot. 16 to *De exsecutione*, chap. 1: *JvS* 2, 79. To the evidence I gave there from *De civitate* 22, 30 (*CChr* 48. 863.27), may be added that the Augustinian context is cited in *Nachfolgung*, chap. 10: Knaake (as in fn. 37), 74.33ff.

Even Steinmetz's detour via Anselm can be justified from the Tübingen sermons, see *TS* 12, 477–8.

[41] Steinmetz, *Misericordia Dei*, 37 n. 4.

[42] *TS* 4, 263; *TS* 6, 29, 35ff, 65, 94; probably also *TS* 15, 138.

[43] Steinmetz, *Misericordia Dei*, 44–50.

[44] The formula mentioned above (2.2.), *mali causa non efficiens* concern evil and *TS* 3, 215–217 (= Augustine), quoted by Steinmetz, *Misericordia Dei*, 47 n. 3 concern the infallibility of God's will.

[45] Steinmetz, *Misericordia Dei*, 48, n. 1 discussing Wolf, *Staupitz und Luther*, 80 and 121.

[46] It is rather in *Staupitz und Luther*, 73 n. 3 on p. 74, line 12–3 that I see Wolf emphasizing the difference between being-good and *misericordia* than on p. 80 and 121 where the being-good is opposed to "wirklich persönlich verstandener Liebe"—a deficiency common to all scholastical thought, not a specifically Thomistic one. In my opinion, Wolf has not appreciated the portion of personal religiosity which Augustine in despite of his metaphysics passed on to Staupitz's—and his coevals'—theology.

(= Augustine); *TS* 12, 328–333 and *TS* 12, 353–369, esp. 368–9 (from Augustine).[47]

Inversely, *misericordia* itself as *misericordia duplex* (*TS* 16, 92ff, 96ff = Augustine) comprises both aspects, in Augustinian terms *esse* and *bene esse*,[48] just as the *amor* of *sponsus* in *TS* 7, 165ff (= Augustine) delivers gifts to the bride (church or soul) with both hands (cit. Canticles 2.6).

To judge by these findings the fact that in the section titled "Problem of Divine Bonitas", Steinmetz focuses on the question of whether Staupitz saw the will of God in the Thomistic or Scotist sense, does not seem cogent but rather far-fetched.[49]

---

[47] See annot. 93 and 113 to *TS* 12: *JvS* 1, 226, 228.

[48] These complementary terms, which are like a primary rock in Augustinian thought, are used by Steinmetz in *Misericordia Dei*, 59 without any evidence and in *MD* 68 and 71–2 without recourse to Augustine and without reference to the Tübingen sermons.
Concerning the comments of Wolf, *Staupitz und Luther*, 73 n. 3, I would like to direct the reader's attention to annot. 12 to *De exsecutione*, chap. 1: *JvS* 2, 78. Even at the time I could not agree with Wolf's attempt to assign one part of Staupitz's *bene-esse* sayings to the area of the ontological being-good, as expressed in the formula "inquantum sumus, boni sumus" (see above footnote 37). If he was correct, one would also have to criticize Augustine for his imprecision.
The fact that *gratia* also comprehends both areas is noted by Steinmetz, *Misericordia Dei*, 60 n. 1. For *misericordia* in parallel to creation as a benefit see *TS* 23, 279–282 with Steinmetz, *MD* 58 n. 3.

[49] And this would be true even if the answer suggested by Steinmetz were correct. Staupitz's sentence: "Sola divina voluntas est regula sui actus, quia non ordinatur ad superiorem finem" (*TS* 3, 16–17) which Steinmetz cites programmatically in *Misericordia Dei*, 27 along with n. 1, and argumentatively in *MD* 49 n. 3 in order to prove Staupitz's Scotist-nominalist understanding of God's will, is not only formally marked by Staupitz as a citation from Thomas Aquinas, but Staupitz is also telling about the difference between divine will and human will, not about the relation between divine will and divine intellect, since Staupitz continues: "Sed homo non est deus" (*TS* 3, 17–18).
Steinmetz's statement does not become more true by repeating it explicitly or implicitly, see *MD* 30; 48 n. 1; 51 n. 1; 56; 156 n. 1; cf. *Luther and Staupitz*, 28 along with n. 100.
The only other instance to be seriously examined in this respect is: "Neque enim tibi placent hominum facta, quia bona sunt, sed potius ideo sunt bona, quia tibi placent" (*TS* 15, 202–3, quoted by Steinmetz *MD* 27 n. 1; 50 n. 1; 95 n. 3). As the passage *TS* 23, 188ff (= Gerson), put in parallel by Steinmetz in *MD* 95 n. 3 (cf. annot. 36 to *TS* 15 and annot. 36 to *TS* 23: *JvS* 1, 270 and 355), in my opinion shows, the former text is concerned with the same relationship between creator and creature, not with that one within God between will and norm. To confirm this result one may compare the quasi patient version of this concept to be found in *TS* 18, 264–266: "Si igitur iusta deo placere scimus, pati autem nulla nisi quae domino placuerunt possumus, iusta sunt cuncta quae patimur . . ." (= Gregory the Great) and inversions which seem similarly paradoxical, as *TS* 11, 185–188 and 188–190 (both = Augustine via Lombard or Giles); see below 6.3.4.
I can't see what *TS* 3, 187–189 (= Augustine via Lombard) should add to this question (see Steinmetz *MD* 27 n. 1 and 49 n. 4 on p. 50), since it contrasts *prima causa* to secondary causes.
It is surprising that although Steinmetz (*MD* 95 n. 3 starting with line 6, and 73 n. 1) cites the two passages *TS* 23, 188–193 and 206–211 (albeit in a different question), they nevertheless are not utilized in the discussion of the relation of the intellect and will of God. The keyword of this discussion, *recta ratio* (*MD* 49), is echoed there several times,

The Augustinian sense of *bonitas dei* in Staupitz comes to light even more clearly when seen as a divine motif of creation. However, out of the following four weighty passages, *TS* 13, 44–50 (= Augustine referring to Plato); 172 (= Augustine), 184–187 (= Augustine critically referring to Origen), and 195–198, Steinmetz briefly touches the first one only without mentioning Augustine in this context at all.[50]

2.4. I discontinue my secondary reading here, albeit somewhat haphazardly. Neither Steinmetz in *Misericordia Dei* nor Wolf in *Staupitz und Luther* have adequately appreciated the position Staupitz granted Augustine in his Tübingen sermons. In my view, such an appreciation requires that the researcher enters into the intentions of the author he examines, whether they suit modern tastes or not. A remark such as the following one made by Steinmetz in his second book, *Luther and Staupitz* (1980), shows little will to do just this: "Quotations from theological authorities buttress his exegetical points just as illustrations from life or pious tales from the ever-present collections of exempla might support the far simpler homily of a village parson."[51] This information about the role of authorities, and Augustine as their vanguard, is not satisfactory, at least not for me. The problem is made even more poignant by the quantitative increase of borrowings (see below 3.). Authorities are never simply accumulated, and *TS* 25, 165–192 with the heading *rememoratio alieni exempli* is an exception that confirms the rule. But Staupitz makes a point of giving precedence to them: "magis placet ... uti quam propriis speculationibus," and he states why he does so: "intellectu profundissimus, sermone lepidus, allegatione authenticus." The authorities give glory and substance to the whole. Steinmetz states this as well, but finding fault: "The power of these tracts (see 4.1.1.) derives from the ideas they propose and the authorities they cite. In form they are unremarkable."[52] This comes close to a much older verdict in which the researcher views the Tübingen sermons as a mere collection of material. (With my thesis of the consciously borrowed eloquence,[53] I have tried to make a virtue of necessity in order to help

---

see *TS* 23, 190–1 (divina ratio et voluntas), 207 (recta ratio), 210 (rectissima iuris ratio), esp. 239–40 (sit pro ratione voluntas) and 245 (ratio . . . iustitiae).

[50] In Steinmetz, *Misericordia Dei*, 58 n. 2 "Cf. *Hiob* (1497–8) 12.117.23–8" to be corrected "... 13 ...". With the exception of *TS* 23, 279–282 (see footnote 48), the Tübingen sermons are not mentioned there. Wolf, *Staupitz und Luther*, 80 n. 3 does not mention Augustine explicitly.

[51] Steinmetz, *Luther and Staupitz*, 48.

[52] Steinmetz, *Luther and Staupitz*, 50.

[53] Richard Wetzel, "Staupitz antibarbarus: Beobachtungen zur Rezeption heidnischer Antike in seinen Tübingen Predigten," in *Reformatio et reformationes*, Festschrift für Lothar Graf zu Dohna, ed. Andreas Mehl and Wolfgang Christian Schneider, THD-Schriftenreihe Wissenschaft und Technik 47 (Darmstadt, 1989) (abbr. *Staupitz antibarbarus*), 117.

the modern reader who might have difficulties in understanding this
kind of writing by citing.) First and foremost, when Steinmetz puts on a
par with "the ever-present collections of exempla" Staupitz's recourse
to Augustine's works at the very moment they appeared for the first
time in print, he to my mind totally misses the historical *Kairos* of this
act of reception.

Before moving from the secondary to the primary sources I would like
to retract one of the few Augustinian heirlooms which Steinmetz con-
cretely treated in his *Luther and Staupitz*. Particularly since it jointly
serves as a prelude to what will be said on Staupitz's use of Augustine's
Enarrationes in Psalmos. In the second chapter, entitled "Hermeneutic
and Old Testament Interpretation," he mentions one of the two tools
Staupitz is said to have received from Augustine via Gregory the Great,
the *caput-corpus-membra* schema.[54] As for Augustine Steinmetz verifies
it from *De doctrina christiana*[55] and as for Staupitz he asserts that it is
impossible to determine whether he learned it from Augustine directly
or through Gregory, or via the medieval tradition of exegesis. Bio-
graphically speaking, this may be correct. The Tübingen sermons,
however, permit a more precise statement. Steinmetz's references are
the following: *TS* 30, 316–318; *TS* 31, 241–244 (= Gregory), 244–258
(247–257 = Pseudo-Augustine[56]) and *TS* 32, 83ff. Even though these
references justify the maintained vagueness, the third one already
intimates direct reception: It is framed by two sentences from *Enarratio*
on Psalm 21,[57] the Psalm about the Lord's suffering, where Augustine
states the change of subject from *caput* to *corpus* at the very beginning
of his comment on verse 2.[58] *Enarratio* 90, sermon 2 is straightly
introduced with some instructions concerning this rule of interpretation.[59] And it is from this *Enarratio* that *TS* 11, 561–575 and
611–621 are quoted. The same thought can be found in *Enarratio* 127.3
where it is based on Ephes. 5.30 together with 1.Corinth. 12.27.[60] And it
is out of this *Enarratio* that Sermon 4 uses the paragraphs 7, 8, 9
throughout. Even if Staupitz may not have read all this, there still
remains *TS* 3, 32–34 which he copied from Augustine and *TS* 11, 450
where he ratifies Augustine's use of caput by exchanging it for *Iesum*

---

[54] Steinmetz, *Luther and Staupitz*, 42 along with n. 35.
[55] See, however, footnote 24.
[56] In Buchwald/Wolf 241, 26–34 it is not yet identified as a quotation from the
pseudo-Augustinian *Meditationes*, see annot. 61 to *TS* 31: *JvS* 1, 447.
[57] The second sentence, *TS* 32, 90–93, in Buchwald/Wolf 243, 31–34 is not yet identified, see annot. 31: *JvS* 1, 451.
[58] *Enarr.Ps.* 21, e. 2, 3 (*CChr* 38. 123.6–7, 15–24).
[59] *Enarr.Ps.* 90, s. 2, 1 (*CChr* 39. 1265–6.13ff, esp. 31ff, and above all 63ff).
[60] *Enarr.Ps.* 127, 3 (*CChr* 40. 1869.3–12, esp. 9–10), cf. 127, 7 (1871.1–3).

Christum.[61] *TS* 11, 600 (= Bonaventure) may be added for the sake of completeness.

3. According to the genre, the introduction to my new edition of the Tübingen sermons had to be limited to update the statistical findings which Wolf had based on those of Buchwald and his own. The immense increase of quotations (as distinguished from Staupitz's own words) had to be opposed by a sharp decrease in the number of books he read personally.[62] Here, I want to continue the deliberations of my article *Staupitz antibarbarus*[63] and show in more detail which ideas Staupitz finds in Augustine, where and possibly through which mediators this happens, and finally where and how he uses them in his cycle of sermons, adapting them to his intentions.

As I showed in section 3.5. of the cited article, the Tübingen sermons have four principal parts (*partes*, *TS* 15, 18ff):

I. *Ante temptationem* (*TS* 15, 34) (Sermones, 1–10)
on Job-Everyman's[64] well-being (*de fortuna*, *TS* 15, 19) as a result of a perfect inner life (*dispositio mentis*, *TS* 6, 4) (Sermones 1–5) and unchallenged (*pacis tempore*, *TS* 11, 5) use of the outer goods of happiness on earth (*bonorum terrenae felicitatis usu*, *TS* 6, 100, 103) (Sermones 6–10)

II. *De temptatione* (Sermones 11–14)
on the providential sense of interior and exterior challenge (*de temptationis et adversitatis consideratione*, *TS* 15, 19–20)

III. *In temptatione* (*TS* 15, 34) (Sermones 15 to end)
on the temptations and how to withstand them (*de temptationis atque passionis et belli exercitatione et conflictu*, *TS* 15, 20–1)

IV. *Post temptationem* (missing)
on the triumph over temptations (*de triumpho*, *TS* 15, 21)

In the following these principal parts will be analyzed passing from groups of sermons distinguishable within them down to the individual sermon to allow the reader to become familiar with their content[65] and

---

[61] Shortly before Staupitz begins his quotation from *Enarr.Ps.* 55, 9 (*TS* 11, 443 = *CChr* 39. 684.23), Augustine writes (*Enarr.Ps.* 55, 8): "Non dedignetur ergo corpus quod praecessit in capite, ut corpus haereat capiti" (683, 15–6).

[62] See *JvS* 1, 14ff. The increase of borrowings from Augustine's *Enarrationes in Psalmos* is gathered there on p. 17 n. 72, that of those from *De civitate* on p. 17 n. 71. Here, these passages newly identified as quotations will be marked in each case.

[63] Wetzel, *Staupitz antibarbarus*, 113–116.

[64] "Neque enim de Iob ut de singulari persona singula dicere intendo . . ., sed magis volo de eo loqui, ut personam cuiuslibet temptati gerit quem propter deum temptatio arripuit." *TS* 14, 190–193.

[65] The only attempt to do this was made by Alfred Jeremias, *Johannes von Staupitz:*

also to let the structure of the cycle emerge as a well-conceived, albeit not always equally well executed, whole. A preliminary evaluation can then be made as to frequency, length, and competence of authorities other than Augustine.[66] Then I will list all the borrowings from Augustine in nearly every sermon in order to show the portion of profundity, persuasiveness, impressiveness, and elegance Staupitz owes to this Father. These results can only be achieved by scanning the sermons several times. The reader is invited to do just this.

4.1. As for the first five sermons of Pars I

—which may be entitled[67] 1) *De misericordia dei in perfectione*[68] ... *Iob* ... *viri* ... *gentilis ostensa*; 2) *De simplicitate cordis sive de eius evacuatione a plica curiositatis, falsitatis, dolositatis*; 3) *De rectitudine cordis sive de conformatione voluntatis humanae cum divina* ...; 4) *De timore*

Luthers Vater und Schüler. Sein Leben, sein Verhältnis zu Luther und eine Auswahl aus seinen Schriften, Quellen. Lebensbücherei christlicher Zeugnisse ... (Berlin, 1926). This attempt failed such that I can not understand his recommendation in *Wegbereiter der Reformation*, ed. Gustav Adolf Benrath (Bremen, 1967; reprinted Wuppertal, 1988), 133. The excerpt from *TS* 11, 361ff, however, is newly translated (133–135).

Georg Buchwald, "Zwei Erziehungspredigten Johanns von Staupitz", *Allgemeine Evangelisch-Lutherische Kirchenzeitung* (1918), 291–294, is precritical concerning the sources and other introductory questions. He gives a paraphrase of Sermon 10 and of a part of Sermon 22. Cf. Wolf, *Staupitz und Luther*, 26 along with n. 3.

Heiko A. Oberman, "Duplex misericordia: Der Teufel und die Kirche in der Theologie des jungen Johann von Staupitz," in: Festschrift for Martin Anton Schmidt on his 70th birthday, *Theologische Zeitschrift* 45 (1989), 231–243, gives a brief account of Sermons 16–7 to explain on this background the concept of a divine mercy which exceeds all human norms when tolerating a "lupus rapax" even as "vices gerens Christi" (*TS* 19, 147ff). Cf. Wetzel, *Staupitz antibarbarus*, 125. Berndt Hamm, *Frömmigkeitstheologie am Anfang des 16. Jahrhunderts* ..., Beiträge zur historischen Theologie 65 (Tübingen, 1982), 329 n. 161, had already pointed to this passage which is ecclesiologically central.

Adolar Zumkeller OSA, "Johannes von Staupitz und die klösterliche Reformbewegung, "*Analecta Augustiniana* 52 (1989), 29–49, citing *TS* 11, 694ff and Sermon 20 (*De ... zelo praedicatorum*), uses texts which so far have been hidden in the Staupitz literature, see Wolf, *Staupitz und Luther*, 155 n. 1 and Steinmetz, *Misericordia Dei*, 180 n. 2.

[66] I feel to be allowed to pass by Pseudo-Dionysius Areopagita, although Staupitz draws on him as a source for describing the structure of the second hierarchy of angels: *TS* 21, 113. Apart from this he is cited at some other places, always indirectly, see *JvS* 1, 15 n. 63 on p. 16.

As to the scholastic authorities. I can only casually touch them in this study; see, however, sec. 7.

[67] The headings used here and in the following are from my table of contents, *JvS* 1, v–x. They imitate the chapter headings Staupitz uses in his writings published in his lifetime. They are an attempt to provide the reader with short information beyond the bare ordinal numbers above each sermon as exhibited by the manuscript which the edited text, of course, had to reproduce. As far as possible they utilize Staupitz's own phrasings. For easier use, I have shortened them suitably.

In that table of contents p. viii, line 3, "tribus" is to be corrected "quatuor." Concerning "Sermon 29", table p. ix, lines 5ff, see my correcting remark in Wetzel, *Staupitz antibarbarus*, n. 33.

[68] Cf. — as in footnote 77 — Augustine, *Enarr.Ps.* 55, 20 (*CChr* 34. 692.14).

dei servili, initiali, filiali ...; 5) *De malo, de mali causa* ..., *cognitione* ..., *fuga....* —

a summary is to be found in *TS* 6, 4–8, which leaves no doubt: Job, this exception among the heathens[69] (and we are originally no different from these[70]) owes his virtues, *simplicitas, rectitudo, timor dei* and *fuga mali* (or *innocentia*), solely to God's mercy (*donis dei gratuitis*).

The second set of five sermons

—6) *De matrimonio* ...; 7) *De divitiis* ...; 8) *De honore* ...; 9) *De conviviis ... David, Assveri, Christi* ...; 10) *De parentum provisione erga liberos* ... —

represent a base of lay ethics:[71] "quomodo bonis terrenae felicitatis uti liceat" (*TS* 6, 100–103). In his outward appearance, Job is no different from his secular environment. As a married man[72] with many children, wealthy, powerful and held in high esteem, blessed with all happiness, he lives within the world *sub deo* (*TS* 15, 84; *TS* 33, 174). Apart from marriage, possessions, social rank and upbringing, one of the sermons even treats the feast or banquet as the place *par excellence* where power can be displayed, where not only conflicts and treason can develop but reconciliation as well.

4.1.1. In his dedication to Johannes Brüheim, Staupitz describes his task as "aliquam partem sacrae scripturae in aedificationem ecclesiae interpretari" (*TS* D, 6–7). Reading the term "interpretari," one might expect a "commentary on Job" (Wolf). In that case one can take note of the Tübingen sermons with some astonishment[73] as Wolf does, or one may be led to the condescending view as exhibited by Steinmetz in *Luther and Staupitz*, that Staupitz unscrupulously fragmented the Job text and then expatiated on it.[74]

---

[69] Cf. Steinmetz, *Luther and Staupitz*, 43 para. 3.

[70] Therefore Staupitz does not need to bother with Job's *genealogia* (*TS* P, 11).

[71] Cf. Steinmetz, *Luther and Staupitz*, 44 para. 1.

[72] Cf. Gregory the Great, *Moralia*, 1, 14 (20) (*CChr* 143. 34, 34–37, esp. 43–47): "Quid per Iob nisi bonorum coniugatorum vita signatur; qui de rebus mundi quas possident dum pia opera faciunt quasi per terrae viam ad caelestem patriam tendunt?"

[73] Wolf, *Staupitz und Luther*, 21: " ... dass für Staupitz der Sermon offenbar die geeignete Form zur Entwicklung seiner theologischen Ansichten bildet."

[74] Steinmetz, *Luther and Staupitz*, 42: "He ruthlessly atomizes the text he has chosen by focusing on a word or phrase and allowing a fragment of the text to serve as a motto for an essay which, speaking charitably, is only tangentially related to the passage under discussion. For example, Staupitz uses the text, 'And there were born ...,' as an occasion for preaching on the nature of Christian marriage — a worthy subject, no doubt, but hardly a concern uppermost in the mind of the author of Job." See also 48: "... the leisurely pace at which Staupitz strolls through the book of Job. He preaches no less than five sermons on Job 1:1, two on 1:3, and two on 1:7. Obviously no commentaries can hope to provide enough grist for a mill which turns with such monumental deliberation."

The later, German, sermons from those preached at Salzburg in 1512 onward and *De exsecutione* which also emerged from such sermons get better marks (43). Nevertheless the Tübingen sermons viewed by Steinmetz as Staupitz's earliest exegetical work on an

Later on Staupitz claims, it was "post multam deliberationem" (*TS* D, 7–8) that he had chosen Job as a reference text. With the purpose of doing something "in aedificationem ecclesiae" (*TS* D, 6–7) it is logical that he does not merely, not even in the first instance, talk about Job as an individual, but as *persona cuiuslibet temptati*, as an Everyman. The fact that the reader is only later told (*TS* 14, 190–193; cited in footnote 64) does not necessarily imply that the author thought about it at such a late stage. Where did the inspiration come from during his *multa deliberatio* that led him to choose the heathen and layman Job as a model or *speculum*, as he calls him himself (*TS* P, 21; *TS* 11, 11 = Gregory the Great)?

The characteristic feature of *rectus corde* (from >rectus< Job 1.1) and >recti corde< (Ps. 31.11; 32.1) (*TS* 3, 240) is that he does not only praise God in *gaudiis*, but also *in tribulatione* (from Rom. 5.3): *TS* 3, 239–40. For Augustine, from whom these lines are cited, Job is the archetype of *rectus corde*, the saying of Job and motto of the Tübingen sermons "Dominus dedit, dominus abstulit ..." (Job 1.21)[75] is a sort of refrain in his *Enarrationes in Psalmos*. *TS* 3, 246 represents just such an example.[76] In other words, I suppose, the homiletic actualization of the character of Job by Augustine has partially determined Staupitz's choice of matter.

Gaudia, or to say it according to Staupitz's table of contents (see above 3.), *fortuna* (*TS* 15, 19), in the brief exposition of the biblical parable in Job 1.1 is illustrated by a catalogue of earthly goods: children, possessions etc. Staupitz uses each term to deliver an ethical treatise in miniature form. I do believe though that he does not fortuitously find opportunity for this, but rather that he searches for it on purpose.[77] It is true that each "essay ... is only tangentially related to the ... text" and that this is "hardly ... in the mind of the author of Job." It is, however, the interpreter's task to elucidate this and not to make fun of it.

These tracts, for which the text of Job just provides the keywords,

---

Old Testament text, are compared to Luther's *Dictata super Psalterium* which in fact belong to that genre. Even Steinmetz admits they are "not absolutely comparable" (38).

[75] About Staupitz's motto, cf. Steinmetz, *Luther and Staupitz*, 39–40.

[76] As to the lines in which Augustine cites Job 1.21 (*Enarr.Ps.* 31, e.2, 26: *CChr* 38. 243.1–5), Staupitz can omit them for exactly that reason. The lacuna in his citation (*TS* 3, 246) can only be noticed when read carefully, see *JvS* 1, 73 along with annot. 87.

Some of Augustine's own quotations of Job 1.21 are gathered in annot. 27 to *TS* 3: *JvS* 1, 67. They derive partly from *Enarrationes* which Staupitz used (see the list below 6.1.), partly from those he didn't. To the first grouping are to be added the following passages: *Enarr.Ps.* 21, e.2, 5 (*CChr* 38. 124.17ff); *Enarr.Ps.* 37, 24 (*CChr* 38. 398.9–11); *Enarr.Ps.* 55, 19–20 (*CChr* 39. 691.19–693.49, esp. 691–2.27–29 and 693.34–36, not in the index of *CChr* 40!) and *Enarr.Ps.* 90, s.1, 2 (*CChr* 39. 1255–6.16).

[77] This is said against Steinmetz, *Luther and Staupitz*, 42 (partially cited in footnote 74), 50 on top of page and similar statements elsewhere.

make sense only if one considers them as the elements of a larger whole where the brief parable (we can after all trace an analogous procedure in the biblical book of Job) has to carry the weight of the wordy contemplations and discussions. Theodicy, or to say it in a term of Staupitz's own, *divini iudicii rectificatio* (*TS* 23, 171ff) is the dominant scope there as well as here, where a rather rigid homiletic triple triad pattern[78] places *honor dei* as the first *punctus* at the top of every sermon. Staupitz has possibly anchored it even more firmly in the literal-historical stratum of the parable and—likewise—in man's postparadisiac life in a decayed creation, than do the participants of the debate in the subsequent poetical parts of the book of Job. In Job's view (and in ours) they indulge in extensive digressions.

4.2. The four Sermones of Pars II

—11) *De ... tribulationibus sub specie aeternae dei sapientiae, providentiae, praedestinationis consideratis* ...; 12) *De vocatione ad poenitentiam, neque angelis bonis in bono confirmatis, neque diabolo angelisque eius in malo obstinatis, sed soli homini et ad bonum et ad malum vertibili congrua* ...; 13) *De diaboli via hominem intellectu, voluntate, operatione in circuitu captivum ducere conantis* ...; 14) *De adiutorio domini erga servum dei* ...—

beyond the unreliability of all happiness *in mundo*, demonstrate that all suffering *in hoc mundo* (*TS* 11, 396) is provisional, nay, is a sign and indication of a future world where felicity can no longer be lost (407), to which man is on his way (*in via TS* 12, 320, 348), man as opposed to the angel on the one hand, who has already attained (*in termino* 12, 643), and the demon on the other hand, who has finally derailed and turns in a circle around himself. The circle (*circuitus*) appears as a cipher for diabolic purposelessness in man who centers upon himself and worldly goods.

4.2.1. It is the Job parable again which supplies the keywords for this ambitious itinerary from heaven through the world into hell and it is Augustine again who supplies the key texts, which increasingly consist of those from *De civitate* in addition to those from *Enarrationes in Psalmos*. So far, all studies on Staupitz have failed to give an appropriate place to his angelology and demonology, if they notice them at all. Surely, we take the demythologicalization for granted nowadays. Staupitz, however, works on the anthropological assumptions that man, situated on the verge of the realm of the animals (*TS* 6, 409ff; *TS* 7, 185ff), represents but a fraction of the creatures gifted with reason (*TS* 13, 200), that he has only very limited room for action and only belongs

---

[78] For a more detailed description see Steinmetz, *Luther and Staupitz*, 40–1, 44–6 along with nn. 50–55.

to the rear-guard in the great drama in which the creatures decide for or against their creator. The angelic as well as the demonic realms are paradigmatic extremes of lived and forfeited existence. In this context concerning all spiritual creatures we find important statements about freedom and grace; its symmetry constitutes a system stronger than does any scholastic philosophy.

4.3. As to Pars III with the remaining 20 sermons, its structure is more difficult to discern.

Sermon 15 (*De virtute et gratia* ...) stands alone at the center. It is a dispute between the devil and God about the thesis, "Iob donis gratuitis praeditum, gratia gratum faciente ornatum, meritis auctum non vere dici posse virtuosum," i.e., Job does not deserve the praise of God.

Then follow different groups of sermons, all of which treat *potestas* (16), (*im*)*potentia* (17), *licentia* or *libertas* (19–22) and finally *opportunitas temptandi* (23–25), be it actively through the devil himself or passively through his victims. Sermon 18 depicts Job's *animi aequitas* when Satan dispossesses him of goods and chattles, nay even his children *deo semper inamisso* (cf. *TS* 18, 277, 294–5).

The four sermons "de libertate quam suscipit diabolus ex negligentia praelatorum, sacerdotum, praedicatorum, principum, parentum" tell us about the scandalous abuses among the clergy from the priests up to the *vices gerens Christi* and about the vocation of the orders of mendicant friars to *correctio* (19), about the false zeal which falls into schism and heresy while exercising *correctio* (20), about the misuse of secular power (21) and about failed education (22).

The three sermons "de opportunitate quam diabolus sumit ex indispositione temptandorum" speak of the false "consideratio sui et operum suorum" (23), of the lack of respect for authorities which represent God as a master (24), and of sin, especially the sin of the tongue (25).

For the remaining nine sermons of Pars III such structural guidelines are missing. Sermon 26 (*De angelorum cognitione* ..., *de confusione diaboli, de possesione coeli* ...) has a special place. In a similar way as Sermon 14 due to the identity of the text in Job 1.8 and Job 1.1 is a summary and recapitulation of certain elements of sermons 1–5, Sermon 26 thanks to the nearly identical texts of Job 2.1–3b and Job 1.6–8 is a smaller version on the angel-devil-man triptych formed by Sermons 11, 12, 13: The angelic themes of *scientia/cognitio, gaudium* and *missio/ adiutorium* are expanded; the devil's unsuccessful striving for power over the earth, i.e., over man who is made out of earth, mythically speaking, *esca diaboli* (*TS* 26, 218), is stressed; man is presented as a citizen of heaven and a carrier of hope, and therefore placed above Adam (223–4).

Common to the next eight sermons is a further shifting of the scene of struggle against the devil to the inner life. (It is worth mentioning that in this Staupitz received support from Gerson, the extent of which has not yet been recognized sufficiently.[79] Maybe Gerson even influenced the *longa deliberatio* through his *Centilogium de impulsibus*, as Augustine has been shown doing above through his *Enarrationes in Psalmos*. Cf. 4.1.1.) Thus, Sermon 27 (*De ... adversitate carnis ad spiritum Job innata ...*) deals with the agonistic and even meritorious sense of original punishment. Sermon 28 (*De veritate aequanimitatis patientiaeque in iactura universae substantiae et nece filiorum visa ...*) which is a dispute similar to Sermon 15 between the devil and God, removes any suspicion from Job of having acted with a selfish motive.[80] Then Sermon 29 (*De ulteriore potestate seu licentia temptandi diabolo concessa ...*) tells us how Job-Everyman is given up to the devil for a *spiritualis afflictio*, and Sermon 30 (*De vita naturae, gratiae, virtutis, quod non sint in manu diaboli ...*) is about the innermost limits set against the devil's power: life, grace and freedom. Sermon 31 (*De peccati egressione e corde, ordine, collectione ...*), Sermon 32 (*De poena et passione, de peccato cordis, consuetudinis, corruptionis ...*), and Sermon 33 (*De compassione nociva ..., de passionibus seu affectibus secundum deum rectis*) finally treat the root and the kinds of sin, the willingness and even gladness with which punishment is received, the relationship between sin and the passions, the sense and the limitations of asceticism, and the affections proper to the human condition, which the son of God did not disdain but shared with us. In Sermon 34 (*De correptione fraterna, de irrationalitate (blasphemiae) ...*) the Tübingen sermons come to an abrupt end.

5.1. Jerome, along with some passages which are falsely attributed to this Father, is rarely cited at all. The quotations are brief and although they appear in nearly one third of the sermons, they never shape more than a small part of a sermon.

Staupitz clearly sees Jerome's competence in the following fields: asceticism ("Pallebant ora ieiuniis et mens aestuabat desiderio ..." *TS* 6, 461–464; "Venter mero aestuans ..." *TS* 10, 420–1 = *TS* 19, 82–3, the latter via Gratian; "Nimia corporis debilitas ..." *TS* 32, 215–218), the discipline of the members of an order ("O summa libertas ..." *TS* 3, 203–4; "Vox praelati ..." *TS* 3, 264–266) and of the clergy in general ("Non tenera vestis ..." *TS* 19, 199–200, via Gerson), how to use the Holy Scriptures ("Ciceronianus ..." and "Vitiosissimum dicendi genus ... ad voluntatem suam sacram scripturam trahere ..." *TS* 31, 155–6 and 157–164), and the connection between scholarship and morality

---

[79] *TS* 27, 32ff along with annot. 5, 10, 16, 19, 25: *JvS* 1, 396–7. Cf. *JvS* 1, 18 along with n. 79 and the index 517a.

[80] See Wetzel, *Staupitz antibarbarus*, 122–3.

("Sancta rusticitas ..." *TS* 11, 700–702 = *TS* 19, 113–115). Some of these familiar quotations could not be identified word for word.[81]

5.2. Ambrose, along with one passage falsely attributed to him about man as a pilgrim (*TS* 12, 335–346), speaks even more rarely, although a few topics are dealt with more extensively, namely in three sermons: In 7 (*De divitiis* ...) he talks about how enjoying material goods is bound to reason which must not forget their real master (*TS* 7, 182–199), culminating in a drastic image: "Nulla discretio inter cadavera ..., nisi forte quod gravius foetent ... divitum"; about the indivisible possession, common even to the pennyless, of heaven and earth, elements and stars, down to such simple pleasures as sleep, something which the rich often can no longer enjoy, as anxious about their wealth (*TS* 7, 272–289). In 13 (*De diaboli via ... in circuitu* ...) he discusses the educational role of the noisome vermin in the fallen creation (*TS* 13, 219–242) and in 25 (*De ... peccato cordis oris operis* ...) about the virtues of discretion (*TS* 25, 145–50).

5.3. Boethius has a singular position. Indirectly quoted from a dictum about the frontiers of the glory of Rome (*TS* 8, 309–10 via Giles) and from a poem about modesty (*TS* 23, 118–125 via Gerson), he is quoted directly only in Sermon 7 (*De divitiis* ...), but throughout several pages in the parenetical part: lines 340ff about the inconstancy of *fortuna* and 425ff about the goods which do not make their owner good (424), e.g. money, jewellery, estates, clothes, and servants. The fact that Boethius is referred to may have been inspired by Thomas Aquinas.[82]

5.4. As to Gregory the Great, Staupitz primarily uses the *Moralia*, and recourse to this work is missing in three sermons only: 6 (*De matrimonio* ...), 8 (*De honore* ...) and 25 (*De ... domini dei dominio* ...). As far as Staupitz interprets the Job text at all, he simply borrows from Gregory rarely failing to mark the reference correctly.[83] While Gregory expounds each verse of the book of Job in all scriptural senses, historical (meaning Job), allegorical (meaning Christ or Church), and moral (meaning man), Staupitz deals with them in a rather eclectic way: In 24 sermons he makes use of the historical sense, in nine of which exclusively; in 15 sermons he uses the allegorical one, in two of which exclusively; in 12 sermons he uses the moral one, in two of which exclusively. There are only five sermons — 1 (*De misericordia dei in ... Iob viro ... gentili ostensa*), 11 (*De ... tribulationibus ... sub specie*

---

[81] Cf. annot. 89 to *TS* 3: *JvS* 1, 74; annot. 59 to *TS* 32: *JvS* 1, 455.

[82] See annot. 113 to *TS* 7: *JvS* 1, 136.

[83] Splinter-like quotations in which Gregory is not named are: *TS* 1, 90–1; *TS* 10, 527; *TS* 17, 56–7. Other nameless quotations in a context already deeply indebted to Gregory are: *TS* 18, 159–60, 214–218, 225–229, 317–321. Remarkable are only *TS* 26, 194–197 and especially *TS* 33, 41–68.

aeternae dei scientiae ...), 17 (*De diaboli potentia ... qua non potest, nisi deus permittat* ...), 31 (*De peccati egressione* ...) and 32 (*De poena et passione* ...) — in which he uses all three senses. This, however, is not done in analogy to the division of the individual sermons into three articuli.[84]

The sermon with the highest number of borrowings from Gregory the Great is 18 (*De animi aequitate qua amissio rerum ... ferenda sit*) of which Staupitz says in *TS* 19, 35–6 that it is conceived as *litteraliter*; except for one allusion in *TS* 18, 82–3 it is indeed drawn from Gregory's historical interpretation. Then follow, though with a far smaller number, Sermon 23 (*De ... consideratione sui et operum* ...) where he only makes use of the moral interpretation, and finally the sermons mentioned above with passages drawn from all three scriptural senses.

I detect two cases where the influence of Gregory is an architectural one that goes beyond the glossing and paraphrasing function to be found in the preceding examples. This occurs firstly in the antithetical parallelization of God's question to Satan >Unde venis< Job 1.7 to God's call >Adam< together with his question >Ubi es< Gn. 3.9 put to man (*TS* 12, 23–32 in Staupitz', 33–44 in Gregory's phrasing). Extended by the *argumentum e silentio*, i.e., God's silence-concerning the angels, this antithesis is the origin for the great angel-man-devil triptych (see above 4.2.–4.2.1.) in which the figure of the middle-piece is represented by Sermo 12 (*De vocatione ad poenitentiam, ... soli homini ... congrua*) and the side panels by Sermons 11 (*De ... missione angelorum* ...) and 13 (*De via diaboli ... in circuitu* ...).

Secondly, the sequence of Sermons 19–22 *ad mysticum sensum* (*TS* 19, 36–7) was inspired by Gregory's interpretation of >frater primogenitus< Job 1.13 with respect to *praelati* (*TS* 19, 25), >coelum< Job 1.16 with respect to *praedicatores* (*TS* 20, 12, 17) and >Chaldaei< Job 1.17 with respect to *principes* (*TS* 21, 14, 24–5). Staupitz can also use him as a basis for his idea of the devil's special *licentia* (*TS* 19, 26) exercised over and through these groups. Even in Sermon 22 (*De negligentia parentum* ...) where Gregory does not offer any obvious help, Staupitz knows how to make use of him: " ... haec acceptio magis ... deservit" (*TS* 22, 177).

Staupitz never anticipates any verse of the Job text,[85] as little as he does concerning Gregory, with the one exception of *TS* 2, 108–111. Two other occurrences, *TS* 10, 337–8 = 19, 352–3 ("Cuius vita despicitur, restat, ut eius doctrina contemnatur") turn out to be familiar quotations

---

[84] As seems to suggest Steinmetz, *Luther and Staupitz*, 41.
[85] Even unambiguous quotations from or allusions to the Job text are not marked, see Job 7.1 in *TS* 12, 347 and Job 28.28 in *TS* 24, 132 (= Augustine); Iob 36.15 in *TS* 33, 190–1 and Job 42.10 in *TS* 15, 310.

which also appear in the *Constitutiones* published in 1504.[86]

Similar maxims stem from other works by Gregory the Great. One is from a letter in *TS* 19, 128–130 ("Bonorum auctori adhaerere non possumus, nisi ...", via Gratian), and another from the commentary on Ezekiel in *TS* 20, 109–10 ("Nullum deo acceptius sacrificium quam zelus animarum", via Gerson). Some passages from the commentary on various Gospel readings can be found in *TS* 9, 60–63 ("Cum augentur dona, rationes etiam crescunt donorum", also quoted in *De exsecutione*, para. 7[87]) and 148–9 ("Terrena substantia aeternae felicitati comparata pondus, non subsidium"), *TS* 19, 225–6 ("Sic opus fiat in publico, ut intentio maneat in occulto", via Gerson), and *TS* 20, 62–3 ("Qui caritatem non habet, praedicationis officium suscipere nullatenus debet").

6. Augustine, as could be expected from Staupitz's characterization as "pater et doctor meus, immo et sanctae ecclesiae, intellectu profundissimus, sermone lepidus atque allegatione authenticus" (*TS* 7, 94–96), is nearly omnipresent. Not only the most numerous, lengthiest, the most important, and most beautiful passages in the Tübingen sermons derive from him, but also those which are hardly tolerable. Staupitz succeeds in finding a suitably illustrative, if not always fundamental text for almost each of his objects. He does so with a sure instinct for the impressive Augustinian formulas (like the already mentioned *uti–frui, causa efficiens–deficiens, esse–bene esse*) including his puns (*sartago–Carthago*), his imagery (*cor rectum–distortum, timor castae–adulterae*) as well as his allegories (Christ the camel, Christ sleeping in the storm, the left hand and the right hand of the lover, the imminent judgement as the drawn bow), and even scenes (Christ in Gethsemane). He neither left out the *facetissima urbanitas* in *TS* 13, 320 nor sarcastic expressions such as *vita quieta–nequitia secura* in *TS* 34, 278, nor *misericordes nostri* in *TS* 12, 247–8, and did not even shy away from using thoughtless or tasteless remarks as we find in *TS* 6, 418–425 and 516–518 (cf. below 6.3.5. para. 4 *lepra*; 6.2.3. para. 3 *Diogenes*).[88]

This is true for Pars I (*de fortuna*) without reservation, both for the

---

[86] *Constitutiones*, chap. 36, final remarks. I had an early look at an electronic editing output of this text by Wolfgang Günther, prepared for *JvS* 5 (Gutachten und Satzungen).

[87] See annot. 22 to chap. 2: *JvS* 2, 82–3.

[88] In the following examination, passages are not taken into account which, although verifiable from Augustine as to the expressed idea, I could not trace back to a specific work of his, such as the harmony of spirit and flesh in the *iustitia originalis* (*TS* 3, 144–46 and 146–7, along with annot. 45, 46: *JvS* 1, 69), or the *numeri rerum* (*TS* 12, 145 with annot. 128: *JvS* 1, 230). Or metaphors such as *amaritudo medicinae* or *testae* (*TS* 11, 402ff with annot. 96 and 98: *JvS* 1, 200). Or a familiar saying such as "cui servire regnare est" (*TS* 24, 115 with annot. 36: *JvS* 1, 365).

first group of five sermons (*de perfecta mentis dispositione*) and for the second group (*de bonorum terrenae felicitatis usu*). It is true as well for the first three of the group of four sermons which constitute Pars II (*de temptationis ... consideratione*), but in Sermon 14 (*De adiutorio domini ...*) Augustine is missing.

In Pars III Augustine is totally absent in four sermons (15, 20, 22, 30). In sermon 23, he is represented by a sole sentence and in six other sermons (17, 18, 19, 21, 25, 31) only single sentences can be attributed to him, and they mostly came to Staupitz via an intermediary. In nine sermons only is Pars III comparable to Pars I. However, these findings are very surprising in only two sermons, 15 (*De virtutue et gratia ... sive: libertatem arbitrii non cogi*) and 23 (*De consideratione sui et operum suorum, ... de proprii meriti vilificatione*). And indeed, as Gerson is about to pelagianize[89] in the latter sermon (*TS* 23, 284ff), Augustine is called upon via Lombard and Giles to help out with a clear *votum*: "Quid est meritum hominis ante gratiam, cum omne bonum meritum nostrum non in nobis faciat nisi gratia?" (*TS* 23, 320–1).

6.1. The first printed edition of Augustine's *Enarrationes in Psalmos* was published by Amerbach in 1489, the same year as was that of *De civitate*. As Staupitz's *Enarrationes* text has common readings, but no common errors like those found in Sermon 28, 164ff citing *De civitate*[90], his use of the Amerbach *Enarrationes* print can not as yet be proved unambiguously.[91] While I was editing the Tübingen sermons, I consulted the old edition. But as it lacked help in *TS* 3, 255 and did not offer the same text Staupitz has in lines 23ff either, I dismissed it—unjustly. The exact collation[92] shows that consequently taking in consideration

---

[89] Steinmetz, *Misericordia Dei*, 54 along with n. 1, draws attention to the fact that Staupitz circumspectly omits a Gersonian sentence such as: "Nolo tamen negare quin anima possit ex sua vita naturali bene moraliter agere et, faciendo quod in se est, se ad vitam gratiae disponere." To my mind, it would only repeat in other words what Staupitz had already let Gerson say uncensured in *TS* 23, 284ff. I can not see that "Staupitz rejects this idea" here. On the other hand, *De exsecutione*, para. 19 indeed most probably must be interpreted in the way Steinmetz suggests.

[90] See footnote 13 para. 2.

[91] I made the following observations in a copy of the UB Heidelberg, Inc. Q 1095 1/X Quart. Important evidence for Staupitz's use of a copy of this early print is the marginalia "alia littera >confringes<", apposed to Augustine's lemma >deduces< Ps. 55.8 in order to point to the Vulgate reading instead of Augustine's Vetus latina reading. This information can be found in Staupitz vice versa: *TS* 11, 467–8.

Staupitz has certainly not used the only other print available at this time besides the edition by Amerbach at Basel in 1489, namely the print which the *Gesamtkatalog der Wiegendrucke* lists as n. 2908, presumably printed in the "Niederlande oder Niederrhein," by the "printer of Augustine's *Explanatio psalmorum* (Copinger n. 741)", around "1485?." Of this latter I examined a copy in Darmstadt, Hessische Landesbibliothek, Inc. IV. 265. In this printed edition, the entire colon "quia a deo ea petunt" (*TS* 16, 113) is missing; and there is no marginal note referring from >deduces< Vet. lat. to the Vulgate.

[92] Collation table of *TS* 3. 23–48 (= Augustine, *Enarr.Ps.* 32, e.2, s.1,2):

the old print, no matter whether Staupitz actually used it or not, I would have been helped in controlling and constituting the text of his borrowings from *Enarrationes*.[93] As a whole the print confirms after all that a great number of surprising readings in Staupitz's text of Augustine are not arbitrary, but representative of an assured tradition.[94]

line(s)	TS	Niederl.? 1485?	Basel 1489	CChr
26	autem	autem	autem	enim
	quo	quo	quo	quod
27	conveniant	conveniant	conveniant	conveniat
28	praeponunt	proponunt	proponunt	praeponunt
32	quam	quam	quam	qua
36	recto	recto	recto	rectum
	qui quod	qui quod	qui quod	ut quidquid
	in illa	in illa	in illa	in illo
37	eum	illum	illum	illum
38	possit	possit	possit	posset
39	male	mali	mali	mali
44–5	illum supra,	illum supra,	illum supra,	illum supra te,
	te infra	te infra	te infra	te infra
		illum	illum	illum

I do not take into account the inversion of "dispar esse" (line 40) and "eius voluntati" (46–7).

In addition, I have compared all the other *Enarrationes* quotations in the Tübingen sermons listed in the following synopsis with the Basel edition of 1489. I have also checked clm 18760 (as mentioned in footnote 4) throughout the corresponding passages.

A by-product of this recent examination is to be noted here, so that I can be *prior accusator mei iustus*: Correctly speaking, the quotation in *TS* 1, 38 between *Utique* and *si*, and in line 40 between *sit* and *punire* as well as between *pertinuit* and *iustificare* must be discontinued; in *TS* 3, 24, *suum* must be excluded from the quotation, in line 45 the quotation must be discontinued between *te infra* and *illum creatorem*, and in 255 it must be discontinued between *erit* and *Vis*; in *TS* 4, 41 *forte* must be excluded from the quotation; in *TS* 5, 283, the quotation must be discontinued between *sequitur* and *affectus*; in *TS* 7, 103, *abundas* (instead of *ardes* Augustine) must be excluded from the quotation and in line 159 *enim* must be included, in 173 the quotation must be discontinued between *praeponetur* and *ut*, in 174 *ergo* must be excluded, in 312 *superbia* must be signed as a quotation; in *TS* 11, 563, *suas* must be excluded; in *TS* 32, 130, *ergo* must be excluded.

[93] As has been done with the quotations from Gerson, since the texts as being presented by Glorieux can only with the greatest reservations be used as a secondary transmission in the way defined in my introduction (*JvS* 1, 14 and 27). Cf. the textcritical apparatus in *JvS* 1, 57, 74, 163, 309, 320–322, 352, 355–6, 365, 396–7, 413, 475.

[94] In addition to those obvious from my collation table in footnote 92, the following readings are confirmed by the edition printed by Amerbach at Basel in 1489: In *TS* 3, 242: *quisque*, in line 251 *impiis* and *filiis*, in 252 *Ne* thus to be included in the quotation, and in 253 *cogites*; in *TS* 4, 38: *accedat*, in line 42 *moritur*; in *TS* 7, 107: *praenuntiaret*, in line 123 *sinu*, in 126 *et*, in 162 *affluant* thus to be included in the quotation, in 177 *in* thus to be included, in 403 *invenitis*, in 403–4 *superabundantem divitiis* thus to be marked as a quotation; in *TS* 11, 420: *erit* thus to be included in the quotation, in line 436 *patiuntur*, in 437 *tribulationem* thus to be included, in 464 *abscondat* and *intrent tribulae*, in 471 *omnes* thus to be included, in 500 cadit, in 561 *Qui*, in 615 *perierant*; in *TS* 16, 104: *quo*, in line 112 *ergo* and in 113 *ea* thus to be included all three, in 118 the first of the three *colunt*.

It also confirms that "eos" in *TS* 11, 413 must be omitted which I felt compelled to add following *CChr*. The same applies to for "vel" (before "lingua") in line 491 where the quotation is thus not to be discontinued.

In the following, I list Staupitz's quotations. In column 2 the synopsis shows in which *articulus* and *punctus* (or *principium* or *effectus*) or, in other words, in which field of the triple triad pattern a quotation is placed. '+' before column 4 indicates when the quotation has been identified by me. These incidences are not very weighty (with the exception, perhaps, of *Enarratio* 59), but their number, nearly one third, is considerable.

col.1 serm.	col.2 art. ...	col.3 lines		col.4 (= Augustine)
TS 1,	1.1	29–31, 36–41		(= *Enarr. Ps.* 62, 12)
TS 2,	3.2	216–7		(= *Enarr. Ps.* 95, 4)
TS 3,	1.1	23–48		(= *Enarr. Ps.* 32, e.2, s.1, 2)
		88–103		(= *Enarr. Ps.* 31, e.2, 25)
	2.3	238–256		(= *Enarr. Ps.* 31, e.2, 25–6)
TS 4,	1.1	37–50		(= *Enarr. Ps.* 127, 7)
		59–63		(= *Enarr. Ps.* 127, 9)
		100–130		(= *Enarr. Ps.* 127, 8)
TS 5,	2.3	281–285		(= *Enarr. Ps.* 188, s.8, 4)
TS 7,	1.1	96–135		(= *Enarr. Ps.* 51, 14)
	1.2	156–178		(= *Enarr. Ps.* 143, 18)
		201–208	+	(= *Enarr. Ps.* 85, 3)
	2.1	291–307		(= *Enarr. Ps.* 125, 13 and 12)
		310–313	+	(= *Enarr. Ps.* 136, 13)
	2.2	315–326		(= *Enarr. Ps.* 48, s.1, 9)
		327–8	+	(= *Enarr. Ps.* 136, 13)
	3.1	397–406		(= *Enarr. Ps.* 85, 2–3)
TS 11,	1.3	409–427	+	(= *Enarr. Ps.* 59, 6)
		433–476		(= *Enarr. Ps.* 55, 4, 9, 11, and 13)
		488–501		(= *Enarr. Ps.* 55, 10)
		513–517		(= *Enarr. Ps.* 55, 14)
	2.1	561–575		(= *Enarr. Ps.* 90, s.2, 9)
	2.3	611–621		(= *Enarr. Ps.* 90, s.2, 11)
		642–644	+	(= *Enarr. Ps.* 17, 31)
TS 16,	1.1	72–80		(= *Enarr. Ps.* 125, 14)
		96–122		(= *Enarr. Ps.* 35, 7 and 8)
TS 32,	1.1	54–56		(= *Enarr. Ps.* 37, 24)
		85–87		(= *Enarr. Ps.* 21, e.1, 16)
		90–93	+	(= *Enarr. Ps.* 21, e.2, 16)
	1.2	130–146		(= *Enarr. Ps.* 50, 19)

In the edition printed in the Netherlands(?) around 1485(?), I have not checked the two quotations found in *TS* 4 and the last two in *TS* 11 as listed in the synopsis. Among all the other *TS* readings just enumerated as being confirmed by the edition printed at Basel in 1489, the Netherlands(?) print of around 1485(?) does not support the following three only: *TS* 3, 251 "-iis" and "-iis," *TS* 7, 177 "in" and *TS* 11, 500 "cadit." As to *TS* 16, 113, see footnote 91.

According to this list Staupitz quotes more than 30 passages of between 2 and 60 lines from 20 different *Enarrationes* in nine of his sermons. These quotations appear in quite varied density, and he does not always explicitly refer to their source. Let us first have a look at the three sermons which are most indebted to Augustine.

6.1.1. Sermon 7 (*De divitiis* ...). After long and important passages derived from *De civitate* about the power fallen man still holds over the natural wealth of creation, though it is restricted in order to punish and try him, Sermon 7, with a total of 503 lines,—speaking about artificial wealth (to use a *distinctio* by Thomas Aquinas) and its responsible use—quotes 84 lines taken from six (2 more than identified before) different *Enarrationes* in eight (four more) passages,[95] each having a length between 5 and 39 lines. This is an echo of the great number of times Augustine himself treated this subject from different viewpoints: Can rich men go to heaven at all? (110). In his conversation with the rich young man (104ff) Jesus does not pass sentence on money but on the greediness, which can possess rich as well as poor men (116). The old question *Qui dives salvetur?* is answered with the vision of poor Lazarus in the lap of the formerly rich Abraham (119ff). The rich shall be rich in good acts (1.Tim. 6.17) (130), then the camel Jesus Christ, together with the burden of his passion, will have gone through the needle's eye for them, too (132ff). The gifts of the right and left hand (146–7) with which the bridegroom Christ endows his beloved, must not be mistaken for each other; desire (>cor< Ps. 61.11 = *desiderium*) which is reserved for eternity must not be lost to the needs of everyday life (156ff). One does not need to worry about salvation because of riches, but because of the arrogance, into which the rich are almost necessarily seduced (201ff, 310–313). Sometimes, a poor man can help a rich man, be it by an act (293ff) or by giving advice (301); even beggars can help each other (302ff). The treasures in heaven are the most secure way of investment (323ff). The poor man (Ps. 85.1) whom God hears favourably, is the humble one, be he poor or rich in secular possessions (397ff).

The loci of these passages except for one are to be found *ad vocem* '*divitiae*', and this one is *ad vocem* '*elemosyna*' in the *Principalium sententiarum in Explanationem libri Psalmorum ... comprehensarum summaria ordinataque annotatio* of the Amerbach edition of 1489 (hereafter called *Tabula*), no matter whether Staupitz used this or other tools.[96] Sermon 7 shows the quotations from Augustine's *Enarrationes*

---

[95] One is also tempted to attribute to Augustine passages presented in an ingenious lighter tone such as *TS* 7, 328–330: "Ne cogites perpetuare divitias quas deus corruptibiles creavit ..."

[96] Considering the otherwise very precise résumé of the history of the Amerbach edition given by Hamm, *Frömmigkeitstheologie* (as in fn. 65), 320 n. 115, one could

to be distributed fairly evenly on (five of) the nine fields of the triple triad pattern (which he sometimes extends), while in the second triad he also integrates Ambrose and the third is nearly entirely given to Boethius.

This type of collecting and redistributing quotations is particularly obvious in this sermon. Except for the most impressive allegory of the bridegroom's left and right hand (*TS* 7, 165ff), an abstract variation of which is placed additionally before and labelled as a familiar biblical usage (*TS* 7, 145–147), all the other quotations, though integrated on purpose, can easily be isolated, as they merely serve as illustration.

6.1.2. Sermon 11 (*De temptationibus tribulationibusque sub specie aeternae dei scientiae, providentiae, praedestinationis consideratis ...*). Besides an introduction to the topics of *praedestinatio–vocatio–iustificatio* which comprises more than half of the sermon and includes arguments from Giles, Thomas Aquinas and Bonaventure, Sermon 11, with a total of 763 lines, quotes 100 lines from *Enarrationes*, plus a nameless 2 line quotation not identified before (*Enarratio* 17). 16 lines are taken from *Enarratio* 59, which have not been acknowledged hitherto; 60 lines in several small portions come from *Enarratio* 55 and 24 lines, distributed over two passages, from *Enarratio* 90.[97] Compared to the keyword *divitiae*, there is an even greater number of occurrences, according to the *Tabula* mentioned above, where Augustine in his *Enarrationes* speaks about *temptatio* and *tribulatio*. The passages quoted here concentrate on a few sequences of evidently central sentences which are located on a few fields of the triple triad pattern. The quotations from *Enarratio* 59 and 55 are restricted to one field (*TS* 11, art. 1, pct. 3) and those from *Enarratio* 90 to two fields (*TS* 11, art. 2, princ. 1 and 3). All three *Enarrationes* are referred to in the *Tabula ad voces 'temptari'* or *'tribulari'*. Staupitz does not merely use them to illustrate something he had already explained sufficiently in simple words interpreting Rom. 8.30. They rather add to the development of his thoughts, since the passages borrowed from Augustine *ad vocem 'tribulatio'* likewise reach their inner goal in Rom. 8 and by means of a tiny redactional addition their outer goal as well. It is impossible to isolate small abstracts and add them up here, as I did in the case of Sermon 7.

Praedestinatio ad conformitatem >imaginis filii< (cit. Rom. 8.29) (364) means first and foremost for all (379)—who believe—*prae-*

---

assume that the printed edition of 1489 was published without a *Tabula* and that it was only added in the later one of 1497 (*GKW* 2911; Heidelberg UB, Q 1095 1/12 Quart). The edition of 1489, however, contains a *Tabula* (placed ahead in the Heidelberg copy) which runs through each letter three times, once for every quinquagena separately, just as the *Tabula* does in *GKW* 2908 (as cited in footnote 91) which seems to have served as a model. On the contrary the print of 1497 summarizes the entries for each vox from all 150 Psalms.

[97] For the connection of *Enarrationes* 55 and 90 to Job, see footnote 76.

destinatio to *imitatio*, and even *communicatio passionum Christi* (cit. 1.
Pet. 2.21 and 4.13) (374ff). The *regula* (366) prescribes that Christ's
>discipulus< must be like Christ (cit. Luke 14.27) (383), and that we
must be like our Head (*caput* 449 = Augustine).[98] Those who do not
suffer in this world are threatened with eternal pain. "Verissimum
signum itaque praedestinationis et immediatum est conformitas passionis Christi" (397–399) which means suffering like Christ, and does
not mean suffering against one's own will and without faith (395–6),
which is perhaps even deserved. And the >passiones huius temporis<
are not very burdensome compared to the future >gloria< (Rom 8.18)
(406–408). This is said by Staupitz.

Now follows Augustine's *Enarratio* 59: For the House of the Lord,
judgement already begins now (1.Pet. 4.17) (409). This word, originally
said as a comfort to the martyrs (410) (who had shared Christ's suffer-
ings more than anyone else), is true in general: The *tribulationes* >huius
temporis< (from Rom. 8.18, inserted by Staupitz!) (425) are a sign
(>significationem dedisti< Ps. 59.6) (424) for those who believe that
through their temporal trial (*exercitatio* 425) they will escape the full
impact of the final judgement (>ut fugiant a facie arcus< Ps. 59.6)
(424–5), i.e., the eternal damnation which awaits the non-believers
(426).

The quotation from Augustine underlines the comfort (405, 408)
which has already been hinted at in >gaudete< (1.Pet. 4.13) in the text
by Staupitz (376) and makes the threat which is dominant in 1.Pet. 4.17
more bearable with the aid of Ps. 59.6. Staupitz's and Augustine's
thoughts meet in *signum* (398) and >significatio< (424) for the first
time, and finally in Rom. 8.18 (406–408 and 425).

In the description of *exsecutio praedestinationis*—this borrowing from
De exsecutione is allowed by line 479—through *vocatio* (429ff) and
iustificatio (481ff) Staupitz carefully integrates into his own text at first a
sequence of four shorter passages (433ff) and then a longer (488–501)
and a shorter (513–517) passage, all from *Enarratio* 55.

Staupitz: Nobody should think that a calling (cit. Rom. 8.30) to
belief is without *tribulatio* (430–1). Augustine: Do not think you can
live piously in Christ without suffering persecution (paraphrase of
>tribulavit< Ps. 55.2–3 through 2.Tim. 3.12); particularly by false
brothers (2.Cor. 11.26) (441ff) who have unhindered access (on Ps.
55.7) (444), as it happened to the Head, Christ (449–50),[99] through

---

[98] Shortly before Staupitz begins his quotation from *Enarr.Ps.* 55.9 (*TS* 11, 443),
Augustine writes (*Enarr.Ps.* 55.8): "Non est discipulus maior magistro suo, non est servus
maior domino suo." (Matt. 10.24 combined with John 13.16) (*CChr* 39. 683.19–20). The
sentence cited above (in footnote 61) preceeds this.

[99] Cf. above at the end of 2.4.

Judas and the Jews, though they could not rob him of heaven (457). We shall edify (449) our neighbours, when they see wine being pressed from grapes (439–40, 448) in the winepress (on >conculcavit< Ps. 55. 2–3) (439) or the wheat (465)[100] being sifted from the chaff (464) on the threshing floor (on >tribulavit< Ps. 55.2–3) (464). Ultimately it is not man (>caro< Ps. 55.5) (446–7) who is at work but God (447) who in his wrath educates his people: "irasceris et deducis (from Ps. 55.8 Vet. lat.), saevis et salvas, terres et vocas (from Rom. 8.30)" (469). Everything is pervaded with *tribulationes*, causing everyone to seek refuge in God and to shun enjoyment and security, "tribulationibus territi et fide impleti" (476). In this sentence which sounds reformatory Staupitz and Augustine meet again. They had both previously used >vocavit< (429–30) and *vocas* (469) as well as *fides* (430 and 476) as keywords.

With this procedure, which I have sketched, Staupitz consciously or unconsciously imitates the method used in *Enarrationes* with regard to their basic text and applies it to the former: like threads, Augustine spins the verses taken from the Psalms (Ps. 59, Ps. 55) on the one hand and from the New Testament on the other (1.Pet. 4.17, Rom. 8.30, 2.Tim. 3.12, 2.Cor. 11.26, [Rom. 8. 18]). All the passages used by him coincide in a portion, be it in the literal or metaphorical sense, be it by equality or contrast or with regard to other rhetorical loci, and can thus be intertwined. The common denominator in this case is sometimes called *tribulationes, conculcationes* and at other times *passiones, persecutiones, pericula*. Staupitz then interlaces the resulting range of biblical-Augustinian thoughts with his own—more direct and often less ingenious—paraphrases of partially the same passages from the New Testament—1.Pet. 4.13, Rom. 8. 29–30—by means of drawing on others—1.Pet. 2.21; 1.Pet. 5.8, 9; Matt. 16.24; 10.38; Luke 14.27; Matt. 11.28—and using *passio* and *crux, tribulari* and *cruciari, tribulari* and *laborare* as synonyms. Although one can easily distinguish and continuously read Staupitz's own writing as opposed to his quotations from Augustine, both are properly interlinked, not simply added one after the other alternatively.

There remains the paragraph about *iustificatio*. Staupitz: We gain justification through the sacraments in which the power of the suffering of Christ becomes effective, baptism and repentance. We require repentance as we inevitably still sin after baptism (482–487). Augustine, or rather Staupitz through him, then continuing to use *Enarratio* 55 describes (488ff) the devil's ambush from which nobody can escape. Who

---

[100] The meaning of this very abbreviated part of the quotation (*TS* 11, 464–5) can be elucidated without doubt through *TS* 29, 61–2: "Sub eadem tribula stipulae comminuuntur, frumenta purgantur."

would not sin through one wrong word (cit. Jam. 3.2)? Even the just
falls seven times (Prov. 24.16), but he gets up again because he—
repents (cit. Ps. 55.9) (501–503). Here Staupitz explicitly expresses a
thought Augustine had only initiated. He is given the right to complete
this transition by the second quotation from Augustine occurring in the
iustificatio paragraph (513–517): "Inveni te misericordem in repromit-
tendo (from Ps. 55.9), veracem in reddendo" which is exemplified by
the confession of Paul in 1.Tim. 1.13. In between (504–513), Staupitz
talks about the so-called three parts of the sacrament of repentance:
contritio, confessio, and *satisfactio*. In the *contritio* as *dolor cordis* (505,
522) the value of the *tribulatio* with respect to *iustificatio* is experienced
and therefore the *tribulatio* is accepted willingly (521–523).

The first quotation from Augustine's *Enarratio* 90 in the parenetical
part of Sermon 11 merely serves as gloss. It is *TS* 11, 561–575 and
explains >leo< and >draco< in Ps. 90.13, the most important biblical
testimony for the existence and the mandate of the guardian angels,
through >leo< in 1.Pet. 5.8 and through >serpens< in 2.Cor. 11.3,
both seen as the violent and cunning face of one and the same
>diabolus<. *Castitas* (from 2.Cor.), as little as poverty (from Ps. 85.1)
above in Sermon 7, must not be understood in the physical sense of the
word, but as poverty there means humility, chastity here stands for
faithful and obedient belief (572, 574).

The other quotation from *Enarratio* 90 in Sermon 11 is *TS* 11,
611–621. It illustrates the scriptural testimony for God's closeness to
those in temptation (>tribulato corde< Ps. 33.9) (610–11) which Staupitz cites directly, through the allegorical interpretation of Christ sleeping (Matt. 8) as faith sleeping which Augustine provides speaking on
>cum ipso sum in tribulatione< (Ps. 90.15). Then we can again pursue
the procedure described earlier where Staupitz spins out a range of
biblical-Augustinian thoughts. The term >eripiam< (Ps. 90.15) which
Augustine takes up by *nec deseruit* (620) and substantiates *corporaliter*
through the three young men in the burning oven and *spiritualiter*
through the Maccabeans, is in turn taken up by Staupitz through the
rhetorical questions in Rom. 8.31–37 (622–631, especially >tribulatio<,
>pericula< and >persecutio<) and through the promise of grace and
life expressed in Rom. 5.8–10 (631–636), the latter being linked back
through >Quis nos separabit ...< (627) and forword through >qui
dilexit nos< (631). According to the same schema, this longest sequence
from the New Testament to be found in the Tübingen sermons is
concluded through Ps. 17.30 along with the pertinent gloss deriving
from Augustine, though not named here.

This entire paraphrase of the Augustinian passages in Sermon 11 may
be considered as an attempt to unfold what Steinmetz had called

"interesting interplay between Romans 8, Psalm 55, and the exegetical comments of St. Augustine" (see at the end of footnote 14).

6.1.3. Sermon 4 (*De timore dei servili, filiali seu casto deque differentiis* ...), with a total of 325 lines, quotes 57, together with the 5 lines transmitted by Lombard in *TS* 4, 27–32 even more than 60 lines from *Enarratio* 127. The original context of the giving side is slightly re-grouped and placed in one of the nine fields on the receiving side again. In every sense of the word, this is the most homogenous borrowing of all. Augustine's comparison (100–105) is unforgettable: Two women, one of whom is faithful whereas the other is an adulteress, both fear their husbands. "Casta timet ne discedat," "adultera ne veniat". The two women symbolize our situation as we await the Second Coming of the heavenly bridegroom (110ff). The comparison, carried through by calling upon Isa. 53 and Matt. 25 to which Staupitz contributes Prov. 7.19–20, is too beautiful to be rendered here in a mutilated form.

It is interesting to read Staupitz's confession that in some earlier sermons *de timore dei* (*TS* 4, 51), he had not clearly acknowledged the salient point about sinning, although even then he must have known the distinctions by Lombard and Bonaventure, which are placed ahead now (23ff and 15ff), the latter of which presupposes the former, and which are both based on Augustine (27–32). Now he fully understands (53–55) and can ask his own heart the crucial question: Would you want to sin if you got off unpunished? (55ff). An affirmative answer reveals the *timor servilis*. Staupitz also takes this question from Augustine (59–63) and does not seem to have taken notice of it before reading *Enarratio* 127 as a whole.[101] In the doublet of this comparison which is in *Tractatus in 1.Ioannis epistolam*, the source for Lombard,[102] there is no similar sentence.

6.1.4. The only other sermon which is comparable with Sermon 4 as to the density and thematic homogeneity of the Augustinian quotations is Sermon 3. Of its 308 lines 58 in three passages are quotations from two *Enarrationes*. Sermon 3 (*De rectitudine cordis sive de conformatione voluntatis humanae cum divina in Christi exemplo visa*) treats a concept equally central for Augustine as well as for Staupitz.[103] In lines 23–48 Staupitz recalls how the Son as the Head[104] accepted the Father's will on the Mount of Olives (cit. Matt. 26.39 parr.): "Quorum una est divinitas, non potest dispar esse voluntas" (40). This example teaches us the

---

[101] Cf. Jeremias, *Luthers Vater und Schüler* (as in fn. 65), 94.

[102] *Tract. in 1.Ioannis epistolam*, chap. 8.6.–7 (*MPL* 35. 2049–50) and the middle of chap. 9 (2051–2, cit. Isa. 53).

[103] Cf. above 2.3. along with footnote 34.

[104] Cf. again above towards the end of 2.4.

regula (30) by which we may overcome the tremendous gap[105] between creator and creature (45):[106] "Quomodo disiunctus es a deo, qui iam hoc vis quod deus?" (48).

The other two quotations extend this basic concept: *rectus homo conformis voluntati divinae*.[107] Firstly, in *TS* 3, 88–103 Staupitz takes up one of Augustine's favourite counter-images. The *cor distortum* or *pravum* is like a piece of wood that won't fit into the parquet, i.e., man who asks the old question of theodicy ("doctrina philosophorum") (90): Does God exist? And if he exists, does he care what happens in the world? Why do I have to suffer, whereas others who are worse do not? This is a prelude to the dinner speech (*TS* 9, 223) in Sermon 9, 199ff, esp. 218–220, 223–232 (= *De civitate*, see below) and the teaching of *duplex misericordia* in Sermon 16, 96ff, esp. 114, 118 (= *Enarrationes in Psalmos*, see below).

Secondly, the association of son (*TS* 3, 238–256, esp. 251ff,[108] cit. Heb. 12.5–7) and heritage "Ne[109] te sine flagello speres futurum, nisi forte cogites exheredari" (252–3) throws a revealing light on the profitability (197, 236) and even necessity[110] of *temptatio* or *tribulatio in hoc mundo*, as they represent the alternative to *aeternaliter cruciari* dominating Sermon 11[111] and in Sermon 16 also pointed to (127, 221). In the sentence "Nec diabolus tibi aliquid facit, nisi ille permittat qui desuper habet potestatem aut ad poenam, aut ad disciplinam, ad poenam impiis, ad disciplinam filiis" (*TS* 3, 249–50), Staupitz on the one hand announces the object of Sermons 16, 17 and 19, i.e., the reasons wherefore and the limits to which God lets the devil do his work; on the other hand, he announces the object of Sermon 24, i.e., God as master retaining his rule through and despite man's apparent rule over man.

6.1.5. In the following I want to discuss a group of sermons which are characterized by only one passage where Augustine is unmistakeably

---

[105] Cf. "Homo non est deus," *TS* 3, 17–8, cf. also *TS* 5, 49ff. Cf. especially Augustine, *Enarr.Ps.* 32, e.2, s.1, 2: "Quantum enim deus distat ab homine, tantum voluntas dei a voluntate hominis" (*CChr* 38. 248. 12–3) which Staupitz passes by before "unde gerens" (*TS* 3, 30).

[106] "Per voluntatis conformationem, non substantiae identitate," *TS* 3, 205–6.

[107] In *TS* 3, 53ff, Giles is not introduced as the originator of this thought but as a supplier of arguments for its binding force. This is stated against Wolf who gradually shifted the emphasis from the second (*Staupitz und Luther*, 90) to the first (p. 95, p. 98 at the end of his long note 5 beginning on p. 92, and p. xi). It escaped him that *TS* 24, 318–328 also has its origin in Giles.

[108] For the connection to Job, see again footnote 76.

[109] Cf. footnote 94.

[110] "Temptari oportet," *TS* 11, 535; "temptari debere" *TS* 14, 54.

[111] ">Non est servus maior domino<" (1.John 13.6) (*TS* 3, 303) is taken up again by "caput" on the one hand and "discipulus" on the other hand (cf. above near footnote 98 and fn. itself).

quoted and where the quotation directly refers to the subject-matter of the sermon.

Sermon 1 (*De misericordia dei in perfectione virtutum Iob viri utique gentilis ostensa*), 36–41 are about the lack of a cause for God's mercy. If there is any ground for his acting, he would have every reason to inflict punishment. He has to create the prerequisite for reward himself: "Invenit in nobis delicta quae donaret, sed non invenit iustitiam quam coronaret. Utique si punire vellet inventa delicta, non esset iniustus; cum ergo iustum sit punire peccatorem, ad misericordiam pertinuit iustificare ipsum". In the frame or introduction to these deliberations (29–31) the use of a more glossing kind is shown. When separated from its biblical origin (Ps. 62.4), it can be taken as a maxim in its own right: "Dono tuo te laudo, per misericordiam tuam te laudo."

Sermons 16 and 32 both contain one long quotation and one or more short ones. With the basic distinction of a *duplex misericordia*, Sermon 16 (*De potestate seu licentia temptandi* ...) in 96–122 teaches the educational intention of the withdrawal of God's care here on earth, and in 72–80 offers an aphorism about *misericordia crudelis* which depends on its *miseros* as a medical art which needs the sick.

In Sermon 32 (*De poena et passione, de peccato* ...) all quotations are glosses. In 130–146, the longer text speaks about the >sanies< (Job 2.8). The two shorter texts, which could also exist on their own are about our perverse feeling of pain (*TS* 32, 54–5): "Dolemus de flagello, non de causa" and about virtue (*TS* 32, 85–87, 90–93): "Testa fit igne firmior" (the latter not recognized before).

6.1.6. With both such glosses as well as maxims of this kind, it is reasonable to assume that Staupitz received them indirectly. "Dolemus de flagello ..." may have been mediated by Gerson.[112] Another gloss, referring to Ps. 118.20, found in Sermon 5 (*De malo* ... *eiusque fuga*), 281–285: "... Praevolat intellectus, et tarde sequitur et aliquando non sequitur affectus ...", is probably received through Lombard.[113]

Maxims are the two quotations in Sermon 2 (*De simplicitate* ...), 216–7: "Tanto amplius laudabitur medicus, quanto plus desperabit aegrotus" and in Sermon 34 (*De correctione fraterna* ...), 126: "Corripiat iustus in misericordia." The latter is unambiguously mediated by Thomas Aquinas[114] (without a title, from *Enarratio* 140; not included in my list).

One of the few quotations from *Enarrationes* which (similarly to that one in *TS* 4, 27–32; cf. 6.1.3.) have been borrowed complete with its

---

[112] See annot. 10 and 12 to *TS* 32: *JvS* 1, 449.
[113] See annot. 99 to *TS* 5: *JvS* 1, 98.
[114] See annot. 29 to *TS* 34: *JvS* 1, 475. This is the only instance where Thomas Aquinas appears in this function.

frame is to be found in Sermon 6 (*De matrimonio* ...), 489–495. It is embedded in a quotation of Lombard and therefore not included in my list. The contents are as follows: Abstinence must not be practised at the cost of adultery by one spouse (*Enarratio* 149, 15).

A maxime shaped by the Augustinian spirit is: "Non est misericordia nisi miserorum" in *TS* 12, 368–9.[115] The request "ure, seca" in a prayer in *TS* 16, 220 draws on a concept which frequently occurs in *Enarrationes* about the doings of the divine doctor.[116]

6.2. Despite the overwhelming number and length of Staupitz's quotations derived from Augustine's *De civitate*, it is in this case easier to establish a general view than in the case of those from *Enarrationes in Psalmos*, even without a synopsis.

6.2.1. Out of the 22 books, 12 are quoted in 16 sermons, though in completely different ways. In Sermon 10 (*De parentum provisione* ...) where Staupitz draws extensively on Giles's *De regimine principum*, a work imbued by Aristotelian thought, he inserts the shocking example of Terence's unchaste youth who refers to Jupiter, found in *De civitate* 2, 7 (*TS* 10, 392–404). At the same time, in what I have called the "political" sermons in my article *Staupitz antibarbarus*[117]—Sermons 8 (*De honore, fama, potestate* ...), 28 (*De ... oppositione diaboli qua nititur exemplis Romanae antiquitatis probare, Iob neque honorem dei procurasse nec virtuose egisse nec proximum aedificasse* ...), and 34 (*De ... falsis Romanorum diis* ...)—, entire pages are dominated[118] by Augustine's demystification of Roman antiquity (books 1–5). One would scarcely have expected Staupitz to be interested in this particular complex of Augustine's monumental work, no matter how we interpret it.

For an explanation it neither suffices to point to Boethius, who says in *TS* 8, 309–10: "Nec Romani populi fama transivit Caucasum montem" (via Giles), nor to Gregory the Great's inherent criticism of stoic insensitivity found in *TS* 18, 134–136. Only Augustine is sufficiently outspoken when talking about "falsissima beatitudo" and "quanto superbior tanto mendacior virtus": *TS* 6, 87–89; see also *TS* 28, 192–194. Most important of all, Job, willing to suffer (*dolens TS* 1, 90–1, from Gregory the Great), is the anti-hero in the first book of *De civitate* from which in Sermon 29 (*De ulteriore postestate seu licentia temptandi diabolo concessa ... spirituali afflictione* ...) Staupitz quotes lines 58–68 and, especially as they expressedly refer to Job, lines 95–99:[119] "Manet

---

[115] See above 2.3. near footnote 47 and fn. itself.

[116] See annot. 44 to *TS* 16: *JvS* 1, 282.

[117] Wetzel, *Staupitz antibarbarus*, 119–125. I can skip a listing of quotations here.

[118] Newly recognized as borrowings from *De civitate Dei* in this grouping are: *TS* 8, 143–147, 147–158; *TS* 33, 197–199; *TS* 34, 233–244, 268–278, 307–323.

[119] *TS* 29, 95–99 is newly recognized as a borrowing, see annot. 18 and 25: *JvS* 1, 418–9. "Rutilat" also in *TS* 11, 8 and *TS* 27, 114.

dissimilitudo passorum in similitudine passionum ... sub uno igne aurum rutilat et palea fumat ... Amisit Iob ... omnia quae habebat. Numquid fidem?" (The rule quoted in this context: "Ne credatur semper factum cum mentis voluntate quod fieri fortasse sine carnis aliqua voluptate non potuit" in 104–106 seems like a direct quotation, but has probably been transmitted by Gerson.[120]) About Aeneas, who would fit in well here, he only says that he bragged about the adultery of his mother (*TS* 34, 225). He therefore is not an *anima naturaliter christiana* for him.

6.2.2. The other big complex in *De civitate* of which Staupitz makes ample use are books 10–12 and 13–14 about the creation and fall of the angels and of man, including book 21 about the eternity of hell. This is not surprising as they aid him in grandly presenting the different possibilities for all creatures gifted with reason in Sermons 12 (*De vocatione ad poenitentiam* ...) and 13 (*De diaboli via ... in circuitu* ...): Creatures may maintain their original status, leave it and return, or lose it forever.

More in detail. In Sermon 12, lines 247–294 with some short interruptions are about eternity of punishment; 302–304 are about God's knowing question to Adam in Gen. 3.9. Lines 379–406 deal with the "non >adhaerere< velle" (from Ps. 72.78, *leitmotif* in book 10) of the noblest, i.e., angelic creature and the self-complacent (397) surrender of its peace with itself (410–413);[121] 420–467, the longest continuous quotation from Augustine of all, deal with the enigmatic groundlessness of its *defectus* (425), its *mala voluntas* (429), or *perversio* (465–6). In contrast to this abundant direct use of books 21, 13 and 12 in Sermo 12, there is only one sentence from book 11 about the *beatitudo innocentiae* in lines 538–540* which has been transmitted via Giles.[122] The passage about man's destiny to die (666–690)—culminating in "Numquam igitur in vita homo est, ex quo in isto corpore moriente potius quam vivente ..." (688–690) (from book 13)—is again directly borrowed.

In Sermon 13 direct quotations are found in lines 44–50 about the threefold question: by whom, how and why the world was created, the third member of which is answered in Plato's words: "... ut a bono deo bona opera fierent" (from book 11). In 81–108, the interpretation of Eccl. 1.9–11 contradicts Plato's teachings on the eternal recurrence (from book 12). Lines 111–140 are about Christ as the way—back—to God (126, 131) and as a way out of the *circulus vitiosus* of a disbelieving conception of life. Lines 159–179 are about the error of the Manicheans who understand creation as a mixture of good and bad to which a helpless demiurge was forced, and 180–205 are about Origen's error of viewing

---

[120] See annot. 20, 21 to *TS* 29: *JvS* 1, 419.

[121] In this grouping are newly recognized: *TS* 12, 385–392, 393, 394–406, 410–413.

[122] The * behind the reference indicates that the Lombard, Giles or Gerson context is newly recognized.

the fall and creation as one and the same thing (both from book 11).

6.2.3. Long passages adopted from the Augustinian books about creation and fall are used as the basis for Sermons 7 (*De divitiis* ...) and 26 (*De angelorum cognitione diurna et vespertina*, ...) on the one hand, and for Sermons 5 (*De mali causa* ...), 6 (*De matrimonio* ...), 26 (*De ... possessione coeli* ...), 27 (*De ... peccato originali* ...) and 33 (*De ... passionibus seu affectibus secundum deum rectis*) on the other.

The creatures of lower ranking, without prejudice to *decus universi* (*TS* 7, 48), are not only there to serve man but also to contribute to man's "humilitatis exercitatio" (62ff) and "elationis attritio" (45). The aspect of the execution of punishment in man's existing in the body and in the world is expressed clearly ("iusto supplicio" 30). Man masters his own flesh no better than he masters lowlier creatures. The flesh's unruliness to the spirit is experienced by him as an adequate punishment ("reciproca poena") for the disobedience of the spirit to God (*TS* 6, 314–316; *TS* 27, 85–6).

In Sermon 6, lines 164–179 prove that the blessing >Crescite et multiplicamini< Gen. 1.28 also includes the marriage in paradise. Lines 181–193 defend procreation of a "sanctorum numerus ... complendae illi ... beatissimae civitati" without "pudenda libido;" 308–316 describe how the original parents acquired their sense of shame[123] and 316–338 are about the place of this sense of shame in public and home life. Line 401 tells via Giles about the use of the genitals "ad voluntatis nutum." Lines 418–425 disseminate the anecdote according to which the Cynic philosophers derive their name from the Greek word *kynes*, in so far as their founder Diogenes is said to have had shameless intercourse with his wife in public (all from book 14).

The borrowing in Sermon 5, 90–107 which can be summed up in the formula *mali causa non efficiens sed deficiens* has already been noted above before and in footnote 31. To be joined to this are 133–147 about the character of *defectus* and *privatio*: "Deficitur non ad mala sed male ..." (133–4); "... qui perverse amat cuiuslibet naturam bonam ... ipse fit in bono malus et miser ..." (145–6) (both from book 12).

In Sermon 26, apart from 44–63 about the "cognitio diurna" and "vespertina" of the angels, we must also mention 213–227 concerning the "praemium perseverantiae" which is the "omni molestia carens societas angelorum in participatione summi dei" (from book 11).

As to Sermon 27, apart from 79–95 ("reciproca poena", see above), we should mention lines 128–138 about human nature which "in illo uno" (from Rom. 5. 12), i.e., Adam "seminaliter" (132) and "velut radice" (136) is destined to die and be condemned, and lines 177–186

---

[123] Newly recognized as a borrowing from *De civitate*: *TS* 6, 308–316.

and 194–203 about its agonistic-meritorious value:[124] "Gratia salvatoris in usus iustitiae poena peccati (from Rom. 6.23, 20) conversa est" (194–5) (all from book 13).

In Sermon 33, lines 89–133[125] concerning the affections as a constitutive part of human being are to be noted.

6.2.4. From book 19 of *De civitate*, Staupitz quotes the depressing litany of the "miseriae huius vitae" (*TS* 6, 24–97),[126] functioning there in a typology of ways of life which he uses as a common introduction to the five sermons about happiness on earth (6–10). For Sermon 24 (*De ... domini dei dominio regnante de humanis dominis et malis et bonis ...*) he borrows the Augustinian concept that the "condicio servitutis" is one kind of punishment for sins, in order to legitimize and, at the same time, to put limits on every kind of power of man over man through the Lord's power (36–119).[127] In Sermon 3, 168–9 Staupitz presupposes that his readers know that book 19 is about *pax*. Definitions of *pax* concerning different realms can be found in *TS* 28, 280–285.[128]

A splinter from book 22 is "praemium virtutis" in *TS* 2, 141.

6.2.5. Even a brief survey like this demonstrates the great importance of *De civitate*. (This work again became equally influential nearly 20 years later in Staupitz's little book *Von der nachfolgung des willigen sterbens Christi*.[129] But here the anthropological aspect outweighs the cosmological.) The passages quoted from *Enarrationes*, especially in Partes I and II, have more the effect of a brushstroke in a painting or ornaments of a house, whereas the citations derived from *De civitate*, especially in Partes II and III, contribute to the structure and architecture of the work. The function of the first is rather parenetical, the function of the other is rather doctrinal. In the former, the focus is on our existence and the earth, in the latter it is on the whole history of salvation, including heaven and hell.

De civitate is an apology which surpasses its primary motive, i.e. to

---

[124] *TS* 27, 177–186 newly recognized. It is a self-account of *De baptismo parvulorum*, see annot. 68: *JvS* 1, 401.

[125] Newly recognized: *TS* 33, 117–120, 120–122, 122–135.

[126] New: *TS* 6, 90–97.

[127] New: *TS* 24, 44–50, 110–114, 117–119.

[128] New: *TS* 28, 294.

[129] The first five chapters — 1) *Von dem herkommen zeitlichs sterbens* 2) *Von der vorwurkung dreifaltigen todtes*, 3) *Von dem angeerbten schaden des ersten ungehorsams*, 4) *Von dem tode des leiblichen todes*, and 5) *Von dem angeerbten nutz des neugebornen Christo* — are closely related to *De civitate* 13, and far more extensively than the few marginalia of the original print lead us to believe. Apart from this, explicit reference is only made to *De civitate* 22.22 from which in chap. 3 (see Knaake, as cited in footnote 37, p. 57, 9ff) passages of up to nine lines are translated from a catalog of ills and pains, similar to that one found in Sermon 6 of the Tübingen sermons from *De civitate* 19. The borrowings deriving from books 12 and 14 which can be documented remain tacit.

defend the Christian God and the Christians against the accusation that
the negative contemporary political situation is their fault (allusion to
this is made in *TS* 34, 276–278),[130] and becomes a justification of God:
God is the master of history (*TS* 9, 199–220) no less than of all other
events in the world which is his creation. And he is the good creator of a
good creation. The creatures are the only ones guilty of any corruption
in the—smaller part of—creation (*TS* 13, 199–201). Thus Adam, the
man placed in paradise to "reparatio ruinae angelorum" (*TS* 30, 56; cf.
TS 11, 603 = Bonaventure), formerly lighthearted and now repentant
(*TS* 12, 214ff, 298–9 = Giles and Lombard, partially from Augustine), is
less guilty than the splendidly gifted Lucifer (*TS* 27, 111; cf. *TS* 4, 225 =
Gerson). And wherefrom does stem the evil, "malum culpae" (*TS* 1,
121)? It is nothing (*TS* 23, 58). It has no roots, it has settled in the good
and leads a parasitical life (*TS* 12, 420ff; *TS* 5, 90ff). The creatures,
however, are not the only ones hit by "malum poenae": ">Quae non
rapui, tunc exsolvebam<" (Ps. 68.5) (*TS* 26, 206), the "unicus sine
peccato" (*TS* 3, 255–6) was punished most severely. Therefore man
should willingly contribute his own part to this (*TS* 27, 190ff, esp. 197ff,
204ff).

6.3. In this attempt to characterize the most influential concepts
Staupitz took from *De civitate*, some elements from several other
writings of Augustine have been intermingled.

6.3.1. *Confessiones*. The two longest quotations in the Tübingen
sermons, *TS* 6, 353–383 about the difficult marriage of Augustine's
parents Monica and Patricius, and *TS* 13, 376–398 about Augustine's
self-indulgent flirtations in hurly-burly ("sartago" 377) of Carthage,
come from the *Confessiones*. A shorter narrative piece (*TS* 10, 482–499)
about his own weakness in being seduced ("seductilis eram" 499)
reveals that it is by assonance ("iuvenes ductiles" 472) that it got into
the educational doctrines Staupitz was actually copying from Giles. The
liberated shout of the one who found peace (cit. Ps. 4.9) may similarly
have found its way into *TS* 9, 164–167. The story about the apple theft
out of presumptiousness (see footnote 34 at the end), hinted at in *TS* 24,
275–277, as well as Augustine's saying about Catiline's causeless malice
("gratuito malum fuisse," 279) are both related by Gerson. "Taceat
laudes tuas qui miserationes tuas non considerat" is a familiar quotation
Staupitz utilizes in *TS* 5, 203–4 and in *TS* 23, 252–254—in the latter,

---

[130] Augustine's attack against such accusers who he claims to be not concerned about
everyman's *quieta vita*, but about their own *secura nequitia* — an understandable criti-
cisme of the imperialistic Roman peace from a provincial Roman —, can be found as a
religious variation in *TS* 3, 307–8: "Maledicti sunt pedes ambulantes in deliciis sub capite
spinis coronato."

Sermon 23 (*De ... divini iudicii rectificatione ...*) it is the only quotation from Augustine. "Sumenda sunt alimenta tamquam medicamenta" is used as a maxim in *TS* 7, 459.

The most beautiful and bold sayings Staupitz incorporates from the *Confessiones* are, curiously enough, quotations in quotations by Giles: "Est inquietum cor ..." (*TS* 29, 50–1*), "Pondus meum amor meus; eo feror, quocumque feror" (*TS* 12, 580–1) (serving for Giles as the nucleus to his argument why Satan remains trapped in self-love) and "Duo fecisti, domine, unum prope te, aliud prope nihil" (*TS* 5, 55–57, taken up again in *TS* 12, 85 and in *TS* 27, 111). A nameless quotation is "(Habemus) palatum non sanum et aegros oculos" (*TS* 29, 189–90), namely, when we do not feel the punishing hand of the father in God's judgement. These borrowings from *Confessiones* to be found in nine sermons are widely scattered: however, they clearly focus on the subject of education.

6.3.2. *De Genesi ad litteram.* The quotations from this work are concentrated in two sermons. In Sermon 6 (*De matrimonio eiusque bonis et de virtutis generativae usu in actu ...*) these borrowings appear as short word for word quotations or short accounts and are always surrounded by texts from Giles. They are alleged in order to prove, firstly, the high ranking of an immortal society which should have been realized in paradise (194–199*); secondly, the subordination of procreative power under "dictamen rationis" which would had been valid there in contrast to overpowering desire in actual condition (401–404*); and thirdly, the difference between man and animal concerning their respective freedom towards the goods they desire (410–415*). The last one is also in *TS* 25, 53–4 in the context of the willfullness of sin. In Sermon 12 (*De vocatione ad poenitentiam, neque ... diabolo angelisque eius in malo obstinatis, sed soli homini ... congrua ...*) an Augustinian passage is embedded in Lombard which Staupitz brings into play (54–66) to show that the devil is not bad by creation but that he was a good angel who fell at an early stage. Other Augustinian citations with an Aegidian surrounding help him to make appear plausible (182–183, 189–90, 190–193* and 202–209*) how Adam deceived himself when not taking God's prohibition and the consequences seriously enough and how he was too lenient with Eve, the treasure ("deliciae" 193). And finally, an Augustinian quotation serves Giles and Staupitz as a basis (536–538*) for the distinction between "beatitudo innocentiae" which the devil lost, and "beatitudo excellentiae" which the devil maintained. Giles is also called in *TS* 17, 139ff for the more difficult task of harmonizing two quotations, one from *De Genesi ad litteram* and the other, a pseudo-Augustinian one from *De dogmatibus ecclesiasticis*, both of which discuss the question concerning which aspects of our thoughts the demons are able to guess and which not.[131] The Augustinian sentence "Nisi deus operaretur interius ..., exstincta esset omnis operatio ..." is used as an axiom in *TS* 12, 633–635* where it serves Giles and Staupitz to prove that Satan will be eternally excluded from any "impulsus divinus ad gratiam", and in *TS* 30, 230 to argue that he has no power to inhibit the divine influence on the "numerus electorum" (281*). Apart from Sermons 6 and 12 there is only Sermon 3 where is found a similarly axiomatic sentence from *De Genesi ad litteram*: "Homo sibi deo praesente illuminatur, absente autem continuo tenebratur" (20–1); it looks like a direct quotation, although is most probably not.

6.3.3. There are two groups of quotations of approximately equal size, taken from the *Enchiridion*. One group consists of direct quotations. Those of the second group have been mediated, in one case even twice. The definition "Hominis sapientia pietas" (from Job 28.28) in *TS* 24, 132–3 and "Pietas dei cultus est" in 135–6, to which can be added "(deus) fide, spe et caritate colendus" in *TS* 2, 26–7, are part of the first group. In Sermon 2 (*De simplicitate cordis ... a plica curiositatis ...*), 52–67, we also find the program which can easily be misunderstood as obscurantistic: "Non est rimanda rerum natura, quem ad modum ab eis quos physicos Graeci vocant ... Satis est christiano, rerum creatarum causas ... non nisi bonitatem intelligere creatoris ...,"[132] which is the only quotation from Augustine in this sermon otherwise deeply influenced by Gerson. There is one last quotation in the first group, *TS* 1, 55–58 which probably is also direct and which, as to its content, introduces the second. All quotations of this group are brilliant versions about the power which always intends evil and through which or despite which God perpetually creates the good. This group is thus entirely concerned with God's omnipotence both in his actions and his permission: *TS* 1, 119–20 (via Lombard or Giles), *TS* 3, 216–225 (strictly speaking, 221–225, via Lombard), 233–235 (via Lombard) and *TS* 24, 245–251* (via Giles). One gloss in *TS* 21, 246–249 about the meaning of >lignum, foenum et stipula< (1.Cor. 3.12) is not recognized as a quotation from the *Enchiridion* by Staupitz who believes it to derive from Lombard. There is one maxim in the clerical code in *TS* 19, 119–121: "Qui emendat verbere ..., misericordiam praestat" (via Gratian). The important concept that body and soul are created "propter dei laudem et finaliter pro supplenda ruina angelici casus" (*TS* 30, 54–57) may also be traced to the *Enchiridion* (via Lombard).[133]

---

[131] Cf. Wolf, *Staupitz und Luther*, 26 along with n. 4.

[132] The whole passage reads like a parody of Pliny, see Melanchthon to John Hess, April 27, 1520: "Animantium, gemmarum, herbarum, elementorum, fulminum ac ventorum naturas Plinius suppeditat ... " (*CR* 1, 156; *MBW* 84.3).

[133] See annot. 16 to *TS* 30: *JvS* 1, 426.

6.3.4. The use of *De trinitate* is the least homogeneous. I can detect but three direct quotations and they all stem from book 13. In *TS* 13, 314–333 an anecdote is narrated as a facetious proof that men know each other's most secret thoughts. In *TS* 10, 177–192 the thesis is stated that the satisfaction of immoral wishes does not make people happier but unhappier. And in *TS* 26, 202–210 there is the thought that the devil loses his grip by which he legitimately holds us, when we believe in him who, though without guilt (cit. Ps. 68.5 >Quae non rapui ...<), was killed by the devil. In *TS* 22, 78–9 we find a reference to book 15 but I cannot see the connection. The idea is that those who pray for the removal of all that separates them from God early enough, will lose nothing when their request is finally granted; on the contrary, such a person will receive lavish gifts (70ff). All the other quotations, and there are not many, have been transmitted via Lombard or Giles. Through Lombard, in *TS* 3, 182–189, Staupitz received the axiom: "Non nisi dei voluntas causa est prima sanitatis, aegritudinis ...". Through Giles, in *TS* 11, 185–188, he received the axiom: "Non haec quae creata sunt ideo sciuntur a deo, quia facta sunt, sed potius ..." and similarly in 188–190: "Universas creaturas suas ... non quia sunt, ideo novit, sed ideo sunt, quia novit." In *TS* 12, 553–4* he also adopts the thesis that the devil, if he ever tells the truth, will do so in the intention to betray us. Furthermore, in *TS* 17, 95–97* he is aided by the basic concept usable to explain how the demons read our thoughts, i.e., the teaching of a "species (intelligibilis)." And finally, in *TS* 25, 59–60 he is provided with the definition of sin as an inversion of *uti* and *frui* mentioned earlier (see above along with footnote 28).

6.3.5. Nearly 30 scraps remain to be gathered and put into baskets, i.e., pieces from 20 genuine (among them 3 letters counted separately) and pseudo-Augustinian (among them 1 letter) writings. Although it is not always obvious, Staupitz received most of these quotations through one or two mediators.

Some passages have already been touched, e.g. the hidden quotation in *TS* 31, 247–257 from the pseudo-Augustinian *Meditationes* (see above near footnote 56 and fn. itself) and the argument Giles uses against himself in *TS* 17, 144 from *De dogmatibus ecclesiasticis* (see above near footnote 131). Other passages enrich topics meanwhile familiar to my reader, such as the praise of God by the entire creation found in *TS* 7, 20 (pseudo-Augustinian Sermon 315); the self-love of Satan: "Ille angelus magis frui voluit sua potestate quam dei" in *TS* 12, 500* (*De vera religione*, via Giles); the *duplex misericordia* in *TS* 13, 280–309 and the "consolationes huius mundi pro sempiterna contemnere" in 360–372 (both from pseudo-Augustinian *Soliloquia*).

However, among these are also important definitions and distinctions such as, in *TS* 11, 275–6, 278–9, the different aspects *dispositio* and *gubernatio* in their relation to the term *providentia* (from *De Diversis quaestionibus LXXXIII*, via Giles); in *TS* 4, 147–154, the distinction of *bona magna—media—minima*: "Virtutes quibus recte vivitur magna bona sunt, ... corpora ... minima, potentiae vero sine quibus recte vivi non potest media ..." (self quotation from *De libero arbitrio* in *Retractationes*, via Lombard, via Bonaventure); the conclusion of this passage "Virtutibus nemo male utitur" can also be found in *TS* 34, 174–176. In *TS* 18, 289–90 we find the formula expressing the onto-axiological difference:[134] "Boni sumus, inquantum sumus" (*De doctrina christiana*,[135] via Lombard). In *TS* 5, 26–34 we read the criticism of the error of the Pythagoreans who not only postulated ten good principles of being, but ten bad ones as well (from *Contra Epistulam fundamenti*, via Giles). In *TS* 31, 77–8* we come upon the definition: "Malum nihil aliud (est) quam carentia vel modi vel speciei vel ordinis" (*De natura boni*, via Giles); in *TS* 25, 43–45* the following one: "Peccatum adeo voluntarium, quod, si non est voluntarium, non est peccatum" (without a title, from *De vera religione*, via Giles); the latter is one of the few quotations which still recurs in the *Salzburg sermons*.[136] In *TS* 23, 58 we find the quasi-definition: "Peccatum nihil est" (Augustine is not named, this is from the *Tractatus in Ioannem*; the two peccatum sayings were already mentioned at the end of 2.2.) In *TS* 23, 320 there is the definition (already mentioned at the end of 6.): "Quid est meritum hominis ante gratiam ..." (*Epistola* 194 *ad Sixtum presbyterum*, via Lombard, via Giles) and in *TS* 32, 250–259* the determination of the effect of concupiscence in the state of grace: "Per gratiam hoc agitur, ut vetus homo crucifigatur et corpus peccati destruatur (from Rom. 6.6), non tamen ita, ut in ipsa vivente carne concupiscentia respersa et innata repente absumatur et non sit, sed ne obsit" (*De peccatorum meritis*, via Lombard). The self-account from the same chapter in *De civitate* has been noted earlier (see above near footnote 124 and fn. itself).

I would like to add two less important definitions to this group: *TS* 14, 153–4: "Proprium est servorum timere" (without a title, from the *Tractatus in Ioannem*) and *TS* 8, 320*: "Gloria clara cum laude notitia" (Augustine is not named, from *Contra Maximinum*, via Giles). Also, I do not want to pass over in silence Staupitz's annoyingly light-minded use of an *auctoritas* in *TS* 6, 516–518: "Lepra coloris vitium est, non valetudinis vel integritatis sensuum atque membrorum" (adopted

---

[134] See footnotes 37 and 48.
[135] See footnote 24.
[136] Cf. *Salzburger Predigten 1518*, serm. 3, conclusion (Salzburg St. Peter, Cod. b V 8, fol. 65r). The text was available to me in an electronic editing output by Wolfram Schneider-Lastin, prepared for *JvS* 3 (Deutsche Schriften I).

together with the imprecise reference provided by Thomas of Strassburg: "in quadam Homilia super Lucam", probably *Sermon* 176).[137]

The remaining 10 of these widely scattered leftovers concern the area
of discipline. One of them derives from *De moribus ecclesiae* and is in
TS 32, 181–187: "Quod ad corpus medicina, ad animam disciplina;" one
is from *De libero arbitrio* in *TS* 32, 164–5: "Non est in potestate nostra,
quibus visis tangamur;" four draw on the *Regula Augustini* in *TS* 8, 176:
"Honorate in vobis deum invicem," in 332: "Magis amari quam timeri
..."; in *TS* 21, 102: "Communia propriis anteponere ..." and in *TS* 34,
131–2*: "Ne nimia servetur humilitas, ubi nulla est quae frangi timeatur
regendi autoritas." The latter was transmitted by Gerson. He is also the
mediator of the following three: *TS* 19, 215–217*: "Bonam conscientiam
deo, proximis vero famam bonam debemus", 192–194*: "Pretiosa vestis
non decet hanc confessionem ..." (both from the Augustinian *Sermones*) and, concerning the principle of the true zelus, *TS* 20, 100–1*:
"Qui scandala quae videt in ecclesia tollere vult, si potest, si non potest,
tolerat et gemit" (from the *Tractatus in Ioannem*, via the *Ordinary Gloss*
on John 2.17). For this quotation Alfred Jeremias, who did not know
about its origin, criticized Staupitz as being a "quietist."[138] From the
pseudo-Augustinian *Sermones ad fratres in eremo* derive the tacit quotation in *TS* 25, 189–192 and the open one in 207–214, both of which are
about the value of silence.

7. I am well aware of the fact that in listing all these references I have
already excessively imposed on the reader's patience. I feel that the
whole business about sifting them may be interpreted as a paraphrase of
my register of authorities and sources, hopefully somewhat more pleas-
ant than the register itself. However, we must go even one step further
and attempt an ever so brief characterization of the mediators.

Gratian is the one who contributes least to Staupitz's collection of
Augustinian quotations: *TS* 19, 119–121. (Gratian himself is only referred to in Sermon 19 for the clerical code.) Then there is Thomas
Aquinas, who also supplies just one Augustinian dictum: *TS* 34, 126.
(Thomas himself is mentioned far more rarely than we might have
assumed after reading Wolf and Steinmetz's criticism of Wolf.) Bonaventure delivers a clarifying amplification of the Augustinian-
Lombardian distinction *timor servilis–filialis*: "... timoris intueri tria:
poenam ..., ut fugiat; offensionem, ut illam caveat; maiestatem sum-
mam, ut illi ... exhibeat reverentiam" (*TS* 4, 14–18). Similarly, Thomas
of Strassburg in a discussion of marriage, an institution which he

---

[137] See annot. 140 to *TS* 6: *JvS* 1, 120.
[138] Jeremias, *Luthers Vater und Schüler* (as in fn. 65), 88–9.

fundamentally approves in Sermon 6 (*De ... actu matrimoniali non solum licito, sed etiam bono atque meritorio*), by establishing a parallel to the Aristotelian triad "bonum honestum, bonum utile, bonum delectabile" (289–292), confronts Augustine's paradisiac "bona matrimonii: fides, proles, sacramentum" (283–4) with the actually existing forms of decay this institution was undergoing: "Nunc vero honestas fidei verecundia permiscetur, utilitas prolis damno et indissolubilitas laboribus et taedio" (305–307). Instead of delight, there is shame and inordinate desire. Instead of blessings, health as well as wealth are being damaged. There is fidelity but weariness and even disgust (*TS* 6, 308ff, 316ff, 339ff, 345ff). This is one of the gloomy highlights of the Tübingen sermons. Apart from this Thomas of Strassburg supplies some key words for a number of direct borrowings, especially in *TS* 6, 318ff.

The Augustinian quotations Staupitz derived via Gerson are already of a different magnitude. More than one of them can be found in the *scandalum* context of Sermons 19 and 20 (see 6.3.5. last paragraph). Gerson is followed by Lombard whose knowledge of and fidelity to Augustine is so outstanding that one can only be surprised about the bad press he gets from Melanchthon.[139] Lombard is inimaginable as absent from sermons 1, 3, 4, 5, 6, 11, 12, and is also important for some statements in sermons 18, 23 and 32. Especially in Sermon 4, he inspires Staupitz to direct reception (see 6.1.3., esp. near footnote 102 and fn. itself).

Giles, however, surpasses all the previously mentioned authorities. There are only 11 sermons in which he is not present. In 12 of the 23 remaining sermons, he is also a mediator, partly as he leads Staupitz to his own reception,[140] partly in that he provides him with passages from Augustine's less known writings. He thus introduces him not only to the *Augustinus receptus*, but also to the very origins of thoughts such as primitive state and first sin, i.e., *De Genesi ad litteram* (see 6.3.2). In his dual role as a guide and supplier on Staupitz's way to Augustine, Giles appears so often and he is of such great importance, that I feel justified in saying that he must not be viewed as a disciple (or a rival) of Thomas

---

[139] See Melanchthon in the same letter (as cited in fn. 132): "Ego in obeliscis sententiarum ostendam, quibus locis in natura hominis hallucinati sint magisterculi . . .," *CR* 1, 157; *MBW* 84. Cf. Melchior Lotter to the reader (author is Melanchthon), prologue to *Epistola Pauli ad Romanos D. Erasmo interprete* (Wittenberg, 1520): "... Longobardi ... equidem sedulitatem probarem, nisi a divinis literis magna ex parte christianas mentes commentariis suis avocasset." *CR* 1, 276; *MBW* 94a.

[140] Although Giles's quotations are often very extensive, Staupitz chooses even longer passages. See *TS* 5, 90ff along with annot. 31: *JvS* 1, 91; *TS* 6, 164ff, 181ff with annot. 42 and 48: *JvS* 1, 106–108; *TS* 24, 59–75 with annot. 26: *JvS* 1, 363; probably also *TS* 24, 36ff, 44ff, 81ff along with annot. 31: *JvS* 1, 362, 364; and *TS* 29, 58–68 with annot. 17: *JvS* 1, 418.

Aquinas only. For the Staupitz of the Tübingen sermons, he fairly fulfills the function of a preserver of the Augustinian heritage in the Augustinian order, in which one may with better reason judge him to have failed otherwise.[141] Unlike Lombard, however, he is never mentioned as a mediator of *Enarrationes in Psalmos* and hardly plays a role in Staupitz's reception of the Roman antiquity in Sermons 8, 28, and 34.[142] At the same time, Staupitz adopts the topics of *De regimine principum* (in Sermon 10), whereas he does not touch on *De ecclesiastica potestate*.

Although there were many guides who led Staupitz to Augustine, he made the most of the way himself. But which Augustine are we talking about? Owing to the intensive use of *Enarrationes*, the impression is justified that in a more than stylistic sense, Staupitz's Tübingen sermons are shaped by the "Augustinian homiletical literature" (see Steinmetz cited in footnote 14). While he no less intensively used books 13 and 14 of *De civitate*, as these were conceived at the beginning of Augustine's dispute with the Pelagians, we find through them a fullfledged doctrine of the primitive state and the original sin present in the Tübingen sermons. The outspokenly Augustinian shade of a predestination doctrine at least is present in bud thanks to the idea of a *numerus sanctorum* or *electorum* (*TS* 6, 187–188; *TS* 30, 281). This may comfort the friend of Reformation thought who otherwise misses the properly antipelagian writings, with the sole exception of *De peccatorum meritis* (see 6.3.5. para. 3 at the end). It would, however, be surprising if Staupitz, the rapacious user of the first volumes of the Amerbach edition, had given up his studies after the latter one appeared. With the booklet *De exsecutione aeternae praedestinationis* and the contemporary testimony of Karlstadt,[143] this appears to be quite improbable. Unfortunately, philological evidence as has been presented throughout these pages, will never be possible in this question.

---

[141] Cf. Hamm, *Frömmigkeitstheologie* (as in fn. 65), 303ff.

[142] Cf. Wetzel, *Staupitz antibarbarus*, 124.

[143] Ernst Kähler, *Karlstadt und Augustin: Der Kommentar des Andreas Bodenstein von Karlstadt zu Augustins Schrift De Spiritu et littera*, Hallische Monographien 19 (Halle, 1952), 5.15–21.

STAUPITZ AND LUTHER:
CONTINUITY AND BREAKTHROUGH AT THE BEGINNING OF THE REFORMATION[1]

LOTHAR GRAF ZU DOHNA

Now more than five hundred years ago, in 1483, a young Saxon entered the world. Johann von Staupitz was enrolled as a student at the University of Cologne—the first mention of the young nobleman who was at least fourteen years old. It is not a particularly important date, but it is historically well-documented. Presumably in the same year, although not mentioned in contemporary sources, Martin Luther was born. He himself took 1484 to be the year of his birth. But such a date was of little importance to him or his contemporaries and had no historical significance.

If I speak today on the subject of Luther, it is because I am concerned about the issue, what does Luther stand for, and about the continuing historical reality of the Reformation. Thus, I am not merely speaking of personalities by talking about "Staupitz and Luther" in this lecture. Moreover, I put the historically less important personality, Staupitz, first in the title, not simply because he is the older of the two. I can with a high degree of probability assume a knowledge of Luther, a man of world-wide, historical significance, so that I need to say much less about him than about his teacher, who deserves our attention precisely because of his student. Above all, I am in a position to talk about some hitherto unknown things about Staupitz, which I can report fresh from the most recent research.[2] These reflections grew out of labor on the

---

[1] An expanded version of this lecture was held at a meeting of the Religionspaedagogisches Institut in Loccum on August 19, 1983. This lecture was also given in its current form as part of a lecture series on the Luther year sponsored by the department of theology and social ethics and the department of history at the Technischen Hochschule in Darmstadt. It was delivered in English translation at the New York State University (Buffalo, New York) and at Tennessee State University (Knoxville). I wish to thank the participants and audiences for their stimulating discussion and most particularly my dear friend, the late Professor Robert L. Hiller, who provided the original translation into English and Timothy J. Wengert for the improved final English version including the footnotes. This article remains in lecture form, and was expanded here only through a few references to the sources and to literature on Staupitz. The article has appeared in German in *Pastoraltheologie* 74 (1985), 452–465.
[2] In this lecture I base my remarks on L. Graf zu Dohna and R. Wetzel, "Die Reue Christi: Zum theologischen Ort der Busse bei Johann von Staupitz," *Studien und Mitteilungen zur Geschichte des Benediktiner-Ordens* 94 (1983), 457–482. To sources and literature cited there I will not refer here every time.

critical edition of Staupitz's works[3] and thus include the results of many conversations with the Tübingen co-editors.[4]

In general, Johann von Staupitz is treated only within the framework of Luther's life. He appears at very particular moments in that life: as Luther's superior (that is, as the Vicar-general of the German congregation of the Augustinian Eremites), and as pastor and mentor of the young monk whom he comforted and whom he selected for a career as professor of theology. But I am not concerned about the biography of either Luther or Staupitz.[5] As the sub-title indicates, this article concerns central questions of the Reformation. To put it more pointedly, on the basis of one example I would like to try to show that the history of the Reformation cannot be written simply as Luther biography.

To be sure, it is a truism that one cannot portray historical figures in isolation from their environment or without considering the history which preceded them. However, all too often the Reformation is described as the action of a single man, Martin Luther, as the unique spiritual breakthrough to a new era which occurred in a scholar's study. And this action is painted on the backdrop of both a church ossified in its abuses and a fallen, scantily sketched scholasticism.

Now I do not intend to go into all the external preconditions, knowledge of which is necessary for an understanding of the Reformation. They include long-overlooked economic and social factors that played an important, though in no way exclusive, role. I merely wish to pose the question: was it really so self-evident that Luther's theological realization would meet with such a lively response and would produce such a far-reaching and revolutionary movement? Is not another turn of events imaginable?

---

[3] Johann von Staupitz, *Sämtliche Schriften: Abhandlungen, Predigten, Zeugnisse*, eds. Lothar Graf zu Dohna and Richard Wetzel (Berlin: 1979–). As of this writing volumes one and two have appeared as volumes 13 and 14 of the series Spätmittelalter und Reformation (Berlin: 1987 and 1979). The next to appear will be volumes 3–5.

[4] I am especially grateful to the current co-editors, Richard Wetzel, Wolfram Schneider-Lastin, Berndt Hamm and Wolfgang Günter and the former co-editor Albrecht Endriss, as well as to the founder of the Tübingen Sonderforschungsbereich "Spätmittelalter und Reformation," Heiko Augustinus Oberman, now of Tucson, Arizona. Through reciprocal encouragement and critical discussion we were all able to refine our findings.

[5] For biographical information about Staupitz, see the overview entitled "Der Autor in seinen Werken," in Johann von Staupitz, *Sämtliche Schriften*, eds. Lothar Graf zu Dohna and Richard Wetzel, vol. II: *Libellus de exsecutione aeternae praedestinationis*, eds. Lothar Graf zu Dohna, Richard Wetzel and Albrecht Endriss, trans. Christoph Scheurl, Spätmittelalter und Reformation 14 (Berlin, 1979), 4–9 (hereafter cited as *De exsec.*), and the literature referred to there. I was unable to use the most recent articles by H.A. Oberman and R. Wetzel in *Reformatio et reformationes*, Festschrift für Lothar Graf zu Dohna zum 65. Geburtstag, eds. Andreas Mehl and Wolfgang Christian Schneider, THD-Schriftenreihe Wissenschaft und Technik 47 (Darmstadt, 1989).

To put it another way, if a Luther with his theology had come on the scene a hundred years earlier during the Council of Constance, which had been called for the purpose of church reform, would he not have been burned at the stake like Jan Hus? Or, after the Council of Basel, would he not have been neutralized like Nicholas of Cusa, who was packed off to reform the monasteries?

The ground must have been prepared in a quite different way to receive the seed of Luther's message so as to produce such a rich harvest. Many Christians clearly saw in his message the "longed-for Reformation," as Heiko Oberman has called it.[6] However, Luther's actual religious intent was soon to reveal itself as the "unexpected Reformation."

I

I need not explain in detail here the prerequisites for the "longed-for Reformation," a reform of the institutional church "in head and members." A few key words may suffice: disappointment over the failure of the reform councils, an increase in the secularization and usurious financial practices of the church, Humanism, and a growing national consciousness. In the meantime there were also the first signs of the "unexpected Reformation." For some reform-minded individuals, the realization that a reform of the institutional church was neither sufficient nor achievable was linked to the inadequacy of a theology too philosophically oriented and of religious practices caught in formalities and based upon a self-centered and opportunistic pursuit of salvation that led to moral laxity. A new practical, pastoral theology of piety developed.[7] While one of its representatives, Johann von Paltz, in his desire to popularize God's grace actually decided to promote the sale of indulgences, his Augustinian brother, Staupitz, paved the way for the "unexpected Reformation."

At first Staupitz also strove for the reform of the Augustinian Order, that is, an institutional reform. But even this shows a change in the concept of reform, something which has not been noticed by past scholarship.[8] Protestant scholars have taken over the Roman Catholic

---

[6] H.A. Oberman, *Luther: Mensch zwischen Gott und Teufel* (Berlin, 1982). This lecture is more indebted to this important book than is apparent in the formulation which is quoted here. It does justice to the meaning of Staupitz more than any previous biography of Luther. The 1982 essay cited above (footnote 2) could not yet refer to Oberman's book on Luther.

[7] Berndt Hamm, *Frömmigkeitstheologie am Anfang des 16. Jahrhunderts*, Beiträge zur historischen Theologie 65 (Tübingen, 1982).

[8] For this and what follows see Lothar Graf zu Dohna, "Von der Ordensreform zur Reformation: Johann von Staupitz," in *Ordensstudien VI*, edited by Kaspar Elm (Berlin, 1989). The lecture which served as a basis for this article was held in Berlin in 1981.

point of view that looked at only one kind of reform, namely, the restitution of the perfection of the Order. This accorded to the basic meaning of the Latin word "Re-formatio," that is, the observance of the Rule. In contrast Staupitz does not envision the retreat out of the world into seclusion by an elite striving for personal sanctification. Instead he desires the monks work in the world through preaching and pastoral care, thereby making the monastery into a leaven for the reform of Christendom.

In this connection Staupitz brought about a concept which appears unusual, the uniting under his leadership of both branches of his Order: the unreformed, Saxon province of the Augustinian Eremites with the German congregation of the strict Observants. Although it was a victory for the reform, seven "renitent Monasteries" of the strict Observants, for whom purity was more important than unity, protested.[9] Luther journeyed to Rome as spokesman for the renitent monastery in Erfurt.

Staupitz, the vicar-general, did not regard the mere externally strict observance of the Order's rule as an end in itself. A great deal of experience, even self-critical experience, echo in his comments. He saw that it is impossible to become holy on the basis of one's own effort. He said to Luther, "I promised God a thousand times that I would become holy .... I do not wish to lie to God any longer."[10] To be sure, this pastoral consolation of the fanatical ascetic, Luther, suffering from an exaggerated sense of guilt, is perhaps for this reason somewhat overstated. But Staupitz, the pastor, was serious about keeping himself and others from placing their trust in their own efforts rather than in the grace of God. Here it becomes quite clear how strongly Staupitz's concept of a reform of an Order is influenced by his theology, which, proceeding from Augustine, develops into a theology of grace based on the Bible and, in particular, on Paul.

It is well-known what an influence the pastoral ministry of Staupitz had on Luther and what a significance the theological insights of the older man grew to have for the younger.[11] Thus, it is not surprising that in the political fight within the Order, the head of the Order drew to his

---

[9] The conceptual pair "purity" and "unity" accords with Oberman's analysis of Luther.

[10] In this way I attempt to reconstruct Staupitz's words from Luther's comments made under varying circumstances and handed down in various ways. See *WA* 33, 431. (= 0. Scheel, *Dokumente zu Luthers Entwicklung* (Tübingen, 1929), 66, lines 28–31); *WA* 40/2. 92, 4–6, 24–26 (= Scheel, *Dokumente*, 76, 17f., 34f.); *WA TR* 2, No. 2797a (= Scheel, *Dokumente*, 101, 26–29).

[11] Ernst Wolf, *Staupitz und Luther*, Quellen und Forschungen zur Reformationsgeschichte 9 (Leipzig, 1927). Even more strongly concerned than Wolf for Luther's originality is David C. Steinmetz, *Luther and Staupitz: An Essay in the Intellectual Origins of the Protestant Reformation*, Duke Monographs in Medieval and Renaissance Studies 4 (Durham, North Carolina, 1980).

side the radical Observant monk from Erfurt. The Franciscan scholar, Weijenborg regards this abandonment by Luther of the classical Observance as an act of disobedience which logically will lead to his apostasy from the Roman Catholic church.[12] In my opinion the actual case is precisely reversed: that it is Luther's complete and utter domination by a rigorous Observantism which led him later as Reformer to such a rigorous condemnation of monasticism. Therein he condemned his own belief in a "monkery" understood as a "sure path to salvation" (Paltz). For Staupitz, on the other hand, the fulfilling of monastic asceticism had never been an end in itself. He had never thought that by such means he could win over a gracious God. Precisely because of this Staupitz can in 1524, the year of his death, entreat Luther as his friend not to reject external things such as the monk's habit and vows, which may be joined to faith, nor to judge the thing itself just because of its abuse.[13]

In this his last letter to Luther, Staupitz confesses not only that his faith in Christ and the Gospel remained unchanged but also that he was the forerunner of evangelical doctrine (olim praecursor exstiti sanctae evangelicae doctrinae). Luther says exactly the same thing himself: "Staupicius started this doctrine (doctrinam)."[14] It is really strange that this clear statement of Luther is not generally taken seriously in Luther scholarship.[15] There are a whole host of statements by Luther which express the same or something quite similar. Thus he testifies in 1532, "From Erasmus I got nothing (Ex Erasmo nihil habeo). I got everything from Dr. Staupitz; he gave me the *occasionem* (motivation)."[16]

In this way Luther attributes the essential element in his evangelical teaching to Staupitz, that is to say not to Staupitz the pastor but clearly to Staupitz the theologian. Otherwise he would not have contrasted him

---

[12] Reinhold Weijenborg, "Neuentdeckte Dokumente im Zusammenhang mit Luthers Romreise," *Antonianum* 32 (1957), 147–202. On this point see Franz Lau in *Luther–Jahrbuch* 27 (1960), 64–107.

[13] A letter from April 1, 1524, *WA BR* 3. 263f.

[14] *WA TR* 1, No. 526 (Spring, 1533).

[15] In any event one cannot play off Luther's other statements, which exhibit criticism of Staupitz's later behavior, against this one. Two sentences from letters to Link with judgments concerning an "unintelligible" letter and a "lukewarm," but nevertheless "printable" writing of Staupitz do *not* present a counterbalance ("must be balanced against ..."), as Steinmetz suggests. (Steinmetz, *Luther and Staupitz*, 3). The two letters are dated, March 19, 1522 (*WA BR*, 2. 632) and February 7, 1525 (*WA BR*, 3. 437). Such expressions of displeasure, conditioned by the changed situation particularly in the period between 1521 and 1523, do not contradict the judgment concerning Staupitz's doctrine and its importance for the beginnings of Reformation theology. Thus Luther is able in one and the same letter dated September 17, 1523, his last to "his father and teacher," Staupitz, to exact bitter criticism and thankfully to acknowledge, "through you the light of the Gospel first began to shine out of the darkness into our hearts, "*WA BR*, 3. 155–156. (cf. 2 Cor. 4.6).

[16] *WA TR* 1, No. 173, (February or March, 1532).

with Erasmus nor have specifically spoken of "doctrina." Luther's opponents certainly saw it from the same point of view. The well-informed papal nuntio, Aleander, reported after the Diet of Worms that Staupitz, Luther's teacher, was the first to begin speaking out against the overall teaching of the theologians, even if not as spiritedly as Luther.[17] Scholars often quote testimonies to the pastoral council and consolation that Staupitz gave to Luther at decisive moments. However, it must be noticed that they also give testimony to the theology which stands behind them. Thus Luther himself quotes a consoling word from Staupitz that expressly summarizes the teaching of the master and the pupil as "*our* teaching": "At the beginning of my case Staupitz said, 'This comforts me that this our doctrine of grace gives God the entire honor and everything and gives nothing to human beings.'" This is in the first printing of the commentary on Galatians (1535).[18] It is striking that in the later printings after 1538, which Luther did not oversee directly, the text is completely changed to read, "the doctrine which you preach." Here the early instituted tendency toward a Luther cult becomes visible, which lifts Luther out of the historical conditions of his existence and is concerned to give him alone the glory. It is a tendency in which the Reformer himself does not participate. Even a year before his death he writes, "Doctor Staupitz, whom I must praise (if I do not want to be a damned, ungrateful papist jackass) that he right from the start was my father in this doctrine and gave (me) birth in Christ."[19]

Should we not take Luther at his word? It was certainly not only "ungrateful papist jackasses" who thrust aside these facts. Then, too, it is not only the literary genre of biography which leads to such an absolutizing of the "hero" that he has only his own effort to thank and is not allowed to have experienced any influences upon his own thinking. On the one hand, Luther is contrasted with a church portrayed in the worst light and with a decadent scholastic theology. On the other, the Reformer is seen as an instrument of God, directly inspired by the Holy Spirit, in fact a most un-evangelical "Saint" Luther.

In addition, Staupitz, because of his position on the edge of two

---

[17] Aleander writes about the Cardinal Archbishop of Salzburg, Lang, whose courtiers (familiares) present in Worms were all Lutherans, or in any case enemies of the Roman church: "Illud certissimum est, eum (scil. Lang) domi fovere Stapitium ord. erem., Lutheri praeceptorem, qui primus contra communem theologorum scholam exercere linguam cepit, quamvis non tanto, quanto Lutherus spiritu." Paul Kalkoff, *Aleander gegen Luther: Studien zu ungedruckten Aktenstücken aus Aleanders Nachlass* (Leipzig/New York, 1908).

[18] *WA* 40/1.21–25 131. (Scheel, *Dokumente*, 62 lines 10–14). I will come back to this below.

[19] *WA BR* 11. 63.

different eras, had no lasting effect on either.[20] For the Roman Catholics
he was too close to Luther. And the Protestants, in the process of
becoming a confessional church, viewed him as someone who had
prematurely left the battlefield or, at best, as a forerunner, who had not
quite risen to the fully developed Lutheran doctrine. But, among the
heirs of the Reformation, the ones who preserved and cultivated the
heritage of Staupitz, repeatedly published his "spiritually rich tracts" far
into the nineteenth century, and even translated them into English and
French were the mystics and pietists, the "Stillen im Lande," for whom
a doctrinally frozen Lutheran orthodoxy offered too little direction in
Christian living.

The development of exclusive confessional points of view has blocked
not only any lasting effect but also a clear understanding of Staupitz's
theology. All too often the inquiry, proceeding from a list of precon-
ceived notions, has sought after the doctrine of this less than doctrinaire
preacher and pastor, intent especially on spiritualization. For a biblical
theologian like Staupitz, who was seeking an alternative to Scholasticism, a method of inquiry oriented towards scholastic formulations of
doctrine would have proved as much a Procrustean bed as a method of
inquiry oriented towards the measuring stick of the developed Lutheran
structure of doctrine.

II

Any research really concerned with taking seriously the historical pe-
culiarity of Staupitz, the theologian, must proceed from his own writings. Unfortunately, it is not possible within the limits of a lecture to
develop directly the theology of Johann von Staupitz on the basis of his
own writings, a good portion of which are unpublished. I wish to
attempt to summarize the most important elements in a concise and
comprehensive manner.[21]

In his theology Staupitz proceeds not from man but from God, not
from the creature but from the Creator. Thus, at the beginning we do
not find the human question, "how can I find a gracious God?" which
was the late-medieval question with which Luther also started. For
Staupitz it is never even a question that man can do anything at all, that
by any kind of effort he had to earn God's grace. God's love preceded
everything: creation, election, redemption and justification. Thus, Staupitz not only rejects the scholastic doctrines of merit and virtue, he even

---

[20] On this and what follows, compare the section, "Von der Wirkungsgeschichte zur
Forschungsgeschichte," in *De exsecutione*, 9–15.
[21] For what follows I refer in general to: Graf zu Dohna and Wetzel, "Die Reue
Christi," where the individual sources are also noted.

'reforms' its conceptual language. He turns on its head the concept of the "grace which makes acceptable" (gratia gratum faciens). This grace does not cause man to become pleasing to God, as the scholastics claim, since God already loves man, instead it causes God to become pleasing to man, something that is impossible without grace.

Staupitz consistently goes back beyond Augustine to the promises of God himself as found in the Bible, particularly in the Gospels and Paul. In the writings of his mature period from 1512 on, no "authorities" are cited, only the Bible. He re-estabishes the Holy Scriptures both as the basis for theology and as the measuring stick for the evaluation of ecclesial praxis. This leads to the exclusion of the church's and the priest's mediating function and to the relativizing of the sacramental means of grace. He stresses the sole effectiveness of Christ, who bestows on us faith, hope and love. No human effort, no good works, can earn justification. It occurs through faith, which God gives to the sinner by grace alone. He does not define the concept of faith narrowly as an accepting of Christian doctrine as true. Faith *in* Christ (not 'about' Christ) is the unconditional trust in God and in Christ who justifies us, as is possible only by the penitent recognition of oneself as sinner. Thus Staupitz can also speak of justification "sola fide" (by faith alone), although he prefers expressions that preclude an understanding of faith taken in isolation, such as "faith active in love" (Galatians 5:6) and in particular the Pauline triad, faith, hope and love (1 Corinthians 13:13).

Human works remain ever finite (finita) and thus never suffice as the basis for a righteousness of infinite merit and hence of an infinite reward. Even *the* works performed by living faith, which can be called works of Christ, are finite. Thus good works are not minimized by Staupitz—they are the fruits of faith and consequently part of the glorification that, according to Romans 8:30, necessarily follows justification. Here Christ works in us in truth. As a result, man remains conscious of his sins. It is the most dangerous temptation of Satan when, in the guise of an angel, he seeks to seduce man to trust in his own righteousness. For Christ, the bridegroom, bestows his own righteousness on the bride, the sinful soul, in their marriage. The righteous man accuses himself first of all and thereby justifies God. The importance of works for the Christian life is thus protected, once Staupitz has excised them from the event of justification, thereby abandoning the entire scheme of necessary preparation, of a "disposition," as the late-medieval doctrine and practice of penance characterized it.

Staupitz views penance not as a formal act consisting of contrition, confession and satisfaction, which must precede justification, but as an imitation of Christ or, more precisely, of the "contrition of Christ." The discovery and interpretation of this (until now) unknown, surprising and, one must say, strange idea are a result of our editing the heretofore unpublished Salzburg sermons of 1512.[22] Their importance lies in the fact that Staupitz already during Passiontide, 1512, before Luther became a professor of Bible at the University of Wittenberg, presented the essential elements of his Reformation theology while preaching to the people in German at a parish church.

Staupitz argues that the suffering of Christ reached its first high point on the Mount of Olives. Here he breaks through to obedience of God; here he agrees to die; here he takes all the sins of all people upon himself and repents so completely that he sweat drops of blood; here he suffered death, not of the body, but of the soul, namely the abandonment (Verlassenheit) by God. By doing all this he gave man an example of suffering contrition, that is, true contrition. Man cannot accomplish such contrition by his own effort, but he can and should imitate Christ, in that he experiences deep pain over his sins and in faith delivers himself over to the grace of God. By appropriating to himself the contrition of Christ man can partake in perfect contrition and with it in salvation. Man can and should ceaselessly imitate the suffering of Christ, which culminates in the contrition of the God-man. Man can only imitate the death of Christ's body once and then only in the face of his own death. But the entire life of the believer should be one of penance, as Luther then says in the first of his 95 theses.

With this concept of the contrition of Christ I have attempted to present an original idea that demands in-depth interpretation. This idea proves to be the key to the interpretation of repentance and justification in the theology of Johann von Staupitz. This idea already shapes the Salzburg sermons of 1512, which stand at the beginning of his mature period, and still play an important role in his last extant sermons as abbot of St. Peter's in Salzburg from 1523, which also have not yet been printed. Moreover, the Nuremberg sermons from Spring, 1517, which have long been well-known, contain a section on contrition that agrees with the above. Until now it has only been interpreted contrary to the actual text, in order to explain it in the light of scholasticism.

The continuity of his theological thought as demonstrated in Staupitz by this "leitmotif" is important in two ways. First, it leaves little room for the contention that Staupitz had adopted anything decisive from Luther. Second, it helps to refute the opinion that as preacher and abbot in Salzburg Staupitz had undertaken a break with his former theological stance. This observation agrees with another finding of our editing, that the so-called "second opinion" from the heresy proceedings against

---

[22] The edition of Wolfram Schneider-Lastin will soon appear as volume three of Staupitz's complete works.

Stephan Agricola in 1523 was, contrary to the prevailing judgement, not written by Staupitz. With this fact the "King's evidence" of his supposed transformation into a rigid persecutor of heretics disappears. The *real* opinion of Staupitz was until now hardly comprehensible. Only after the archival discovery of some documents, which make possible an approximate reconstruction both of inquisitors' questions which were not transmitted and of the answers of the accused, does this opinion of Staupitz bear witness to the continuity of his views.[23]

It is important to comprehend the singularity of Staupitz's theology, in order to understand the content and intent of his transmitted statements.[24] On the other hand, it is historically incorrect to apply to these testimonies of a theological movement still in flux the later rigid alternatives, "Roman Catholic" or "Lutheran." Thus, the attempts of confessional theologians to mark Staupitz as an adherent of one confession or the other have achieved rather unconvincing results. One must take seriously the various attempts at reform of Christian faith and life, rather than regard in isolation and on the basis of its results Luther's particularly fundamental and consequently overthrowing approach that ultimately succeeded. Staupitz and Luther both give answers to the same questions which oppressed people in the late Middle Ages and which arose out of a search for the sure way to eternal salvation. Staupitz, too, wanted to reform theology on the basis of the biblical principles. For him the central point here was the Pauline doctrine, passed on through Augustine, of the grace of God. More pronounced, I dare say, than in Luther was his attempt at the same time to overcome the old controversy between the schools.

In addition to this parallel striving by both reformers—despite the obvious generation gap—there was also a reciprocal sharing of ideas as well as influence on the younger man by the older.[25] Luther explicitly attests to his dependence on Staupitz's concept of the essence of repentance in his 1518 *Resolutiones*. True penance begins with the love of righteousness and of God; this is the source of penance and not its aim or completion.[26]

---

[23] My edition of the "Consultatio super confessione fratris Stephani Agricolae" will appear soon in volume 5 of Staupitz's complete works.

[24] This aim is understood to be complementary to the undertaking of D. Steinmetz which organized individual doctrines (loci) in the context of scholastic theology. David C. Steinmetz, *Misericordia Dei: The Theology of Johannes von Staupitz in its Late Medieval Setting*, Studies in Medieval and Reformation Thought 4 (Leiden, 1968).

[25] R. Wetzel recently called attention to texts of Luther clearly dependent upon Staupitz in his lecture, "Staupitz und Luther," held on November 10, 1983 in Tübingen and now published in *Martin Luther: Probleme seiner Zeit*, ed. V. Press and D. Stievermann (Stuttgart, 1986), 75–87.

[26] *WA* 1. 525, 4–14 (= Scheel, *Dokumente*, 9, lines 28–10, line 3).

In his conception of penance Staupitz begins with the two elements, namely contrition and satisfaction, which during the late Middle Ages— in a peculiar interaction between praxis and doctrine—had resulted in an undesirable development. He avoided the two-fold danger of the late-scholastic doctrine that viewed contrition as a precondition for justifying grace. This led, on the one hand, to a deemphasis among the Scotists of the demands for contrition, so that a truly penitent attitude became dispensable. On the other, it opened up the danger, found among the Occamists, that an insistence upon real, heart-felt contrition brought with it the notion that this contrition must be viewed as a possible achievement of human nature itself. Staupitz also recognizes both dangers present in satisfaction. Consequently, he warns against the easy solution of indulgences as a cheap pay-off, as it were, as well as against the valuation of works of satisfaction as meritorious achievement.

Thus Staupitz's theology of contrition, by disregarding the whole system of disposition and achievement as well as sacramental mediation of grace, leads out of the dead end of late scholastic "accounting" back to the gospel, just as do Luther's teachings about indulgences and penance. Now we can understand the lively response to Staupitz's sermons in Salzburg and Munich and the enthusiasm of the audience in Nuremberg, who considered Staupitz the reformer of theology.[27] His sermons were from 1512 copied down. He was asked to have them published, as did indeed occur in more than one edition in 1515, 1517 (January), and 1518. Even his "Tabletalk" was regarded as so important that it was noted down in 1517, something which first began in Luther's case fourteen years later. When the members of the Nuremberg "Stau-pitz society" then heard that a student of their master by the name of Luther was teaching in Wittenberg, correspondence was initiated with him, too. And when this student composed in Latin a series of theses dealing with indulgences, they translated them into German, whereby they then achieved their tremendous circulation and impact.

It is not possible for me in this limited space to trace Luther's step-by-step development into the Reformer. But we must at all costs

---

[27] The most important source is Christoph Scheurl's *Briefbuch*, 2 vols. eds. F. Freiherr von Soden and J.K.F. Knaake (Potsdam, 1872; reprint ed. 1962), esp. II, 1, 4f., 6, 8f., 35f., 42, 60f. Notice the programatic phrase, "Christi theologiam restaurare," in the letter of November 3, 1517 (II, 35), which identifies the efforts of the Augustinian family and of Staupitz as well as the mood in Nuremberg and is in any case not only to be applied to the recipient of the letter, Luther. The expressions, with which Staupitz is singled out as preacher "never before heard" overall his contemporaries as "versus theologus"—"Pauli lingua," "evangelii praeco," "omnis ... hunc colit, adorat" (II, 1)—return again at the end of 1518 and 1519, in order to designate the role of Luther as Reformer (II, 60, 62, 90). Beyond that Staupitz is praised by the Nurembergers—in an almost messianic way—as if he were the one "qui salvum faciet populum Israhel" (II, 4f.).

shield ourselves from the penchant of many Luther experts to assume that Luther's known teaching was already fully developed, or at least outlined in its essentials, where its first traces become visible. In reality this development occurs gradually, even though in spurts. Often, consequences of a discovery are deduced much later. Today it can be established that by the Spring of 1518 Luther has united the "three building blocks of the Reformation," as Oberman called them:[28]

1. The unmerited grace (sola gratia)
2. The clear Scripture (sola scriptura)
3. God demands no preparatory effort (no definite degree of contrition), but faith alone, that is, faith defined as trust (sola fide).

If these are the three basic tenets of the Reformation, and I am convinced that they are, then the theology of Johann von Staupitz is reformational.

Therefore Luther was right. Staupitz did start this "doctrinam." Luther had the greatness to recognize the achievements of his teacher. Should we be any less generous? It is now possible to prove a considerable number of individual dependencies of Luther on Staupitz.[29] That is here neither possible nor necessary. My intention is to stress the main lines of the argument.

III

Finally only the question of Staupitz's importance for the Reformation as an historical event remains. In the first place, there is his immediate influence on Luther as theologian and pastor. Next in importance is his influence upon other theologians.[30] In 1517 Karlstadt himself testifies how a writing by Staupitz led to a decisive change in his theological outlook. Melanchthon also expresses his admiration for Staupitz in a prefatory dedication. Caspar Guettel, the reformer of the county of Mansfeld, confesses his dependency on Staupitz. Above all others, it was the Augustinian Eremites who carried and spread the Reformation. Generally it is stated that these were brothers in Luther's Order. But, starting in 1503, the Reformed Augustinians were influenced by the reform of the Order and the reform theology of their vicar-general, Staupitz. He was to a large degree responsible for the fact that the members of the Order became "cadres of the Reformation." After all,

---

[28] Oberman, *Luther*, 204.
[29] See above, footnote 25.
[30] For what follows see "Von der Wirkungsgeschichte zur Forschungsgeschichte," in *De exsecutione*, 9f.

he appointed Luther district-vicar and also named him his successor to the professorship in Wittenberg.

Staupitz's support was decisive precisely during this critical period. In 1518 the vicar-general obtained for Luther a forum for his message at the Heidelberg disputation. A little later he accompanied his pupil to Augsburg for the examination by Cajetan and while there had great influence upon the Elector, Frederick the Wise. And even in his later years in Salzburg he did not, as is generally assumed, reject Luther's teaching or declare it to be heretical.

His influence on the public at large was also of enduring importance. Due to the great success of Staupitz's preaching and writings, that public was prepared in quite a different way for Luther's attack than would have been the case without him. In this respect, such educated laymen as Pirckheimer and Duerer must be mentioned, but also a much wider audience. The fact that Luther's initially academic statements found such resonance among the laity, may well have been decisive for the success of the Reformation.

I reiterate: Staupitz already brought an essential part of that which is called the "unexpected Reformation." Thus, Luther's "unexpected Reformation" was not completely without preparation. Staupitz, however, did not bring the other, "longed-for Reformation," that is, the long desired reform of the clergy, the papal church.

With this we arrive at a very important point for our second, concluding question. Why did Luther's Reformation succeed? Why did the second great surge engulf the first wave of Staupitz's attempt at the Reformation? Luther was in many ways more medieval than Staupitz. For this reason he could better address his contemporaries, who were still overwhelmingly medieval in thought and attitude. Luther himself says that he had been a papist.[31] He continued to take the pope seriously; he viewed him as the anti-Christ, a most medieval idea! With Staupitz the pope played no role at all. In faith there are only Christ and the Christians. Staupitz had abandoned all vestiges of clericalism. But then where was that "image of the enemy," without which a revolution can hardly win over the masses? The devil belongs to that, too, as Oberman has impressively demonstrated.

Furthermore, Luther attacked indulgences, a particularly blatant excess, the denunciation of which was exceptionally popular, not least because of the wide-spread anti-Rome syndrome. Luther, or at least the public Luther, arrived at theological fundamentals by way of attacking an abuse. Staupitz wanted to reform theology in its fundamentals; the abuses, even an out-dated form of a vegetating church in Babylonian

---

[31] WA 40.1 134, 3–7. (= Scheel, *Dokumente*, 62, 17–22) et passim.

captivity, would then disappear on their own. We have discovered only recently in the Salzburger Gutachten (legal depositions), of how little importance the Mass and the other pillars of the institutional church were for him.[32]

Finally, through the object of Luther's criticism, indulgences, the question concerning papal authority, although not posed by Luther, was nevertheless touched upon. From this arose the deep reaction of the papalist theologians; from this Luther came very quickly into the role of a defendant and polemicist and found himself questioning papal authority. For this reason a reformation inside the existing church became impossible. With his theology alone, especially with what was most peculiar to it, Luther would neither have given such strong offense to the Renaissance church, nor would he have found such broad public support.

The historian cannot answer the question whether a successful Staupitzian reformation, which would have allowed unity to take precedence over purity, would be thinkable. The historian's task is to point out that what actually happened is not always the only possible alternative among the manifold effects of historical factors.

The historical alternative which did not happen is easily forgotten. Not the liberal, La Fayette, but the radical, Danton, influences our image of the French Revolution. There was a reform movement (in the Eleventh Century) which actually conquered the church from within, in that it even occupied the papal throne. Therefore it appears to us today less revolutionary than it really was. Looking back inclines one toward the hasty judgment that those currents which did not meet with success had no chance at all to succeed in the first place.

It is not in any way the purpose of this paper to play Staupitz off against Luther, as has been so often the case in reverse. It is much more a matter of taking Luther seriously, especially taking Luther's own statements seriously, if one recognizes in Staupitz a key figure of the Reformation in the decisive years of its preparation and breakthrough.

This recognition does not alter the fact that Luther is *the* Reformer, the initiator and carrier of the earth-shaking event which we call the Reformation. But our knowledge of Staupitz helps us understand *how* Luther became the Reformer and *why* the Reformation prevailed to such an astounding degree. This knowledge of the role of Johann von Staupitz gives us a clear view of a more historical and, thereby, a more human Luther.

---

[32] See above, footnote 23.

THE AUGUSTINIAN THEOLOGIAN
KONRAD TREGER (ca. 1480–1542) AND HIS
DISPUTATION THESES OF MAY 5, 1521

ADOLAR ZUMKELLER, O.S.A.

In 1521 the Augustinian Konrad Treger, or Träyer of Fribourg, Switzerland, known as the defender of Catholic doctrine in both Strasbourg and in his home-land,[1] defended thirty theses on predestination and reprobation, justification and merit, grace and freedom in a disputation at the Augustinian cloister in Strasbourg, three years before the beginning of his controversial theological work. The disputation was held on May 5 of that year in connection with the Provincial Chapter of the Rhenish-Swabian Province and the theses have been preserved. Treger himself, who had been *magister regens* of his Order's *studium generale* in Strasbourg since 1517 and in 1518 became Provincial of the Rhenish-Swabian province, presided at the disputation while the Augustinian Gallus Wagner was the *respondens*.[2]

The following is known about Treger's early theological education:[3] from 1509 to 1512 he studied in Paris. In the summer of 1514 at the Provincial Chapter in Strasbourg, he was appointed to lecture on the Bible and on the *Sentences*.[4] Soon afterwards, on September 3, 1514, he matriculated as *baccalaureus biblicus* at the University of Fribourg in

---

[1] For the literature about Treger and his work, see N. Paulus, "Conrad Treger: ein Augustiner des 16. Jahrhunderts," in *Der Katholik* 79 no. 1 (1889), 439–477, 511–534; Fr. Niggli and B. Wild, *Konrad Treyer, Augustinerprovinzial*, (1944, unpublished manuscript at Augustinus-Institut Würzburg); H. Wicki, "Der Augustinerkonvent Freiburg im Üchtland im 16. Jahrhundert," extract from *Freiburger Geschichtsblätter* 39 (1946), 49 ff.; A.F. Vermeulen, *Der Augustiner Konrad Treger: die Jahre seines Provinzialats (1518–1542)* (Rome, 1962); Adolar Zumkeller, "Konrad Treger OESA, (ca. 1480–1542)," in *Katholische Theologen der Reformationszeit*, ed. E. Iserloh (Münster, 1988), V, 74–87.

[2] Printed in J.E. Kapp, *Nachlese nützlicher Reformationsurkunden* (Leipzig, 1727), II, 450–458.

[3] A. Höhn reports on this in *Chronologia Provinciae Rheno-Suevicae Ordinis FF. Eremitarum S. Augustini* (Würzburg, 1744), 150, and refers to the records of the Provincial Chapter which are lost today: "Conradus Tregarius, ab aliis Torniatoris latine, germanice Treer dictus, de Friburgo Helvetiorum, studiorum causa Parisios missus anno 1509, mansit ibidem ad triennium, tam vitae sanctimonia, quam doctrinae praestantia extitit commendatissimus: anno 1514 ... ad Lecturam Bibliorum et Sententiarum promotus, in Provincia inter ceteros Doctorali Laurea insignitos patres eminuit."

[4] Cf. Höhn, *Chronologia*, 150, reports that this occurred in 1514 when the Provincial Chapter took place in Strasbourg.

Breisgau. He became *baccalaureus sententiarum* on September 20, 1515. On September 22, 1516, he obtained the licentiate and received his Doctorate of Theology on the following day.[5] Unfortunately, neither his lectures on the Bible nor those on the *Sentences* are preserved. Moreover, his teachers in Paris and in Fribourg are not known. We do know, however, that he journied to Italy during the years of his studies in Fribourg, at which time he came in contact with Giles of Viterbo, the General of the Order and a highly regarded theologian. In the summer of 1515, he was the *discretus* of the Rhenish-Swabian Province at the General Chapter in Rimini.[6] A year after he became Provincial of his Province, he once again took part in the General Chapter of the Order in Venice, in June 1519.[7]

That theological disputations took place during the Provincial Chapters of the Rhenish-Swabian Province seems to have been the custom.[8] At the Disputation of 1521, the Provincial Konrad Treger himself was the *praesidens*. This designation in the extant text clearly indicated that Treger was responsible for the theses presented; they reflect his theological doctrine. Later, in fact, he acknowledged them as his own work. He gave the thirty propositions the Greek title, Παράδοξα. With this denomination he clearly wanted to express that although the theses seem contradictory, with closer analysis they are in keeping with the truth.[9] As he states in his conclusion, with the term *Paradoxa* he did not wish to propose new and unusual doctrine (*nova et inusitata*), but rather to present propositions that agreed with Paul, the *doctorum princeps*, and with Paul's *interpres divus*, Augustine. The thirty theses are known today only through the 1727 edition of Erhard Kapp. Kapp used a copy of the theses published by Treger in 1521 which had been in the possession of George Spalatin.[10] Since the Latin text forms the foundation for

---

[5] H. Mayer, *Die Matrikel der Universität Freiburg* (Freiburg, 1907), I, 216. The so-called "Conrad Dreger" reportedly was a student at Tübingen in 1498. According to Paulus, he is not identical to the Augustinian since there is proof that he was born in Oftertingen while our Augustinian comes from Fribourg/Switzerland. Paulus, "Ein Augustiner des 16. Jahrhunderts," 439. Cf. Vermeulen, *Der Augustiner*, 19f.

[6] Höhn, *Chronologia*, 156: "Discretus Generalis anno 1515 adiungebatur praeclaro P. Magistro Hieronymo Candelphio Priori Constanciensi et Diffinitori Generali ad expendiendas Provinciae causas apud Reverendissimum Patrem Generalem, et ubicunque necesse fuerat."

[7] *Analecta Augustiniana* 9 (1921–1922), 32. In the list of the participants of the chapter, he is mentioned as "Provincialis Magister Conradus Trigarius," of the Rhenish-Swabian Province of the Order.

[8] Cf. Höhn, *Chronologia*, 119 (Provincial Chapter at Breisach, 1483) and 134 (Provincial Chapter at Colmar, 1503).

[9] He also described his 100 statements on the authority of the church and councils as "paradoxa."

[10] Kapp shows this in the title of his treatise on Treger: "Bruder Conrad Trögers, Augustiners und Provincials 30 Sätze von der Vorhersehung und Verwerffung, darüber

further investigation and can be obtained now only with difficulty, it is reprinted here in full.

Παράδοξα

Positiones presidente F. Chonrado Tregario, Theologo Augustiniane familie, Priore Provinciali et respondente F. Gallo Vagnero, apud S. Augustinum Argentine III. Non. Maji hora XII. disputate. M.D. XXI.
1. Ab eterno predestinatos fuisse aut reprobatos omnes mortales, cum ex Bibliorum canone, tum ex infallibili divina cognitione, atque immutabili ejus voluntate, luculenter accipimus.
2. Verum cum non sit "volentis nec currentis sed miserentis Dei" (Rom. 9:16), manifestum est, neminem ob sua merita predestinatum, neque aliquem propter sua delicta reprobatum.
3. Predestinatio cum sit Dei voluntas immutabilis, qua vult hominis misereri, eumque sua munificentia felicitati donare, hinc est, vitam eternam nullis humanis meritis consequi posse.
4. Reprobatio contra est nolle misereri, neque homini velle vitam dare atque eodem modo sequi videtur, nullum a vita rejectum ob sua delicta.
5. Non igitur quod homo mandata Dei, quantum fieri potest, observat in finem usque, aut alius transgreditur ob hoc vel illud, ille vitam meretur, hic ab ea excluditur.
6. Hec omnia predestinationis et reprobationis effectus et apertissima indicia sacris canonibus (quibus ex animo refragari impium) divulgatum est.
7. Non tantum ad rem faciunt opiniosissimi quique, quantum illud Pauli (Rom. 9:18): "Cui vult miseretur, quem vult, indurat," et id genus alia.
8. Certus autem et infallibilis est predestinatorum et reprobatorum numerus, nec incrementum illum neque hunc decrementum sumere posse, ex sacris literis compertum habetur.
9. Atque de necessitate absoluta ob id non eveniunt omnia, sed potest selectorum quilibet damnari et rejectus salvari.
10. Et quanquam Christum communem carnem et sanguinem cum omnibus habuit, non tamen eodem modo pro omnibus vitam, sanguinem, carnem, crucis passionem Deo Patri obtulit.
11. Immo plerosque absque propria commissa culpa a facie Dei expulsos et ejectos, vel inviti cogimur asserere.
12. In multis igitur Sacratiss. Christi sanguinis effusio ad vitam eternam non operatur, quo peccatorum remissionem et beatitudinem perpetuam consequantur.
13. Quanquam autem Christus ob id non veniat culpandus, eorum tamen perditio ex ipsis non est.
14. Qui dicit, Christum solum principium omnibus vitam eternam meruendi, meruisse, Christum, Servatorem nostrum, impudenter conspurcat et contaminat.
15. Totaque errat via, qui bona opera nostra in Christi passione efficaciam sortita esse contendit, quo peccatorum remissionem et eternam vitam mereamur.
16. Quippe Christus sua nobis passione et remissionem ipsam criminum et bona opera, gratiam et vitam eternam meruit.
17. Atque hec omnia gratis et libere nobis donata: "Non ex operibus iustitie,

---

den 5. May 1521 zu Strassburg im Augustiner-Closter disputiret worden ist, aus dem von Spalatino rubicirten Exemplar." Kapp, *Nachlese*, 450.

que facimus nos, sed secundum suam magnam misericordiam salvos nos fecit" (Tit. 3:5).

18. Falso igitur nobismetipsis blandimur propter opera nostra, quantumcunque bona, cum scriptura dicat (1 Cor. 4:7): "Quid habes, quod non accepisti?"

19. Ob id ruit hoc commentum (etiamsi peculiare est doctoribus) mereri de congruo et condigno.

20. Bona opera, status innocentie, et quicquid boni primus parens noster habuit, misericordie Dei erat donum.

21. Homo ante lapsum suis relictus viribus, sicut stare non potuit ita multominus in bonis (corr. ex: nobis) promovere.

22. Adeo autem primorum parentum peccato humanam naturam corruptam esse, scimus, ut homo non possit nisi in malum.

23. Hujusmodi autem primigenum peccati genus, non justicie originalis carentiam, sed morbum et appetitionem dicimus, quo sensus adversatur spiritui juxta Paulum (cf. Gal. 5:17).

24. Digladiari autem, an hujusmodi membrorum lex et tyrannis post Baptismi Sacramentum peccatum sit appellandum [etiamsi consonum sit scripture (cf. Rom. 6:12–14)] non magnopere probamus.

25. Hunc peccati fomitem nec parvuli nec adulti animam (si desit actuale peccatum) morari ab ingressu celi dicimus.

26. Ad institutum dicimus hominem, nec ad gratiam se disponere posse, nec a peccatis resurgere, nec tentationibus, quantumvis parvis, prevalere, imo nec quicquam boni cogitare sine Dei adjuvamine.

27. Per hujusmodi autem adjuvamen nos non generalem illam influentiam, aut etiam gratiam Dei assistentem intelligimus, sed specialem Dei motionem, aut verius Deum hec omnia nobis gratis donantem.

28. Ob id non ita Deo opera nostra adscribimus, ut etiam voluntatis non sint nostre, quippe active omnes nostras operationes saltem suas attingit voluntas, nec ad bonum in subjectiva tantum potentia se habet.

29. Proinde de nostra adjecta forma inquit Propheta (Eccl. 7:21): "Non est justus, qui faciat bonum et non peccet." Item (Isa. 64:6) "Justitie nostre tanquam pannus menstruate" etc.

30. Cum autem scriptura appellat opera nostra quantumcunque bona, et bona mala: delirum et anxium, videtur, tam acerbe de voculis disceptare, maxime vero cum de re constet.

Quum sepe multa a majoribus meis fuisse disputata non ignoramus, et nos quoque illorum exemplis excitati: hec Paradoxa ita disputanda suscepimus, ut non videamur Predestinationis ac reprobationis divina oracula temere ad nostrum torquere sensum, asserendo nova et inusitata. Sed ea maxime, que doctorum principi Paulo, atque ejus interpreti Divo Augustino consentanea videntur. At apud optimum quemque libera sit potestas judicandi, ut volet. Modo permittat et nobis hec nostra, qualiacumque sunt disputationis capita, pie tractare.[11]

Not without importance for understanding these theses are Treger's own explanations that he gave three years after the disputation and which should be presented before we examine the content of the

---

[11] According to a note of Kapp, the concluding section is written in Spalatin's hand but in view of its tenor, the real content is authored by Treger. Kapp, *Nachlese*, 457.

propositions more closely. In Strasbourg on March 12, 1524 our Augustinian published one hundred new *Paradoxa* on the authority of the
Church and Councils which he intended to dispute in Fribourg,
Switzerland.[12] In these theses he sharply attacked Reformation teaching. Wolfgang Capito, who had proclaimed the new doctrine in Strasbourg with success since 1523, reproached Treger because, among other
things, in his new publication he had "not intended such theses for the
discovery of the truth since two years ago here in Strasbourg he debated
many points concerning grace and free will that entirely contradict his
current position."[13] Treger considered this a calumny to which he gave
the following reply and rectification:

> They write that I have not always been of this opinion, that I had not
> intended that disputation for the proclamation of the truth when some
> years ago I debated here in Strasbourg on many points of grace and free will
> which completely contradict my present position.
>
> Good Christian, I am convinced that these evangelical gentlemen have
> disgraced themselves and their spirit urges and forces them to lie so
> publicly. For I base my case on the very articles disputed by me at that time,
> which without a doubt are even now in the hands of many (as in my own),
> namely that I had said nothing at all about the present issues and so little
> thought in a Lutheran way that I had disputed against his doctrine in at least
> five articles, namely, in the ninth, the twenty-fourth, the twenty-seventh,
> the twenty-eighth, and in the thirtieth. And even if something was debated
> at that time that Luther also wrote and taught, I nevertheless had disputed
> the same or similar issues at Paris, Venice, and other places before I had
> even heard of Luther. I can show which points and articles were debated at
> such places. But these gentlemen are so learned that they consider anyone
> who teaches or disputes a word that is not explicitly against the Lutheran
> doctrine to belong to their crowd. As if Luther has not taught and written
> many things that have been taught and written for a thousand years that are
> also good and useful—as all heretics have done. For indeed, one cannot sell
> the bad unless it is mixed with the good, and poison mixed with honey.[14]

---

[12] "... *paradoxa Centum fratris Conradi Tregarij Heluecij ... de ecclesie Conciliorumque auctoritate,*" printed sine loco 1524.

[13] [Wolfgang Capito], *Verwarnung der diener des worts und der Brüder zu Strassburg ... Wider die Gotslesterige Disputation bruder Conradts Augustiner Ordens Provincial,* printed sine loco (April) 1524, fol. B 2a, quoted from Paulus, *Treger,* 443: "solches nicht fürgenommen zu Erkundung der Wahrheit; denn von der Gnade und dem freien Willen hat er vor zwei (!) Jahren hier in Strassburg in vielen Punkten disputiert, das jetziger Meinung gerichts entgegen ist."

[14] *Vermanung Bruder Conradts Treger ... an ein lobliche gemeyne Eydgnoßschafft von der Boᵉhemschen ketzerey vnnd antwurt Vff ein lugenthafft gotslestrig buch von etlichen so sich diener des worts heissen ...,* (written April/May, printed in August) sine loco 1524, fol. C III r-v: "Sie schreyben, ich sey nit allwegen diser meynung gewesen, ich hab solche disputation nit zů verkündung der wahrheit fürgenommen, dann ich vor etlichen jaren hie zů Strassburg in vil puncten von der genad vnd freyen willen disputiert, diser yetzigen meynung gantz entgegen.

Frummer Christ, ich acht, das dise Ewangelischen herren sich gar verschampt habenn, vnd sie ir geist so offenlich zů liegen für vnd für zwingt vnd tringt; dann ich bezeüg mich vff

Thus Treger asserts: 1) that he held no teachings of Luther in his theses of 1521, but had opposed Luther's doctrines already at that time with propositions 9, 24, 27, 28, and 30. 2) If some of these theses were also being taught and written by Luther, he (Treger) had already debated them or similar ones in Paris, Venice, and in other places, even before he had heard them from Luther. Evidently he refers to disputations during his years of study in Paris, 1509–1512, and to theological disputations in which he had taken part at the General Chapter in Venice of 1519. Regrettably, he did not mention which theses were treated at that time. 3) In any case, much that was written and taught by Luther was good traditional teaching of the Church.

Turning now to the contents of Treger's theses, we can categorize them in four groups:

I. Propositions 1–13 clarify questions concerning predestination and reprobation.
II. Propositions 14–21 treat the doctrines of justification and merit.
III. Propositions 22–25 deal with the Fall of Adam and its consequences.
IV. Propositions 26–30 concern the necessity of grace and human cooperation.

I. *Predestination and Reprobation*

Treger emphatically teaches predestination and reprobation from eternity. He claims that it is clearly evident in sacred Scripture, and stems from the infallible knowledge and unchangeable will of God (Proposition 1). He defines predestination as God's unalterable will to show mercy to a man and to give him eternal life (Proposition 3). By the same token, he understands reprobation as God's will not to show mercy to a man and not to give him eternal life (Proposition 4). Appealing to Romans 9:16–18, he teaches that predestination and reprobation are

---

die selbigen artickel, datzumalen durch mich disputiert, die on zweyfel noch bey vilen (vnd auch bey mir) funden werden, das ich der yetzigen materi mit keinem wort nye gedacht hab, vnd so wenig Luthersch vff solch zeyt, das ich auch vnder anderm fünff artickel zům wenigsten wider die Luthersch ler datzumal disputiert hab. Namlich den Neünden, Vierundtzweintzigsten, Sybenundtzweintzigsten, Achtundtzweintzigsten vnd den Dreyssigsten. Vnd wie wol auch etwas vff sollich zeyt disputiert worden ist, das der Luther auch schreybt vnd lert, hab ich doch das oder dem gleychfoᵉrmlich zů Paryss, zů Venedig vnd an anderen orten vnd enden disputiert, ee ich vom Luther gehoᵉrt hab. Woᵉlche puncten vnd artickel an sollichen orten disputiert, ich antzeygen kan. Aber dise herren sind so hochgelert, so bald ein wort gelert oder disputiert wirt, der Lutherschen ler nit wider, achten sie den der sollichs leret oder disputiert, von irem hauffen zů sein. Als ob der Luther nit vil geleret vnd geschriben het, das vor Tausent jaren gelert vnd geschriben wer worden, das auch gůt vnd nützlich, wie dann alle ketzer gethon haben. Dann ye das boᵉss mit dem gutten vnd das gifft vnder dem honig verkaufft muss werden."

independent of man's merits or demerits (Propositions 2 and 7); or put another way: neither one's merits nor fulfilling God's commandments are the real grounds for obtaining eternal life. Likewise, neither one's sins nor one's transgression of God's commands are the true basis for one's exclusion from eternal life (Propositions 3–5). Treger thus adopts the doctrine of unconditional predestination and reprobation which was put forward in the Middle Ages already in the *Sentences* of Peter Lombard in close connection with the later Augustine, and in the latter Middle Ages—in contrast to Thomas of Strasbourg—was championed by Gregory of Rimini and his followers. A group of German Augustinian theologians also adopted it, such as John Klenkok, John Hiltalingen of Basel, Angelus Dobelin and John Zachariae.[15]

As Hiltalingen, Treger shows that Thomas of Strasbourg, with his doctrine of predestination and reprobation *post praevisa merita* and *post praevisa demerita* respectively,[16] had hardly any followers even in his own province of the Order.

Completely in keeping with Augustine's interpretation, Treger further taught that the number of the predestined and reprobated can neither increase nor decrease (Proposition 8). Yet, he immediately makes the qualification that it is not *de necessitate absoluta*; anyone predestined could be rejected, and the damned could be saved (Proposition 9). Gregory of Rimini and several of his disciples, following Duns Scotus, had taught analogously, as did the German Augustinians Dobelinus and Zachariae mentioned above.[17] With the reference to *necessitas absoluta*, Treger may well have been alluding to the distinction between the *potestas Dei absoluta* and the *potestas Dei ordinata*, which Zachariae also employed for this problem. In any case, in 1524 Treger declared with justification that he had intended his ninth thesis against Luther. In Luther's *Disputatio contra scholasticam theologiam* of 1517, article 31 states: "Vanissimo commento dicitur: praedestinatus potest damnari in sensu diviso, sed non in composito."[18] With the aid of the distinction between the *sensus divisus* and the *sensus compositus*, Gregory of Rimini, Hugolino of Orvieto, and John Zachariae, among others, had determined this question.[19] It is possible that Treger also had recourse to this distinction in the oral presentation of his thesis.

The further consequences which Treger derived from his doctrine of

---

[15] Cf. Adolar Zumkeller, *Erbsünde, Gnade, Rechtfertigung und Verdienst nach der Lehre der Erfurter Augustinertheologen des Spätmittelalters* (Würzburg, 1984), 68ff., 143, 147ff., 247ff.

[16] Cf. J.L Shannon, *Good Works and Predestination according to Thomas of Strassburg OSA* (Baltimore, 1940), 75ff and 96ff.

[17] See Zumkeller, *Erbsünde*, 159ff and 253ff.,

[18] *WA*, I, 225.

[19] Zumkeller, *Erbsünde*, 159, 254.

predestination and reprobation sound harsh: on the cross Christ did not offer his life to his heavenly Father for all men equally (Proposition 10), since for many people his shed blood does not bring about the forgiveness of sins nor the reception of eternal life (Proposition 12). Indeed, there is a large number of people who are rejected from the sight of God without having contracted any guilt (Proposition 11). This does not mean that there is any fault on the part of Christ (Proposition 13). These seemingly harsh *paradoxa* are too short to allow a clear reconstruction of Treger's doctrine which was based on and expounded in oral debate. In any case, with Proposition 10 he could not have wanted to deny that Christ died on the cross for all men. In keeping with Augustine, he understood Proposition 11 as referring to little children who die unbaptised.

II. *Justification and Merit*

Treger then turns to the questions of justification and merit. He maintains that through his suffering, Christ has earned for us the forgiveness of sins, good works, grace, and eternal life (Proposition 16). It would be, therefore, a great insult to Christ if one claimed that he had only earned for all men a beginning (*principium*) with which to earn eternal life (Proposition 14). It would also be a great offense to assume that our good works receive their potency through Christ's suffering so that we merit redemption and eternal life on their account (Proposition 15). Treger, rather, calls on Titus 3:5: "He has saved us not because of righteous works that we do, but in accordance with his great mercy", as evidence that justification and eternal life are given to us by God with no obligation (*gratis et libere*) (Proposition 17). Invoking 1 Cor. 4:7, he explicitly emphasizes that our good works are a gift of God, and therefore we have no grounds for pride in them (Proposition 18). He considers the two-fold concept of merit (*mereri de congruo et condigno*) employed by the *doctores* a superfluous invention (Proposition 19). In addition, he sees the good works and the *status innocentiae* of the first man as a gift of God's mercy. (Proposition 20). With Augustine, Treger taught that before the Fall, Adam on his own could not remain, muchless progress in the good (Proposition 21).[20]

Thus, Treger strongly emphasizes the complete gratuitousness of justification and eternal life. He knows nothing of meriting eternal life. Man's good works as well, which he acknowledges as such, are seen so entirely as God's gift that it is questionable whether Treger ascribed any merit to them. It is possible that he is close to the Augustinianism of Gregory of Rimini and his adherents, Hugolin of Orvieto, Alfons

---

[20] Cf. Augustine, *De Correptione et gratia*, 11.32 (*PL* XLIV, 935ff.).

Vargas, Angelus Dobelinus, and John Zachariae, who maintained similar views on this question.[21] Gregory explicitly taught "that a human act, which is inspired by love in any way, is in and of itself meritorious in God's sight neither for eternal life nor for any other eternal or earthly reward."[22] In addition, Gregory also supports his position with reference to 1 Cor. 4:7, and to Augustine's statement that all our merits are exclusively God's gifts.[23]

III. *The Fall and its Consequences*

Treger teaches that through the sin of our first parents, human nature was so vitiated that fallen man has power only to do evil (Proposition 22). The *peccatum originale*, or *primigenum peccati genus* as Treger puts it, is not to be understood as the absence of original righteousness, but as that *morbus* and *appetitio* because of which, according to Gal. 5:17, the senses are in conflict with the spirit (Proposition 23). Treger had a number of predecessors in his strong emphasis on the *corruptio* of human nature resulting from the Fall: the Augustinian Giles of Rome and other theologians of high scholasticism, as well as his German confrere, Angelus Dobelinus.[24] John Klenkok had already held the thesis that fallen man could only do evil by his natural power.[25] With his view that original sin consists not in the lack of original righteousness, but in *morbus* and *appetitio*, Treger is close to the doctrine of Gregory of Rimini. Gregory, with his appeal to Augustine and Paul, saw the essence of these sins in concupiscence, while in the lack of original righteousness he saw only their *effectus*.[26]

Whether this *tyrannis* of the body's members should still be called "sin" in the baptized, which seems to be in accord with Scripture, Treger—as he implies in the following thesis—does not want to make this an issue of fierce controversy. In any case, he would be of the opinion that this *fomes peccati* prevents neither children nor adults from entering heaven, provided there is no "actual sin" (Proposition 25). As he explained in 1524, he directed this thesis against Luther. Indeed, in his *Disputatio et excusatio ... adversus criminationes D. Joannis Eccii* of 1519, Luther had declared: "... in puero post baptismum peccatum

---

[21] See Adolar Zumkeller, "Hugolin von Orvieto über Prädestination, Rechtfertigung und Verdienst," *Augustiniana* 4 (1954), 109–156; 5 (1955), 35–39; and also *Erbsünde*, 8ff, 207–209, and 287ff.

[22] *Lectura*, 1 Sent. dist. 17 q. 1 art. 2 (II, 237).

[23] Augustine, *De Trinitate*, 13.10.14 (CCL. 50a, 400).

[24] For references to Aegidius Romanus see Zumkeller, *Erbsünde*, 15f, to Angelus Dobelinus, 146ff.

[25] See Zumkeller, *Erbsünde*, 58.

[26] *Lectura*, 2 Sent. dist. 30–33 q. 1 art. 2 and 4 (VI 182–184, 194–195). Cf. the literature on Gregory's doctrine in Zumkeller, *Erbsünde*, 5f n. 22.

remanens negare, hoc est Paulum et Christum semel conculcare."[27] In addition, already in the previous year he had stated in his *Resolutiones disputationum de indulgentiarum virtute*: "... cum nisi ipse (scil. *fomes*) sanetur, impossibile sit intrare caelum, etiam si nullum adsit actuale."[28] We do not know whether Treger quoted these propositions from Luther's original writings, or simply based them on the list of errors in the bull *Exsurge Domine* of June 15, 1520. The latter seems more likely since in the bull both propositions are found in this close association as numbers two and three, that is, in immediate succession.[29]

IV. *The Necessity of Grace and Human Cooperation*

Treger teaches that man needs a certain *Dei adiuvamen* in order to dispose himself for grace, to rise up from sin, to resist temptations— even the little ones—and indeed, even to think anything good (Proposition 26). What does he mean by this *Dei adiuvamen*? Treger answers that it is not the *generalis influentia*, nor the *gratia Dei assistens*, but a *specialis Dei motio*, or more correctly, that God himself gives us everything *gratis* (Proposition 27). In this, he is close to the position of Gregory of Rimini, who insisted that for every *actus moraliter bonus* of man, there is a *specialis Dei auxilium*.[30] This is also characteristic of Hugolin of Orvieto, John Hiltalingen, and John Klenkok.[31] Very much like Treger, Klenkok describes the *adiutorium Dei speciale* as a "specialis Dei assistentia sive gratis iuvando ad bene agendum et volendum et ad non peccandum sive non permittendo nos temptari ultra virtutem nobis ab eo praestitam."[32]

Despite all these declarations, Treger stresses expressly that works are not only God's work, but are also the work of our will. The will actively plays a part in all our works rather than being only *in subjectiva potentia* toward the good (Proposition 28). In 1524 Treger claimed that this thesis was directed against Luther. In his disputation at Heidelberg in 1518, Luther had presented the following conclusions: "Liberum

---

[27] *WA* 2. 160.

[28] *WA* 1. 572.

[29] H. Denzinger and A. Schönmetzer, *Enchiridion Symbolorum* (Freiburg,[32] 1963), Nrr. 742ff/1452ff.

[30] See Christoph Peter Burger, "Der Augustinschüler gegen die modernen Pelagianer: Das 'auxilium speciale dei' in der Gnadenlehre Gregors von Rimini, in *Gregor von Rimini: Werk und Wirkung bis zur Reformation*, ed. Heiko A. Oberman (Berlin, 1981), 195–240. See more literature in Zumkeller, *Erbsünde*, 50 n. 188.

[31] Cf. Adolar Zumkeller, "Hugolin von Orvieto über Urstand und Erbsünde," *Augustiniana* 3 (1953), 41–44. Also A. Zumkeller "Der Augustinertheologe Johannes Hiltalingen von Basel über Urstand, Erbsünde, Gnade und Verdienst," *Analecta Augustiniana* 43 (1980), 104–107 and Zumkeller, *Erbsünde*, 50–60.

[32] Zumkeller, *Erbsünde*, 50 n. 192.

arbitrium post peccatum est de solo titulo et dum facit quod in se est, peccat mortaliter (13th conclusion). Liberum arbitrium post peccatum potest in bonum potentia subjectiva, in malum vero activa semper (14th conclusion)."[33] In the *probatio* of his fifteenth conclusion, Luther clarified what he meant by *potentia subjectiva* and *activa* respectively as follows: Augustine said of Adam: " 'Acceperat posse, si vellet, sed non habuit velle, quo posset'[34] per 'posse' intelligens potentiam subjectivam et per 'velle, quo posset', potentiam activam."[35] Accordingly, Treger intended to express in Proposition 28 that the will, aided by God's *adiuvamen*, not only has the subjective ability to will, but also the active power to will to the extent that it is capable.

From this cooperation of man (*de nostra adiecta forma*), Treger continues to claim that all our works are still faulty, and he quotes Eccl. 7:21 and Isaiah 64:6 as proof: "our righteous deeds are like the cloth of a menstruating woman" (Proposition 29).[36] Treger concludes with the statement that since sacred Scripture calls our works good, and good works evil, it seems foolish and embarassing to debate words so strenuously, especially since the fact itself clearly remains (Proposition 30). What he probably wanted to say was that Scripture acknowledges our good works, but at the same time speaks of the deficiencies of our works. These two facts should be recognized and not questioned further. As he himself declared in 1524, this thesis was directed against Luther, who in 1518 had declared in conclusion 58 (among others) of his *Resolutiones disputationum de indulgentiarum virtute*: "Verum etiam opus bonum optime factum est veniale peccatum."[37]

Conclusion

In conclusion it can be said that the thirty theses of Treger prove that he based his treatment of predestination and reprobation entirely on the teachings of the later Augustine. Not without reason did he emphatically claim in his concluding remarks—preserved for us by Spalatin—that in his *Paradoxa* on predestination and reprobation he did not want to teach *nova et inusitata*, but only what agreed with the teaching of the apostle Paul and his *interpres* Augustine. However, since the details of the individual arguments of his theses are not preserved, it is impossible to determine how far Treger made use of Augustine's original works.

---

[33] *WA* 1. 354.

[34] Augustine, *De correptione et gratia*, 11.32 (*PL* XLIV, 936).

[35] *WA* 1. 360.

[36] Cf. Adolar Zumkeller, "Das Ungenügen der menschlichen Werke bei den deutschen Predigern des Spätmittelalters," *Zeitschrift für katholische Theologie* 81 (1959), 265–305; and Zumkeller, *Erbsünde*, 289ff, 379ff.

[37] *WA* 1. 608.

For the same reason, it is not clear whether Treger was directly influenced by Gregory of Rimini or one of his followers. Nevertheless,
there is a number of striking similarities with the Augustinianism of
Gregory, not only in the doctrine of predestination and reprobation, but
also regarding Treger's denial of the possibility of merit for eternal life,
his understanding of original sin, his doctrine of the necessity of a
special help of divine grace, and his emphasis on the deficiencies of
human works. Evidence that Gregory of Rimini was not forgotten in the
Augustinian Order in the later fifteenth and sixteenth-century is found
in the decrees of the General Chapters of 1491 and 1497, which permitted the Order's *magistri* to read *extraordinarie* the works of Gregory and
other theologians of the Order, in addition to the works of Giles of
Rome.[38] Indeed, in 1509 the *magister regens* in Bologna entirely put
aside the *Sentences* commentary of Giles and read Gregory instead.[39]
Unfortunately, there are as yet no studies of the theology of the
Augustinians in Paris at the end of the fifteenth century. Still it is
noteworthy that in Treger's day Gregory's *Sentences* commentary already existed in various printings, some of which appeared in Paris.[40]

Moreover, it is certain that in 1521 Treger already had some knowledge of Luther's teaching. Whether the two ever met personally,
however,—which could have occurred at the Heidelberg Disputation—
remains uncertain. Since the individual arguments of the thirty theses
are not preserved, the extent of his knowledge of Luther's doctrine
cannot be clearly determined. It is possible that he himself had read very
little of Luther's writings and had based his knowledge on the list of
condemned propositions in the bull *Exsurge Domine*. In any case,
Treger was already very critical of his Wittenberg confrere at that time.

---

[38] Cf. Zumkeller, *Erbsünde*, 434 n. 566f.

[39] Zumkeller, *Erbsünde*, 435.

[40] Damasus Trapp, Gregory of Rimini's Manuscripts, Editions and Additions," *Augustiniana* 8 (1958), 430.

CALVIN AND THE NATURAL KNOWLEDGE OF GOD

DAVID C. STEINMETZ

The problem of the natural knowledge of God in Calvin's theology was sharply posed in the 1930's in a famous debate between Karl Barth and Emil Brunner.[1] In his little book, *Natur und Gnade*, Brunner argued for what he called a "Christian natural theology."[2] By the use of this somewhat ambiguous phrase, Brunner meant to suggest that the image of God had not been completely destroyed by human sin and disobedience. Remnants of the image were still present in human nature and formed a point of contact for the gospel. Furthermore, the revelation of God in nature was not lost to Christians, who, by using the spectacles of Scripture, could once again know God in and through his works. In all these contentions Brunner claimed Calvin as his ally and mentor.

> Calvin considers this remnant of the *imago Dei* to be of great importance. One might almost say that it is one of the pillars supporting his theology, for he identifies it with nothing less than the entire human, rational nature, the immortal soul, the capacity for culture, the conscience, responsibility, the relation with God, which—though not redemptive—exists even in sin, language, the whole of cultural life.[3]

Brunner's book met with an immediate and harsh answer from Barth in a pamphlet, *Nein: Antwort an Emil Brunner*. The unusual heat of Barth's response was due in part to the political situation in Germany, where natural theology had been exploited by pro-Nazi Christians. Against Brunner's reading of Calvin, Barth argued that Calvin constantly pointed to the Bible as the true source of the knowledge of God.

> The possibility of a real knowledge by natural man of the true God, derived from creation, is, according to Calvin, a possibility in principle, but not in

---

[1] This essay was written with the aid of a grant from the Herzog August Bibliothek in Wolfenbüttel, West Germany, and is dedicated to Father Trapp, whose research in the theology of the late medieval Augustinian Order has proven invaluable to me in my study of the theologies of Staupitz and Luther. In this essay, however, I proceed to examine whether Augustine's exegesis of Paul, and not the Pauline exegesis of the Augustinian Order, found a resonance in the exegesis of John Calvin and the early Protestant interpreters of Romans 1.

[2] Emil Brunner and Karl Barth, *Natural Theology*, trans. Peter Fraenkel (London, 1946), 37.

[3] Brunner and Barth, 41.

fact, not a possibility to be realized by us. One might call it an objective possibility, created by God, but not a subjective possibility, open to man. Between what is possible in principle and what is possible in fact there inexorably lies the fall. Hence this possibility can only be discussed hypothetically: *si integer stetisset Adam* (Inst., I, ii, 1).[4]

Because the human race has fallen into sin, the content of its natural knowledge of God is nothing more than idolatry and superstition.[5] Therefore, the revelation of God in nature, whatever its original purpose may have been, serves only to render fallen human beings inexcusable and to justify the wrath of God against them.[6] As Barth understands Calvin, there is no knowledge of God the creator apart from the knowledge of God the redeemer.[7]

In his recent book, *John Calvin: A Sixteenth Century Portrait*, William J. Bouwsma, whose interest in Calvin's thought is more historical than theological, touches briefly on the problem of the natural knowledge of God in the context of Calvin's indebtedness to his cultural tradition. Unlike Karl Barth, Bouwsma is convinced that Calvin does in fact advocate a natural theology based on natural insight and innate religious instinct.[8] While Calvin is not altogether certain "how far or how deep the natural knowledge of God could go," he is convinced at the very least that nature unremittingly demonstrates God's existence.[9]

On the question of God's essence, Bouwsma believes that Calvin is more ambiguous. On the one hand, Calvin warns against speculative theology that attempts to know the essence of God from his works; on the other hand, he regards "every aspect of external nature" as "redolent with religious instruction."[10] Rivers and mountains, birds and flowers, even the human body itself, are important sources for the natural knowledge of God. Calvin is particularly interested in the heavenly bodies as theological tutors and regards astronomy as the alphabet of

---

[4] Brunner and Barth, 106.

[5] Brunner and Barth, 107.

[6] Brunner and Barth, 108.

[7] Brunner and Barth, 108–109: "It is true that, according to Calvin, the knowledge of God in Christ includes a real knowledge of the true God in creation. Includes! This means that it does not, as Brunner seems to think, bring forth a second, relatively independent kind of knowledge, so that the circle would become an ellipse after all—as if our reason, once it had been illuminated, had of itself (*per se*) gained the power of sight (Instit., II, ii, 25)!" The debate prompted by Barth and Brunner was continued and extended by several historians, especially by Edward A. Dowey, Jr., *The Knowledge of God in Calvin's Theology* (New York, 1952) and T.H.L. Parker, *Calvin's Doctrine of the Knowledge of God* (Grand Rapids, 1959).

[8] William J. Bouwsma, *John Calvin: A Sixteenth Century Portrait* (New York, 1988), 103.

[9] Bouwsma, 104.

[10] Bouwsma, 104.

theology.[11] Yet in spite of the fact that Bouwsma has found impressive evidence for a kind of natural theology in Calvin's thought, he nevertheless concludes that the debate between Brunner, "for whom Calvin left a large place for the knowledge of God from nature," and Barth, "for whom he left little or none," "is futile because of Calvin's ambivalence; he can be cited on both sides of the issue."[12]

The appeal to Calvin's ambivalence with respect to the problem of natural theology, while understandable, may not be entirely justified.[13] Calvin outlines the main themes in his understanding of the natural knowledge of God in his earliest theological writings. His views on natural law and the role of human conscience are, for example, already articulated in the 1536 edition of the *Institutes*. While Calvin modifies his views over time, he remains remarkably consistent in adhering to fundamental distinctions first drawn in the 1539 *Institutes* and the 1540 *Commentary on Romans*.[14]

In what follows, I want to examine one of Calvin's earliest discussions of natural theology; namely, his exegesis of Romans 1:18–32, a passage in which the question of the natural knowledge of God is crucial to the development of Paul's argument. What I hope to demonstrate is that Calvin gives this passage a highly original, if problematic, reading that remains crucial to his later thought. In order to assess the originality of Calvin's interpretation of Paul, I intend to compare his exegesis with the exegesis of Augustine and four other well-known and widely cited interpreters, who inhabit to a greater or lesser degree Calvin's own intellectual and spiritual world.[15]

---

[11] Bouwsma, 104.

[12] Bouwsma, 262 n. 51.

[13] The best treatment of the place of nature in Calvin's theology is found in Susan E. Schreiner, "Theater of Glory: Nature and the Natural Order in the Thought of John Calvin," (Unpublished Ph.D. dissertation, Duke University), scheduled to be published in a revised form by the Labyrinth Press as volume three in the series, Studies in Historical Theology. However, while Schreiner focuses on Calvin's thought in the context of ancient and medieval tradition, this essay concentrates primarily on Calvin's thought in the context provided by his contemporaries. See also the essay by Christopher B. Kaiser, "Calvin's Understanding of Aristotelian Natural Philosophy: Its Extent and Possible Origins," in Robert V. Schnucker, ed. *Calviniana: Ideas and Influence of Jean Calvin*, Sixteenth Century Essays and Studies 10 (Kirksville, MO, 1988) 77–92. For a treatment of the distinction between natural and supernatural theology in Reformed theology from Calvin to Protestant Orthodoxy, see Richard A. Muller, *Post-Reformation Reformed Dogmatics*, volume 1: *Prolegomena to Theology* (Grand Rapids, 1987) 167–193.

[14] The critical edition of Romans by T.H.L. Parker contains the revised text of 1556, with variants noted for the 1551 and 1540 editions. While Calvin expands and revises his remarks on the natural knowledge of God in 1551 and 1556, the absolutely crucial distinction between the clarity of divine revelation and the blindness of fallen human reason is already articulated in the 1540 exegesis of 1:20. Similarly 1.5.1–2, 7, 9, 11, 14–15, first appear in the 1539 *Institutes*.

[15] T.H.L. Parker in his book, *Commentaries on the Epistle to the Romans 1532–1542*,

Paul had raised the question of the natural knowledge of God in the context of the problem of the moral responsibility of the Gentiles. If the ancient pagans had a knowledge of the true God, however rudimentary, they could be held responsible for their moral lapses and addiction to idols. By the same token, total religious ignorance would provide them with a legitimate excuse and relieve them of accountability to God.

Paul takes the line that the pagans did have a knowledge of God from nature and conscience. While this knowledge was primitive in comparison with the rich revelation of God entrusted to the Jews, the really decisive question for Paul was not how much the Gentiles knew, but what they did with what they knew. Although the Gentiles admittedly had little, they abused the little they had. God was therefore within his rights to hold them accountable for their sins and to punish them for their disobedience.

I

Augustine in his early commentary on Romans, the *Expositio quarundam Propositionum ex Epistola ad Romanos*, regards 1:18–32 as essentially unproblematic. The wiser Gentiles knew God the Creator through his creation. Their problem was not lack of knowledge, as Paul's sermon in Athens demonstrates (Acts 17:28), but pride, the root of all sins. They did not give thanks to God, who was the source of their wisdom, and so fell foolishly into idolatry. The reprimand of the Gentiles, however, is itself proof that they are not excluded from the realm of salvation but can attain grace through conversion. Augustine does not seem to have in mind a knowledge of God the Creator through creation possessed by all human beings, but only by some. The wiser Gentiles knew in fact what others could, but did not, know in principle.[16]

The late medieval exegetical tradition, of which Denis the Carthusian may be taken as representative, agreed with Augustine that Romans 1 contains no special problems.[17] There were, of course, a number of

---

compares Calvin's exegesis of 1:18–23 with the exegesis of Melanchthon, Cajetan, Bullinger, Sadeleto, Bucer, Haresche, Pellikan, Grimani, and Guilliaud. Parker has collected in one short volume a good deal of valuable information. He is, however, in my judgement overly cautious when he does not take up the idea of natural theology in these authors, because working "with such short passages of commentary ... would fail in almost every instance to do justice to the author." (7). There is, of course, no doubt that Calvin's thought is richer than his few remarks on Romans 1 demonstrate, but what he and the other commentators say is enough, as Parker also observes, to "note agreement in general, agreements in intention and tendency." (7)

[16] "Expositio quarundam Propositionum ex Epistola ad Romanos, 3–7," in *Augustine on Romans*, ed. Paula Fredriksen Landes, Texts and Translations no. 23, Early Christian Literature Series 6 (Chico, 1982), 2–4.

[17] Denis the Carthusian was one of the few medieval authors whose works were collected by the library of the Academy in Geneva. The standard work on the library of

smaller exegetical points on which commentators differed, but the general thrust of Paul's argument seemed clear enough.

Denis admits that God has revealed truth to human beings in a variety of ways: through an infusion of wisdom, through angelic revelation, through the teaching of the saints, and through natural reason. Paul, however, is speaking about natural reason in Romans 1.[18] Through the influence of the light of natural reason, a rational soul can understand the creator by means of the created order, since effects bear some likeness to the cause in which they participate.[19] Specifically, one can know that God is just and wise, that God approves of what is just and disapproves of injustice, and that God deserves reverent worship.[20] One can even know the "invisible things" of God; namely, the perfections such as power, justice and providence that are one in the simple, incorporeal being of God. Furthermore, Denis agrees with John Damascene that all human beings have an innate knowledge of the existence of God.[21] If the Gentiles have merited the wrath of God, it is not because they do not know the truth but because they do not do it.

The themes sounded in Augustine and developed by Denis recur in the three Protestant commentators mentioned favorably by Calvin in the preface to his own commentary on Romans: Philip Melanchthon (Wittenberg, 1532), Heinrich Bullinger (Zurich, 1533), and Martin Bucer (Strasbourg, 1534).[22] But there are other themes as well. Impor-

---

Calvin's Academy is Alexandre Ganoczy, *La bibliothèque de l'Acadèmie de Calvin*, Etudes de philologie et d'histoire no. 13 (Geneva, 1969). Although a beautiful edition of Denis was published in Cologne in 1533, Parker does not mention Denis in his own study of Romans commentaries, though he tracks other non-contemporary commentators such as Thomas Aquinas. Haymo of Auxerre, also unmentioned by Parker and appearing under the false name of Haymo of Halberstadt, is published in Cologne in 1539, *Haymonis Episcopi Halberstatten in d. Pauli Epistolas Omnes Interpretatio* (Cologne, 1539).

[18] Denis the Carthusian, *In Omnes Beati Pauli Commentaria* (Cologne, 1533), Vr.

[19] *Commentaria*, Vr: "Cum enim omnis creatura sit quidam radius sui creatoris, et omnis effectus sit quaedam participata similitudo suae causae (quam unumquodque producit sibi simile) certum est quod ex naturis creatis aliquomodo cognoscatur increatura natura."

[20] *Commentaria*, IIIIv: "per naturalem rationem de Deo scire potest, videlicet quod Deus sit iustus et sapiens, approbans bona, et reprobans mala, et quod ipsi soli sit cultus perfectissimus, utpote honor latriae exhibendus."

[21] *Commentaria*, Vr: "Secundum Damascenum quoque omnibus naturaliter inserta est cognitio existendi Deum."

[22] Parker omits from his discussion of commentaries in the period 1532–42 the posthumously assembled exegesis of Zwingli, *In Evangelicam Historiam de Domino Nostro Iesu Christo, per Matthaeum, Marcum, Lucam et Ioannem conscriptam, Epistolasque aliquot Pauli, Annotationes, D. Huldrychii Zvinglii per Leonem Judae exceptae et editae* (Zurich, 1539) and the commentary by the Lutheran theologian Erasmus Sarcerius, *In Epistolam ad Romanos pia et erudita Scholia* (Frankfurt, 1541). Moreover, Parker is not correct when he asserts that after 1542 and "before the Council of Trent" "no new commentaries came out ..." (p. viii) See Antonio Brucioli, *Nuovo Commento in tutte le celesti et divine Epistole di San Paulo*, 7 vols. (Venice, 1544); John Chrysostom, *In Omnes*

tant to Melanchthon's treatment of Romans 1:18–32 is a Lutheran distinction between law and gospel.[23] As Melanchthon sees it, Paul posits a natural knowledge of God, but it is a knowledge of the law and not of the gospel.[24] What the Gentiles know through nature is that there is a God, that this God is just and requires justice, that he punishes the ungodly, and that he hears and saves whoever is obedient to the law. What cannot be known through natural reason alone is the gospel; namely, that God desires to remit sins, to be reconciled to the unworthy and unclean, and freely to account as just the unrighteous. To the extent that the natural knowledge of God posits the necessity for human worthiness, to that extent it is in conflict with the knowledge of God derived from the gospel.[25]

Melanchthon understands Paul to teach that the natural knowledge of God is implanted in the human mind by God and is not simply a conclusion derived from the observation of nature.[26] Indeed, reason would not marvel at the works of God in nature if it did not already have an innate, proleptic knowledge of God. The rise and fall of nations, the change of times and seasons, the punishment of the wicked and the terrors of conscience are all testimonies that there is a good and just God, to whom all human beings are responsible. By the exercise of reason the human mind can know that things do not exist through themselves but depend on a prior transcendent cause.

This natural knowledge ought not, however, to be confused with speculations concerning the essence of God. Natural knowledge of God is knowledge of God's will toward sinners, not of his hidden nature.[27] Paul is a practical, not a speculative, theologian.

Unfortunately, the natural knowledge of God has been partly obscured by original sin. Human nature is so weakened by the fall into sin

---

d. *Pauli Epsitolas Commentarii* (Antwerp, 1544); and Veit Dietrich, *Annotationes Compendiariae in Novum Testamentum* (Frankfurt, 1545).

[23] Philip Melanchthon, *Commentarii in Epistolam Pauli ad Romanos* (Wittenberg, 1532). References are to Rolf Schäfer, ed., *Römerbrief-Kommentar 1532*, in *Melanchthons Werke in Auswahl* (Gütersloh, 1965). (Hereafter cited as *MW*).

[24] *MW*, 70: "Nam hanc notitiam de Deo naturaliter habent homines, quae quidem est notitia quaedam legis, non evangelii."

[25] *MW*, 71: "Habet enim quandam legis notitiam, non evangelii, sicut in ipso conscientiae certamine experimur, ubi cum notitia naturali et notitia legis acerrime pugnat evangelium.

[26] *MW*, 71–72: "Quamquam enim, ut postea dicit, mens ratiocinatur aliquid de Deo ex consideratione mirabilium eius operum in universa natura rerum, tamen hunc syllogismum ratio non haberet, nisi etiam Deus quandam notitiam *kai prolepsin* indidisset mentibus nostris."

[27] *MW*, 72: "Neque vero notitia Dei intelligi debet de speculationibus, in quibus quaeritur de essentia Dei, sed notitia Dei est notitia voluntatis Dei erga nos et notitia legis Dei, h.e. quod vere irascatur peccantibus, quod vere requirat iusta, quod iniustos puniat, quod exaudiat et servet iustos."

that it neither constantly assents to the knowledge it has nor obeys the eternal law written in the mind.[28] Melanchthon is particularly offended by the position of the Epicureans, who deny the providential care of God for creation, and by the stubborn opacity of idolaters, who cling to a false persuasion of God in their hearts.[29]

If Melanchthon's discussion is dominated by a characteristically Lutheran distinction of law and gospel, Bullinger seems preoccupied with a typically Zwinglian concern with superstition and the cultic use of religious art.[30] Bullinger believes that idolaters are particularly blameworthy because God has richly revealed himself to them in the natural order. Through the visible order they know that the invisible God is the omnipotent, true, wise, just, good, and supreme Being through whom all things subsist and by whom all things are governed.[31] This sentiment is found not only in Paul, but also in the Old Testament and in the writings of the pagan philosophers, especially in the writings of Seneca.[32] The Gentiles did not lack all knowledge of the truth and of true religion; rather, they abused the knowledge they had.[33] For Bullinger it is a short step from the pagan sin of idolatry to the cultic use of images by Christians.

The most extensive discussion of Romans 1 is found in Bucer's lengthy commentary on Romans.[34] Like Melanchthon, Bucer wants to

---

[28] MW, 71: "Quamquam autem naturae hominis quaedam legis notitia de Deo insita est, tamen haec ipsa notitia peccato originis aliqua ex parte obscurata est et nunc obruitur in impiis per alias rationes, ut, cum vident impii bonis male esse, sceleratis bene esse, discedunt a naturali notitia propter has offensiones et iudicant Deum non curare, non respicere humana. Ita delabitur mens humana in Epicureas opiniones." Cf. 74: "Porro haec naturalis notitia aliqua ex parte obscurata est a peccato originis. Nunc enim tanta est imbecillitas naturae, ut non constanter assentiatur huic notitiae, sed patiatur eam nobis excuti. Nec affectus oboediunt isti legi aeternae in animis scriptae, non timent Deum, non confidunt Deo."

[29] MW, 75: "Quod igitur hic dicit: 'Vani facti sunt per cogitationes suas', ad utrosque referatur, ad philosophos et idolatras, quod habuerint vanas, falsas et nihili opiniones de Deo et has falsas opiniones amplexi sint tamquam veritatem, sicut Epicurei mira securutate irrident omnes alios et se solos sapere gloriantur hoc nomine, quod ausint contemnere Deum."

[30] Heinrich Bullinger, In Sanctissimam Pauli ad Romanos Epistolam (Zurich, 1533), see especially 19v–28r. (Hereafter cited as Pauli).

[31] Pauli, 17v: "Et enim omnia in iis intelliguntur nempe si opera Dei exacto iudicio pensitentur. Deus enim per se omnium rerum est subsistentia, omnipotens, summus, verus, aeternus, bonus, sapiens et iustus. Caeterum harum rerum certissimum argumentum est moles mundi, quae in Deo subsistit. Potentia et sapientia eius condita est, iustitia et veritate regitur, bonitate vero et pulcherrima est et utilissima: quae sane non posset nisi aeternus, omnipotens et vere summus esset."

[32] Pauli, 18r: "Certe ut ex multis unum proferam, unus Seneca plus sincerioris theologiae posteritati reliquit, quam omnes fere omnium scholasticorum libri."

[33] Pauli, 18v.

[34] Martin Bucer, Metaphrases et Enarrationes Perpetuae Epistolarum d. Pauli Apostoli (Strasbourg, 1536), 82–100 (hereafter cited as Enarrationes).

emphasize both the external revelation of God in creation and the internal conception of God imprinted on the human mind. This innate *notio Dei* is so firmly implanted that it can never be expunged from the mind.[35] Bucer cites as proof of his contention the speech of the Stoic philosopher, Lucilius Balbus, in book two of Cicero's *De natura deorum*. For Bucer as for Melanchthon it is the innate knowledge of God that predisposes the mind to see the handiwork of God in nature.

Because God has revealed himself through nature and the human mind to the Gentiles, who do not worship him, it would seem that this revelation was given in vain. Bucer, however, wants to underscore Paul's point that God cannot be blamed for the failure of the Gentiles to make proper use of the witness of God in nature. Indeed, natural revelation takes away every human excuse.[36]

In his *Conciliatio locorum* Bucer distinguishes between two kinds of knowledge of God (*duplex notitia Dei*): (1) a general or natural knowledge of God given to all human beings who are sound of mind and body and (2) a full and solid knowledge of God, given by the Holy Spirit only to the elect, that generates love and reverence for God.[37] The former undercuts human excuses; the latter leads to eternal life. Therefore it can be rightly argued that the Gentiles both know God and do not know him.[38] They know God sufficiently to condemn themselves, but have no efficacious knowledge. While they know that God exists and glimpse something of his essence, they do not embrace and honor him as God.

The discussion has now moved far beyond the observation of young

---

[35] *Enarrationes*, 84: "Cum enim Deus se ipse hominibus revelet, ea quae de ipso fas est homines cognoscere, non possunt eos latere. Sic certe haec notio Dei, eum in omnia habere potestatem, et esse summum bonum, impressa et infixa est mentibus omnium, ut nemo, qui quod sentit verum, fateri velit, queat negare eam inditam divinitus. Quae enim non ab ipso naturae conditore in nobis notiones informantur, incertae, nec diuturnae, et eadem apud omnes esse solent. At Deum esse, omnibus innatum et quasi in animo insculptum est, et non solum una cum saeculis, aetatibusque hominum inveteravit, sed confirmatum auctumque semper est adeo, ut quamvis multis multo studio annitantur, nequeant tamen hanc Dei notionem ex animo expungere." See also the comments of Parker, *Commentaries on Romans*, 108–110 on Bucer's adaptation of the Stoic concept of *notio* to Paul's argument.

[36] *Enarrationes*, 86: "Omnis siquidem peccati defensio eo constat, quod quis non volens peccarit, viam quod quis ignorat non potest eligere, eoque videtur non volens peccare, quod peccat ignorans. Hinc Paulus veniam se consequutum scribit, quod Christum blasphemasset per ignorantiam. Proinde ubi Deus tollit sui ignorantiam, tollit simul nobis omnem excusationem contemptus sui apud nos."

[37] *Enarrationes*, 87–88.

[38] *Enarrationes*, 87–88: "Ex hiis iam satis liquet, utrumque vere dici, impios nosse Deum, et non nosse. Norunt siquidem Deum, norunt quae recta sunt, quantum ad id sufficit, ut seipsi condemnare compellantur. Rursus non norunt, quia non norunt efficaciter, ita ut spiritus Domini, quo ista Dei notitia constat, praevaleat, et diversum carnis iudicium opprimat, sed praevalet hoc illi, omneque quod a spiritu Dei est veri iudicium profligat."

Augustine that wiser Gentiles knew God the Creator through creation but abused that knowledge through pride. Nevertheless, if we compare the exegesis of Denis the Carthusian with the exegesis of Melanchthon, Bullinger, and Bucer, we can, I think, point to a general consensus on the meaning of Romans 1 that incorporates Augustine's point in a more complex and nuanced vision. All agree that there is a general knowledge of God from creation that is accessible to human reason apart from grace. This knowledge rests in part on inferences drawn from observation of the created order (Denis, Melanchthon, Bullinger, Bucer) and in part on an innate knowledge implanted in the human mind by God (Denis, Melanchthon, Bucer).

All agree that human reason, on whatever grounds, knows that God exists. Melanchthon insists that what fallen human reason knows is God's will toward us and not God's essence, though the qualities Melanchthon insists are knowable—that God is just, that he punishes the ungodly, that he hears and saves whoever is obedient to the law— are simply accepted by other theologians as perfections belonging to the divine essence.

All agree that while the natural knowledge of God is not saving—and may even need to be corrected by the gospel (Melanchthon)—it is, nevertheless, real knowledge. The problem is not with the quality or even the quantity of knowledge gained by human reason through the natural order. The problem is human sin, which has so weakened human nature (Melanchthon) that it rejects or abuses the knowledge that it has (Denis, Melanchthon, Bullinger, Bucer). As a result, the natural knowledge of God serves only to render fallen human beings inexcusable. A sub-theme in this discussion is a preference for Stoic philosophers (Bullinger, Bucer) and a distaste for Epicureans (Melanchthon, Bucer).

II

While Calvin repeats many of the themes developed by Denis, Melanchthon, Bullinger, and Bucer in his own exegesis of Paul, it is clear that Calvin intends to take the discussion in a somewhat different direction by focusing on the knowing subject and the noetic effects of sin. Calvin certainly agrees that human beings were "formed to be ... spectator[s] of the created world" and endowed with eyes to see "the world as a mirror or representation of invisible things" and so to be led through the contemplation of creatures to the praise of their divine Author.[39] While

---

[39] Translations into English are quoted from John Calvin, *Calvin's Commentaries: The Epistles of Paul to the Romans and to the Thessalonians*, trans. by Ross Mackenzie (Grand Rapids, 1973), 29–39. The Latin text was edited by T.H.L. Parker, *Iohannis Calvini*

Calvin, unlike Melanchthon and Bucer, does not speak of an innate knowledge of God, he does mention "a manifestation of God's character which is too forceful to allow men to escape from it, since undoubtedly every one of us feels it engraved on his own heart."[40] On the other hand, he immediately qualifies his sole reference to a knowledge "that God has put into the minds of all men," by adding, "He has so demonstrated his existence by His works as to make men see what they do not seek to know of their own accord, viz. that there is a God."[41]

Calvin repeats Paul's argument that pagans naturally know there is a God but "suppress or obscure" his "true knowledge."[42] While the natural order demonstrates the existence of God, it reveals, not God's essence, but knowledge accommodated to the limited capacity of human beings to comprehend God.[43] Calvin calls this a revelation of God's glory, which he defines as "whatever ought to induce and excite us to glorify God."[44] Calvin insists that all the works of God "clearly demonstrate their Creator."[45]

At this point Calvin breaks with the exegetical tradition since Augustine by distinguishing sharply between what is offered to natural reason and what is received. On the one hand, Calvin wants to insist that "the manifestation of God by which He makes His glory known among his creatures is sufficiently clear as far as its own light is concerned."[46] On the other hand, he wants to point to the fact of culpable human blindness. The difficulty is not with what is shown to fallen human reason through the natural order; the difficulty is with human organs of perception.[47]

Commentarius in Epistolam Pauli ad Romanos, Studies in the History of Christian Thought 22 (Leiden, 1981), 29.

[40] *Calvini*, 29: "hic tamen videtur voluisse indicare manifestationem qua proprius urgeantur quam ut refugere queant: ut certe eam cordi suo insculptam quisque nostrum sentit."

[41] *Calvini*, 30: "Hic aperte testatur, Deum omnium mentibus sui cognitionem insinuasse: hoc est, sic se demonstrasse per opera, ut illi necessario conspicerent quod sponte non quaerunt, esse scilicet aliquem Deum ..."

[42] *Calvini*, 29: "Veritas Dei, veram Dei notitiam significat. Eam continere, est supprimere, seu obscurare ..."

[43] *Calvini*, 29: "Quo verbo significat, Deum quantas est, minime posse mente nostra capi: sed aliquem esse modum intra quem se cohibere debeant homines: sicuti Deus ad modulum nostrum attemperat quicquid de se testatur. Delirant ergo quicunque scire appetunt quid sit Deus ..."

[44] *Calvini*, 29: "Intelligit autem id totum quod pertinet ad gloriam Domini illustrandum: vel (quod idem est) quicquid nos movere excitareque debet ad Deum glorificandum."

[45] *Calvini*, 29: "Deum per se invisibilis est: sed quia elucet eius maiestas in operibus et creaturis universis, debuerunt illinc homines agnoscere: nam artificem suum perspicue declarant."

[46] *Calvini*, 30: "Sit ergo haec distinctio: Demonstrationem Dei qua gloriam suam in creaturis perspicuam facit, esse, quantum ad lucem suam, satis evidentem: quantum ad nostram caecitatem, non adeo sufficere."

[47] In his treatment of Romans 8:20–22 Calvin admits that nature has been damaged by the fall, but that God preserves it from collapse until its renewal at the end time.

The metaphor of blindness, however, is too strong. If blind, then ignorant; if ignorant, then not culpable. The earlier exegetical tradition did not have this problem because it admitted that natural reason knows both that God exists and that God is just, powerful, and providential. Such knowledge is not saving, but it is nevertheless authentic. Calvin realizes that blindness overstates Paul's case and retreats to the metaphor of severely damaged sight. "We are not so blind," he concedes, "that we can plead ignorance without being convicted of perversity."[48] Or, as he says elsewhere, "we see just enough to keep us from making excuse."[49]

The thrust of his argument, however, is that, while human beings know that God exists, they misperceive his self-revelation in nature because of the noetic consequences of human sin. Since sin is a condition which is not natural to the human race, but a consequence of Adam's fall, the misperceptions of the revelation of God in nature are inexcusable. Fallen human beings therefore create fictitious new Gods, imaginary pictures, insubstantial phantoms, which they worship in the place of God.[50] Since all human beings, and not merely philosophers and intellectuals, seek "to form some conception of the majesty of God, and to make Him such a God as their reason could conceive Him to be," their "presumptuous attitude to God is not ... learned in the philosophical schools, but is innate, and accompanies us, so to speak, from the womb."[51] Even Plato, "the most sound-minded" of the philosophers, disappoints Calvin, because he "sought to trace some form in God."[52] In the end, the content of the natural knowledge of God expressed as natural theology is idolatry.

One further note, mentioned by Calvin but not developed, is introduced by a reference to Hebrews 11:3, which "ascribes to faith the light by which a man can gain a real knowledge [of God] from the work of

---

[48] *Calvini*, 30: "Caeterum non ita caeci sumus, ut ignorantiam possimus praetexere quin perversitatis arguamur."

[49] *Calvini*, 30: "Neque abs re: caecitate enim impedimur ne pertingamus ad scopum. Videmus eatenus nequid iam possimus tergiversari."

[50] *Calvini*, 31: "Eiusmodi virtutes quum non recognoverint homines in Deo, sed somniarint tanquam inane phantasma: merito dicuntur illum sua gloria improbe spoliasse." Cf. 31–32: "Postquam Deum talem finxerunt, qualem carnali suo sensu apprehendere poterant, longe abfuit quin verum Deum agnoscerent: sed factitium et novum Deum, vel potius eius loco spectrum sunt fabricati."

[51] *Calvini*, 31: "Nemo enim fuit qui non voluerit Dei maiestatem sub captum suum includere: ac talem Deum facere qualem percipere posset suopte sensu. Non discitur inquam haec temeritas in scholis, sed nobis ingenita, ex utero (ut ita loquar) nobiscum prodit."

[52] *Calvini*, 32: "Atqui talis audaciae scelere nemo eximi potest: non sacerdotes, nec legislatores: non philosophi, quorum maxime sobrius Plato, formam ipse quoque in Deo vestigat."

creation."[53] Calvin suggests that creation, which is no longer an effective source of the knowledge of God for fallen human reason, can be reclaimed as a source by believers who view the world with the light of faith and not merely with the light of natural reason.

If we compare Calvin's exegesis with the exegesis of Denis, Melanchthon, Bullinger, and Bucer, we find some points of agreement between them. All agree that the created world demonstrates God's existence and that human beings without exception know by nature that there is a God. Calvin even agrees that the world is a mirror of God's glory, and that it reveals enough of God's will and nature to stimulate human beings to praise and glorify God.[54]

However, Calvin demurs when the other interpreters of Paul argue that human beings have a reliable, if rudimentary, knowledge of the will or essence of God.[55] The problem is not with the objective revelation of God in nature but with the perception of God by fallen human reason. Human beings are very nearly blind because of sin. Since they know that there is a God and since they misperceive the self-revelation of God in creation, they worship idols in place of God. There is even a suggestion, not echoed by the other commentators, that faith will correct human blindness and enable human reason to reclaim creation as a reliable source for the knowledge of God.

III

These ideas, sketched in all too brief a form in the commentary on Romans, are expanded and developed in successive editions of the *Institutes*, beginning with the 1539 edition. For example, in the *Institutes* Calvin adopts the theme of an innate knowledge of God's existence (*sensus divinitatis*), advocated by Denis, Melanchthon, and Bucer, and missing or at best only hinted at in his interpretation of Romans 1.[56]

---

[53] *Calvini*, 30: "Quare Apostolus ad Hebraeos, fidei tribuit istud lumen, ut in mundi creatione vere proficiat."

[54] In this connection Muller, *Prolegomena*, 185, rightly observes: "The Barthian readers of Calvin go to great lengths to deny the existence of natural theology, while all that Calvin does is declare such theology useless to salvation. Calvin, in fact, consistently assumes the existence of false, pagan natural theology that has warped the knowledge of God available in nature into gross idolatry. Calvin must argue in this way because he assumes the existence of natural revelation which *in se* is a true knowledge of God. If natural theology were impossible, idolatrous man would not be left without excuse. The problem is that sin takes the natural knowledge of God and fashions, in fact, an idolatrous and sinful theology. The theology exists and man is to blame because it is sin and sin alone that stands in the way of a valid natural theology."

[55] *Calvini*, 30: "Concipimus Divinitatem: deinde eam quaecunque est, colendam esse ratiocinamur. Sed hic deficit sensus noster, antequam assequatur aut quis, aut qualis sit Deus."

[56] *Instistutes* 1.3.1. Muller, *Prolegomena*, 174, in discussing *cognitio insita*, prefers to

Furthermore, his clumsy use of a blindness "not so blind" is replaced by a more satisfying appeal to the metaphor of sight dimmed by age.[57] Blindness is now an acute astigmatism that can be corrected by the light of faith and the spectacles of Scripture.

What is striking, however, is the singularity of Calvin's reading of Paul. In the judgment of Calvin's contemporaries, Paul does not stress an acute noetic impairment because of sin or distinguish sharply between what is revealed in nature and what is perceived by fallen human reason. The thrust of Paul's argument, indeed, runs in the opposite direction. The point that Paul makes is not how little the Gentiles knew, but how much, considering the circumstances, they did know and how little use they made of it. By stressing the damage human reason has incurred through sin, Calvin makes the argument for the moral responsibility of the pagans all the more difficult to sustain.

Other Protestant theologians, of whom Melanchthon may be taken as representative, tend to argue that God is revealed in nature, that this revelation, however limited and inadequate, is nevertheless perceived by fallen human beings, who, precisely because of their sinfulness, proceed to suppress, distort, deny, ignore, forget, and abuse what they know.[58] Calvin argues, rather, that God is revealed in nature, that this revelation is misperceived by fallen human beings, who, precisely because of their sinful and culpable misperception, proceed to suppress, distort, deny, and abuse the true knowledge of God offered to them through the natural order.

Calvin avoids the difficulties he has placed in his own path by arguing that human blindness is culpable; but it is an argument which, in the form Calvin presents it, is not embraced by Denis, Melanchthon, Bullinger, or Bucer. These four commentators are joined in their dissent by Desiderius Erasmus,[59] Faber Stapulensis,[60] Martin Luther,[61] Huldrych Zwingli,[62] Johannes Oecolampadius,[63] Erasmus Sarcerius,[64] Andreas Knöpken,[65] Johannes Bugenhagen,[66] Thomas de Vio (Cajetan),[67]

---

speak of an intuitive knowledge basic to the mind to distinguish it both from innate knowledge in the Platonic sense and from discursive knowledge acquired by ratiocination.

[57] *Institutes*, 1.6.1.

[58] *MW*, 71, 74.

[59] Desiderius Erasmus, *In Novum Testamentum Annotationes* (Basel, 1535), 346–347.

[60] Jacobus Faber Stapulensis, *Epistole divi Pauli Apostoli: cum commentariis praeclarissimi viri Jacobi Fabri Stapulen* (Paris, 1517), 54v–56r.

[61] *WA* 56, 11–13, 174–179.

[62] Zwingli, *In Evangelicam Historiam*, 409.

[63] Johannes Oecolampadius, *In Epistolam b. Pauli Apost. ad Romanos Adnotationes* (Basel, 1525), 12r–15r.

[64] Erasmus Sarcerius, *In Epistolam ad Romanos*, on Rom. 1:18–32.

[65] Andreas Knöpken, *In Epistolam ad Romanos Interpretatio* (Nuremberg, 1524), on Rom. 1:18–32.

Johannes Lonicer,[68] Jean de Gagney,[69] Jacopo Sadoleto,[70] Ambrosius Catherinus Politus,[71] Marino Grimani,[72] Johannes Arboreus,[73] Claude Guilliaud,[74] Conrad Pellikan,[75] Alexander Alesius,[76] Wolfgang Musculus,[77] Johannes Brenz,[78] Peter Martyr Vermigli,[79] Domingo de Soto,[80] and Andreas Hyperius.[81]

There are, of course, repeated expressions of concern by Calvin's contemporaries about the inadequacy of the natural knowledge of God. The Dominican theologian, Ambrosius Catherinus Politus, for example, is troubled by the fact that, even if the Gentiles knew something about God through the natural light of reason, they could not glorify God without the supernatural gift of grace. If God therefore commanded the Gentiles to do what they could not do without grace, how could they be held responsible for their failure? Catherinus resolves his dilemma by arguing that the Gentiles knew enough about God to ask for divine aid and that God would have gladly given his grace to any who sought it.[82]

---

[66] Johann Bugenhagen, *In Epistolam Pauli ad Romanos Interpretatio* (Hagenau, 1527), on Rom. 1:18–21.

[67] Thomas de Vio, Cardinal Cajetan, *In Omnes d. Pauli et Aliorum Apostolorum Epistolas Commentarii* (Lyon, 1639), 5–7.

[68] Johannes Lonicer, *Veteris cuiuspiam Theologi Graeci succincta in d. Pauli ad Romanos Epistolam Exegesis, ex Graecis Sacrae Scripturae Interpretibus desumpta* (Basel, 1537), 6–7.

[69] Jean de Gagney, *Brevissima et facillima in omnes d. Pauli Epistolas Scholia* (Paris, 1629), 2r–2v.

[70] Jacobo Sadoleto, *In Pauli Epistolam ad Romanos Commentariorum Libri Tres* (Venice, 1536), 22v–23r.

[71] Ambrosius Catherinus Politus, *Commentaria in omnes divi Pauli et alias septem canonicas Epistolas* (Venice, 1551) 16–18.

[72] Marino Grimani, *In Epistolas Pauli, ad Romanos, et ad Galatas Commentarii* (Venice, 1542), 13r–14v.

[73] Johannes Arboreus, *Doctissimi et lepidissimi Commentarii in omnes divi Pauli Epistolas* (Paris, 1553), 4v–5r.

[74] Claude Guilliaud, *In omnes divi Pauli Apostoli Epistolas Collatio* (Paris, 1548), 6v–7v.

[75] Conrad Pellican, *In omnes apostolicae Epistolas, Pauli, Petri, Jacobi, Ioannis et Iudae Commentarii* (Zurich, 1539), 15–17.

[76] Alexander Alesius, *Omnes Disputationes de tota Epistola ad Romanos* (Leipzig, 1553), on Rom. 1:18–32.

[77] Wolfgang Musculus, *In Epistolam Apostoli Pauli ad Romanos* (Basel, 1555), 30–31.

[78] Johannes Brenz, *In Epistolam, quam Apostolus Paulus ad Romanos scripsit, Commentariorum Libri Tres* (Basel, 1565), 55–66.

[79] Peter Martyr Vermilgi, *In Epistolam S. Pauli Apostoli ad Romanos* (Basel, 1560) 57–67. See also the discussion by Muller, *Prolegomena*, 170–172.

[80] Domingo de Soto, *In Epistolam divi Pauli ad Romanos Commentarii* (Antwerp, 1550), 41–48.

[81] Andreas Hyperius, *Commentarii in omnes d. Pauli Apostoli Epistolas* (Zurich, 1584), 22–26.

[82] Ambrosius Catherinus Politus, *canonicas Epistolas*, 18: "Sicut enim Deus illuminavit eos, ut intelligerent quid esset eis faciendum ad salutem, ita non defuisset in praebendo opportunum (quo ea facere poterant) auxilium, si poposcissent."

Similarly, the Lutheran theologian, Johannes Brenz, agrees with Calvin that the natural knowledge of God was obscured by original sin. The fact that God gave Israel the Law and the prophets in order to clarify and confirm the natural knowledge of God impressed on human reason is an incontrovertible argument for its inadequacy.[83] Nevertheless, the Gentiles, who had no knowledge of the Mosaic Law, the prophets, or the Gospel, knew that God exists, that God is eternal, powerful, wise, good, and the governor of all things.[84] The obscurity which Brenz bemoans is a good deal clearer than the near blindness deplored by Calvin.[85]

The distinction between what is offered by God and what is received by fallen human beings is echoed in Calvin's eucharistic theology. The question had been posed many times whether unbelievers receive the body and blood of Christ when they take the elements of bread and wine. Calvin argues that the substance of Christ's body and blood is offered to the congregation in the eucharist, whenever it is celebrated, but can only be received by faith. Men and women who lack faith participate in the simple meal of bread and wine and but not in the spiritual real presence of Christ. Christ is truly offered, whether faith is present or absent; Christ is truly received, only when faith is present.[86]

In short, Calvin draws a distinction between what is offered and received that becomes a guiding principle of his thought, even outside the context of natural theology. In spite of the human fall into sin, the created order continues to function as a theater of God's glory. The whole world is, to use Bouwsma's phrase, "redolent with religious instruction." While fallen human reason perceives that God exists, it misperceives what God is like. Only when reason is illumined by faith, can it once again see the world for what it is, a mirror of divine glory. On this fundamental point Calvin is, I think, sometimes ambiguous but never ambivalent.

---

[83] Brenz *In Epistolam ... Romanos*, 62–63: "Indigemus igitur sacris literis, quae hanc obscuritatem et tenebras discutiant. Et in hunc usum promulgatus est Decalogus, et postea Prophetica scriptura explicatus: ut quae de Deo impressa erant humani rationi, illustrarentur et confirmarentur."

[84] Brenz, *In Epistolam ... Romanos*, 60: "Ex hoc mundo naturaliter cognosci potest, quod sit Deus, isque aeternus. Deinde ut essentia Dei per se non videtur, ita nec potentia, nec sapientia, nec bonitas, nec severitas eius videntur: proponuntur tamen humanae rationi, ex hoc mundo videnda. Cum enim ex administratione mundi intelligitur quod sit Deus: eodem intellectu comprehenditur etiam, quod is Deus sit potentissimus et sapientissimus."

[85] The same point is made by Melanchthon earlier, *MW*, 71, 74.

[86] *Institutes*, 4.17.33–34.

A LATE MEDIEVAL PARALLEL IN REFORMATION THOUGHT: *GEMINA PRAEDESTINATIO* IN GREGORY OF RIMINI AND PETER MARTYR VERMIGLI

FRANK A. JAMES III

I. INTRODUCTION: VERMIGLI AND GREGORY

More than twenty years ago, Philip McNair described Peter Martyr Vermigli as having sprung "ready-made out of the Alps one September day in 1542 like Minerva from the head of Jupiter."[1] Is this mythological accolade justified? Did Peter Martyr, the Roman Catholic Prior of San Frediano, enter the mainstream of the Protestant Reformation "ready-made?"

The extraordinary welcome that Peter Martyr received from the Zurich and Strasbourg divines provides ample justification for McNair's assessment. In October 1542, just days after Martyr's arrival in Strasbourg, Bucer wrote to Calvin "A man has arrived from Italy who is quite learned in Latin, Greek, and Hebrew and well skilled in the scriptures; he is about forty-four years old, of serious demeanor and keen intelligence. His name is Peter Martyr."[2] Bucer's description of him as being "quite learned," "well skilled" and a "serious" scholar of "keen intelligence" strongly suggests that, upon his arrival in Strasbourg, Martyr was already a theologian of considerable maturity. Bucer's words were followed with swift action. One month later, he arranged for Vermigli to succeed the late Wolfgang Capito at the Strasbourg Academy. The enthusiasm and speed with which Vermigli was welcomed into the higher echelons of Reformed Protestantism is staggering, especially when he had been so recently a prominent theologian in the Roman Catholic Church. This study is a preliminary exploration of the early intellectual and theological context which came to bear upon Vermigli and which warrants his being portrayed with such a provocative appelation as "ready-made."

It does not require great imagination to realize that Vermigli's chief

---

[1] Philip McNair, *Peter Martyr in Italy: An Anatomy of Apostasy* (Oxford, 1967), xiii.

[2] John Calvin, *Opera quae supersunt omnia*, eds., William Baum, Edward Cunitz and E. Reuss (Brunswick, 1863–1900), XI, c. 450, Bucer writes to Calvin, Oct. 28, 1542: "Advenit ex Italia vir quidam graece, hebraice, et latine admodum doctus, et in scripturis feliciter versatus, annos quadraginta, quatuor, gravis moribus et iudicio, acri, Petro Martyri nomen est."

theological qualification for the Strasbourg teaching post must have
been his profound Augustinianism.[3] All of the exegetical skills in the
world could not have merited Bucer's approval without an intensive
Augustinian theological perspective. While it must be recognized that
the meaning of Augustinianism in late medieval thought is multi-
dimensional,[4] our particular interest is drawn to the so-called *schola
Augustiniana moderna*, an intensive academic Augustinianism dedicated to the revival of the genuine theology of Augustine.[5] This theological tradition was imbued with the soteriology of Augustine and
especially associated with the name of Gregory of Rimini.[6] Within this
tradition, the doctrine of predestination is especially important, partly
because Gregory's exposition of this doctrine itself encompasses virtually every characteristic feature of the *schola Augustiniana moderna*,[7]
and partly because soteriological concerns are at the heart of Gregory's
Augustinianism. A careful examination of this tradition, especially the
doctrine of predestination will suggest that Peter Martyr Vermigli's
ready acceptance into Bucer's affections was due in large measure to
Vermigli's earlier absorption of the *schola Augustiniana moderna*.

Our point of departure in this study is a single comment from
Vermigli's funeral oration delivered by his disciple and successor at the
Zurich Academy, Josiah Simler. The funeral oration, which provides a
brief and remarkably accurate biography of Vermigli, recalls that, while
studying at the University of Padua, Martyr chiefly studied the theology

---

[3] Augustine was for Martyr, *summus theologus*. In Martyr's loci on predestination there
is an explicit correlation between Augustine and Martyr's doctrine of predestination. On
the opening pages Martyr specifically states he is following in the footsteps of Augustine
and cites two works in particular. See *In Epistolam S. Pauli Apostoli ad Romanos ...
Commentarii* (Basel, 1558), 405: "At rationes, quibus Augustinus se defendit, nostrum
quoque institutum tuerti postunt. Quare, quae hoc loco dicturi sumus, ea ex duobus eius
libris breuiter colligemus: quorum alter inscribitur, *De Bono perseverantiae*: ... alter *de
Correptione & Gratia*."

[4] David Steinmetz distinguished five meanings in the term "Augustinian." See David
Steinmetz, *Luther and Staupitz: An Essay in the Intellectual Origins of the Protestant
Reformation* (Durham, North Carolina, 1980), 13–16. Jaroslav Pelikan distinguishes a
three-fold use of the term "Augustinian". See Jaroslav Pelikan, *The Christian Tradition:
A History of the Development of Doctrine*, vol. 4: *Reformation of Church and Dogma
(1300–1700)* (Chicago, 1984), 17–19.

[5] For background concerning the *schola Augustiniana moderna* see the following:
Damasus Trapp, "Augustinian Theology of the Fourteenth Century: Notes on Editions,
Marginalia, Opinions and Book-Lore," *Augustiniana* 6 (1956), 146–274; Adolar Zum-
keller, "Die Augustinerschule des Mittelalters," *Analecta Augustiniana* 27 (1964):
167–262; Heiko A. Oberman, *Werden und Wertung der Reformation: Vom Wegestreit zum
Glaubenskampf* (Tübingen, 1977); Alister E. McGrath, *The Intellectual Origins of the
European Reformation* (Oxford, 1987).

[6] Heiko A. Oberman, *Masters of the Reformation: The Emergence of a New Intellectual
Climate in Euorpe*, trans. Denis Martin (Cambridge, 1981), 64.

[7] See Zumkeller, "Augustinerschule," 217–223; Cf. Martin Schüler, *Prädestination,
Sünde und Freiheit bei Gregor von Rimini* (Stuttgart, 1934), 39–70.

of Thomas Aquinas and Gregory of Rimini.[8] Modern scholars have focused their attention on the first part of Simler's comment, we shall pursue the other parallel between Vermigli and Gregory of Rimini.[9]

Simler's *Oratio* provides substantial evidence, that Vermigli encountered the writings of Gregory at the University of Padua and thus during the formative stage of his theological development. Two lines of Gregorian influence at Padua are probable. The first line of influence is somewhat unexpected. Simler informs us that Martyr studied under "two Dominicans" at the University of Padua, one of whom was Gaspare Mansueti da Perugia.[10] Although Gaspare was a Dominican, and therefore in the shadow of Thomas, nevertheless he was a probable source of Gregorian influence since he and his tutor in Perugia, Paolo da Soncino, admired and were well acquainted with Gregory's commentary on Lombard's *Sentences*.[11] A second line of probable influence is suggested by the fact that Vermigli also studied theology under an unidentified Augustinian Ermite.[12] Since Gregory was *Doctor Authenticus*[13] of the Hermits of St. Augustine, it is likely that the Ermite mentioned by Simler would have been well versed in the writings of Gregory of Rimini, especially since they were readily accessible.

Corroborating these two lines of Gregorian influence is the fact that Gregory's Commentary on the *Sentences* was frequently reprinted as a textbook and readily available in northern Italy. It was reprinted eleven times at major educational centers in Europe from 1481 to 1522. Of these reprintings, four were in northern Italy.[14] It is worth mentioning that Vermigli was not unique in acquiring an appreciation for Gregory

---

[8] Josiah Simler, *Oratio de vita et obitu viri optimi, praestantissimi Theologi D. Petri Martyris Vermilii* (Zürich, 1562), reprinted in *Loci Communes D. Petri Martyris Vermilii* ed., Robert Masson, (London, 1583), fourth page. (The *Oratio* is unpaginated) All subsequent citations of the *Oratio* are from this edition of the *Loci Communes*.

[9] See John Patrick Donnelly, *Calvinism and Scholasticism in Vermigli's Doctrine of Man and Grace* (Leiden, 1976), 27; Richard A. Muller, *Christ and the Decree: Christology and Predestination in Reformed Theology from Calvin to Perkins* (Grand Rapids, 1988), 61ff; Joseph C. McLelland, "Peter Martyr Vermigli: Scholastic or Humanist?" in *Peter Martyr Vermigli and Italian Reform*, ed., Josepch C. McLelland (Waterloo, Ontario, 1980), 141–151.

[10] Simler, *Oratio*, third page: "Debebam hoc loco Theologica quoque illus studia commemorare: tres enim Patuaij Theologos audunt, Heremitanum unam & duos Dominicani ordinis." McNair, 104, informs us of the name of the Dominican, Alberto Pascaleo da Udine (Albertus Vtinensis).

[11] McNair, 103–104. cf. Donnelly, 36.

[12] Simler, *Oratio*, second page.

[13] *Analecta Augustiniana* 7 (1917/18), 425.

[14] See F. Stegmüller, *Reportorium Commentatorum in Sententias Petri Lombardi* (Würzburg: 1947), VI, 178. It is noteworthy that in the late fourteenth century, the Florentine *Studio* contained a copy of Gregory's commentary on the *Sentences*. See also N. Bretano-Keller, "Il libretto di spese e di ricordi di un monaco vallombrosano per libri dati e avuti in prestito (sec. XIV; fine)," *La bibliofilia* 61 (1939), 145, 157.

while at Padua. About thirty years earlier, Giles of Viterbo, later Prior General of the Augustinian hermits, also studied at Padua (1490–1493) and like Vermigli, appreciated the thought of Gregory.[15]

II. GREGORIAN PARALLELS IN VERMIGLI'S DOCTRINE OF PREDESTINATION

In the course of his work on the new critical edition of Gregory's commentary on the *Sentences*,[16] Father Trapp offers this *caveat* to unwary readers: "Leafing through Gregory's pages one may be shocked by the predestinarianism, and ask oneself whether Gregory's God was the Mexican War God."[17] Gregory was probably unfamiliar with Mexican deities, but there was indeed a militancy in his defense of Augustine's doctrine of predestination. Gregory was the standard bearer of Augustinian thought, and prepared to engage all comers. As he makes clear in *distinctio* 40–41 of his commentary, Peter Auriole, Archbishop of Aix, was the latest reincarnation of Pelagius and the object of Gregory's theological chastisement. Gregory could hardly contain his contempt for Auriole whose theological position he judges, "does not escape the bounds of the Pelagian heresy."[18]

Peter Martyr was an heir to this Gregorian polemic. He takes the same antagonistic posture in defending Augustine's doctrine of predestination. Indeed, he was one of the early Reformation's principal apologists for a distinctively Augustinian doctrine of predestination. Over a century ago Charles Schmidt concluded that, after Calvin, Vermigli did more than any other Protestant theologian to establish this doctrine.[19] At three important junctures he championed the doctrine of predestination. In 1553, Peter Martyr jumped from the fire into the frying pan when he fled the reign of Mary Tudor and a re-Catholicized England to a Strasbourg increasingly dominated by contentious Lutherans. There he defended his doctrine of predestination against the Lutherans, who were led by Johann Marbach.[20] Matters seemed unresolvable when, in

---

[15] John W. O'Malley S.J., *Giles of Viterbo on Church and Reform: A Study in Renaissance Thought* (Leiden, 1968), 60–63.

[16] All citations include volume and page number according to Trapp edition of Gregory's commentary on Lombard's *Sentences*.

[17] Damasus Trapp, "Notes on the Tübingen Edition of Gregori of Rimini," *Agustiniana* 29 (1979), 238.

[18] *Lectura*, 1 Sent. dist. 40–41 q. 1 art. 2 (III, 335): "... quod forte non exit pelagianae heresis metas ..."

[19] Charles Schmidt, *Peter Martyr Vermigli: Leben und ausgewählte Schriften* (Elberfield, 1858), 106: "Da Martyr, neben Calvin, am meisten zur Festestellung dieser Lehre beigetragen hat ..."

[20] Simler, *Oratio*, thirtieth page.

1556, Martyr accepted Bullinger's invitation to succeed Conrad Pellican at Zurich.

If Vermigli thought Zurich a refuge from the storm, he was mistaken. Martyr arrived in July and soon thereafter found himself embroiled in a full blown "prädestinationsstreit."[21] Bullinger, while not a rigorous predestinarian, was respectful of Vermigli's view.[22] Theodore Bibliander, Bullinger's colleague at Zurich, was not so respectful. The Zurich theologians sided with Vermigli and Bibliander was eventually dismissed from his duties in February, 1560.

Even with Bibliander's dismissal, Martyr still was to see a third stage of controversy over predestination which required his intensive attention. After Vermigli left Strasbourg in 1556, Zanchi inherited the Reformed cause against the increasing influence of Marbach. To bolster his view, Zanchi composed fourteen theses on predestination[23] and turned to Vermigli and Zurich for theological support. The result was the Zurich confession on predestination of which Martyr was the principal author. Although this document was broader than Vermigli's own view, it affirmed support for Zanchi against the Strasbourg Lutherans. Throughout the course of his academic life, the doctrine of predestination proved to be nearly as constant a companion to Vermigli as his beloved Julius.[24] His willingness to defend it indicates the depth of his conviction.

Although dealing with different historical manifestations of perceived Pelagianism, there are remarkable parallels between the fourteenth century Augustinianism of Gregory and the sixteenth century Augustinianism of Vermigli. Time and again, the same issues are isolated and resolved with the same theological conclusions, often employing the same terms, and always based upon the same twin sources of Scripture and Augustine. What is perhaps the most significant parallel between the two theologians is the construction of the doctrine of predestination within a causal nexus. Indeed, both treatments are, at their core, extended theological essays differentiating the *causa* of predestination

---

[21] Joachim Staedtke, "Der Züricher Prädestinationsstreit von 1560," *Zwingliana* 9 (1953), 541.

[22] For an assessment of Vermigli's influence on Bullinger see Peter Walser, *Die Prädestination bei Heinrich Bullinger im Zusammenhang mit seiner Gotteslehre*, Studien zur Dogmengeschichte und systematischen Theologie (Zürich, 1957), 182ff; see also Staedtke, "Der Züricher Prädestinationsstreit von 1560," 543. A more recent analysis is J. Wayne Baker, *Heinrich Bullinger and the Covenant: The Other Reformed Tradition* (Athens, Ohio, 1980).

[23] For the full text of the Zurich Confession on Predestination see Johann H. Hottinger, *Historiae Ecclesiasticae Novi Testamenti* (Zürich, 1667), VIII, 843–847.

[24] McNair, 271–274.

from the *effectus* of predestination. The causal orientation had been dictated largely by the Pelagians who, according to both Martyr and Gregory, confused the two. In order to argue the Augustinian case properly, they turned to the *ordo salutis* schema in Romans 8:28–30, for the constitutive framework for the doctrine of predestination.

A comparison of their formal definitions of predestination illustrates the structural parallel. Gregory's formal definition of predestination is patterned after Augustine and closely parallels that of Vermigli. After accepting Augustine's classic definition (*quod praedestinatio est gratiae praeparatio*), Gregory offers his own more elaborate definition of predestination:

> the eternal purpose of God (*propositum Dei*) concerning the grace to be given and this grace, which Augustine tells us is the "effect of predestination," is threefold: calling, justification and glorification.[25]

Vermigli's formal definition is more detailed but follows precisely the same cause-effect structure.

> Predestination is the most wise purpose of God (*propositum Dei*) by which He has decreed firmly from before all eternity, to call those whom He has loved in Christ to the adoption of sons, to justify faith, and subsequently to glorify through good works, those who shall be conformed to the image of God, that in them the glory and mercy of the Creator might be declared.[26]

Both definitions represent the eternal *propositum Dei* as the ultimate cause of predestination which in turn produces the following soteric effects: vocation, justification and glorification. This overhearing structure governs both conceptions. Our analysis draws principally upon this causal nexus, in accord with which we will explore the doctrine of predestination under three headings: *propositum Dei*, *praedestinatio* and *reprobatio*.

A. *Propositum Dei*

To describe the very center of the causal framework, which provides the ground for his conception of predestination, Gregory employs the Augustinian phrase, *propositum Dei*.[26] A comparative glance at each

---

[25] *Lectura*, 1 Sent. dist. 40–41 q. 1 art. 2 (III, 321): "... id est praeordinatio vel electio seu propositum dei aeternum dandae gratiae, et ideo ipsa, ut ibi dicit Augustinus, 'est praedestinationis effectus'. Haec autem gratia in generali est triplex, scilicet vocatio, iustificatio et glorificatio ..."

[26] *Romanos*, 411: "Dico igitur, praedestinationem esse sapientissimum propositum Dei, quo ante omnem aeternitatem decreuit constanter, eos, quos dilexit in Christo, vocare and adoptionem filiorum, ad iustificationem ex fide, & tandem ad gloriam per opera bona quo conformes fiant imagini filij Dei, vtque in illis declaretur gloria & misericordia Creatoris."

formal definition reveals that it is precisely the same phrase which describes the causal foundation upon which Vermigli erects his doctrine. The *propositum Dei* is exclusively identified with the divine will;[27] but more than that, it is the *sovereign* will of God that dominates Gregory's and Vermigli's thinking about predestination. This is especially evident from the repeated reference to Romans 9, with its imagery of the potter and the clay, which nourishes both visions of the *propositum Dei*. Three characteristics stand out in their respective conceptions of the eternal will of God: it is free, omnipotent and all its actions are a matter of divine prerogative.

That God's will is absolutely free is clear from Gregory's reliance upon the powerful imagery of the Potter and the clay. "From the same lump of clay, which is wholly uniform, the potter selects one part sheerly according to His free will so that it may receive a perfect form sheerly according to His will and dismisses the rest."[28] This imagery also projects the immeasurable "power" (*potestate*) of the divine will to fashion his creation as he pleases.[29] So imbued with power is the divine will, Gregory declares: "*impediri non potest.*"[30]

Not only does Gregory's vision of the *propositum Dei* include divine freedom and omnipotence, but implicitly has to do with the divine *right* to exercise his will in any way He pleases. God, according to Gregory, has the ontological and moral right of the Creator-Potter to do with His clay what He wills. Like Vermigli, Gregory's understanding of the *propositum Dei* gets beyond the matter of freedom and power, to the matter of divine right.

The parallel between Gregory and Vermigli concerning the *propositum Dei* is nowhere more conspicuous. In sandwiching his *locus de praedestinatione*[31] between chapters 9 and 10 of his commentary on Romans, Vermigli clearly intended the reader to come to his theological treatment of predestination immediately after having encountered chapter 9 with its riveting imagery of the potter and the clay and the haunting Old Testament refrain, "I will have mercy upon whom I will have mercy" [Ex 33:19]. As with Gregory, Vermigli identifies the *propositum*

---

[27] *Lectura*, 1 Sent. dist. 40–41 q. 1 art. 1 (III, 323): "Est ergo praedestinatio ipsum velle seu propositum dandi vitam aeternam ..."

[28] *Lectura*, 1 Sent. dist. 40–41 q. 1 art. 2 (III, 345): "Talis autem electio utique potest esse inter aequales, sicut patet in exemplo Apostoli de figulo, qui ex eadem massa penitus uniformiter pro libito partem unam eligit, ut perfectam recipiat formam, et reliquam dimittit informem."

[29] *Lectura*, 1 Sent. dist. 40–41 q. 1 art. 2 (III, 340): "Et postea adhibuit exemplum de figulo, in cuius potestate est 'ex eadem massa facere vasa in honorem et vasa in contumeliam.'"

[30] *Lectura*, 1 Sent. dist. 40–41 q. 1 art. 3 (III, 349): "Tum quia voluntas dei impediri non potest."

[31] *Romanos*, 414: "Cum praedestinatio sit propositum seu voluntas Dei ..."

Dei exclusively with the divine will.[31] With such images and ideas permeating his thought, it is not at all surprising that his understanding of the *propositum Dei* is characterized by the same three features as Gregory. According to Vermigli, "God is a potter who has the power (*potestatem*) to make from the same lump of clay one vessel for honor and another for dishonor."[32] Moreover, the potter fashions the clay without any external constraints or any consideration beyond his own purposes. The sovereign will of God is indisputably free to elect Jacob and to reject Esau without considering their good deeds or mitigating circumstances.[33] The essence of the *propositum Dei* lies in the sovereign right of the Creator to do as he wills with his creation. Again the illustration of the potter and the clay in Romans 9 figures prominently. In a revealing passage, Vermigli juxtaposes divine power, divine liberty and divine right. Opponents, he replies, "rob God of his legitimate power (*potestate*) and liberty (*libertate*) in election, which are set forth by the Apostle when he says that God has no less of a right (*iuris*) over men than the potter has over the vessels which he makes."[34]

Although living in different eras and facing different philosophical and theological challenges, still the principal question surrounding the doctrine of predestination for Gregory as well as Vermigli was fundamentally one of causality. As was the case with Vermigli in the sixteenth century, the terms of the theological debate were drawn by the Pelagian opponents. In particular, Gregory developed his soteriological perspective against the background of two contemporary late medieval concepts, the *causa positiva* and *causa privitiva*.[35] The former represents a straightforward semi-Pelagian understanding of predestination: God predestines on the basis of foreseen good actions. These morally good human actions constitute the *causa positiva*.

But it was the second theological perspective identified with Peter Auriole that commanded most of Gregory's attention. Auriole accepted the notion of a foreseen *causa positiva* for reprobation, but he added a new theological twist on the matter of predestination. Instead of a *causa positiva*, Aureole posited a foreseen *causa privitiva* for predestination.

---

[32] *Romanos*, 415: "Nam, vt Paulus nos docuit in hac epistola, Dei solius est hoc efficere. Is enim tanquam figulus, habet potestatem ex eadem massa, faciendi vas aliud ad honorem, aliud ad contumeliam."

[33] *Romanos*, 417.

[34] *Romanos*, 418: "Nec animaduertunt isti, se, vt satisfaciant humanae rationi, & libertatem nescio quam, hominibus asserant, Deum sua legitima potestate & libertate in eligendo expoliare: quam tamen Apostolus praedicat, aitque non minus Deo iuris esse in homines, quam figulo in vasa fictilia."

[35] *Lectura*, 1 Sent. dist. 40–41 q. 1 art. 2 (III, 326): "Demum alii dixerunt [Auriole] quod praedestinationis nulla est in praedestinatis causa positiva, sed privativa tantum, scilicet absentia finalis obicis per culpam originalem vel actualem respectu gratiae dei, reporbationis vero est causa positiva in reprobis, scilicet talis obex peccati gratiae."

Under the inspiration of Paul's first epistle to Timothy (2:4), with its universalistic flavor fully appreciated, Auriole proposed the following salvific scheme. Auriole supposed that the first and most basic instinct of God is to will a universal salvation. However, Auriole was also a realist since God's will in this respect is not always effectual. If an obstacle develops, in the form of man's active resistance to God, then God's salvific intention will be frustrated in that case. Auriole retains enough of an Augustinian view of original sin to admit that there is no positive dignity in man which warrants predestination. However, in the absence of a foreseen obstacle, God's salvific will takes effect. Although one may not actively turn to God in faith and repentance, by simply not rejecting God, he will avoid eternal reprobation. In other words, as long as one does not positively resist God's salvific will, he will receive eternal life. While no man is in himself worthy of God's grace, some are not unworthy. The foreseen absence of unworthiness is sufficient to serve as the just basis for eternal predestination.[36]

In response to this Auriolean scheme, Gregory formulates five conclusions to refute what he considers to be nothing more than a variation on a Pelagian theme.[37] Three of the five theological conclusions are directed to the matter of predestination and may be summed up succinctly. Predestination, as Gregory sees it, is neither a matter of foreseen *causa positiva* nor foreseen *causa privita*, but of God's mercy alone. In the first conclusion, Gregory considers various opposing views, and whatever shape they take, he essentially counters with the same fundamental axiom: all human salvific involvement is in reality an effect of predestination not the cause. Indeed, no one can perform a good deed unless specially helped by God.[38] Advocates of the *causa positiva* are

---

[36] *Lectura*, 1 Sent. dist. 40–41 q. 1 art. 2 (III, 343), Auriole's view according to Gregory: "Secundo, 'agens universale agit in omne, quod non habet impedimentum', sicut patet de sole, qui in omnem partem aeris diffundit radios suos, nisi sit impedimentum. Sed, 'deus est ex sua bonitate agens universale volens omni creaturae rationali gratiam et salutem, offert enim, quantum est ex se, gratiam suam omnibus, 'qui solem suum facit oriri super bonos et malos'. Igitur omnibus dat gratiam et salutem nisi in illis sit impedimentum. Igitur quod aliquis careat salute et sit reprobatus, 'causa est positio impedimenti ab aeterno praevisa', quod vero alius sit praedestinatus, causa est negatio talis impedimenti."

[37] *Lectura*, 1 Sent. dist. 40–41 q. 1 art. 2 (III, 326): "Mihi autem videtur quod ex dictis scripturae et sanctorum sequuntur quinque conclusiones, cum quarum omnium veritate non stat veritas alicuius modi dicendi de praedictis. Harem prima est quod nullus est praedestinatus propter bonum usum liberi arbitrii, quem deus praescivit eum habiturum, qualitercumque consideretur bonitas eius. Secunda, quod nullus est praedestinatus, quia praescitus fore finaliter sine obice habituali et actuali gratiae. Tertia, quod quemcumque deus praedestinavit, gratis tantummodo et misericorditer praedestinavit. Quarta, quod nullus est reprobatus propter malum usum liberi arbitrii, quem illum deus praevidit habiturum. Quinta, quod nullus est reprobatus, quia praevisus fore finaliter cum obice gratiae."

[38] *Lectura*, 1 Sent dist. 40–41 q. 1 art. 2 (III, 331): "Multae aliae auctoritates possent

attacked under Gregory's banner which reads: "*Prima igitur est gratia, secunda sunt opera.*"[39]

In the second conclusion, Gregory performs corrective surgery upon what he views to be Auriole's defective concept of *causa privitiva*. In rather prolix fashion, Gregory refutes Auriole's contention that baptism is ultimately due to the impersonal "course of nature."[40] Baptism, whether of infants or adults, counters Gregory, is the *effectus praedestinationis*. The theological explanation why some infants die before baptism, while others die after baptism is bound up with the sovereign judgement of God.[41] Gregory's third conclusion merely states positively what he has already maintained negatively: "Anyone predestined was predestined from the mercy and gracious will of God alone."[42]

Like Gregory, Vermigli devotes the vast majority of his time in a *negative* effort to debunk what Pighius and the Pelagians have posited as the *causa* of predestination. In particular, Vermigli forcefully argues that the *causa* of predestination cannot be theologically construed in such a way that the divine will is conditioned upon future human actions, whether foreseen works or foreseen faith. Stated positively, the exclusive *causa* of predestination is the sovereign will of God. Whether intentionally or not, Vermigli's polemic against Pighius provides a remarkable parallel with Gregory's remonstrance against Auriole, not merely in temperament, but also in theological content.[43]

One noteworthy Vermiglian characteristic, reminiscent of Gregory's battle against Aureole, is the repeated use of the sacrament of infant baptism as a counter example. Vermigli's surfeit of scriptural references are bolstered by this sacramental scenario: a baptized (and presumably therefore redeemed) infant, who dies before performing any good works, illustrates that the salvation of such a one can not be based upon

---

adduci ad ostendendum quod ad nullum bonum actum agit homo vel coagit, nisi ad coagendum moveatur et iuventur a deo. ... Sed constat quod talis motio et divinum adiutorium respectu taliter boni usus est effectus praedestinationis, et non causa."

[39] *Lectura*, 1 Sent dist. 40–41 q. 1 art. 2 (III, 330.)

[40] *Lectura*, 1 Sent dist. 40–41 q. 1 art. 2 (III, 334): "Cum igitur non sit iustificatus nisi per baptismum, sequitur quod ideo fuit baptizatus, quia fuit praedestinatus, et sic non ex cursu naturae, sed ex divina praedestinatione consecutus est sacramentum."

[41] *Lectura*, 1 Sent. dist. 40–41 q. 1 art. 2 (III, 336): "Ex quibus verbis patet quod talis discretio est non naturali cursui, sed divino iudicio tribuenda."

[42] *Lectura*, 1 Sent. dist. 40–41 q. 1 art. 2 (III, 337): "Tertia conclusio, videlicet quod quilibet praedestinatus fuit praedestinatus ex sola misericordia et gratuita voluntate divina ..."

[43] Compare Gregory with Vermigli. *Lectura*, 1 Sent. dist. 40–41 q. 1 art. 2 (III, 337): "... probatur primo quidem ex praecedentibus, per quae monstratum est quod nec propter bona opera aut bonum usum liberi arbitrii nec propter carentiam culpae aut cuiuscumque reddentis hominem indignum vitae aeternae, quae deus praevideret futura, quisquam est praedestinatus, sed potius eius praedestinationem talia consequuntur." *Romanos*, 415: "His ista iam consititutis, reddendae sunt rationes, propter quas negamus, bona opera praeuisa esse causa praedestinationis."

foreseen works, since the infant performed none. Salvation must therefore be based upon the sheer grace of God. To those who rejoin: the infants predestination, in that scenario, would be based upon foreseen potential works that *would* have been performed had they survived into adulthood. Martyr surrejoins: "This is even more ridiculous!"[44]

In his classic work, *Justification et prédestination au XIVe siècle*, Paul Vignaux captures Gregory's predestinarian spirit with the appellation: "*Le Mystérie de la Prédestination.*"[45] For Gregory, the outworking of predestination in time is observable from its effects, but the mysterious cause lies in the ineffable and incomprehensible *propositum Dei* which lies back of predestination.[46] Vermigli's thought is suffused with the same sense of mystery. Referring to Romans 9, Vermigli asks:

> How in God's name can he [Paul] seem not to have resolved the question when he reduced it to the highest cause, namely the will of God? And this shows that we should not go any further. When God had appointed limits at the foot of Mt. Sinai, if any man had gone beyond those limits, he was by law punished. Therefore let these men beware when they boldly go beyond what Paul says."[47]

Vermigli and Gregory genuflect before the mystery of what they term the "deep wisdom of God"[48] and the "deep judgement of God"[49] respectively.

B. *Praedestinatio*

In a significant shift in late medieval orientation, Gregory parts company with Thomas by removing predestination from its Thomistic *loci* in

---

[44] Compare Gregory and Gregory on the topic of baptized infants who die. *Lectura*, 1 Sent. dist. 40–41 q. 1 art. 2 (III, 326–327): "Antecedens patet de pueris baptizatis morientibus in aetate infantili. ...

Ad hoc tamen conati sunt aliqui respondere dicentes quod, licet parvuli tales non fuerunt praedestinati propter usum bonum liberi arbitrii, quem habituri fuerunt, fuerunt tamen praedestinati propter eum, quem habituri fuissent, si ad aetatem debitam pervenissent.

Sed ista responsio nulla omnio est." *Romanos*, 417: "Neque enim quicquam habent, quod respondeant de paruulo, qui insertus in Christum infantili adhuc aetate moriatur. Nam si eum volunt esse seruatum, necesse est, vt fateantur, eum fuisse praedestinatum. At cum in illo nulla opera bona sequuta fuerint, Deus ea praeuidere certe non potuit: ... Ridiculum autem est, quod objiciunt, Deum preuidisse quid ille fuisset facturus, si diutius viuere contigisset."

[45] Paul Vignaux, *Justification et prédestination au XIVe siècle: Duns Scot, Pierre d'Auriole, Guillaume d'Occam, Grégoire de Rimini* (Paris, 1934), 165.

[46] *Lectura*, 1 Sent. dist. 40–41 q. 1 art. 2 *ad passim*.

[47] *Romanos*, 417: "Et quomodo tandem videri potest non soluisse, cum eam deduxerit vsque ad supremam causam? nimirum ad voluntatem Dei, ... Cum Deus posuisset terminos ad radices Sinai, si quis eos fuisset transgressus, legibus dedisset poenas. Videant ergo isti qua audacia longius ausint progredi, quam Paulus voluerit."

[48] *Romanos*, 423: "profoundissima Dei sapientia."

[49] *Lectura*, 1 Sent. dist. 40–41 q. 1 art. 2 (III, 340): "alta iudicia dei."

theology proper and relocating it to the realm of soteriology.[50] Nowhere in his formal discussion does Gregory categorize predestination in Thomistic terms—as *pars providentiae*. It is precisely this soteriological shift that characterizes Vermigli's doctrine of predestination.

Modern Vermigli scholars have tended to stress Thomistic[51] elements in Martyr's doctrine of predestination, in which case, one would expect predestination to be viewed as a sub-compartment of providence, hence a category of theology proper. While there are parallels and even formal doctrinal agreements at certain points, it cannot be denied that a profound difference of orientation exists between Thomas and Vermigli. However, the context in which Vermigli treats predestination demands a soteriological orientation. Unlike Gregory or Thomas, Vermigli chose to place his formal theological analysis of predestination within his scriptural commentary on Paul's epistle to the Romans. The *loci* on predestination is strategically placed at the end of the ninth chapter where soteriological concerns are paramount, at least according to Vermigli's exegesis. Indeed, for Vermigli the placement of predestination indicates his fundamental belief that it derives directly from Romans 8:28–9:33. Martyr does briefly touch on the relationship between providence and predestination, where it is quite clear that he does not follow the Thomistic view of predestination as *pars providentiae*. Indeed, Vermigli lays stress on the differences between providence and predestination. Providence, as he understands it, is a broader concept having to do with "God's governance and administration of His creation."[52] Vermigli's conception of predestination has a much narrower soteriological focus, which is clearly exhibited in his formal definition of predestination.

As an outworking of the soteriological context, both Augustinians understand predestination to be a purely and exclusively salvific expression of the divine will. Throughout his discourse, Gregory confines predestination exclusively to the elect.[53] Besides his formal definition, Gregory provides several abbreviated summations of predestination, which illustrate his usage. For example, he places himself squarely in the Augustinian tradition when he explains predestination as: "the eternal decree of God by which He decides beforehand to give grace to certain

---

[50] Oberman, *Masters*, 70.

[51] Donnelly, 27: "Martyr's career shows clearly that a Protestant theology could rest on a Thomistic base."

[52] *Romanos*, 410: "prouidentia omnes creaturas complectitur. ... Quod diximus, prouidentiam ad omnia pertinere. ... Obiter sic definiri potest prouidentia: est Dei ordinata, immobilis, & perpetua vniuersarum rerum administratio."

[53] *Lectura*, 1 Sent. dist. 40–41 q. 1 art. 1 (III, 322): "... praedestinatio vero de bonis tantum." Again in art. 1 (III, 323): "... Unde ille dicitur praedestinatus, cui proposuit deus dare vitam aeternam ..."

ones,[54] and as "the decree of giving eternal life."[55] From these summations, it is clear that Gregory understands *praedestinatio* in an exclusively positive sense of *praedestinatio ad vitam aeternam*. Any one of these summations could have come from the pen of Peter Martyr.

Vermigli's more elaborate treatment distinguishes between *praedestinatio communiter* and *praedestinatio proprie*, but reaches the same conclusion as Gregory. Perhaps out of deference to Calvin, Vermigli acknowledges that one may speak of *praedestinatio communiter* in which both the elect and the reprobate are included.[56] In this sense, "neither the wicked nor the devil himself, nor sins can be excluded from predestination."[57] From this perspective, it is virtually indistinguishable from providence. However, Vermigli adds that the scriptures "do not often use predestination in this sense," and hence, he confines himself to *praedestinatio proprie*, which refers to "the elect only."[58] Predestination then is presented as an exclusively soteric expression of the *propositum Dei*.

Christological concerns within the soteriological scheme are particularly important to both Gregory and Peter Martyr. At this point one must carefully determine whether it is the *propositum Dei* or *praedestinatio* which is in view. When speaking of the *propositum Dei*, both Vermigli and Gregory inalterably employ the unqualified designation "God," indicating the entire Godhead is in view, not just God the Father. Here, because the *propositum Dei* is *ab aeterno*, the Godhead is envisioned before specific functions are distinguished and, therefore, no particular person of the Trinity steps out for individual attention. There is for Gregory and Vermigli a theocentric orientation regarding the *propositum Dei*. Moreover, the Gregorian and Vermiglian conception of the divine purpose is properly viewed as the *voluntas Dei essentialis ad intra*, that is, the one, undivided, immanent will of the Godhead. It is an unconditional divine willing, logically antecedent to all things, predicated upon nothing but the nature of the divine essence.[59]

---

[54] *Lectura*, 1 Sent. dist. 40–41 q. 1 art. 1 (III, 322): "Patet ergo, quid nomine praedestinationis proprie datur intelligi, quia scilicet aeternum dei propositum, quo quibusdam gratiam dare praestitut."

[55] *Lectura*, 1 Sent. dist 40–41 q. 1 art. 1 (III, 323): "Et dico quod praedestinatio est propositum dandi vitam aeternam ..."

[56] *Romanos*, 409.

[57] *Romanos*, 409: "Hac ratione nec impij, nec diabolus ipse, neque peccata excludi possunt a praedestinatione: omnibus enim ijs rebus Deus vtitur, quomodo voluerit ..."

[58] *Romanos*, 410: "Caeterum Sacrae literae hanc vocem non facile vsurpant, nisi de electis."

[59] Both Gregory and Vermigli identify the *propositum Dei* with God Himself. *Lectura*, 1 Sent. dist. 40–41, q. 1 art. 2 (III, 325): "... quod non est intentio articuli ... quarere, utrum in praedestinatio sit aliquid quod sit causa illius entitatis, quae est praedestinatio, quae non est nisi dietas ipsa ..." *Romanos*, 414: "Cum praedestinatio, sit propositum seu

However, when the focus is on *praedestinatio*, there is a Christological undercurrent that swells to the surface. In the course of his argument against Auriole's notion of *cursu naturae*, Gregory makes it abundantly clear that Christ is the mediatorial centerpiece of predestination.[60] Accordingly, those baptized, whether as infants or adults, are in union with Christ their head, not because of the randomness of nature but because they are predestined to be "members of Christ."[61] It is through this soteric membership in Christ that all the effects of predestination are distributed to the elect.

Vermigli's understanding of the mediatorial role of Christ in *praedestinatio* finds both a conceptual and verbal correspondence to that of Gregory. "None," declares Vermigli, "is predestined except to this end, namely to be a member of Christ."[62] In this soteriological vision, Christ is the exclusive mediator through whom all of the soteric effects of predestination come to the elect, namely vocation, justification and glorification. Vocation, as Vermigli conceives it, has specific reference to the inward call of God whereby the mind is moved to contemplate the promises of God. Justification is a forensic declaration in which sins are forgiven and one is reconciled with God. Glorification essentially refers to the believer's sanctification, in which good works and holiness of life are progressively manifested. To Vermigli's mind, glorification also exhibits an eschatological quality, which begins as temporal sanctification and stretches into eternal glorification.[63]

By his collimation to the Gregorian emphasis on this point, Vermigli is distinguished from at least one notable Protestant Reformer, John Calvin. The Genevan Reformer envisions Christ not only as the mediator and object of predestination, but also as the author of predestina-

---

voluntas Dei, ea autem sit omnium rerum prima causa, quae idem est cum substantia Dei ..."

[60] *Lectura*, 1 Sent. dist. 40–41 q. 1 art. 2 *ad passim*.

[61] *Lectura*, 1 Sent. dist. 40–41 q. 1 art. 2 (III, 334): "Constat autem quod per baptismum fimus membra Christi. ... Ex his omnibus multipliciter patet evidenter quod, sicut humana natura in Christo ex aeterna gratuita praedestinatione divina unita est verbo et absque peccato concepta et nata, sic quicumque baptizati sunt, sive antequam crederent ut pueri sive postquam crediderunt ut adulti, hoc ex gratuita eorum praedestinatione consecuti sunt."

[62] *Romanos* 412: "Quos dilexit in Christo: Hoc addimus, quia quicquid Deus donat, aut se decreuit donaturum, dat id & daturus est per Christum. ... nos electos & praedestinatos esse in Christo. Is enim Princeps est, & caput omnium praedestinatorum: Imo nemo praedestinatur nisi ad id, vt efficiatur membrum Christi."

[63] *Romanos*, 320: "Hic [Rom 8:30] docemur, quae sint principia Ecclesiae, & elementia populi Dei. Est autem Ecclesia coetus, non humana ratione coactus, sed collectus praescientia, praedestinatione, & vocatione Dei. Ita respiciunt non succesiones vllus naturae, aut praerogatiuas, aut conditiones locorum: nam tantum pro Dei iudicio, & beneuolentia distribuuntur. Post vocationem statim subijcitur iustificatio. Inter quas cum nihil intercedere possit, nisi sola fides merito per eam dicimur iustificari: non quod ea sit, iustificationis nostrae causa: sed quod instrumentum sit, quo apprehendimus vocationem

tion, actually involved in the choosing of the elect.[64] Vermigli, on the other hand, does not view Christ as the author or cause of predestination. When contemplating the causal origins of predestination, the first cause is always ascribed to the *propositum* of the unparticularized designation "God," referring to the whole Trinitarian Godhead. Vermigli pictures God, in this unparticularized sense, actively electing certain ones, who are subsequently entrusted to Christ the mediator to accomplish redemption.

Martyr makes an interesting qualification regarding the role of Christ in election. When he denies that Christ is the *cause* or author of predestination, he carefully restricts himself to the "humanity of Christ."[65] He does not specifically address the role of the preincarnate second person of the Trinity. Presumably, logic would compel him to concede that the role of the preincarnate second person of the Trinity, insofar as he is undifferentiated from the other members of the Trinity, did also function as the "author" or cause of predestination. In the Vermiglian conception then, the mediatorial function of Christ in predestination is logically subsequent to the electing function of the Trinity.

Furthermore, the unique role of Christ (as distinguished from the other members of the Trinity) is, as Vermigli states, the "first and principal effect of predestination."[66] All the soteric benefits of predestination that come to the elect are mediated through the person and work of Christ, who is "the prince and head of all the predestined." In the Vermiglian conception, Christ is "*medius* and *mediator*, the midpoint and the go- between."[67]

As mediator, Christ is the guarantor and connecting link between the eternal cause and temporal effect of predestination. Following this Christocentric logic, Martyr views predestination not as a single act but a series of acts or links in a "golden chain"[68] of cause and necessary effect. Each effect of predestination in turn becomes the cause of the

---

nobis exhibitam per promisiones. Proprie vero causae iustificationis illiae sunt, quas Paulus hic assignauit, praescientia, praedestinatio, vocatio. Sita autem in eo est iustificatio nostra, vt nobis peccata condonentur, nosque Deo reconciliemur. At bona opera, sancta vita, instauratio virium, & dona Spiritus sancti postea consequuntur, & pertinent glorificationem: ad quam etiam ea spectant, quae expectamus danda in alia vita."

[64] John Calvin, *Institutio Christianae religionis* (Genevae, 1559), 3.22.7: "Hoc quidam tenendum est, vbi affirmat se scire quos elegrit, speciem aliquam notari in genere humano: deinde non distingui qualitate suarum virtutum, sed caelesti decreto. Vnde sequitur, multos proprio marte vel indutria excellere, quando se Christus electionis facit authorem."

[65] *Romanos*, 421.

[66] *Romanos*, 421: "Hic nos respondemus, Christum, & eius mortem praedestinationis primum & praecipuum effectum esse ..."

[67] Muller, 19. Although Muller's comment has reference to Calvin, it applies just as well to Vermigli.

[68] *Romanos*, 321: "Est haec graditio Apostoli catena vere aurea, qua homines beandi

subsequent effect.[69] Predestination causes vocation, which causes justification, which, in turn, causes glorification—and back of the entire predestinarian scheme is the *propositum Dei* for which there is of course no cause, since there is no cause of God.[70] Again, Vermigli's conception underscores the structural significance of Romans 8:29–30. His vision of predestination is panoramic, for it includes not only the eternal cause, but also its temporal outworking. Indeed, he insists that any definition of predestination is incomplete, if not improper, if considered in abstraction from its temporal effects.[71] A key to Vermigli's perspective is that the *propositum Dei* knows no essential distinction between the divine intent and its execution.[72] The sovereign will of God comprehends both purpose and accomplishment through the mediatorial work of Christ.

Vermigli's essential conception of *praedesintatio* is a virtual replica of Gregory's. Like Vermigli, Gregory visualizes *praedestinatio* as the first expression of a four-part diaphony of salvific events, including *vocatio*, *iustificatio* and *glorificatio*. As his definition suggests, each of these effects of predestination maintain a causal relationship to the other effects.[73] Especially noteworthy is the parallel vision in which predestination is not viewed piecemeal, but as a connected whole. Christ is for Gregory, as well as Vermigli, the inseparable connection between the eternal cause and its temporal effect. The *ordo salutis* provides the organizational framework for this soteriological understanding of predestination and informs his entire discussion. Underlying the causal structure of Gregory's doctrine of predestination is the *propositum Dei*, by which God intends to save those whom He has elected in Christ, and whose sovereignty invariably assures implementation.[74]

Although Gregory does not devote a separate article to the effects of predestination, as does Vermigli, he is nevertheless very concerned throughout his discussion to differentiate the proper causes from proper

---

trahuntur in coelum, multo praestantior, quam est illa Homerica, qua Iuppiter fingitur, orbem vniuersum regere."

[69] *Romanos*, 414: "Fieri quidam potest, vt effecta praedestinationis sic inter se conferantur, vt vnum sit causa alterius. Diuini autem propositi non possunt esse causae: Nam vocatio, quae est effectum praedestinationis, causa est vt iustificemur. Iustificatio etiam causa est bonorum operum: & bona opera tametsi causae non sunt, media tamen sunt, per quae Deus nos traducit ad vitam aeternam."

[70] *Romanos*, 414.

[71] *Romanos*, 412: "Quod autem effecta praedestinationis in eius definitione exposita sint, nihil est mirum. Haec enim definitio dari non potest, nisi correlatiua, vt vocant, experimantur."

[72] *Romanos*, 436: "... nihil enim potest extare, nisi quod Deus voluerit, & quod Deus vult, id nobis efficit."

[73] *Lectura*, 1 Sent. dist. 40–41 q. 1 art. 1 (III, 321ff).

[74] *Lectura*, 1 Sent. dist. 40–41 q. 1 art. 3 (III, 349): "voluntas dei impediri non potest."

effects. Gregory maintains that calling, justification and glorification are the proper effects of predestination.[75] It should be noted that while he does explicitly affirm that glorification is an effect in the definition, Gregory inexplicably devotes less attention to glorification as an effect of predestination. It appears that what is said of calling and justification he naturally assumes the reader will understand also applies to glorification.

There are other effects of predestination mentioned by Gregory. Absolution is described as an effect,[76] and Gregory, with reference to the apparent purification resulting from the martyrdom of the infants slaughtered by Herod, concludes that such cleansing is also an effect of predestination.[77] And for those who survive infancy to exercise faith, Gregory insists that such faith is itself a "gift of God."[78] Furthermore the "*divinum adiutorium*," without which no one performs good works, is itself an effect of predestination.[79]

It is noteworthy that Gregory, like Vermigli, does not include foreknowledge in his formal definition of predestination. It appears that *praedestinatio* and *praescientia* are so intimately bound up together in the eternal divine will that there is no need to give special treatment to foreknowledge.[80] Prescience does come to the fore when it touches Gregory where he is most sensitive, namely the cause of predestination. Indeed, he takes considerable pains to refute what he views to be a Pelagian notion, that foreknowledge, in any of its many forms, determines election. Suffice it to say, Gregory adamantly resists any suggestion that divine foreknowledge is the cause of divine predestination.

Peter Martyr's more sensitive understanding of the relationship of foreknowledge to predestination, however, does present him with an

---

[75] *Lectura*, 1 Sent. dist. 40–41 q. 1 art. 2 (III, 330): "Et confirmatur, quia, ut sancti et doctores communiter dicunt, vocatio et iustificatio sunt effectus praedestinationis .."

[76] *Lectura*, 1 Sent. dist. 40–41 q. 1 art. 2 (III, 333): "Ex quo sequitur quod absolutio et puritas a tali culpa est praedestinationis effectus."

[77] *Lectura*, 1 Sent. dist. 40–41 q. 1 art. 2 (III, 336–337): "Praeterea, quid dicetur de sanctis innocentibus, quos constat per martyrium fuisse ab originali culpa mundatos, si qui eorum non fuerant circumcisi, sicut forte plures eorum non fuerant, upote interfecti ante octavum vitae suae diem, quo secundum legem circumcidendi erant? ... Unde oportet hoc reducere solum in impietatem Herodis, quod insanissimum est, vel, quod verum est, in divinam providentiam, quae eos hoc modo salvare disposuit et ab originali culpa mundare, et per consequens talis mundatio est divinae praedestinationis effectus."

[78] Both Gregory and Vermigli stress that faith is a gift of God. *Lectura*, 1 Sent. dist. 40–41 q. 1 art. 2 (III, 332): "... fides sit donum dei." *Romanos*, 414: "fidem esse donum Dei."

[79] *Lectura*, 1 Sent. dist. 40–41 q. 1 art. 2 (III, 331): "... divinum adiutorium respectu taliter boni usus est effectus praedestinationis, et non causa."

[80] *Lectura*, 1 Sent. dist. 40–41 q. 1 art. 1 (III, 323). Gregory cites Augustine with approval. "His concordat sententialiter Augustinus in libro *De dono perseverantiae*, circa medium, ubi ait: 'Namque in sua, quae falli mutarique non potest, praescientia opera sua futura disponere, id omnino nec aliud quicquam est praedestinare.'"

intriguing dilemma. In Romans 8:29–30, the Apostle Paul had placed *praescientia* before *praedestinatio* in the *ordo salutis* sequence, therefore suggesting that foreknowledge acts causally to predestination. And yet, Vermigli's formal definition of predestination makes no mention of foreknowledge. This is especially noteworthy since he does in fact understand the *ordo salutis* as a causal sequence. According to his exegesis, Martyr resolves the tension as follows: *praescientia* (even though it is prior in the soteric sequence), functions conjunctively not causally.[81] Although *praescientia* is joined (*coniuncta*) to *praedestinatio*, it has primary reference to divine knowledge (*intelligentiam Dei*), which relates only to things future. On the other hand, *Praedestinatio*, although joined to *praescientia*, properly pertains to the divine will. In Vermigli's theological construction then, *praescientia* is viewed from two perspectives. First, from one perspective, *praescientia* and *praedestinatio* form an essential union. Second, within this union, *praedestinatio* is given logical priority to *praescientia*. Vermigli's reasoning is that divine knowledge of the future events is logically dependent upon a prior divine will to create such feature events. Therefore, although fundamentally joined together in the *ordo salutis*, *praedestinatio* is logically prior to *praescientia*.

Surveying the respective soteriological conclusions with regard to *praedestinatio*, one cannot avoid recognizing the extraordinary degree of correspondence in all essential matters. *Praedestinatio* is for both Gregory and Vermigli the positive soteric expression of the *propositum Dei*, which is portrayed within a causal nexus and revolves around a Christological axis.

C. *Reprobatio*

The idea of predestination, considered by itself, is unremarkable in late medieval thought. Some medieval theologians, including the mature Thomas, had clearly articulated a *praedestinatio ad vitiam aeternam* based solely on the sovereign mercy of God.[82] However, many other late medieval theologians nuanced the doctrine of predestination in such a way as to stress the efficacy of the human will, which was indicative of

---

[81] *Romanos*, 410: "Et idcirco praescientia requirit voluntatem, quae praecedat: nihil enim futurum est, nisi Deus id esse velit: Nam alioqui impediret. Praescit ergo Deus ea, quae vult esse futura: Deinde non omnes quos Deus praescit, eos etiam praedestinat: praescit enim reprobos, quos scit esse damnandos. Sed quemadmodum praescientia Dei voluntatem coniunctam habet, & tamen ad notitiam seu intelligentiam Dei pertinet: ita e diuerso praedestinatio, etsi absque praescientia esse non possit, tamen proprie ad voluntatem pertinet."

[82] See Thomas Aquinas, *Summa Theologiae*, 1a. 23. 2: "Unde manifestum est quod praedestinatio est quaedam ratio ordinis aliquorum in salutem aeternam in mente divina existens." cf. *Quaesto Disputate de Veritate*, q. 6 art. 1.

the general trend away from semi-Augustinianism toward a semi-Pelagianism, *de facto* if not *de jure*.[83] Gregory's Augustinian soteriology in general and his treatment of the dark side of predestination, that is, reprobation, represented one of the most substantial rebuttals to this trend in late medieval theology. Indeed, Gordon Leff suggests that the primary reason that Gregory is remembered in later generations is primarily because of this foreboding doctrine.[84]

Reprobation, as envisaged by Gregory and Vermigli, follows closely the Augustinian line. Gregory defines reprobation as "the eternal purpose of God (*propositum Dei*) whereby He preordained not to give grace, moreover He preordained a just eternal punishment for sins."[85] Vermigli's definition is more elaborate but presses in the same Augustinian direction:

> We may define reprobation as the most wise purpose of God (*propositum Dei*) whereby He has before all eternity constantly decreed without any injustice, not to have mercy on those whom he has not loved, but passes over, that by their just condemnation, he might declare his wrath toward sins and also declare his glory.[86]

At four crucial junctures, these definitions run parallel. First, the *propositum Dei* is the ultimate cause of reprobation. Second, reprobation is construed passively, that is to say, it is a withholding of divine mercy. Third, reprobation is distinguished from punishment which is based on sins. Finally, eternal reprobation is absolutely just. Each of these parallels will be considered in turn.

Many late medieval theologians and even some early Protestant theologians exhibited a certain reticence when it came to formulating a doctrine of reprobation, especially where it touched on the matter of divine causality.[87] Neither Gregory nor Vermigli follow this tendency. Both are unequivocal in their assertion that reprobation is not dependent upon foreseen sins and that the sovereign will of God is the ultimate and exclusive cause of reprobation. Gregory again develops his doctrine of reprobation against the backdrop of the *causa positiva* of the Pelagians and the *causa privitiva* of Aureole. His response to both is

---

[83] See Pelikan, 10ff.

[84] Gordon Leff, *Gregory of Rimini: Tradition and Innovation in Fourteenth Century Thought* (Manchester, 1961), 196.

[85] *Lectura*, 1 Sent. dist. 40–41 q. 1 art. 1 (III, 322): "... aeternum dei propositum, quo praeordinavit talem non dare gratiam, praeordinavit autem iustam pro peccatis aeternam poenam."

[86] *Romanos* 413: "Sit igitur reprobatio, sapientissimum Dei propositum, quo ante omnem aeternitatem decreuit constanter, absque vlla iniustitia eorum non misereri, quos non dilexit, sed praeterijt: quo iusta illorum condemnatione iram suam erga peccata & gloriam declaret."

[87] See footnote 22 for references to Bullinger's view of predestination.

nothing short of an extended exegesis of Romans 9, supported with the authority of Augustine. He maintains that, just as there is no foreseen *causa positiva* or *causa privitiva* for predestination, neither are there causes for reprobation. With the example of Jacob and Esau firmly in view, Gregory resolutely declares: "Just as God predestined eternally those whom He willed and did this not because of some future merits of theirs, so also He eternally reprobated those whom He willed, not because of their future demerits."[88]

Although two centuries had passed, Gregory and Vermigli upheld the same Augustinian soteriology against what they judged to be hetero-dox forces. Exhibiting much the same temperament as Gregory and very nearly the same words, Vermigli declares: "What we have already demonstrated with regard to predestination, that it does not depend on foreseen works, we also affirm with regard to reprobation, that it does not depend on foreseen sins."[89] And with a slight hint of sarcasm Peter Martyr sums up: "if sin were the true cause of reprobation, then no one would be elect."[90]

The matter of divine causality in reprobation naturally gives rise to the even more perplexing question of God's relationship to human sin. Gregory and Vermigli walk the same razor's edge, balancing the sover-eignty of God with human accountability. On the one hand, God does not "impose" sin upon earthlings who are fully responsible for their sinful actions. On the other hand, neither could deny that, in some sense, God is the cause of sin. With Romans chapter 9 as their common theological referent, both Gregory and Vermigli develop their analysis along the same theological lines and reached essentially the same conclusion. For Gregory God is the "immediate partial coefficient cause" of sin.[91] For Vermigli, "it can not be denied, but that God in a sense wills ... sin."[92]

---

[88] *Lectura*, 1 Sent. dist. 40–41 q. 1 art. 2 (III, 343): "Concludo igitur una cum Magistro distinctione 41 quod, sicut deus, quos voluit, ab aeterno praedestinavit et non propter merita aliqua futura, ita, quos voluit, ab aeterno reprobavit non propter demerita eorum futura."

[89] *Romanos*, 426: "Quod hactenus probauimus de praedestinatione, eam videlicet ab operibus praeuisis non pendere: idem etiam de reprobatione asserimus, quoniam nec ipsa pendet a praeuisis peccatis, modo intelligas per reprobationem non extremam damna-tionem, sed illud imum aeternum Dei propositum non miserendi ..."

[90] *Romanos*, 426: "Ad haec si peccatum esset vera causa reprobationis, tum nullus eligeretur ..."

[91] *Lectura*, 2 Sent. dist. 34–37 q. 1 art 3 (VI, 257): "Est ergo conclusio probanda quod actus mali, quem efficit peccator, deus est immediata causa, partialis tamen, coefficiens actum eundem. Hanc probo primo sic: Omnis actus malus iam factus, quamdiu est, immediate conservatur a deo; igitur omnis actus malus, dum fit, immediate fit a deo."

[92] *Romanos*, 423: "Vt huic difficultati satisfiat, primum meminisse debebunt, negari non posse, Deum quoquo modo velle, aut quemadmodum alij dicunt, permittere pecca-tum."

Undergirding this conclusion is the same basic presupposition, namely that all things without exception derive their existence and sustenance from the divine will or the *propositum Dei*. In Gregory's conception, divine causality of sin is linked to God's role as the ultimate ground of existence. Insofar as God is the creator and *conservator* of all things, He is the cause of all human actions, of sins no less than good works.[93] According to Vermigli, God is the cause of sin in the sense that he creates and "governs" (*gubernat*) all that comes to pass, including sinful men. "There can be nothing," asserts Vermigli, "except that which God wills to be."[94] The parallel extends beyond the divine creation and governance of sin. There is also the concern to remove from divine governance of sin any connotation of divine compulsion to sin. Exhibiting the same concern in very nearly the same words, Gregory's assertion, "God does not reprobate anyone by imparting malice (*malitiam*)."[95] is echoed by Vermigli: God does not "pour into us any new malice (*malitia*)."[96] For both Augustinians, the divine governance of sins is simply an acknowledgment that the overarching providence of God encompasses not only good works but also human sin.

Even the various refinements on this theological conundrum exhibit the remarkable degree to which Vermigli's theological perspective parallels that of Gregory's. We note three of the more important parallels:

(1) Both adopt Augustine's dual understanding of sin as *actus* and sin as *privati boni*. Insofar as sin is an act in distinction from what it produces, it is something in which God is the partial coauthor. But sin as privation is nothing, that is, something which has no existence and as such, it has no cause properly speaking.[97] In other words, God is not the author of sin as sin, but God is the partial coauthor of the act [as act] which produces sin. As L. Davis states it, "to sin is *agere male*; God is responsible for the *agere*, not the *male*."[98]

(2) Both acknowledge a certain divine asymmetry between the production of good and bad acts. In the production of good acts, God not only creates and sustains the act in itself, but God also actively moves the will to good acts. However, in the production of evil acts, divine causality is

---

[93] *Lectura*, 2 Sent. dist. 34–37 q. 1 art. 3 (VI, 258).

[94] *Romanos*, 436.

[95] *Lectura*, 1 Sent. dist. 40–41 q. 1 art. 2 (III, 347): "Non enim deus aliquem reprobat impartiendo malitiam, sed non impartiendo gratiam ..."

[96] *Romanos*, 413: "Quanquam nihil opus est, vt ab illo nobis infundatur noua malitia."

[97] Compare Gregory with Vermigli on sin as *actus* and as *privati boni*. *Lectura*, 2 Sent, dist. 34–37 q. 1 art. 2 (VI, 271–280); *Romanos*, 37.

[98] Leo Donald Davis, "Man, Intellect, and Will in the Writings of Gregory of Rimini," (Ph.D. dissertation, University of Wisconsin-Madison, 1981), 327.

confined to the existence and sustenance of the act in itself.[99]

(3) The most significant refinement made by both Gregory and Vermigli is the recognition of a deeper dimension to the relationship of the divine will and human sin. Although present in both, it is given more stress in Vermigli.

If the foregoing analysis is complete, as Leff seems to suggest with regard to Gregory,[100] then it would present in effect a deistic conception of God's relationship to human sin. In that case, God creates and sustains all human acts, good and bad, but is entirely removed from any real participation in the evil acts. This is true but incomplete. Gregory does acknowledge at least one sense in which God takes a more active role in human sin, that is, in some oblique way, God brings about sin as punishment for previous sin. The "hardening" in Romans 9:18 seems to have brought Gregory to this conclusion. In the fifth conclusion of article 2, he points out that both Augustine and Lombard interpret Paul's meaning as a temporal hardening, rather than eternal reprobation, an interpretation with which Gregory agrees. After citing Lombard, Gregory asserts that the hardening of Pharaoh's heart, is not only divinely wrought, but is also a merited punishment (*meruit poenam*) because of previous sins.

> The master does not take hardening to mean eternal reprobation but rather temporal obstinacy or hardening of the heart, whose merit (*meritum*) frequently is preceding sin (*praecedens peccatorum*), as is clear in the case of Pharaoh ... because of the cruelty which he inflicted on those to whom he owed humanity and mercy, he merited punishment (*meruit poenam*).[101]

This temporal hardening is sin (*peccato*) as Gregory makes plain.[102] All of this is not to suggest that Gregory understood God to be evil, but that his analysis is more complex than Leff admits.

---

[99] On divine asymetry in Gregory, see Davis, 328. For Vermigli, see *Romanos*, 423: "Deinde non est iusta collatio, quam isti faciunt, inter bona opera & peccata. Sic enim Deus facit in nobis opera bona, vt nobis gratiam & spiritum suppeditet, quibus illa fiant: nam ea bonorum operum sunt principia, quae profecto ex nobisipsis non habemus. Peccata autem ita gubernat & quodammodo vult, vt nihilominus illorum principia, hoc est caro corrupta & vitiata natura, non in Deo sint sed in nobis."

[100] Leff, 104–216. Davis, 326 criticizes Leff for not appreciating the "deeper level" in Gregory's understanding of God's relationship to human sin. In my judgement Davis is quite correct. Indeed, I wonder if Davis fully appreciates the depth of Gregory on this point.

[101] *Lectura*, 1 Sent. dist. 40–41 q. 1 art. 2 (III, 348): "Ad ultimam dicendum quod Magister non accipit obdurationem pro aeterna reprobatione, sed pro temporali obstinatione vel induratione cordis, cuius meritum est frequenter praecedens peccatum, sicut patet in Pharaone, qui, sicut dicit Augustinus ... propter crudelitatem, quam 'exercuit in eis, quibus humanitas et misericordia debebantur, meruit poenam ...'"

[102] Gregory identifies this temporal hardening as sin. See *Lectura*, 1 Sent. dist. 40–41 q. 1 art. 2 (III, 346).

Vermigli's analysis at this point parallels Gregory and differs only in that Vermigli gives it greater emphasis. At certain points in his treatise, Martyr employs language which goes beyond governance. Sins may be "inflicted" (*infliguntur*)[103] or "imposed"[104] upon men by God as divine punishment for prior sins. With rather striking directness, Vermigli writes:

> He [God] is the cause of those actions which in us are sins. Insofar as those actions are of God, they are justice, for God punishes sins by sins (*Deus enim peccata alijs peccatis punit*). Therefore sins as punishment (*Peccata ergo quatenus sunt poenae*) are laid (*infliguntur*) upon men by God as a just judge.[105]

The infliction of additional sins upon sinners is the sovereign prerogative of the potter over the clay.

Vermigli's treatment of God's role in Adam's sin is especially poignant. Adam's fall did not catch God unaware, for Vermigli observes, "God knew that Adam would fall if not confirmed by the Spirit and granted more grace and yet God did not help him or stop him from falling."[106] Moreover, it was within God's power to prevent Adam's fall, "but God did not."[107] Martyr does not claim to provide an explanation as to why God did not help Adam, he only defers to the sovereign prerogative of the Creator to do as He wishes in accord with his "hidden and unspeakable wisdom."[108] Neither does Vermigli shy away from the logical conclusion of his analysis for he states: "God in a sense (*quodammodo*) willed that first sin and was in a sense (*quodammodo*) the author."[109] Even more striking is Vermigli's three-pronged assertion

---

[103] *Romanos*, 413: "Peccata ergo, quatenus sunt poenae, hominibus a Deo, vt a iusto iudice infliguntur."

[104] *Romanos*, 414: "Nam peccata, & si, vt peccata sunt, a Deo legibus condemnentur: quantenus tamen sunt iustae poenae, ab eo irrogantur pro malis impiorum merits."

[105] *Romanos*, 413: "Certe, non potest Deus si recte ac proprie loqui velimus, causa peccatorum pronounciari: quem tamen a peccatorum gubernatione ac regimine haudquaquam possumus prorsus excludere, causa quippe illarum actionum est, que nobis peccata sunt: quamuis vt sunt a Deo, sint mera iustitia. Deus enim peccata alijs peccatis punit. Peccata ergo, quatenus sunt poenae, hominibus a Deo, vt a iusto iudice infliguntur."

[106] *Romanos*, 427: "Quo tamen ad peccatum primi hominis, animaduertendum est, illud non potuisse dici alterius peccati poenam. Si enim primum fuit, aliud ante se non habuit. Deum vero peccatum illud prorsus noluisse minime dici potest, eo enim inuito qui committi potuit? Porro videbat illum casurum, si spiritu & gratia opulentiori non confirmaretur: non occurit, non supposuit manum suam ne caderet."

[107] *Romanos*, 427: "Reprobatio vero si comparetur primo homini, Deus illum ab aeterno decreuit producendum, vt libero arbitrio & aliqua gratia sibi adiuncta stare posset, si vellet: potuissetque illi maiorem conferre gratiam, ita vt neque cadere posset, verum noluit."

[108] *Romanos*, 431: "... quare non immerito dicimus ipsum decreuisse quosdam eximere, alios autem relinquere, idque iuste: cuius tamen iustitiae causae non sunt ex operibus nostris quaerendae, quum ipsi Deo constent ex eius arcana ineffabilique sapientia."

[109] *Romanos*, 427: "Vnde apparet Deum illud peccatum quodammodo voluisse, ac eius quadantenus fuisse authorem, licet non fuerit poena praecedentis peccati."

that God presented Adam with the "opportunity to sin," "a wife who enticed him to sin," and finally, "the act of disobedience itself could not have occurred without the power of God."[110] Not only did God permit and sustain Adam's sin, but God intentionally presented Adam with an opportunity for sin as well as an enticement to sin.

The second major parallel derived from their formal definitions, is that both interpret reprobation as a passive expression of the sovereign will of God. For both, the essence of reprobation is found not in what it does, but in what it does *not* do. In both cases, reprobation is characteristically described as "not to have mercy," or "passing over" (*praeterit*).[111] Reprobation in neither instance conjures up visions of a dispassionate deity arbitrarily hurling helpless victims into a lake of fire. Rather the image is one in which God actively rescues some sinners, but mysteriously passes by others.

The third major parallel gleaned from their respective definitions, is that both Gregory and Vermigli adopt precisely the same distinction between reprobation and condemnation. According to Gregory, there is a difference between the cause of *reprobatio* and the cause of condemnation. Reprobation is passively understood as the eternal will of God not to bestow mercy on some. The divine will acted in absolute freedom, according to the divine inscrutable wisdom and without giving any consideration to foreseen meritorious deeds. The cause of reprobation is very clear for Gregory: "God purposed *not* to be merciful to some. This is properly the reason (*ratio*) for reprobation. Why He purposed, we are not able to assign any reason outside His own good pleasure."[112] There is however, a different cause for eternal condemnation. The reason for God's punishment is sin (*peccatis*). "On account of their guilt (*culpas*), original or actual or both, He wills to give them punishment."[113] Of course, those on whom God does not bestow mercy

---

[110] *Romanos*, 427: "Diabolus praeterea, nisi Deus voluisset, illum non ausus esset tentare. Destinauerat praeterea suam bonitatem & seueritatem ex illo declare: occasionem dedit, Legem dum posuit, quam sciebat non seruandam, nec non vxorem dando, quae alliceret. Et denique actio ipsa, quam priuationem rectitudinis, vt subiectum sustinuit, citra Dei vim & virtutem produci non potuit."

[111] Compare Gregory with Vermigli. *Lectura*, 1 Sent. dist. 40–41 q. 1 art. 1 (III, 323): "Reprobatio vero est velle non misereri seu, quod idem est, propositum non dandi vitam aeternam ..." *Romanos*, 413: "His verbis significatur, omnes natura sua esse in miseria. ... Ex hac miseria Deus aliquos liberat, & hos dicitur diligere: Alios praeterit, & illos odisse dicitur, cum eorum non misereatur. Quo iusta illorum condemnatione iram suam erga peccata, & iustitiam declaret."

[112] *Lectura*, 1 Sent. dist. 40–41 q. 1 art. 3 (III, 353): "Unum est quod deus proposuit se aliquorum non misereri, et in hoc proprie consistit ratio reprobatiois. Et cur sic proposuerit, non est aliquam causam praeter suum placitum assignare ..."

[113] *Lectura*, 1 Sent. dist. 40–41 q. 1 art 3 (III, 353): "Aliud est quod talibus, quorum proposuit non misereri, praeparavit etiam pro peccatis poenam debitam. Et ideo, quamvis non propter eorum culpas nolit deus misereri, id est dare vitam aeternam, tamen propter

will inevitably sink in the quicksand of original sin and commit innumerable actual sins for which they must be punished. There is then for Gregory, a difference between the passive divine will not to show mercy and the active divine will to punish sinners.

Vermigli's theory of causality in reprobation maintains the same theological distinction between *reprobatio* and *condemnatio*.[114] Reprobation has reference only to the decision not to have mercy in eternity past, and its cause lies in the inscrutable sovereign will of God. Condemnation, on the other hand, has a temporal referent whose cause lies within the matrix of original and actual sins. "Sins are the cause of damnation but not the cause of reprobation."[115] Divine willing in the case of condemnation is reactionary rather than initiatory. God's role in condemnation is confined to the institution and execution of the general principle that sins are to be punished. Condemnation, as we will see, is the expression of divine justice. So then, the "true cause" of condemnation is sinful man, but the true cause of reprobation is the mysterious and unfathomable *"propositum Dei."*[116]

The fourth and final parallel we observed concerns the matter of divine justice in reprobation. As both formal definitions indicate, there is a concern to protect the judicial-ethical integrity of the divine will. Vermigli echoes Gregory in maintaining that the divine will is just in condemnation as well as in reprobation. In condemnation, God's will exercises a forensic justice. God holds man accountable for his violations of divine standards and is just in condemning all sins, whether original sin or actual sin.[117]

Moreover, both theologians also insist that the reprobative will of God is just, even though it is expressed in eternity past before the existence of human sin. In this sense a forensic justice is not in view but an essential justice. In other words, God's will by its very nature is just. On this point, Gregory's analysis is somewhat less developed than Vermigli. Yet, there can be little doubt, that for Gregory, God's will is,

---

eorum culpas originales vel actuales aut utrasque vult eis dare poenam. Et ista voluntas iustissima est."

[114] *Romanos*, 425: "Neque adeo absurdum est, vt ipse fingit, peccata cadere sub reprobationem: non quidem vt eius causam, sed vt condemnationis & aeternae miseriae causam."

[115] *Romanos*, 414: "... peccata causae quidem sunt, cur damnemur, non tamen cur a Deo reprobemur.

[116] *Romanos*, 413: "Nec tamen propter haec omnia, peccatorum nostrorum vere causa dici potest, cum veram peccatorum causam satis in nobis ipsis habeamus."

[117] *Romanos*, 413: "Iusta dicitur horum damnatio, quoniam propter peccata illis infligitur. Neque tamen hinc inferre debemus, peccata praeuisa causam esse, cur quisquam reprobetur. Ea enim non efficiunt, vt Deus proposuerit nolle misereri. Causa tamen sunt damnationis, quae sequitur vltimo tempore, non autem reprobationis, que fuit ab aeterno."

by its very definition, just in all its willing. He writes: "it stands firm that he [God] reprobates some and finally willed that they not be saved, which He wills by His incomprehensible and irreprehensible just judgement (*justo judicio*)."[118] Gregory's affirmation of this essential justice of the divine reprobating will is, in the final analysis, an act of faith. Vermigli is more explicit: "God does no injustice to any man although he does not bestow his mercy on some. For God is not bound to any law nor is He compelled to have mercy on any man. God says in the Gospel [Matt 20:15] 'Is your eye wicked because I am good? Is it not lawful for Me to do with My own what I will?'"[119] The divine reprobating will is just because it is a rightful exercise of its inherent prerogative as Creator. Once again the imagery of the potter's right over the the clay looms large in Vermigli's thought. At this point the essential justice of God's will blends into divine right.

III. Gemina Praedestinatio

From the preceding analysis it should be clear that both Gregory and Vermigli taught a thoroughgoing doctrine of *gemina predestinatio*. Neither conception quite approaches the double predestination of Calvin, but they genuinely qualify as double in view of the salvific polarity that issues from the one will of God. The key difference between our Italian Augustinians and Calvin is that the former takes a distinctively passive approach to reprobation, distinguishing between preterition (the will to bypass some) and condemnation (the will to punish those who are passed by for their sins), while Calvin, on the other hand, tends to minimize the passive understanding of reprobation in favor of an active stress on condemnation. It is clear, however, that both Gregory and Vermigli accept as valid the same Calvinistic line of reasoning, that if the divine will, possessed of perfect wisdom, power and sovereignty, predestines some, it necessarily implies a corresponding reprobation of the rest. With all three, this logic is nurtured by the Pauline juxtaposition of Jacob's election and Esau's rejection with the imagery of the potter and the clay in Romans chapter 9.

Modern interpreters of Gregory, while differing on many other interpretative points, nevertheless agree that Gregory teaches a doctrine of

---

[118] *Lectura*, 1 sent. dist. 40–41, q. 1 art. 2 (III, 348): "Cum istis autem stat quod aliquos reprobavit et velit finaliter non salvari, quod etiam ipsum velle incomprehensibili et irreprehensibili suo iusto iudicio ..."

[119] *Romanos*, 413: "Non enim obstringitur cuiquam vllo iure, aut tenetur ex debito cuiusquam misereri. Itaque; respondet Deus in Euangelio [Matthew 20:15]. An oculus tuus nequam est, quia ego bonus sum? Nonne licet mihi facere quod volo de meo? Idem Paulus docuit ex potestate figuli. Asserit tamen nullam ea causa iniustitiam cadere in Deum."

gemina predestintio.[120] There is not quite the same unanimity concerning Vermigli's doctrine of predestination. Although there is a general consensus among Vermigli scholars that his doctrine of predestination should be properly designated double,[121] there has been one dissenting vote. Joseph C. McLelland, over thirty years ago denied that Vermigli taught double predestination.[122] Based upon the preceding analysis we are compelled to agree with McLelland's critics on this point.

What is more debatable and more complicated is the correlative question of whether their doctrines of double predestination are oriented toward supra- or infralapsarianism. There is something of an interpretive dilemma because both Gregory and Vermigli adopt apparently conflicting orientations. At one point Gregory sounds remarkably infralapsarian while at other points he appears to be a convinced supralapsarian. The parallels between Gregory extend even to this soteriological ambiguity, for Vermigli gives the same conflicting impressions. Others have recognized this problem with regard to both Augustinians. Heiko Oberman touched on this question in his book on Bradwardine and concluded that there is a sense in which Gregory is both supra- and infralapsarian.[123]

Vermigli scholars are divided as to the proper categorization of his doctrine of double predestination. Reinhold Seeberg describes Martry's doctrine of predestination as "extreme supralapsarian."[124] Donnelly concurs in this assessment.[125] But more recently, Richard Muller's analysis of Vermigli's doctrine of predestination has challenged this traditional characterization. While acknowledging the overarching sovereignty of the *propositum Dei*, Muller insists that Martyr's view "presses ... toward a purely soteriological and essentially infralapsarian definition of predestination."[126]

The ambiguity can be resolved, I believe, by recognizing the distinction between *sub specie aeternitatis* and *sub specie temporis*. When addressing the *causa* of predestination or reprobation, both Gregory and Vermigli express themselves from the vantage point of eternity and

---

[120] See Schüler, *Prädestination*, 46ff. Cf. Heiko A. Oberman, *Archbishop Thomas Bradwardine, a Fourteenth Century Augustinian: A Study of His Theology in its Historical Context* (Utrecht, 1958), 219; and Gordon Leff, *Gregory of Rimini: Tradition and Innovation in Fourteenth Century Thought* (Manchester, 1961), 197.

[121] See Muller, 66–67 and Donnelly, 132.

[122] Joseph C. McLelland, "The Reformed Doctrine of Predestination According to Peter Martyr," *Scottish Journal of Theology* 8 (1955), 259.

[123] Oberman, *Bradwardine*, 220.

[124] R. Seeberg, *The History of Doctrines* (Grand Rapids, Baker Book House, 1952), II, 421.

[125] Donnelly, 137.

[126] Muller, 65.

the *propositum Dei aeternum*. From this perspective, the divine will acts prior to anything temporal, including the fall and its consequences. Speaking *sub specie aeternitatis*, there is a supralapsarian orientation. However, the *propositum Dei aeternum* is carried out in history, and this is the principal theological sphere in which Gregory and Vermigli develop their doctrine of double predestination. Therefore, when addressing the question of predestination and reprobation *sub specie temporis*, the Adamic fall is the fundamental presupposition before all soteriological discussion. In this sense, which is most often the case in both treatments, there is a distinctly infralapsarian cast to their thought. It is also worth noting that Vermigli's Christological orientation inclines him toward a more infralapsarian conception. Since Christ is the first effect of predestination and is exclusively associated with saving sinners, Vermigli's primary emphasis in predestination tends to infralapsarianism.[127]

Although Gregory never specifically addresses the issue of the order of the decrees, the distinction between *sub specie aeternitatis* and *sub specie temporis* is implicit throughout. Pighius, however, forced Vermigli to address this issue by directly raising the question of sequence in eternity with regard to reprobation. Vermigli's response evidences this same perspectival distinction.[128] On the one hand, the basic soteriological movement in Vermigli's thought is infralapsarian, that is, to see predestination as the rescue of sinners, and correspondingly, he stresses condemnation as a just punishment of sinners, rather than reprobation *in se*. On the other hand, he only reluctantly moves into the realm of the *propositum Dei aeternum* where none dare tread unless pressured by Pighius!

Interestingly, when Vermigli does enter the dominion of the *proposi-*

---

[127] For Vermigli's infralapsarian orientation see *Romanos*, 411: "Meminisse etiam debemus amorem, electionem, & praedestinationem Dei ita inter se ordinari certa ratione consequantur. Primum notitiae Dei offeruntur omnes homines non foelices, imo egeni & miseri, quos Deus pura simplicique misericordia diligit, eis bene vult, illosque discernit ab alijs, quos praeterit, & sua beneuolentia non complectitur, atque hac discretione dicuntur eligi: electi autem ad finem destinantur."

[128] *Romanos*, 425–426: "Fingit postremo loco Pigghius absurda a nobis dici, quod homines doceamus prius esse in massa vitiata & corrupta peccato originis quam a Deo praedestinentur, quasi velimus hic Dei propositum iustificare: cum tamen in consilio praedestinationis prius ponamus condemnationem & aeternam infoelicitatem, quam ipsa peccata & vitiatam nostram originem, atque ita iustificamus quod est prius per posterius. Addit etiam ita quo ad Dei propositum nostra ipsorum sententia finem praestitui, & ea quae ad finem perducunt: vnde cum peccatum originis vnum sit ex medijs quo condemnamur, non posse, quemadmodum fingimus, reprobationem antecedere: cum sub illa cadat & comprehendatur quasi medium ad aeternam condemnationem. Verum haec ostendunt hominem istum non intelligere quid a nobis dicatur. Nec Augustinus neque nos vnquam diximus originalem culpam antecessisse praedestinationem, cum praedestinatio sit ante omnem aeternitatem, & Adamus in tempore lapsus fuerit."

tum Dei aeternum, he tends to leave behind the scriptures and depends on logic.[129] It is within the realm of the *propositum Dei* that supralapsarian tendencies emerge. And since this is not the realm in which he is most comfortable, Vermigli only enters rarely. The sphere in which he is most comfortable is Scripture and the effects of predestination in time, which propel him toward a more evident infralapsarian perspective.

For these two Italian Augustinians, the central core of the doctrine of double-predestination is the *propositum Dei*. With equal ultimacy, divine reprobation and divine predestination issue from the same *propositum Dei*. It is this remarkable parallel that forms the nucleus of their soteriological outlook.

IV. Epilogue

The head of Gregory of Rimini has worn many crowns, not all of his own choosing: *tortor infantium, antesignanus nominalistarum* and *Doctor Authenticus*, but of all the laurels bestowed on him, none has been more fitting than that granted by Damasus Trapp: "the first Augustinian of Augustine."[130] Although the authority of Augustine was never lacking in the Western medieval church, it had suffered a relative eclipse by the end of the 13th century. Illustrative of Augustine's slippage in stature is the fact that the Bishop of Hippo is virtually absent from the Thomistic hierarchy of Dante's *Divine Comedy*. But in the meridian of the 14th century. Bouwsma observes, "a fresh breeze had begun to blow in the old European atmosphere."[131] The authority of Augustine reemerged triumphantly borne on the wings of two Italians—Gregory of Rimini and Francesco Petrarch. If Dante's world relegated Augustine to the shadows, Petrarch's *Secretum* made him the very embodiment of wisdom.

Gregory figured prominently in the Augustinian resurgence on two fronts: the recovery of the whole corpus of Augustine's writings, thus freeing theologians from reliance on various medieval compendia, and the critical excision of apocryphal material. What is more, Gregory inaugurated a distinctive tradition, especially within his own order, but also finding a wider audience among certain Italian humanists for whom Augustine's theology, especially his soteriology, was the measure of true Christianity. Among the characteristic features of Gregory's purified

---

[129] *Romanos*, 425ff. In this section, Vermigli refers to not one scriptural passage, which is quite out of character.

[130] Trapp, "Augustinian Theology of the 14th Century", 181.

[131] William J. Bouwsma, "The Two Faces of Humanism: Stoicism and Augustinianism in Renaissance Thought," in *Itinerarium Italicum: The Profile of the Italian Renaissance in the Mirror of its European Transformations*, ed. Heiko A. Oberman with Thomas A. Brady Jr. (Leiden, 1975), 35.

Augustinianism, also designated the *schola Augustiniana moderna*, was the doctrine of predestination.

Any attempt to understand Peter Martyr Vermigli's doctrine of predestination must begin by appreciating his late medieval intellectual context. It should not be forgotten that Vermigli was born in Florence, where Augustinianism was no less prominent than humanism. One need only be reminded that in the century before Vermigli's birth, Florence was governed by the Augustinian humanist Caluccio Salutati.[132] Florence was also touched by Gregory's influence. One of Salutati's intimate friends was Luigi Marsili an Augustinian monk who studied under Gregory at Paris.[133] Perhaps it was Marsili, who placed a copy of Gregory's commentary on the *Sentences* in the Florentine *Studio*.[134] If McNair is right, Vermigli's decision to enter the Canons Regular of St. Augustine at Badia Fiesolana was inspired by another famous Florentine Augustinian, Fra Mariano Della Barba da Genazzano.[135] With such an Augustinian heritage in Florence, it is not surprising that Vermigli found Gregory congenial during his theological studies at Padua.

The Florentine environment had predisposed young Vermigli to a general appreciation of Augustine, but it was in the rarefied atmosphere at Padua that Augustine became the brightest star in Vermigli's patristic galaxy. Simler's *Oratio* provides us with strong evidence that it was Gregory who directed Vermigli to the intensive study of Augustine as an interpretative guide to holy scripture. Gregory's battle cry was, after all, *ad fontes Augustini*. What is especially significant is that Vermigli's decisive encounter with Augustine under the tutelage of Gregory, was precisely at the formative stage of Vermigli's theological development. Under the burden of Steinmetz's important reservations concerning the link between Gregory and Luther,[136] Vermigli's early introduction to Gregory of Rimini is a crucial factor in the proper interpretation of the Gregorian parallels in Vermigli's doctrine of predestination.

Steinmetz raised other interpretative concerns which bear upon our analysis of Gregory and Vermigli. Steinmetz rightly points out that the existence of theological parallels may indicate a common theological source rather than direct theological influence.[137] In the case of Vermigli the question may be asked, if Gregory is so important for Vermigli's

---

[132] See Ronald G. Witt, *Hercules at the Crossroads: The Life, Works, and Thought of Coluccio Salutati* (Durham, North Carolina, 1983).

[133] Charles Trinkaus, *In Our Image and Likeness: Humanity and Divinity in Italian Humanist Thought*, 2 vols. (Chicago, 1970), I, 61.

[134] Brentano-Keller, 145, 157.

[135] McNair, 54.

[136] Steinmetz, 16–27.

[137] Ibid.

doctrine of predestination, why then is he never cited? The fact that Vermigli does not cite Gregory in his *loci* on predestination is not in itself decisive. It can legitimately be argued that Vermigli heeded Gregory's call *ad fontes Augustini*, that is to say, Vermigli saw no need to cite the intermediary (no matter how significant), when he could refer more authoritatively to the source. The publication of the Amerbach edition of the *Opera Omnia Augustini* in 1506 greatly facilitated direct access to Augustine.[138] The fact of the matter is that Gregory intended to be a conduit through which his students could encounter the two primary foundations for Christianity: Augustine and Paul. Indeed the very fact that Vermigli does not cite Gregory is, in a roundabout way, an indication of Gregory's influence. Furthermore, as Oberman[139] has shown, historical context is a crucial factor in interpretation. In the case of Vermigli, it needs to be stressed that he had an intellectual context in which Gregory played an important, and perhaps determinative, role in his theological outlook.

There is one final question. Was Vermigli's doctrine of predestination derived primarily from the Protestant Reformation which was already underway when he apostatized? It must be admitted that Vermigli did in fact read Protestant literature while still in Italy.[140] Within Vermigli's intellectual sphere, there were diverse influences which came to bear upon him in varying degrees, including early Protestant writings. There are several qualifications one must also consider when assessing the level of Protestant influence upon Vermigli. (1) There is no evidence that Vermigli encountered Protestant literature during the formative stage of his theological development. Indeed, the only positive proof is that he did read Protestant literature a decade later in Naples while involved in the Valdesian circle. (2) Protestant influence cannot account for the Gregorian parallels in Vermigli's doctrine of predestination. (3) Furthermore, virtually all Vermigli research has turned up one vital fact, namely, that Vermigli's theology was remarkably developed before his entry into Protestantism, a view that Bucer seems to have also held, as his actions in Strasbourg suggest. (4) Finally, Vermigli's doctrine does not appear to be derived from any particular Protestant theologian. It cannot be denied that certain Protestant reformers may have prompted some later refinements, but these were born from the give-and-take interaction of theological peers. There are parallels among the early

---

[138] Oberman, *Masters*, 71.

[139] Heiko A. Oberman, *Forerunners of the Reformation: The Shape of Late Medieval Thought Illustrated by Key Documents* (Philadelphia, 1981), 32–43. See also Oberman, "Headwaters of the Reformation: Initia Lutheri—Initia Reformationis," in *Luther and the Dawn of the Modern Era*, ed. Heiko A. Oberman (Leiden, 1974), 40–88.

[140] McNair, 148–149.

Reformed theologians, but there are also important differences, especially on the matter of predestination. It appears therefore, that a theologian of Vermigli's calibre cannot be accounted for by making him dependent on those for whom he is more likely a source rather than an object of influence. What is being suggested here is that Vermigli's context was one in which the pivotal influence at the formative stage of his theological development was not Protestant theology, but Gregory of Rimini.

Bucer's ready acceptance of the apostate Roman Catholic Prior of San Freidano into the hallowed halls of the Strasbourg Academy calls for an explanation. The answer I believe, lies in the young Vermigli's direct encounter with Gregory's Augustinianism which left its impact upon him throughout his Protestant career and accounts for the Gregorian parallels in his doctrine of predestination. Gregory of Rimini planted Augustinian seeds in late medieval Catholicism that bore fruit in Peter Martyr Vermigli, the "ready-made" Protestant.

HILTALINGER'S AUGUSTINIAN QUOTATIONS

DAMASUS TRAPP, O.S.A.

The biography of Johannes Hiltalinger de Basilea, O.E.S.A., was written half a century ago by Hermann Haupt with such competency that little need be added. In spite of the fact that this biography has been published in two great German Encyclopediae.[1] Hiltalinger to this day remains practically unknown.

Johannes Hiltalinger became Lector at Avignon in 1357, taught as such at the *Studium Generale* in Strassburg, and within a short period gained so great a reputation for learnedness that Jordan of Saxony, O.E.S.A., dedicated to him his *Vitasfratrum*.[2] He read[3] as Baccalarius Parisiensis ca. 1365–66 while Simon de Cremona[4] was probably '*Baccalarius Secundarius Augustiniensium*'.

As Baccalarius Formatus Hiltalinger held his *Decem Responsiones* (10 RR): RR 1–5 in Paris before 1368; R 6 in Toulouse before 1368; R 7 in Avignon probably at the General Chapter on Pentecost, 1368; RR 8–10 in Paris after 1368. The *Magistri Opponentes of the Decem Responsiones* were as follows: Johannes Cusin, O.P. (R 1); Johannes Romani O.E.S.A. (R 2); Johannes de Calore—later Chancellor of the University (R 5); Bartholomaeus de Ripario, O.P. (R 6); Facinus de Ast, O.E.S.A. (R 7); the *Prior de Zerbona* (R 8); Simon Freron of the

---

[1] cf. *Realencyklopädie f. prot. Theologie u. Kirche* VIII (1900) 77–78 and *Allgemeine Deutsche Biographie* L. (1905) 341–342.—H. Haupt's necrologue with a list of his works—several of which are of great interest for scholastic studies on the 14th c.—is found in: *Nachrichten der Giessener Hochschul-Gesellschaft* XI, 1 (1936) 15–28. A copy was graciously forwarded to the writer.—I use this opportunity to thank all libraries which provided microfilms, and all librarians who generously opened their rich stores of knowledge whenever I had to appeal to them.

[2] cf. *Jordani de Saxonia Liber Vitasfratrum*, ed. Arbesmann-Hümpfner, O.E.S.A. (New York, 1943), Introd. XX, XLVII sq., LIII sq., LVI.

[3] By some scholars the *Lectura* of Hiltalinger has been assigned to a rather late date; cf. A. Zumkeller, *Hugolin v. Orvieto u. seine theol. Erkenntnislehre* (Würzburg, 1941) 99–100.—The chronology of the 14th century is complicated by the fact of the 'marginalia shift' as shown later in this article (see: footnote 17).

[4] Simon de Cremona O.E.S.A. has left all his Four Books in the MS Cremona 118. On f. 153ᵛ Simon tells us that he held his *Responsio Prima* under Mag. Johannes Romani O.E.S.A. Under the same Magister Romani, Hiltalinger 'answered' in his *Responsio Secunda* (10 RR r. 2). As Romani was in a great hurry to leave Paris (cf. Denifle, *Chart.* III n. 1291, p. 111), Simon and Hiltalinger chronologically were very close together because only newly created Magistri used to 'oppose' in a *Responsio*.

Navarra College (R 9); the Augustinian Nicolaus de Amatrice '*in Aula*' together with the Magistri Guillelmus Arnaldi and Guillelmus (de Salvarvilla) Cantor Parisiensis (R lù).

In the year 1371 Hiltalinger attained the goal of his scholastic career, the Magisterium. With the title of Magister Parisiensis well earned, he left Paris immediately and repeatedly became Provincial of his home province. Rapidly he rose to greater dignities. At the General Chapter of 1377 he was appointed Procurator General of the Order and by virtue of office was henceforth closely associated with the papal Curia. During the election riots of Urban VI it was Baduario–Peraga,[5] Prior General of the Augustinians, who played his part in tranquillizing the Romans; and right after the election Hiltalinger, Procurator General of the same Order, had the honor of preaching before the new pope.[6]

When the French Cardinals left the obedience of Rome, Hiltalinger followed them[7] and became anti-general of the Augustinian Order under the Avignon obedience. We need not interpret this decisive step in Hiltalinger's career as political opportunism, because even saints like Vincent Ferrer were in the Avignonese fold and promoted its cause. Hiltalinger was such an active agent for Avignon that Rome finally published against him the M a n d a t u m   c a p t i v a n d i,[8] whereupon Avignon made him a bishop at Lombez near Lourdes. He died in 1392 and was buried at Freiburg i. B.

Hiltalinger[9] was a brilliant personality endowed with a surprising capacity for work and organization. He lived in a period of intense literary and theological activity and followed the historical trend of the mid-century theology, leaving us a theological legacy which, without exaggeration, might be called a *Petit dictionnaire de la théologie du XIVe siècle*.

His extant works are a complete *Lectura*, the *Decem Responsiones*, the incomplete *Vesperiae*, and a *Sermo Optimus*. His lost works comprise a *Quolibetum* and a *Lectura super Epistulam*.

---

[5] cf. D. Perini, *El B. Buenaventura Baduario-Peraga* (Santiago de Chile 1925) 39. Perini also publishes (*ibid.* 49–50) the Bull of Clement VII which makes Hiltalinger General under Avignon.

[6] cf. Mich. Seidlmayer, *Die Anfänge des grossen abendl. Schismas* (Münster 1940) 279; 'Et iste testis [fr. Menendus O. Min.] vidit ipsos septem cardinales in missa cum papa in dicto festo. Et fecit sermonem m a g.   J o h a n n e s   d e   B a s i l e a, et Cardinalis Aragonensis [Petrus de Luna] dixit tunc Evangelium'.

[7] cf. Perini, *l.c.*, 49–50.

[8] cf. Gerd Tellenbach, *Repertorium Germanicum II* (Berlin 1933) 25 sq. and 28. The same 'M a n d a t u m   c a p t i v a n d i Roberto [Clementi VII] adhaerentes' is issued twice on the same day: March 7, 1389. On one addressee is living in the diocese of Basel, the other in Prague. In both M a n d a t a 'Johannes de Basilea alias dictus de Hiltelingen' heads a list of fifteen persons to be captured.

[9] A more detailed biography of this great son of St. Augustine will be published apart.

Hiltalinger's manuscripts are few: Clm 26 711, Toulouse 248, Fribourg Cordeliers 26, Basel F II 9; Wien Nat. 4319 (10 *Responsiones* + 3 *Quaestiones* from the Third Book), Einsiedeln 45 (*Sermo Optimus*). All manuscripts are of a date close to Hiltalinger's; two of them (Basel F II 9 and Toulouse 248) were even manuals of Hiltalinger himself.

The manuscripts of Peter Gracilis, O.E.S.A., Jacobus de Altavilla, O. Cist., Henricus de Hassia and Angelus Dobelin. O.E.S.A., are of great help because they often copy from Hiltalinger whose extant works will be published in about five volumes within a few years.

To put Hiltalinger in the correct perspective, it is necessary first to characterize the context and the framework of 14th c. theology. This is not an easy task since sweeping generalizations have created the impression that the mid-century theology is blasé and eclectic, sophisticated and skeptic, fitting into the strait-jacket of n o m i n a l i s m.[10] As a matter of fact, the theology of the 14th century is still under a cloud and could stand further probing.

Tempted to find another common denominator one might identify the mid-century theology as positive and historical-minded. Going through the texts of the 14th century the observing reader cannot fail to ascertain that several of these decried theologians saw the urgent need of revitalizing their speculation through better firsthand research in older sources, especially Augustine, Proclus, Dionysius, Boethius, Anselm, Lincolniensis, etc.

At least t h r e e   f a c t s can be adduced to prove this changed mentality of the 14th century. F i r s t, better facilities for quoting were generally adopted by 1350, especially codified capitulations of those Fathers and *Authentici* whom the scholastics were wont to consult. S e c-o n d, the esteem for older manuscripts, already noticeable at the beginning of the 14th century, was greatly on the increase. T h i r d, there did exist a group of theologians who prided themselves on their accuracy of quoting.

A positive mentality never develops suddenly. When by the mid-century we find that the chapter division of the Fathers and *Authentici* was well advanced in the stage of codification, we must realize that we are approaching the end of a long process which presupposes that the

---

[10] 'Nominalism' as applied to the 14th century seems to be a retroactive terminology. In years of MSS studies I have never found the term 'nominalista' in any MS before 1385. The 15th century used this epithet for the 14th c. theologians who in reality called themselves 'Moderni'. In an article on 'Nominalism' (*Dict. Théol. Cath.* XI, 1: 717–784), P. Vignaux simply postulates

Moderni   =   Occamistae
Occamistae   =   Nominalistae
Ergo Moderni =   Nominalistae Q.E.D.

scribes had consciously and conscientiously copied chapters and chapter numbers for many years. Today, after the advent of print, it would be enough to edit one copy in order to codify chapter divisions. In the age of the manuscript, however generations of copyists had to be convinced of the importance of these numbers; otherwise, they would never have been generally adopted.

The many *Tabulae*,[11] especially the *Milleloquium Augustini* and the *Milleloquium Ambrosii*, would never have been possible without established chapter division. The chapter division in its turn could not have been codified nor widely used without the facile Arabic number system, the triumph of which remains forever the glorious achievement of the 14th century.

'Capitulation' is the basic quoting facility in any period; in the present era of print pagination ranks next. In the age of the manuscript, 'f o l i a- t i o n' corresponded to our pagination. Due to variation in size it was impossible to give each copy of a particular work the same *folia*, and therefore, the m a r g i n a l   c y c l i c   l e t t e r   s y s t e m was invented, which, if generally adopted, would have made quoting independent of the *folium*. When we find that text divisions of certain 14th c. MSS. are marked by recurring letter cycles A-Z, AA-AZ, BA-BZ, CA-CZ, ... ZA-ZZ, we have an indication of erudite concern about convenient quoting facilities.

To illustrate the usage of this scrupulous method of quoting, we note these few examples from Hiltalinger's *Decem Responsiones* (10 RR), where Dionysius is quoted by letter system:

cap. 5 parte 11 vel secundum alium modum

littera L:	10 RR r. 4
cap. 7 littera G:	10 RR r. 4
cap. 2 parte 2 vel littera B:	10 RR r. 4
cap. 5 littera F et littera G:	10 RR r. 4
cap. 5 et signanter circa finem litterae E:	10 RR r. 4
cap. 8 littera D usque F et cap. 7 a littera F usque H inclusive ubi littera G dicit:	10 RR r. 5
cap 8 littera G:	10 RR r. 5

---

[11] About *Tabulae* cf. J. Ghellinck, *Patristique ... au bas moyen âge*, in: *Geisteswelt des Mittelalters* (Baeumker's Beiträge Suppl. III, 1 [Münster 1935] 423 ff.—For the two monumental *Milleloquia* cf. D. Perini, *Bibliographia Augustiniana* I (Firenze 1929) 203 *f:* *Carusi* Fr. Bartholomaeus de Urbino (died 1350). More MSS are indicated by P.B. Ministeri, *De Augustini de Ancona ... operibus*, in: *Analecta Augustiniana* XXII, 2 (1952) 223 f.—Vincent A. Fitzpatrick, M. S. SS. T., has just finished (June 1954) a Dissertation under Dr. B. Peebles of the Catholic University of America, Washington: *Bartholomaeus of Urbino, The Sermons embraced in his Milleloquium S. Augustini* (pp. 124) which blazes the trail for learned research concerning this Milleloquium.

There are numerous other examples, but these may suffice to show that the printers had not to invent any new quoting facilities. Yet the amanuenses of the 14th century by their passive resistance remonstrated against this cyclic letter system[12] and therefore it could not become common usage in all MSS. Thus the quoting facility of the cyclic letter system remained a sporadic and unsuccessful attempt.

Another feature of the 14th century commentaries was much more successful in providing good quoting faculties. Many MSS adopted the mathematical pattern of detailed text division. In his *Quaestiones*, Hiltalinger used the pattern $3 \times 3 \times 3$, which allowed for as many as thirty subdivisions. At the beginning of each Quaestio, we have:

3 *Rationes Principales*, then the *Oppositum* followed by
3 *Conclusiones*, each with some *Contra* and their *Solutio*;
3 *Corollaria* (after each *Conclusio*), also with *Contra* and *Solutio*.

In the *Decem Responsiones* Hiltalinger used the $10 \times 3 \times 4$ pattern which was even richer in quotable subdivisions. Thus at the beginning of each Responsio we find some *Rationes Principales*, then
10 *Notabilia* for term definition, then
3 *Conclusiones* each with
4 *Corollaria*, followed by a report on Hiltalinger's 'R e s p o n s i o-n e s' to the Magister or the Magistri who 'opposed' him.

By its very nature the mathematical text division is sometimes forced.[13] A logical text cannot like molten lead be poured into a pre-

---

[12] From MSS in my possession I give the following examples: Vat. lat. 1083 (Johannes de Ripa, In Primum) where the amanuensis gets tired of the cyclic letters after three pecias.—Erfurt CA 2° 115 (Facinus de Ast) where the copyist gives up on f. 41—A third example is an Augustinian chartulary of Clare (England) MS Harl. 4835 which does not prove very much as the copy is from the 15th century; every item of his chartulary is marked by cyclically returning letters. Among the items is one c o n t a i n i n g   t h e o l d e s t   p r o o f   f o r   t h e   a u t h e n t i c i t y   o f   G i l e s' *De erroribus philosophorum*; MS Harl. 4835 f. 49^r (letter: FO, date: Jan. 15, 1317): 'Ego frater Johannes de Waldyngfelde mutuo recepi Conventu Clare tertium scriptum thome in uno volumine et tractatum Egiddi de erroribus philosophorum, et de materia celi, in alio volumine ad terminum vite mee conservandum atque post obitum meum predicto conventui restituendum ... in die s. Mauri abbatis anno Domini MCCC septimo decimo'.—A fourth example may be found in Vat. lat. 986 f. 73^r–79^v: where eight times the cycle A–G is repeated on the margins by a careless copyist. These eight 'A–G' correspond to eight *folia* in the original, from which the copy was made. It is the cyclic letter system which early prints use to subdivide *one folium* as we see it in the recently reprinted *Summa Gandavensis*.

[13] John of Ripa, in his *Determinationes*, ridicules his opponent [Mag. Ascensius, O. Min.] because Ascensius likes a text division based on the 'p a t t e r n 10'; cf. Vat. lat. 981 f. 24^r = Pal. lat. 566 f. 205^v = Arch. S. Piet. G 37 f. 46^r: 'Sed volebat complere denarium rationum quem numerum etiam in Lectionibus et Tractatibus suo usui dedicaverat; et propter hoc etiam aliquae rationes suae in idem coincidebant'.—For Ascensius see footnote 17.

established number of empty trays. Hiltalinger is honest enough to tell us that many subdivisions were added later for the sake of conforming with the pre-established pattern. In questions like *Prologus* and *Vesperiae* Hiltalinger gave up the strict text division and used a more flexible system though lacking in provision for the same neat quoting facility.

Another quoting facility was the 'f o l i a t i o n' of the manuscripts. By 1350 most MSS had numbered folia. Ordinarily the *folia* are numbered on the *recto*, but in Vat. Lat. 4353 (Rich. Chillington) the *verso* is apparently numbered. 'Foliation' was a quoting facility which benefited only those who had access to one particular manuscript.

At first sight the modern reader is amazed to see Hiltalinger quote the *Postilla super can. Johannis* fol. 7—fol. 12—fol. 34—fol. 41—fol. 42—fol. 45—fol. 65, or the *Postilla super Actus Apostolorum* fol. 56. Both are lost works of Johannes Klenkok,[14] but even if they should be recovered, these quotations would be of little help since each MS must naturally differ in 'foliation'.

To get a better understanding of the meaning of 'foliation', let us take an example from Petrus de Ceffons (*In Quattuor Sententiarum*, MS Troyes 62), which does make sense and explains other instances. Like other scholastics of the 14th century, Petrus sent his *scriptor* out to obtain correct quotations from the desired books in a local library. On fol. 47^v of the Troyes MS 62 this *scriptor*, Guillelmus de Capella (Guilleville ?), is advised to consult the Gregory copy on fol. 28. As the "*scriptor*" well knew which copy was meant the direction was well given.[15]

---

[14] MS Toulouse 248 (Hiltalinger, In Primum et In Quartum) always writes: 'Kleinkoch'.

[15] At the end of 1 Sent. q. 20 Petrus gives a sketchy outline for further development of q. 20: 'Unde contra hoc arguit Chaton q. 2 Prologi art. 1: Recita dicta Chatonis et responde ad argumenta opinionis quam tangit Landulphus. Et move haec duo dubia, primum ... secundum, Utrum brutum formet complexam; quod sic: in Gregorio, per quattuor argumenta, lib. 1 dist. 3 q. 1 f o l i o 28. Et dubita si velis ad illa ... Dubita hic de fascinatione sicut Quol. 3 q. 12 [Henrici Gandavensi]'. Apparently the scriptor Guillelmus preferred to have no doubts; he certainly did not go out of his way to get the texts but was absent-minded enough to copy the Master's directions for the benefit of the modern reader. Several other directions of Petrus remained pious wishes. cf. f. 57^r: 'Ki^{ton} [Chillington] tenet oppositum; cuius dicta per manum scriptoris hic extrahi feci, et hic annecti de verbo ad verbum (o n t h e m a r g i n was the direction which the amanuensis scrambled with t h e t e x t without obeying the direction: Antevertantur haec folia; in quolibet ponantur dicta Ki^{tonis}. Hoc animadverto quia nec laudabile est ... a nimis truncato repetere verba hominum et illa dimittere quae eis possent plurimum suffragari. Ideo communiter feci per alias partes scribi de verbo ad verbum sicut iacebant in scripto dicta illa quae impugnare decreveram, ut totalis eorum panderetur intentio et inspiceretur quomodo res ultimate se haberet'.** The loquacious Petrus certainly was not the only one to feel that the *autoritates* should be looked up carefully in the original sources.—Petrus left us a very large

The example just quoted throws a different light on the case of Hiltalinger, whose 'folium quotations' were personal notes to be deleted from the final edition, as their usefulness would then have ceased. Hiltalinger never found the time to copy the actual texts from the *Postillae* nor to suppress, subsequently, those 'folium quotations'. Thus they remained, characteristically all in the Fourth Book, which when compared with the First Book and the *Decem Responsiones* ranks lower in editorial finesse.

A second fact supporting our conviction that the 14th c. theologians were historical-minded is their love for older MSS which they shared with the primitive humanists. Mention has been made of the humanistic theologian, Petrus de Ceffons. The Augustinian Luigi Marsili[16] is also noted for having mixed theological reasoning with the 'belli e buoni detti' of classical pagans. In Hiltalinger, too, there are traces of a new humanism. Not only did he allow the Muse of the classics and of Petrarch to chime in occasionally, but by his bombastic Latin he also attempted to improve the theological Latin of the 13th century, an attempt which has to be considered as a failure.

An even better argument follows from the fact that humanism originated in an age when education lay in the hands of theologians. To explain the growing love for classical MSS we must postulate love for theological MSS, because only when led by the trend of their theological vocation to appreciate theological MSS could some 14th c. theologians develop an interest in classical MSS as their a v o c a t i o n. Any other explanation is hardly possible.

The third fact alleged in favor of our postulate that a historical mentality existed among the 14th c. theologians, is evident to anyone who reads their texts. The 'Q u i d a m quotations' become increasingly rarer in the 14th century. Their abundance in texts of the 13th century makes editing difficult and evaluating problematical as the authors seem to be the more original the more their sources are unknown. Many a good theologian of the *Antiqui* would be called eclectic if he had indicated his sources as carefully as Hiltalinger did or if the editors had been successful in tracking down all implicit quotations.

Commentary which teems with classical and semi-classical poetry and shows great interest in natural sciences. He read after 1347, his *Socii* being Magister Grimerius, Magister Laurentius, Dominus Prior Magister Johannes. He often vents his resentment against the condemnations of 1347; because he thinks that the venerable Masters of the mid-century and their enthusiastic quest for truth deserved a better fate: approval rather than harsh condemnation.—In his introductory letter which I shall publish, he thunders against three foreign 'Vetulae' whom he expects the king of France to banish because of their share in engineering the condemnations.—One may not be surprised to learn that Petrus never became Magister but remained Baccalarius for life.

[16] cf. Perini: *Bibl. Aug.* II, 182 sq.—For Augustinian humanism cf. R. Arbesmann, *Outstanding Augustinian Humanists*, in: *Tagastan* 10 (1947) 101–112.

In the 14th century the 'Quidam quotations' are more the exception than the rule with a large group of writers. In Hiltalinger they form an insignificant fraction among his five to six thousand quotations.

An old rule prescribed that living authors should not be impugned by budding Baccalarii; for the sake of peace they were to be impugned anonymously. Yet there must have been a tradition, culminating in authors like Hiltalinger, which permitted marginal annotation of the real names during the *Lectura*, and authorized their insertion in the text before publication. This 'marginalia shift' creates one of the most serious problems in dating 14th century manuscripts as many names were shifted into the text body with anachronistic titles, i. e., a Frater Titius could be transferred from the margin to the text as Master Titius, or Cancellarius Titius, or Patriarcha Titius, although he had no such title at the time of the *Lectura* but only chanced to become a dignitary before the date of the work's publication.[17]

Little by little a certain group of theologians expected to find no *Quidam* in their sources. Hiltalinger in 3 Sent. q. 18 once voices his regret in regard to Astensis: 'Et concordat Astensis lib. 1 titulo 19 art. 2 cum doctoribus quos recitat ibidem; non tamen nominat eos'.[18]

---

[17] Some scholars have dated the *Lectura* of Hiltalinger too late because they over-looked this 'marginalia-shift'. If the argument of titles which Hiltalinger gave to Hugolinus at the moment of publication ('Generalis noster', viz., 1368–71) were valid for dating the *Lectura* reading, the Third Book of Hiltalinger w o u l d   h a v e   b e e n   r e a d   a f t e r 1381, as Johannes de Calore is called in the Third Book 'tunc Cancellarius Parisiensis'. [see later in this article].* A beautiful example of 'marginalia shift' we have in the *Determinationes* of Johannes de Ripa. The name of the addressee against whom the *Determinationes* were written, was placed by Johannes de Ripa only on the margins of his copy. On the margins of one MS, viz., Pal, lat. 566 it still occurs, namely M a g i s t e r A s c e n s i u s [Aquitanus de S. Columba, O. Min. cf. Sbaralea 1, 104]. At least twice this important key name was shifted into the text body:

1°	Vat. lat. 981 f. 49[r]:	Magister An[lus]
	= Arch. S. Piet G 37 f. 71[v]:	Magister Au.
	= Pal. lat. 566 f. 259[r]:	Magister Ascen[9]
2°	Vat. lat. 981 f. 51[u]:	Magistrum Austere
	= Arch. S. Piet G 37 f. 74[r]:	Magistrum Aust.
	= Pal. lat. 566 f. 264[v]:	Magistrum Ascen[m]

[18] B.M. Xiberta, *De scriptoribus O. Carm.* (Louvain 1931) 63 mentions a chapter decree of 1416 which reflects upon the 14th century: 'Item quia doctores nostri ordinis propter negligentiam cursorum veniunt in oblivionem quia nolunt eos in suis actibus *sub suis nominibus propriis allegare* ... mandamus omnibus et singulis baccalariis et cursoribus quod deinceps nostros rememorentur doctores *allegando eos* in suis actibus tam in p r i n c i p i i s quam in r e s p o n s i o n i b u s ...'—In the introductory letter of *Petrus de Ceffons* we hear of a 'm a n d a t u m   m a i o r u m'   t o   q u o t e (MS Troyes 62 f. 2[r]): 'Et advertat vestra discretio quod dum festinanter scriberem aliqua de dictis aliorum cum dictis propriis immiscui et multoties allegavi. Haec enim quandoque e x   m a n d a t o feci m a i o r u m; et etiam g l o r i a b a r   priscorum dictis v e r a c i b u s   me q u o-m o d o l i b e t   c o a p t a r e. Ea tamen secundum vestrae discretionis [Guillelmi de Capella] amplitudinem inserere vel rescindere poteritis'.** This gusto for exact quoting

Some commentaries of the second half of the 14th century continue the former custom of quoting most of their 'authorities' under the anonymity of *Quidam*. In the case of Ripa's '*Quidam* commentary', however, we know that it is a *Lectura Reportata*, published 'eodem anno', 1357, without any further editing. The *Quidam* of Ripa's MS therefore remained in his extant *Reportata* copies,[19] while the names, if any, appeared only on the margins of Ripa's own manual copy.

The 'Quidam commentaries' make at least one exception regarding names: they usually give great attention to exactness in quoting from St. Augustine.[20] To this extent they acknowledge the new mentality.

Up to this point we have been dealing with the historical trend among the theologians of the 14th century in general. Later we shall corroborate the third of our alleged facts on the basis of Augustinian quotations in Hiltalinger. The impact of these arguments will make itself felt when the reader is able to check with the forthcoming edition of Hiltalinger's works.

---

makes *Alfonsus Vargas Toletanus* a mine of information; a reprint was therefore made in New York to be released when the MSS check-up is finished. For Alfonsus cf. J. Kürzinger, *Alfonsus Vargas Toletanus*, in *Baeumker's Beiträge* XXII, 5–7 (Münster 1930) 41 ff.

[19] A *Lectura Reportata* was one written by a student in the classroom (ab ore magistri); if copies were made directly from such a *Lectura Reportata* they naturally could not show the wealth and precision of quotations which we admire in the works of an author like Hiltalinger who did carefully edit the first draft, whether *Reportatum* or not.

[20] In *Facinus de Ast* MS Erfurt Amplon, 2° 115, Augustinian quotations are carefully underlined. *Ripa*, too, quotes Augustine with painstaking care.* In two MSS of *Ripa's Lectura* (Vat. lat. 1083, Vat. lat. 6738) the colophon bears the date, Dec. 16, 1357, with the remark 'ab ore magistri'. As each of these two colophons was written by a different writer, the date cannot refer to the time of copying.—If the Four Books were to be read, the First Book had to be finished around the 16th of December.—*Ripa's Lectura* was published 'eodem anno' (1357); see below p. 433. Between 1357 and 1361 (at least) the *Determinations* of Ripa were written because the addressee of the Determinationes— Ascensius [Austensius Aquitanus de S. Columba] who became Magister in 1352—was made bishop in 1361; cf. Sbaralea I, 104. Before 1361 Ripa was Magister; cf. Determinations Vat. lat. 981 f. 69^v = Pal. lat. 566 f. 314^v = Arch S. Piet. G 37 f. 96^r: 'Istam [conclusionem] aliqualiter deduxi in *Vesperiis* [meis].* But is it possible that the Lector Johannes Hiltalinger could have assisted (at Avignon?) at the *Responsiones* of the Baccalarius Formatus, Johannes de Ripa? cf. Hiltalinger's 2 Sent. q. 22: 'Ad hanc rationem *audivi respondere* Johannem de Ripa dicendo quod argumenta fundantur super falso quia imaginantur ... quod *ipse dicebat* esse falsum'.— The feud between Ascensius and Ripa led the antagonists from one university to another; cf. *Determinationes* Vat. lat. 981 f. 21^v = Pal. lat. 566 f. 200^r = Arch. S. Piet. G 37 f. 42^v: 'Alias expresse posuit [Ascensius] et publice *in hac universitate et alibi* me audiente [Johanne de Ripa]'.—After the revocation of *Ludovicus' de Padua* (Vesperiae 1362), it seems, Ripa was considered to have been condemned implicitly; cf. Hiltalinger 10 RR r. 10: 'Ex his evaditur sufficienter error Johannis de Ripa et Doctoris Profundi in materia ista, qui posuerunt intrinsecam contingentiam sive indifferentiam—et hoc in actu voluntatis divinae; ex eidem ostenditur multiplex error *Ludovici de Padua in Vesperiis suis* in materia ista'. cf. A. Combes, *Jean Gerson* (1940) 623–673; and Combes, *Un inédit de S. Anselme d' après Ripa* (1944) 16; both in: *Etudes de phil. médiévale (Gilson)* tom. XXX and XXXIV.

But first a few remarks on the importance of our postulate. If 'Back to the sources' was a characteristic demand with 14th c. theologians, it will shed new light on the puzzle of their so-called e c l e c t i c i s m.

It was in the sources that many new ideas were found which had to act like chemical reagents, dissolving the proud systems of the 13th century. No wonder therefore that in the name of alleged discoveries the *Moderni* started to attack the systems which are dear to us again today. Yet this attack should not leave the casual reader with the idea that theologians like Hiltalinger belonged to a tired group of irreverent eclectics. The *Moderni* themselves would have been amused at such a charge. If ever a theological group was animated by intellectual enthusiasm, it was the pleiad of Masters around 1350 who claimed to have rediscovered many an old truth and therefore felt entitled to insert their 'discoveries' into the lofty structures of 13th century.[21] It is true, they made so many structural additions that the old systems lost character and stability; yet, negative designs did not animate them as they were hoping to construct new systems which, alas, did not materialize.

The *Schola Modernorum* was infected by some dangerous and deadly germs which could have brought about its decay but its collapse is due to a process which might best be described with the quip: 'It was not their theology which ran out first: it was their theologians!'. The Black Death thinned their ranks; the condemnations of the mid-century drove some into other fields like humanism—as we can read between the lines of Petrus de Ceffons. In 1368 the freedom of research was limited by the proclamation of the first *Authenticus*, i.e., 'Doctor of a School' in the modern sense. By 1372 the privileges of the Masters were curtailed, along with their vote in the chapter.

The death knell of the *Schola Modernorum* rang when the schism destroyed the scholastic standards of Paris by subordinating the academic world, its institutions and its magisterial dignities, to political expediency. It was bound to happen that professors of good Parisian

---

[21] Dissent from the Old Masters does not imply irreverence as far as Hiltalinger is concerned. Against *Richard Fitzralph* of Ardmagh [Armacanus] who belittles the Friars as 'Viri illiterati' Hiltalinger observes acidly (10 RR r. 3): 'Quid igitur de S. Thoma de Aquino? Numquid ipsum idiotam reputabit de cuius fructu operum satiata est terra? Quid de Aegidio, Bonaventura, Scoto, et de aliis luminaribus ecclesiae sanctae dei?—When *Bartholomaeus de Castellione* [= Guido Terreni!] in his *De perfectione vitae*, parte 2 cap. 18 (MS Avignon 299 f. 56^r sq.) says that 'Thomas erronee scripsit', Hiltalinger (10 RR r. 5) feels compelled to recast this criticism into a milder form, though a perusal of the Avignon MS shows that Guido had just as much esteem for the recently canonized Thomas as Hiltalinger.—The latter also accords great respect to the Masters of his own Order whom he calls *schola nostra*, *Doctores nostri* (be they Antiqui or Moderni). About 30 times he mentions them as a group with uniformity of habit rather than of doctrine. 200 times he quotes *Aegidius* with flattering titles ('Dominus Aegidius Magnus') which he omits when he contradicts him!

stock became rarer and rarer within one or two generations; the chairs had to be filled by more and more *epigoni* whose literary productions were petering out in a few second-rate manuscripts. Thus the pendulum swang back to the *Antiqui*. Some of the *Moderni* were still copied, but the school was at an end. With the advent of the age of print, the *Moderni* were quickly forgotten. If printing had been invented a hundred years earlier, history might have been different; for a group such as the *Moderni* would surely have seen that the Fathers were printed before the Protestant attack against tradition gained volume.

Even so, we can say that an attempt at historical theology was made in the 14th century, but unfortunately the bud was nipped before it could unfold. All that remained was a bad name.

A postulated historical trend can give its own context also to the so-called 'nominalism' of the 14th century.

From the sources came not only new ideas but new terms and consequently a taste for a new terminology which broke with the crystal clear and homely language of the *Antiqui*. We may call the latinity of the *Moderni* bombastic: Ciceronian tastes may be shocked by it: yet, the learned language of the West was enriched by the abstract terms of this century which had no linguistic inhibitions. The terminology of the *Moderni* required endless *Notabilia* for the explanation of their ever shifting terms. If 14th century theology is to be described as 'nominalism' we must not forget its long-winded logomachies; we come much closer to the truth if we interpret 'nominalism' etymologically as 'terminalism' i.e. a school which had to struggle with the hydra of its own terminology.[22]

'Skepticism' is still the blackest mark on the record of the 14th century theology. Many have made the accusation, some have pleaded for conviction but I hope that the judges will pause before they render the final verdict. What we call 'skepticism of the 14th century' was partly the result of the shocked surprise at the different atmosphere surrounding and pervading the sources; partly it was the consequence of a *Logica Moderna* gone wild; to a large degree it was the outcome of a pseudo-scientific ideal which pretended to treat a theological question 'm o r e g e o m e t r i c o'.

In their enthusiastic quest for truth the *Moderni* hitched their chariot to the proud star of mathematical evidence,[23] depreciating philosophy in

----

[22] cf. Xiberta, *De scriptoribus O. Carm.* (Louvain 1931) 474 n. 2: 'Fortasse in hac ratione quaestionum pertractandarum est insigne [c h a r a c t e r i s t i c], immo et ratio nominis realismi et nominalismi, magis quam in solutione problematis de universalibus, cuius momentum et influxum in totam scientiam plurimi [?] scholastici non assequebantur.'

[23] *Petrus de Ceffons* (MS Troyes 62 f. 1ʳ) describes the mathematical deductive method of the 14th century in many lyrical passages: 'More scientiarum mathematicarum, arith-

favor of theology, depreciating likewise the created in favor of the absolute and eternal. Untroubled by any fears of heresy in a world all Christian, and apparently united forever, the *Moderni* distinguished the mathematical concept of *evidens* from the workaday certainty of *probabile*. Their use of the term *probabile* was the most fatal feature of their system, even though it meant 'p r o v a b l e' rather than 'p r o b a b l e'.

They applied the term *probabile* to a proof for the existence of God, not because a man of healthy intuition cannot be led to the threshold of faith through sound reasoning, but rather because a stubborn unbeliever (proterviens) cannot be forced into intellectual submission. In the dangerous distinction of *evidens-probabile* the *evidens* was too narrow and the *probabile* too broad. Moreover, the term *probabile* was so often abused in arguments of plain theological casuistry that it finally became discredited and assumed the meaning of 'probable'. Nevertheless, it would seem a little slanderous to accuse the whole pleiad of venerable Masters in the fifties and sixties of skepticism, for it is incredible that cardinals, bishops and priors-general should have been guilty of such cynicism without being corrected.

HILTALINGER'S ATTITUDE TOWARDS QUOTING

I

In his more than five thousand references, Hiltalinger quotes Holy Scripture very often, the scholastics about two thousand times, his own

---

meticae praesertim vel geometriae, quarum dicta sequentia praecedentibus innituntur ... qualiter [in horologio] ex unius rotae circumductae gyro plurium sequitur per intermedia volubilium rotarum motus, tandemque delectabilis harmonia concluditur miro sonitu campanarum! ... S u p p o s i t i o n e s ipsas rotis, c o n c l u s i o n e s seu c o r o l l a r i a sonantibus aequare moliebar campanulis'. Even if Peter had not put it in so many words, this literary ideal would be plain to see in the commentaries of the 14th century with their mathematical text division, their mathematical deductive method, their mathematical examples, and their love for quotations from authors like *Alanus* (Regulae theologicae), *Alexander* (De memoria rerum difficilium = Definitiones XXIV Philosophorum) etc. who reason 'more geometrico'.* *Johannes de Ripa* (In Primum), however, does not think very much of mathematical examples; cf. Vat. lat. 1083 f. 131ᵛ: 'Omnia ista exempla mathematica de figuris et excessibus angulorum sunt multo deridenda si quis cupit attingere ad indaginem veritatis'.—Ripa's system, an enrapturing 'world of light', is an advanced development of the Gandavensis; cf. Vat. lat. 1083 f. 140ᵛ: '[Gandavensis] mihi fuit pater'. A key passage which an opponent singles out for the marginal criticism 'Deberet probare', stresses the a l m o s t   s t a t i c   f e a t u r e s of this visionary 'world of light'; cf. Vat. lat. 1083 f. 43ᵛ: 'Et ideo potius vitalis potentia dicitur l o c u s quam s u b i e c t u m huiusmodi actionum vitalium; immo p e r   a c c i d e n s   e s t   s u b i e c t u m ipsarum inquantum contingit huiusmodi actiones esse qualitates potentiam informantes. Quapropter multo sanius diceretur, secundum meum propositum, deum esse visionem vel notitiam 'o b i e c-t i v a m' creaturae quam 'f o r m a l e m' quoniam per 'f o r m a l e m' communiter intelligitur formalitas inexistentiae communicativae divini esse. Et ideo in hoc verbo <'formalis'> videtur latere venenum. Sed oportet pro nunc termino isto uti'.

Augustinians around one thousand times. Occasionally he is apologetic about his extensive quoting.

At the end of the 10 RR r. 3, he sounds rather fatigued: '*In qua potius volui sententias doctorum recitare quam propria phantasmata multiplicare*'; but then we must not forget that the 10 RR r. 3 deals with the old, mooted question of poverty.

Within the 10 RR r. 3, at the end of the 10 *Notabilia*, he says: '*Nec indignetur aliquis de multitudine remissionis et allegationis, non solum dictorum sed etiam auctorum, quia ut dicit Apuleius De deo Socratis ...*'. The Apuleius quotation, also found with neat cross reference in the dedication of the *Decem Responsiones* to Gyso of Colonia, O.E.S.A., makes it plain that as we have already many perfectly cut stones in our theological tradition, we need only build them into our edifice. In other words, Hiltalinger quotes so often to save the past from oblivion.

Toward the end of 10 Rr r. 2, Hiltalinger defends his many 'r e m i s-s i o n e s' thus '*Sed quia aliquae rationes circa ccl. 1 et 2 communiter moventur, ideo infrascriptas remissiones aestimo in hac quaestione notandas*'. He then 'remits' to Durandus, Aegidius, Petrus de Tarentasia, Richardus de Mediavilla, St. Thomas, Thomas de Argentina etc., evidently a n x i o u s t o p r e s e n t a p o s s i b l y c o m p l e t e '*status quaestionis*'.

In 1 Sent. q. 15, we find another and very natural reason for extensive quoting: '*Et ne videar falsum imponere [Johanni de Ripa], recito verba sua in forma*'. Here as in many other places it is a sense of fairness which makes Hiltalinger quote.

A curious instance of 1 Sent. q. 8 must be mentioned: '*Ad ista respondeo et quia difficilia sunt, appodiabo me ad dicta doctorum*'. After quoting only Anselm and the Gandavensis, Hiltalinger for once seems to restrain his quoting verve by saying: '*Visis horum doctorum dictis, nullius <alterius dicta> sunt valoris*'. But it is certainly amusing to find that he later felt the urge to add more: '*Pro solutione tamen eorum est etiam notandum illud quod ait S. Thomas q. 4 De veritate art. 2*'. This second '*text stratum*', a long quotation from St. Thomas, it already incorporated in all MSS. But the MS Toulouse 248, and it alone, superimposes upon the preceding *strata* still another quotation giving us thereby the example of a triple 'stratification'[24] of Hiltalinger's text. It shows at the same time that quoting had become a habit with men like our Magister Johannes who again and again went over the wide field of theological literature to glean what they could from the mature speculation of the past.

---

[24] cf. F. Petrarca, *Invective contra medicum*, ed. Pier Giorgio Ricci (Roma 1950); introduzione 18.

Hiltalinger's admiration for the past is voiced expressly in 2 Sent. q. 3, where we find him making a bow to the theological erudition of Lombard and Hugo: '*Credo tamen eos [Lombardum et Hugonem] volumina sanctorum tanta diligentia sicut suos posteros studuisse*'.

II

The theologians of the 14th century were 'happy quoters' who carried into their texts quotations upon quotation because in their own minds as well as in those of their contemporaries this feature increased the value of their literary productions. The fact that they had already released their books to the public did not prevent these 'busy bees' from filling the margins of any copy of their works which afterwards chanced to fall into their hands.

Thus Hiltalinger who read the Sentences ca. 1365–66 made marginal annotations as late as 1381. In his 3 Sent. q. 12 we read: '*Sed contra dicta potest argui secundum quod Magister Johannes de Calore, tunc Cancellarius Parisiensis, arguebat*'. The qualification '*tunc Cancellarius*' implies that Johannes de Calore was no longer in office when Hiltalinger was writing this note, and from Denifle we know that the successor of Johannes de Calore was in office on July 15, 1381.[25]

The extensive editing efforts made by Hiltalinger enabled him to quote himself about 200 times with formulas in all three tenses: *Videtur, Videbitur, Visum est*. As regards chronology, these 'self-quotations' serve as a rule no useful purpose. Some are typical examples of the so-called 'stratification' of 14th century texts. Now and then the cross references in Hiltalinger's works yield some general information; from them we glean the titles of works which have been lost: he wrote a *Quolibetum* and a *Lectura super Epistulam*. We learn also that the 14th century *Responsio* could be called *Quaestio Ordinaria* and that it was held in the morning; we hear that the *Quaestio* of a 14th century commentary was called *Lectio* and as a rule was to be read on one day; it is likely then that the whole Four Books of Hiltalinger [36+29+19+26 QQ] were actually delivered in one year.

From a remark in the First Book we construe that it was the author's intention to place the *Vesperiae* '*in fine Lecturae*' where they de facto are found in the Clm 26 711. We are thus left with little hope of finding a more complete edition of the *Vesperiae* than the incomplete one we have.

The most remarkable 'self-quotation' is to be found on the margin of

---

[25] cf. Denifle, *Chartularium* III: n. 1458 and 1461 (p. 298 and 301 respectively). *Johannes de Calore* was still acting on May 6, 1381; and had a new successor on July 15, 1381.

F II 9 f. 140ᵛ, within the *Secundum Principium*, extant only in this Basel manuscript. Unbelievable as it may sound, it is a specimen of Hiltalinger's own handwriting, characterized by the customary illegibility of the scholar who has plied a speedy quill for many years. The marginal note on f. 140ᵛ reads:

> Item Doctor Sanctus lib. 3 dist. 17 q. 1 art. 2 in solutione primae rationis: In Christo sunt duae naturae integrae quarum una non est pars alterius, ex quibus immediate persona componitur.—Item Anselmus 1 Cur deus homo cap. 6 quod incipit 'Ut breviter dicam' vel secundum alium librum, quod incipit 'Sufficere nobis debet':[26] Dominum Jesum Christum dicimus verum deum et verum hominem et unam personam in duabus naturis, et duas naturas in una persona.—Hoc dicit magis expresse[27] De incarnatione cap. 2; et habetur auctoritas in *Tertio meo* dist. 1 concl. 2 corollario 3.

The handwriting of this note is different from that of the text. It also differs from the characters of another amanuensis in the F II 9, who also bears the name Johannes de Basilea.[28]

No one but Johannes Hiltalinger de Basilea was entitled to write '*in Tertio meo*' if Anselm's quotation '*De incarnatione cap. 2*' occurs, as it does, with the same mistake ('cap. 2') in Hiltalinger's Tertio dist. 1 concl. 2 corollario 3.

The note '*vel secundum alium librum*', is typically Hiltalinger's style. A cross reference at the quoted place '*in Tertio*' of Hiltalinger makes the proof more stringent: '*De his plura habentur in Principiis et Vesperiis meis*'. Obviously, this refers back to the *Secundum Principium*—with or without the note—since the text, parallel to the note, pertains to the running feud between Hiltalinger and the *Dominus Michael* (Süchenschatz?) *de Zerbona* over the d u a e   n a t u r a e.[29] The authorship, therefore, is absolutely certain. The penmanship likewise may very naturally be assumed to be Hiltalinger's.

---

[26] Both 'capitulation incipits' and the quoted text are in Anselm's 1 Cur deus homo cap. 8; ed. F.S. Schmitt II (Edinburgh 1946) 59.

[27] 'm a g i s   e x p r e s s e' refers to Anselm's Ep. De incarnatione Verbi cp. 11; cf. ed. F.S. Schmitt II, 28: lines 23–25. The wrong 'capitulation': 'cap. 2' (which also occurs in the *In Tertium*) is not improved by the equally wrong one, found in the *Vesperiae*, i.e., 'cap. 5'. The mistakes go back to a misreading [Roman 2 = 11 = angular Arabic 5].

[28] This s e c o n d   J o h a n n e s   d e   B a s i l e a is a Friar Preacher, Prior of the Dominican House of Wien, AD 1411, the year he holds his Principia at the Austrian University; cf. MS Wien 4593 ff. 100ʳ, 100ᵛ, 106ᵛ, 110ʳ, 110ᵛ (Dominus Prior), 111ʳ, 111ᵛ.

[29] The Socius of Hiltalinger '*Dominus Michael de Zerbona*' may be identified with Michael Süchenschatz of Wien, because he copied Hiltalinger's Decem Responsiones with his own hand (MS Wien 4319) and added some lines at the end which concern the 'd u a e n a t u r a e   i n   C h r i s t o', theme of discussion between Hiltalinger and Michael in their Parisian P r i n c i p i a. The Principia, solemn University Acts which degenerated into mere show-pieces, were held at the beginning of each of the Four Books. The different Baccalarii attacked one another under the anonymity of 'Baccalarius S. Bernardi' 'Baccalarius S. Augustini' etc. and had to exchange their views i n   w r i t i n g, a

There may be the hypercritical '*proterviens*' who maintains that Hiltalinger's little note did not become absorbed into the text in some preceding copy, but was again placed on the margin of the MS F II 9 by some lucky finder of this precious relic. This artificial theory loses all probability when we consider that we have and have always had very few MSS of Hiltalinger, owing to the '*damnatio memoriae*' which followed almost immediately after the editing of his works.

Since F II 9 is a 14th century MS, the time element does not permit the supposition of three successive MSS of the *Secundum Principium*: first, one without the note; second, one which omitted the note; third, one which was belatedly enriched by the note.

While the fragmentary nature of the *Secundum Principium* explains why we have no *Tertium Principium* nor a *Quartum Principium*, it also shifts the *Secundum* Principium toward a very late date; noteworthy also is the fact that the *In Secundum* itself was published by Hiltalinger after the *In Primun* and the *Decem Responsiones*.

An examination of other Hiltalinger MSS does eliminate from our mind any lingering doubt about the penmanship of the precious little note in the F II 9; M S T o u l o u s e 2 4 8 a l s o b e a r s m a r g i-n a l n o t e s o f t h e s a m e p e n m a n s h i p, and as the authenticity of our note in F II 9 is thus accredited, MS Toulouse 248 itself gains in merit as a text witness.

We may conclude by saying that Hiltalinger had the MSS Basel F II 9 and Toulouse 248 in his own hands—a fact which looms highly important for an edition based on so very few MSS.

III

Before examining Hiltalinger's Augustinian quotations, it is necessary to illustrate the new quoting technique of the 14th century with a few general examples. The reader will not fail to note that they are quite different from those of the 13th century.

In the *Secundum Principium* Hiltalinger demands from the *Baccalarius Praedicatorum* the chapter and verse of a quotation attributed to Aristotle:

> Peto quod mittat mihi dicta Philosophi in forma (i.e., literally) cum quotatione capituli quia multum dubito de dicto sicut iacet in forma (i.e., in the preacher's version).

In 10 RR r. 6 Hiltalinger quotes in a vein which betrays scholarly vanity:

---

custom which at Hiltalinger's time was well established.—Hiltalinger left only a complete First Principium, and an incomplete Second Principium. The different 'Baccalarii', u n f o r-t u n a t e l y (!), c a n n o t b e i d e n t i f i e d w i t h c e r t a i n t y i n H i l t a l i n g e r' s P r i n c i p i a.

Quamvis autem Bradwardine et [Johannes de] Braculis saepe allegent Hermetem in libro De verbo aeterno, reperi tamen eadem dicta in libro Hermetis De helica ad Asclepium; et communiter omnia quae hi doctores dicunt ipsum dicere in libro De verbo aeterno, reperi in tertio libro.

In 1 Sent. q. 27, where Thomas de Argentina supports a statement with 'Aegidius 1 Sent. dist. 32', Hiltalinger remarks:

Perlegi Aegidium in ista distinctione 32 per totum nec possum invenire quod hic doctor [Argentinas] dicit.

In 10 RR r. 7 Hiltalinger shows his erudition in the casual manner which is typical of him:

'Aliter habet dicere Haston[30] in materia ista sicut patet in [suo] articulo 1 qui secundum meum librum est [articulus] 2: Utrum inter 'necesse esse' et 'impossibile esse' mediet 'possibile esse'.

An apt demonstration of positive-minded erudition is seen in 10 RR r. 8 in the Notabile 8: '*Immo de facto sic ponitur esse per S. Thomam parte 1 q. 25 art.* [ ]. *Et recitat Adam in Prologo, dubio 8 quaestionis*'. The number of the article was missing in Adam, according to my three MSS; however, Hiltalinger left a blank space [] to supply the number at a later date. Then, toward the end of *Notabile 9*, Hiltalinger in a new stratification communicates the results of his research: '*Tamen nota; dictum S. Thomae sic quotatur in Adam. Sed reperio ipsum hoc dicentem Parte 1 q. 85 art. 4*' (where the passage is actually found today).

This is of capital importance also in the Alfonsus Vargas edition of 1490 (reprint 1952). When the edition omits a chapter number many of the Alfonsus MSS leave a blank for the missing number. This blank seems to prove more than anything else that authors like Alfonsus felt it an obligation to supply missing numbers at a later date. These blanks are mute testimony to the positive-mindedness of the 14th century despite the fact that human frailty and pitiful library conditions made perfection impossible in the Middle Ages.

Others besides Hiltalinger were concerned with the accuracy of their documentation. Thus Conradus de Ebraco, O. Cist., sharply defends his accurate quoting of the *Articuli Parisienses* against Johannes de Braculis (Clm 27 034 f. 66[r]). Conrad had quoted:

---

[30] *Nicolaus de Aston*, O. Min., famous in the 14th century for his '*Achilles Astensis*', i. e., an '*argumentum* invincibile et *insolubile* 'for God's existence, left us *12 Quaestiones* which on account of many cross-references purport to be a complete *Lectura*. The '*articulus 1 = 2*' *is* quaestio 7 in MS Oriel 15 f. 217[r].—The 12 Quaestiones did not fill the reading requirements of a whole year: on 12 days, therefore, Nicholas exhibited his dazzling 'logicistic' fireworks before an admiring audience; on the other days he must have read 'Good old Scotus'.* It is hardly necessary to say explicitly that '*Achilles Astensis*' *is not a person* although this 'literary ghost' [Stegmüller's witty reaction] has already started to haunt the indices of recent books.

Art. 8: 'Quod qui habet meliora naturalia, de necessitate habebit maiorem
gratiam et gloriam, error'.

Against J. de Braculis he shows that an 'Art. 8' is really found among a
group of *'Articuli reperti in Scriptis quibusdam erroneis ut solent a
quibusdam intitulari'*. He indicates the 'Art. 1' of this group[31] as

'Quod divina essentia in se nec ab angelis videtur (f. 66^v) nec videbitur'.

In a recent study on Hugolinus by Adolar Zumkeller.[32] O.E.S.A., we
have a fine example which illustrates Hugolin's attitude. During a
discussion with the Baccalarius Minorum in the *Tertium Principium*,
Hugolin had been reproved for quoting incorrectly. His reaction was
short and definite:

Iste Pater [O. Min.] dicit quod verba allegata [En. in] Psal. 58 non sunt ibi
nec illud Augustini [12 De civitate dei cap. 9] est in isto capitulo sed in
capitulo 10. Respondeo: Videat clarius quia ita inveniet.

The 14th century theologians sometimes manifested outright jealousy in
regard to quotations which they claimed as their own discovery. Johannes de Ripa reminds Ascensius de S. Columba very firmly that certain
'Lux-quotations' from St. Augustine were first discovered by himself.
Because the text is somewhat scrambled, I here give the text according
to three MSS (viz., Vat. lat. 981 f. 64^r; Pal. lat. 566 f. 299^v–300^r; Arch.
S. Pietro G 37 f. 89^v):

Quod vero dicit [Ascensius] adversarios fuisse coactos per *lucem* intelligere
beatitudinem formalem, quia me hic vocat adversarium, falsum dicit; nam
nec fui coactus cum antequam ipse de ista materia somniaret, ipsam in
Lectura Sententiarum tractaverim et communicaverim eodem anno (!)[33] *in
scriptis* ex quibus quia pervenerunt ad ipsum, hausit materiam respiciendi
istos Augustini processus nec ....

Any rediscovered theological work of the past was quoted by these 14th
century theologians to such an extent that posterity should find no
excuse for being ignorant of its first 'rediscoverer'. As examples we find
that Ripa e x p l o i t s   t o   t h e   v e r y   l i m i t an opuscule of

---

[31] Such a little group of '11 Articuli' exists, in the old Lombardus edition 'AD 1513
apud Lodovicum Hornken Agripensem', on the last flyleaves ['P']: 'condemnati ab
episcopo Parisiensi et Magistris theologiae Regentibus Parisius AD MCCCXL [?] in
octava Epiphaniae Domini'. I think it is valuable information to know that condemnations
could cover anonymous groups of writings. Perhaps Johannes de Ripa was condemned
this way? (see footnote 20).

[32] cf. Adolar Zumkeller, *Hugolin v. Orvieto über Urstand u. Erbsünde*; offprint (from
Augustiniana 1953, 4) [Leuven 1953] 67.

[33] See footnote 20.

Anselm;[34] Bradwardine an opuscule of Hermes; and Hiltalinger some small treatises of Alanus and Alexander.

IV

Let us now make a study of the new quoting technique of the 14th century in Hiltalinger's Augustinian quotations. Of course, we do not claim that each of these 800–1000 quotations prove a personal acquaintance with the sources. That would be a far too optimistic evaluation.

1. *Stock Quotations*

First of all, there was then as now a stock of Augustinian quotations which, like so many theological proverbs, passed from one generation to the next. They are also found in Hiltalinger where they stand out because of their colorless, vague or incorrect connotations.

In 1 Sent. q. 2, and again in 3 Sent. q. 11, Hiltalinger quotes: *'Cetera potest homo nolens, credere nonnisi volens'*—once under the name of 'Augustine' and in the other instance merely with the vague indication *'in quadam Homilia super Johannem'*.[35] It is taken from Augustine's In Jo. Ev. tract. 26 (Pl 35: 1607), had already been vaguely alluded to in Lombard II n. 234, and passed from scholastic to scholastic.

We find another example in Hiltalinger's I Sent. q. 36: *'Prima veritate quae deus est vera sunt omnia'*. Both Hiltalinger and Hugolin cite as source 'Super psalmum 3'. Actually it is 83 QQ q. 1 (Pl 40: 11), and occurs in Lombard[36] I n. 426: *'Omne verum a veritate est verum; est autem veritas deus'*. In the original text of Augustine there are three or four lines inserted between the two short sentences of Lombard. As the original was not consulted, theological tradition recast the two sentences of Lombard into one: *'Prima veritate quae deus est vera sunt omnia'*.

In all fairness to Hiltalinger it must be admitted that the colorless and obscure quotations are an insignificant fraction of the large number of Augustinian *dicta* he quotes. Some quotations seem vaguer than they are. When Hiltalinger 1 Sent. q. 2 alleges Augustine *'in multis locis'* for

---

[34] cf. A. Combes, *Un inédit de S. Anselme d'après J. de Ripa* (Paris 1944), in: *Etudes Gilson* XXXIV.

[35] This quotation is also found in *Hugolinus* who is much more exact in supplying the source; twice he gives the reference 'Super Johannem hom. 27'; cf. A. Zumkeller, *Hugolin v. Orvieto* (Würzburg 1941) 357 and 363.

[36] Lombard's vague if correct reference 'in libro 83 QQ' underwent a curious change at the hands of the copyists: '83' became 'Sr' [super] and 'qq' became 'ps' [ps. 3?].—The Augustinian *Angelus Dobelin* has the correct reference '83 QQ q. 1' but the same wrong text: 'Omne verum veritate prima est verum'; cf. MS Jena Univ. El. Fol. 47 f. 6[r].

the statement: '*Omne quod est, est deus vel creatura*', he has in mind the many beautiful *apophthegmata* of the *Milleloquium, vocabulo* 'E s s e E n s   E s s e n t i a' I (1672) 389 sq. Or when, at the end of 1 Sent. q. 13, he defends himself against the charge of being a '*contemptor doctrinae Augustini*', he shows his acquaintance with Augustine by supporting the criticized doctrine with: '15 De trinitate cap. 27 de magnis circa finem cap. 79 de parvis ... in fine illius parvi capituli ... Et subdit infra cap. 80 de parvis ...'.

2. Overt Indirect Quotations

Among the 800–1000 Augustinian quotations in Hiltalinger's works, about 200 are marked 's e c u n d u m   a l l e g a t i o n e m' of other authors.[37] They are accredited to:

Peter Lombard over 70 times;

James of Viterbo, Thomas of Strasbourg, Gregory of Rimini, Alfonse of Toledo, Bonsimilant and John Romani (all Augustinians) over 20 times;

Giles of Rome, 17 times;

Adam, Alanus, Armacanus, Astensis Aureolus, Brinkil, 'Bartholomaeus de Castellione', Climenton (Richard of Chillington), 17 times;

Henry of Ghent, 6 times;

Hugolin, 16 times;

Johannes de Marchia, Johannes de Calore, Scotus, John XXII and Benedict XII about 25 times;

Klenkok and Bradwardine about 20 times;

Canon Law about 7 times; and

St. Thomas, 5 times.

We see, therefore, that Hiltalinger feels obliged by a then common standard of literary honesty not to claim any merit for some 200 quotations which are not the result of his own research. It may safely be assumed that about 200 more Augustinian quotations were taken from other scholastics because many of them occur close to texts which are selected from authors famous for their Augustinianism. As Hiltalinger expected his readers to consult the quoted scholastics, he knew that these untagged indirect Augustinian quotations would not go to his own credit.

There are various reasons for indirect quoting. In the case of Peter Lombard and other popular works it was accessibility which justified

---

[37] It was not uncommon for scholastics to quote from secondary sources; cf. Hiltalinger 10 RR r. 6: 'Patet per Doctorem Subtilem lib. 2 q. 1, ubi tria vituperat quae ponit idem Doctor [Sollemnis] 6 Quol. q. 3 diffuse quorum primum—secundum recitationem Doctoris Subtilis ... —'.

this method. The medieval student had no Migne on his shelf. If he was to love Augustine he had first to acquire a taste for the Augustinian texts within his reach. Since Lombard was so easily accessible, he could lead the beginner to the less accessible Augustinian original.

Another reason rose very naturally from the interpretation of Augustinian texts. Other scholastics had interpreted famous quotations from Augustine: if Hiltalinger did not agree with them, or if their authority was great enough to lend support to his own explanation, they had to be cited by chapter and verse.

Sometimes Hiltalinger quotes Augustine indirectly only to prove that he went directly to the sources. A telling example is found in his *Decem Responsiones* (10 RR r. 6, shortly before concl. 1):

> Patet hoc per Augustinum 5 De trinitate cap. 17 quia sicut Pater et Filius sunt unum principium Spiritus Sancti, sic omnes tres personae sunt unum principium creaturae—s i c u t   p o n i t   D o c t o r   S u b t i l i s libro 2 q. 1 in fine art. 2— ... S c i a t   t a m e n   l e c t o r   qu od   i l l a   v e r b a A u g u s t i n i   q u a e   r e c i t a t   S c o t u s   n o n   r e p e r i   u b i e s t   d i c t u m. Nam totus liber 5 non plura quam 16 capitula habet secundum libros quos vidi; et in cap. 17 de parvis nulla fit mentio de his quae possent ad istud propositum esse. Habentur plura pro his cap. 13 et 14 de magnis, et signanter 33 de parvis, quod est circa finem 14 de magnis' (cf. PL 42: 921).

Another example is found at the end of 10 RR r. 6, Notabile 8, where Hiltalinger quotes three passages of Augustine on Aeternitas. Although the source is not indicated these three are taken from the *Milleloquium*. Then he continues:

> Ex his sequitur primo quod anni dei qui non transeunt, idest aeternitas dei, non aliud sunt quam essentia dei, sicut aeternitas dei ipsa substantia dei est, nihil habens mutabile. V e r b a sunt Magistri lib. 1 dist. 19 cap. 2 (I n. 169) et originaliter sumuntur ab Augustino 7 Confessionum, ubi tractat illud Psal. (101, 25) 'In generatione et generatione anni tui', s e c u n d u m   q u o t- a t i o n e m   M a g i s t r i.

Hiltalinger must have been unsuccessful in tracing this last quotation for reasons shown by the Quaracchi edition of Lombard (I n. 169). Hiltalinger continues:

> Bradwardine lib. 1 parte 34 cap. 1 dicit esse illa verba Augustini super Psal. 101 serm. 2 et 1 Confess. cap. 6.

Apparently he was satisfied with the reference 'Psal. 101 serm. 2' because the *Milleloquium* vocabulo 'A e t e r n i t a s' lists 'Psal. 101 serm. 2' immediately after the o t h e r   t h r e e *dicta* which Hiltalinger quoted as mentioned above. He also checked the reference '1 Confess. cap. 6' but found there only the Psalm quotation (101, 28): 'Anni tui non deficient' (PL 32: 665). We know of this check-up because shortly afterwards in the same *Notabile 8* he uses a beautiful passage from 1 Confess. cap. 6 (PL 32:664).

3. *Bi-serial Quotations*

In some works of St. Augustine, especially in the *De trinitate*, and to a lesser degree in other books such as *De civitate dei*, *De libero arbitrio*, and *De Genesi ad litteram*, we find two 'capitulations' quoted side by side, e. g., 'cap. ... de magnis *et* cap. ... de parvis' or either of the two alone, i.e., 'cap. ... de magnis' or 'cap. ... de parvis'. The 'capitulation' 'de magnis' on the whole corresponds to the 'capitulation' of *Migne*; such however is not the case when we meet the 'cap. ... de parvis'.[38]

Hiltalinger uses this meticulous manner of double citation almost exclusively when taking a text from the *De trinitate*. In the case of the *De civitate dei* only ten such cases have come to my attention while in *De trinitate* the bi-serial system occurs 60 times, viz., 28 times in Hiltalinger's First Book, 19 times in the *Decem Responsiones*, 10 times in the unfinished *Vesperiae*.[39]

Ignoring the instances of single quotation 'de parvis' and the very few cases when 'de magnis' is just added to our vulgate chapters, a few examples of the bi-serial system may be cited. They are taken from the *Decem Responsiones* (10 RR r. 6) where we find Hiltalinger admitting that the edited work greatly differs from the actual delivery of the *Responsio*.

In regard to Spiritus Sanctus = Donum, Hiltalinger says:

'Patet per Augustinum 4 De trinitate cap. 52 de parvis et 20 de magnis; vel secundum alios libros 21 d e   m a g n i s   e t   2 8   d e   p a r v i s.[40] Item

---

[38] The 'capitulation': 'de parvis' never reached the stage of codification although it started early; cf. Scotus, Quodl. q. 8 (Vivès XXVI [1895] 343 sq.).—I have not seen the 'editio princeps' of St. Augustine nor the medieval 'Corpus' of St. Augustine (Troyes 40; *Cat. gén des MSS ... des Dep. II* [1885] 33–42). cf. J. de Ghellinck, *La prem. éd. imprimée ... S. Aug., in: Misc. J. Gessler* I (1948) 530–547. Ghellinck, *Une ... collection médiévale ... S. Aug., in: Liber Floridus. Festschrift P. Lehmann* (St. Ottilien 1950) 63–82. Ghellinck, *Patristique et MA*, III (1948) 342.

[39] As a young Baccalarius did not have sufficient time to check the primary sources, we may assume that these 'bi-serial quotations' were inserted prior to publication. This would give us another criterion for establishing the order in which Hiltalinger's works were published: the *In Primum* and the *Decem Responsiones* were first overhauled; then the *In Quartum* and the *In Secundum*, finally the *In Tertium* (the shortest of all, with traces of incomplete editing). The *Vesperiae* were never finished; the *Quolibetum and the Lectura super Epistulam* were never released to the public.—The fact that the unfinished *Vesperiae* are replete with 'bi-serial quotations', may easily be explained by the ambition of a new Magister who wanted to show his erudition before the whole University.

[40] If the numbers '52 de parvis', '27 et 28 de parvis', and '39 de parvis', are correct we are here confronted with t h r e e   d i f f e r e n t   's m a l l   c a p i t u l a t i o n s'; but we have no way of verifying it.

15 De trinitate cap. 17 d e   m a g n i s   e t   5 1   e t   5 2   d e   p a r v i s:
'Non frustra in hac trinitate non dicitur Verbum nisi Filius, nec Donum dei
nisi Spiritus Sanctus'. Istam partem deduxi 1 Sententiarum dist. 18 concl. 1;
et ponit eam Magister ibidem in textu pluribus capitulis'.

This precise 'capitulation' could not have been gleaned from the Magister (I. nn. 109 and 161) because his text does not contain it.

Our next example is found in a discussion on eternity (10 RR r. 6):

Probabitur amplius per Augustinum 4 De trinitate cap. 18 d e   m a g-
n i s,   v e l 19 secundum alios, sed 39 de parvis:[41] 'Non enim proprie,
inquit, vocatur aeternum quod aliqua ex parte mutatur; inquantum igitur
mutabiles sumus in tantum ab aeternitate distamus'. Item in fine illius 4
<De trinitate cap. 18> e t   e s t   4 2   d e   p a r v i s: 'Vera incommuta-
bilitas ipsa est aeternitas' (PL 42: 904 and 905).

The *Augustinian dicta* are not found in Lombard, nor under the *vocabulum* A e t e r n i t a s in the Milleoquium. This surprisingly scrupulous manner of quoting Augustine has nothing to do with an Augustinian's love for the founder of his Order: it is rather a characteristic of many 14th century theologians. The same scrupulosity can be noticed in Hiltalinger when he quotes other authors, and although contemporaries rival with him, he seems one of the outstanding 'quoters' of this positive-minded century.

4. *Uncodified Capitulations*

The 'capitulation' of Augustine's major works was approaching the stage of codification by 1350. Bartholomew Carusi of Urbino has some valuable remarks about this in the introduction to his *Milleloquium* [I (1672) f. a: 4ᵛ]:

Liber de academicis: Omnes <libros tres> sine capitulis reperi.
Liber de origine animae: Allegavi eum indistincte, non per capitula, quia
sic reperi.
Liber de baptismo parvulorum: Non quotavi in allegando capitula quia
celeriter perlegi et sine capitulis reperi.
Liber de unico baptismo ... contra Petilianum: Indistincte allegavi ut
reperi.
Liber de cura pro mortuis agenda: Sine capitibus eum reperi et indistinctum.
Liber de vera et falsa poenitentia: Satis est magnus et per plura capitula
distinctus.
Liber quaestionum ad Orosium: Ego cursim perlegens non bene feci
indistincte allegando.
Liber super totum Evangelium Joannis scriptus per Tractatus sive Sermones: Quod volumen apud aliquos in duas partes dividitur, credo magni-
tudinis causa, et secunda pars incipit in Tractatu XLIIII super illud: 'Ante

---

[41] See footnote 40.

festum Paschae'. Nec hoc mirandum quia etiam reperi opus super Psalterium in tres partes divisum.

Liber super epistulam ad Galatas: Inadvertens fui non allegando[42] distincte hunc librum; sed antiquitas libri et celeritas perlegendi fuit in <mihi>? causa'.

While, generally speaking, the major works used by the 14th century theologians already had a codified 'capitulation', it is true that 'fluctuations'[43] are noticeable in the Augustinian quotations of Hiltalinger, v.g.:

1 Sent. q. 2: De fide [doctrina] christiana cap. 5 secundum unam quotationem, vel capitulo ultimo secundum aliam.

1 Sent. q. 6: 15 De trinitate cap. 14 in fine, vel secundum aliam allegationem cap. 15 in principio.

1 Sent. q. 26: 83 QQ q. 20, vel 25 secundum alios.

2 Sent. q. 28: 19 De civitate dei cap. 23 in fine secundum unam quotationem, vel cap. 24 in principio secundum aliam.

10 RR r. 2: 1 De trinitate cap. 13 secundum aliam (!) quotationem.

10 RR r. 5: 3 De libero arbitrio cap. 23 [c. 15; PL 32: 1293].

10 RR r. 6: 3 De libero arbitrio cap. 23, vel 26 secundum aliam allegationem [c. 15; PL 32: 1293].

10 RR r. 8: 5 Super Genesim cap. 12 [22 ?], vel 24.

---

[42] *Bartholomew Carusi* realizes that the authenticity of an Augustinian work must be supported by the *Retractationes*, and also that the evaluation of a particular text witness must be founded on the '*antiquitas*' of the manuscript. He often mentions the antiquity of his MSS in the Index Librorum [cf. Milleloquium I (1672) f. e: 1ʳ.]: '*Liber de Duodecim Gradibus abusionum*. Et etiam dubium est utrum sit Augustini, quia non nominatur in libro R e t r a c t a t i o n u m et aliqui appropriant Cypriano; ego tamen reperi in a n t i-q u o originali intitulatum Augustino'. *Ibid*. f. e: 4ᵛ '*Liber de Symbolo ad Laurentium*. Non nominatur in libro R e t r a c t a t i o n u m, nonnulli ascribunt Hieronymo; ego tamen reperi in a n t i q u o volumine intitulari Augustino, sed anceps de vero pauca excerpsi de ipso'.** There are many remarks in the Introduction of Bartholomew which have interested the patrologists e.g., *ibid*. f. e: 1ʳ '*Liber Enchiridii*. Unde in Episcopatu Bononiensi, argenteis et aureis literis scriptum reperi'. Or the introductory lines of the *Tabula Sermonum* (*ibid*. f. i: 1ᵛ) which exalt the Sermon collection of *Dominus Robertus Cancellarius Parisiensis*. It seems that Bartholomew was the first to have attempted a 'patrological' treatise on Augustine's works.

[43] Some fluctuations have been observed a n d   r e c o r d e d by the Maurini-Migne edition; cf. PL 40: 231: '[Enchiridion] in scriptis codicibus 'capitulationes' et sectiones non easdem sortitum est. In quibusdam 134, aut 126, vel, ut in editis, 122; in aliis 71, in nonnullis 54 aut rariores, et in quibusdam nullas'. Hiltalinger's 'capitulations' of the *Enchiridion* never agree with Migne's.—Some quotations like Hiltalinger's (10 RR r. 7): '11 vel 12 De civitate cap. 15; p e r l e g a s   t o t u m   c a p u t   q u i a   r e p e r i e s   b o-n a   i b i   a d   p r o p o s i t u m' do not indicate fluctuation of 'capitulation' but only show the erudition of Hiltalinger who could quote from memory in the lecture hall on the spur of the moment, and used every opportunity to encourage his students always to read the whole chapter when consulting the originals.

5. *Personal Acquaintance with Augustinian Originals*

According to the preceding pages one might set the number of Hiltalinger's direct quotations at 400–500; yet a lower number would come closer to the truth. Each quotation would have to be compared with the thousands of *apophthegmata* in the *Milleloquium*, in Lombard, in Canon Law, and in the more known theologians. Such a test is not only difficult but also inconclusive. The presence of an Augustinian *dictum* in the *Milleloquium* does not exclude the possibility of a personal approach to the sources—if general interest in the original sources is postulated or proven for the theology around 1350. I have made a file of all the *apophthegmata* in the Milleloquium and Peter Lombard, but not for Canon Law because Hiltalinger exploited it rather infrequently for his Augustinian quotations. Neither did I prepare a file for the *Glossa Ordinaria*.

6. *The Milleloquium*

In the case of Peter Lombard my file is often conclusive, but the same cannot be said for the *Milleloquium*. I doubt that its use can be definitely proved more than twenty times. Hiltalinger quotes it by name four times: *vocabulo* Christiani, *vocabulo* D i v i t i a e, *vocabulo* L e x N a t u r a l i s, *vocabulo* A s s u m p t i o. He also uses undoubtedly the *vocabulum* C a r i t a s because a long series of quotations in his text is also found in the *vocabulum* C a r i t a s of the *Milleloquium*. In one case he used a passage with many Augustinian quotations from Johannes de Braculis who had taken them from the *Milleloquium*, *vocabulo* F a c i e s.

Only by a happy coincidence can one prove that a particular quotation comes from the *Milleloquium*, if, for instance, the quotation is the very first *apophthegma* under a vocabulum which is really descriptive and indicative, and easily leads to the quotation under discussion. But whoever is acquainted with the *Milleloquium* knows that the *vocabula* contain sometimes whole chapters of Augustinian works whose catalogization is not perfect; for while richness of contents and clearness of indexing are mutually exclusive, the author of the *Milleloquium* preferred richness to clarity.

7. *Proof of Personal Acquaintance with the Sources?*

Instead of indulging in a fruitless search for the extent of direct quoting it is more profitable to determine whether Hiltalinger took over indirect quotations without ever confronting them with the originals. In the preceding pages of this article we have already seen a number of examples which prove his c o n s c i e n t i o u s n e s s t o c o n s u l t the original whenever an indirect quotation had strange connotations. I want to indicate a few more, especially from the Third Book, because if a scholar can detect flaws in an indirect quotation at first sight—and does correct them by an examination of the originals—we have good reasons to suppose that he often went to his patristic library when he quoted in a manner which *seems* to show direct consultation of the primary sources.

In 10 RR r. 5 concl. 2 coroll. 3 Hiltalinger writes:

> Dictum legis naturae in suo proprio 'legali esse' est simpliciter invariabile. Patet corollarium ... per beatum Augustinum 9 De trinitate cap. 6 de magnis et 16 de parvis (PL 42: 966) ubi dicit: 'Viget et claret desuper iudicium veritatis ac sui iuris incorruptissimis regulis firmum est; et si corporalium imaginum quasi quodam nubilo subtexitur, non tamen involvitur atque confunditur' A l i t e r   e t   m a g i s   e x p r e s s e   n o t a t auctoritatem   praedictam   Milleloquium;   sed   non reperi   omnia   quae   Milleloquium   point,   in   textu <A u g u s t i n i>.[44]

This example indicates that Hiltalinger went first to the *Milleloquium* to find a convenient passage about 'lex' under the properly descriptive *vocabulum* L e x   N a t u r a l i s; surprised at some connotations of the *Milleloquium* text—which we can no longer verify—he went to the original, discarded the *Milleloquium* text in favor of the original one, but was scholarly enough to warn against the flaws of the *Milleloquium*. That he actually sought enlightenment in the sources, results from the 10 RR r. 6. Notabile 2 where our Augustinian *dictum* is preceded by a large section of 9 De trinitate cap. 6.

Another example of the conscientious use which Hiltalinger made of his secondary sources, I take from the *Vesperiae* terminus 1 consideratio 3 where Hiltalinger copies a group of Augustinian *dicta* from 'Johannes de Braculis in suo tractatu De videndo deum cap. 7', viz.: 2 2   D e   c i v i t a t e   [d e i]   c a p.   3 2 ... Super Ps. 104, 4 ... 83 QQ q. 31 <52> ... Commentar. ad Fortunatum <Fortunatianum> [ep. 148, olim 111; PL 33: 622 sq.].

---

[44] cf. Milleloquium I (Brixen 1734) 1171; II (Paris 1672) 19, 2 D under the vocabulum 'L e x   n a t u r a l i s'. [The Brixen edition has numbered c o l u m n s; the Paris edition has only numbered the p a g e s each of which has t w o   c o l u m n s. The Brixen edition ends the first volume with the *vocabulum* 'Luxuria', the Paris edition with the *vocabulum* 'J u v e n t u s   e t   J u v e n i s'].—In our Paris edition, the Augustinian quotation under discussion appears as one complete *apophthegma* near the beginning of the *vocabulum* 'Lex naturalis' [II (1672) 19, 2 D]; the Milleloquium and the Migne text do not show variants appreciable enough to warrant the high degree of surprise expressed by Hiltalinger. It may well be that our Milleloquium has undergone overzealous editing efforts. Hiltalinger's manual copy of the *De trinitate* cannot be blamed for the discrepancy because Hiltalinger quotes the same passage in the same words a second time (10 RR r. 6 notabile 2), this time in a much fuller context of 9 De trin. cap 6.

It is interesting that Johannes de Braculis got these quotations from the *Milleloquium, vocabulo* F a c i e s [I (1672) 413, 1 C sq.] where the serial order is the following: 83 QQ q. 52 ... 22 De civitate cap. 29 ... En. in Ps. 104, 4; only the ep. 148 (olim 111) is missing.

When Hiltalinger copied the group of Augustinian *dicta* he saw immediately that the first quotation '22 De civitate [dei] cap. 32' could hardly be correct. Conscientiously he went to his library to solve the problem, and proudly communicated the result of his research:

> Sciendum tamen quod secundum libros quos vidi, 22 liber De civitate [dei] non habet nisi 30 capitula, et in 30 [capitulo] nihil dicitur de ista materia; sed in 29 [capitulo] habetur (PL 41: 797): 'Facies autem dei manifestatio eius intelligenda est'.

8. *Augustinian Quotations of Hiltalinger's In Tertium*

Of all the works which Hiltalinger published the *In Tertium* received least of his care and attention. The Third Book remained with a few exceptions just as the Baccalarius Hiltalinger read it to his students in Paris.

There are about 70 Augustinian quotations in this Third Book; they are usually short, often indirect and seem to compare unfavorably with the wealth of Augustinian texts as contained in other works, esp. the *Decem Responsiones*. Now, if among these 70 unpretentious quotations we still detect a larger number that attest to the new historical attitude of the 14th century, we have a very good argument for our basic assumption; because we then make only a minimum claim, supported by quotations which are less representative and below the average of quotations found in works like the *Decem Responsiones*.

As a matter of fact, about one half of these 70 Augustinian texts show signs of the new quoting habits. E i g h t e e n among them, although taken over from Peter Lombard, indicate a 'capitulation' which is better than Lombard's:

3001 [45] Hiltalinger	3 Contra Maximinum c. 10; PL 42: 765.
Lombard III n. 55	'in libro contra Maximinum'.
3043 Hiltalinger	Enchiridion c. 36 [38]; PL 40: 251.
	Enchiridion c. 37 [39]; PL 40: 252.
Lombard III n. 18–20	'In Enchiridio'.

---

[45] These four-figure numbers are the text numbers of my edition: Book 1 will have the numbers 0001–1999, Book 2: 2000–2999, Book 3: 3000 – ... For reference purposes I indicate the *last number* of each of the 19 Quaestiones Tertii: 3036 – 3068 – 3106 – 3137 – 3176 – 3213 – 3252 – 3288 – 3322 – 3356 – 3392 – 3430 – 3476 – 3503 – 3534 – 3564 – 3605 – 3641 – 3682.

3099 Hiltalinger   Ad Dardanum ep. 44 [ep. 187 (57)]; PL 33:
                                                847.
        Lombard III n. 80   'Ad Dardanum'.

3109 Hiltalinger   Enchiridion c. 36 [38]; PL 40: 251.
        Lombard III n. 18   'in Enchiridio'.

3110 Hiltalinger   1 De trinitate c. 13; PL 42: 840.
        Lombard III n. 47   'in libro De trinitate'.

3144 Hiltalinger   3 De trinitate c. 7 [8]; PL 42: 876.
        L o m b a r d I I n. 5 1 (N o   r e f e r e n c e   n e a r b y).

3180 Hiltalinger   13 De trinitate c. 19; PL 42: 1033.
        Lombard III n. 76   'Augustinus'.

3292 Hiltalinger   13 De trinitate c. 10 de magnis; PL 42:
                                                1024.
        L o m b a r d   I I I   n.   1 3 5(N o   r e f e r e n c e).

3323 Hiltalinger   In Jo. Evang. tr. 47 [n. 13]; PL 35: 1740.
        Lombard III n. 146   'Super Joannem'.

3325 Hiltalinger   12 Sup. Gen. ad litt. v. fin. [c. 35]; PL 34:
                                                483.
        L o m b a r d   I V   n.   4 4 0(N o   r e f e r e n c e).

3403 Hiltalinger   15 De trinitate c. 18; PL 42: 1082

3408   'Nullum est isto die dono excellentius...
                                                [1083]. Sine caritate quippe fides potest
                                                quidem esse sed non prodesse' cf. L o m-
                                                b a r d I n. 1 4 9 where only the first
                                                half is found under the quotation '1 5
                                                D e   t r i n i t a t e'.

3433 Hiltalinger   In Ep. Jo. [tr. 8 n. 9]; PL 35: 2041.
        Lombard III n. 215   'Super Ep. Jo.'.
                                                (But Hiltalinger refers to Decret. De pae-
                                                nit. Dist. 2 Depositum).

3451 Hiltalinger   1 De doctrina christ. ult. med. [c. 27]; PL
        (L o m b a r d I I I n. 2 0 1)   34: 29 ubi dicit 'Ille iuste et sancte vivit etc.
                                                <qui rerum integer aestimator est>'. This
                                                incipit of 1 De doctrina christ. c. 27 is the
                                                only sentence which Lombard [(III n. 201);
                                                n o r e f e r e n c e b u t 'A u g u s t i n u s']
                                                omits in his famous passage on the order of
                                                charity. Yet Hiltalinger expects his students
                                                and readers to identify Lombard's famous
                                                passage by an *incipit* which Lombard omits
                                                and Hiltalinger only gets from the original:
                                                'P a t e t   p e r   M a g i s t r u m   i n   d i s-
                                                t i n c t i o n i b u s   i s t i s'.—The two
                                                vague remarks 'ultra medium' and 'in dis-
                                                tinctionibus istis' sound as if Hiltalinger
                                                q u o t e d b o t h A u g u s t i n e a n d

	Lombard from memory in the lecture hall!
3481 Hiltalinger	2 De lib. arb. [c. 19]; PL 32: 1268
	'Virtutes igitur quibus recte vivitur etc.'.
Lombard II n. 241	1 libro Retract.: 'Virtutes quibus recte vivitur etc.'.
3504 Hiltalinger	15 De trinitate c. 18; PL 42: 1082.
Lombard I n. 149	'15 De trinitate'.
3435 Hiltalinger	1 De doctrina christ. c. 32 [c. 27]; PL 34: 29.
Lombard III n. 201	'Augustinus'.
3540 Hiltalinger	1 De doctrina christ. c. 26 [c. 22]; PL 34: 27.
Lombard III n. 192	(No reference).

The above list creates the impression that Baccalarius Hiltalinger was so familiar with Augustinian sources that he could easily correct Lombard's references; but there remains the possibility that the 14th century text of Lombard was already well equipped with exact Augustinian 'capitulations'. This would give less credit to Hiltalinger, but pay all the more tribute to an entire generation of 14th century theologians. I am inclined to accept this possibility as a probability.

The Fathers of Quaracchi have given us a splendid edition of Lombard, based on the oldest manuscripts, but our problem will not be solved until we can determine just how well documented the 14th century Lombard appeared. Only then can we gauge the personal merit of a 14th century theologian who *seems* to improve Lombard's quotations.

The theory that the 14th century Lombard had already good text verifications, is supported by some facts. In his *Expositio Litteralis*, e.g., Johannes Klenkok O.E.S.A. quotes exactly what Lombard quotes but vaguely. In one place, at least, Klenkok verified a Lombard text better than the Quaracchi edition L: III n. 9:

> Item in libro De trinitate: 'Non esset Dei hominumque mediator, nisi esset idem Deus, idem homo, in utroque unus et verus, quam servilem formam, a solo Filio susceptam, tota Trinitas, cuius una est voluntas et operatio, fecit. Non autem in utero Virginis prius caro suscepta est, et postmodum divinitas venit in carnem, sed mox ut Verbum venit in uterum, servata veritate propriae naturae, factum est caro et perfectus est homo, id est, in veritate carnis et animae natus est'.

In regard to this passage Klenkok says in his *Expositio litteralis*[46]:

---

[46] cf. MS Klosterneuburg 304 f. 135ᵛ and MS Siena G V 16 f. 36ᵛ.—On Klenkok, Johannes de Braculis, Angelus Dobelin cf. my forthcoming article: Teólogos Agustinos alemanes del siglo XIV, *Archivo Agustiniano*.

Auctoritas Augustini non invenitur in libro De trinitate, sed invenitur lib. 2
Sententiarum Hugonis cap. 5

The whole passage is actually found in Hugo's Summa Sententiarum
tract. 1 cap. 16 (PL 176: 72). The fact that the 'capitulation' of Klenkok
does not correspond to our modern one, does not diminish the merit of
his erudition. While the Quaracchi Fathers quote Hugo of St. Victor for
Lombard III n. 10, they do not remit to Hugo in L: III n. 9

In addition to Klenkok other scholastics corrected and improved
Lombard's references; e.g., Richardus Chillington in his *Quaestiones
theologicae*[47] very casually corrects our Lombard:

'*Item in Enchiridio cap. 6 [c. 9], et allegat Magister...*'. He refers to
L: I n. 52 where Lombard does not pretend to quote the *Enchiridion*
but, erroneously, the '*De fide ad Petrum in expositione Symboli*'.

One last example of a 14th century documentation of Lombard's text;
surprisingly it comes from Facinus de Ast, O.E.S.A., who otherwise is
more interested in the speculative problems, raised by the *Quidam*
[Johannes de Ripa] and by many other *Quidam*. A few times, however,
he identifies vague quotations of Lombard. The outstanding instance
occurs in the *In Tertium* of Facinus[48]:

'Item Ad Rom. 8, 3 'Misit Filium suum <in similitudinem carnis
peccati> Glossa; et est sumpta ab Augustino de verbis Apostoli, e t
e a m   d e   v e r b o   a d   v e r b u m   a l l e g a t   M a g i s t e r   3 Sen.
dist. 3 cap. 3: 'Contracta non est de carne peccatrice sed in similitudine
eius per passibilitatem et mortalitatem et alios defectus' 'Cetera vero
[hominum] omnis caro peccati est; sola istius non est caro peccati quia
non eum mater concupiscentia <sed gratia concepit>. Habet tamen
similitudinem carnis peccati'.

The Lombard text (L: III n. 14) gives not the faintest hint of quoting
from Augustine nor have the Quaracchi Fathers tracked down this
implicit quotation; but as a matter of fact, three or four lines of the
Quaracchi edition are literally taken from Augustine's Sermo 152
([n. 8]; PL 38: 823) where Augustine speaks 'de verbis Apostoli',
namely Rom. 8, 1–4.

If it were definitely established one day that the Lombard text of the
14th century incorporated many corrected references, contributed one
by one in slow and patient research, we would have to consider such a
proof as bearing upon the historical attitude of several scholastic generations.

---

[47] cf. Vat. lat. 4353 f. 50^r.

[48] cf. Facinus de Ast, In Tertium q. 6; MS Erfurt Ampl. 2° 115 f. 176^v and MS Ottob.
lat. 446 f. 116^r sq.

Among the 70 Augustinian quotations in Hiltalinger's Third Book there are e i g h t w h i c h m a y b e c o n s i d e r e d a s r e s u l -
t i n g f r o m H i l t a l i n g e r' s p e r s o n a l r e s e a r c h i n
t h e s o u r c e s;

3044 2 De trinitate cap. 10; PL 42: 855–58.

3357 De spiritu et littera ad Marcellinum prope finem ([c. 34]; PL 44: 240. The 'finis' would be c. 36). This quotation is not in Lombard, nor in the Milleloquium; Hugolinus[49] has it, but without reference.

3383 15 De trinitate cap. 4 de magnis et 15 de parvis (PL 42: 1061). Although the Milleloquium has this *dictum* (I [1672] 288, 1 B; first apophthegma, under the obvious vocabulum 'Deus') we cannot credit the Milleloquium for the bi-serial capitulation.

3419 Enchiridion cc. 6, 7, 11 [cc. 4–5]; PL 40: 232–233. Not in L nor in M.

3424 De bono [dono] perseverantiae cap. 19; PL 45: 1024; also quoted by 10 RR r. 5.

3481 2 De civitate dei cap. 21; PL 41: 68 ('Forte nec tunc [fuit] viva moribus sed picta coloribus'). Not in L nor in M.

3482 1 De moribus ecclesiae cap. 14 [cc. 14–15]; PL 32: 1321–22. The quotation is taken from St. Thomas who incorrectly refers to 'Augustinus in quadam epistula'. Cf. Thomas I II q. 65 art. 3.

3540 10 De civitate dei cap. 2 [c. 3 n. 2, olim c. 4]; PL 41: 280 ('Ipse enim fons nostrae beatitudinis, ipse omnis appetitionis est finis'). The M has this passage where no one would normally search for it, viz., II (1672) 7, 1 E *vocabulo* 'Latria'.

Of the remaining 44 Augustinian quotations s e v e n are probably direct ones, some are proverbial commonplaces, t h r e e are neither from Augustine nor Ps-Augustine. About f i v e are from the *Glossa Ordinaria*, t w o are from Richard Chillington,[50] five are from Hugolinus.[51]

One is undoubtedly from the *Milleloquium*: 'Augustinus lib. Meditationum cap. 21 [27]' (cf. II (1672) 571, 2 B). These spurious Meditationes are not in the Maurini edition, nor are they mentioned in the *Clavis Patrum Latinorum*; Bartholomaeus de Urbinio (Index Librorum; I [1672] f. e: 1ᵛ) notes:

Alicubi dicitur '2 liber Soliloquiorum ad deum' de quo Bernardus et Anselmus multa in suos [!] etiam quoad literam transtulerunt. Satis est magnus et 39 capitula distincta continet; et de poenis inferni diffuse pertractat. De quo in libro R e t r a c t a t i o n u m nulla fit mentio. Incipit: 'Eia

---

[49] cf. A. Zumkeller, *Hugol. v. Orvieto* (Würzburg 1941) 359.
[50] cf. MS Bruges 503 f. 103ʳ and 105ʳ.
[51] cf. MS Paris Nat. lat. 14559 ff. 162ʳ, 196ᵛ, 197ʳ.

nunc, homuncio, fuge paululum occupationes tuas'. (The Milleloquium contains around 50 quotations of this devotional treatise).

After this rapid examination of the Augustinian quotations which Hiltalinger incorporated in his Third Book, we may specify the minimum claim that about o n e f o u r t h perhaps o n e t h i r d of Augustinian quotations by authors like Hiltalinger, show connotations of the new quoting attitude of the 14th century.

Considering this fact in connection with the two others which we alleged at the beginning of this article, one has reasons to assume that no appraisal of the 14th century theology is complete, or even just, without properly evaluating this incipient historical consciousness which—if fully developed—could have forestalled attacks against the medieval church in the name of a forgotten or neglected tradition.

BIBLIOGRAPHY OF THE WRITINGS OF DAMASUS TRAPP

1935

"Aegidii Romani de doctrina modorum," *Angelicum* 12 (1935), 449–501.

1954

"Hiltalinger's Augustinian Quotations," *Augustiniana* 4 (1954), 412–449.

"Telógos agustinos alemanes del siglo XIV," *Archivo Agustiniano* 48 (1954), 277–300.

1955

"The Portiuncula Discussion of Cremona (ca. 1380): New Light on 14th Century Disputations," *Recherches de Théologie ancienne et médiévale* 22 (1955), 79–94.

1956

"Augustinian Theology of the 14th Century: Notes on Editons, Marginalia, Opinions and Book-Lore," *Augustiniana* 6 (1956), 146–274.

1957

"Alfonsus Vargas Toletanus," *Lexikon für Theologie und Kirche*, ed., J. Höfer and K. Rahner, 2nd ed. (Freiburg: Herder, 1957–65), I, 334.

"Clm 27034: Unchristened Nominalism and Wycliffite Realism at Prague in 1381," *Recherches de Théologie ancienne et médiévale* 24 (1957), 320–360.

"Peter Ceffons of Clairvaux," *Recherches de Théologie ancienne et médiévale* 24 (1957), 101–154.

"Gregory of Rimini's Manuscripts, Editions and Additions," *Augustiniana* 8 (1958), 425–443.

1959

"Dionysius v. Borgo San Sepolcro," *Lexikon für Theologie und Kirche*, 2nd ed. (1959), III, 405–406.

"Facinus de Asti," *Lexikon für Theologie und Kirche*, 2nd ed. (1959), III, 1337.

1960

"Gerhard v. Siena," *Lexikon für Theologie und Kirche*, 2nd ed. (1960), IV, 722–723.

"Gregory v. Rimini," *Lexikon für Theologie und Kirche*, 2nd ed. (1960), IV, 722–723.

"Jacobus de Appamiis," *Lexikon für Theologie und Kirche*, 2nd ed. (1960), V, 835.

"Jakob v. Viterbo," *Lexikon für Theologie und Kirche*, 2nd ed. (1960), V, 849.

"Johannes Hiltalingen v. Basel," *Lexikon für Theologie und Kirche*, 2nd ed. (1960), V, 1007.

"Johannes Klenkok," *Lexikon für Theologie und Kirche*, 2nd ed. (1960), V, 1050–1051.

1962

"Augustine and His Influence," *A Catholic Dictionary of Theology*, ed., H. F. Davis (London: Thomas Nelson, 1962), I, 209–222.

"New Approaches to Gregory of Rimini," *Augustinianum* 2 (1962), 115–130.

Review of *Gericht und Evangelium*: *Zur Worttheologie in Luthers erster Psalmenvorlesung*, by Albert Brandenburg, Konfessionskundliche und kontroverstheologische Studien 4 (Paderborn: Verlag Bonifacius-Druckerei, 1960), in *Augustinianum* 2 (1962), 546.

1963

"Angelus de Dobelin, Doctor Parisiensis, and His Lectura," *Augustinianum* 3 (1963), 389–413.

"The Quaestiones of Dionysius de Burgo OSA," *Augustinianum* 3 (1963), 63–78.

1964

"Gregorio de Rimini y el nominalismo [Homenaje leido en el Centenario d El Escorial 1563–1963]," *Augustinianum* 4 (1964), 5–20.

"Notes on John Klenkok OSA (d. 1374)," *Augustinianum* 4 (1964), 358–404.

Review of *Archbishop Thomas Bradwardine, a Fourteenth Century Augustinian*: *A Study of His Theology in its Historical Context*, by Heiko A. Oberman (Utrecht, 1957), in *Augustinianum* 4 (1964), 245–246.

Review of *Katalog der abendländischen Handschriften der Östereichischen Nationalbibliothek Neuerwerbungen*, by O. Mazal und F. Unterkircher, Teil 2.1 und 2.2 (Wien, 1963), in *Augustinianum* 4 (1964), 227–228.

Review of *Konrad v. Ebrach S.O. Cist. (d. 1399)*, by K. Lauterer, Editiones Cistercienses (Roma, 1962), in *Augustinianum* 4 (1964), 234–235.

Review of *Latin Manuscript Books Before 1600*: A List of the Printed Catalogues and Unpublished Inventories of Extant Collections, by Paul Oskar Kristeller (New York: Fordham University Press, 1960), in *Augustinianum* 4 (1964), 231–232.

Review of *Problem of Sovereignty in the Later Middle Ages: The Papal Monarchy with Augustinus Triumphus and the Publicists*, by M. Wilks, Cambridge Studies in Medieval Life and Thought 9 (Cambridge: University Press, 1963), in *Augustinianum* 4 (1964), 243.

"Simon v. Cremona," *Lexikon für Theologie und Kirche*, 2nd ed. (1964), IX, 766.

"Simonis de Cremona OESA, Lectura super 4 LL. Sententiarum MS Cremona 118, ff. 1^r–136^v," *Augustinianum* 4 (1964), 123–146.

1965

"Harvest of Medieval Theology [Notes on Heiko A. Oberman's book, *The Harvest of Medieval Theology*]," *Augustinianum* 5 (1965), 147–151.

"'Moderns' and 'Modernists' in MS Fribourg Cordeliers 26," *Augustinianum* 5 (1965), 241–270.

"Notes on some Manuscripts of the Augustinian Michael de Massa (d. 1337)," *Augustinianum* 5 (1965), 58–133.

"Thomas v. Strassburg," *Lexikon für Theologie und Kirche*, 2nd ed. (1965), X, 147–148.

1966

"La tomba bisoma di Tommaso da Strasburgo e Gregorio da Rimini," *Augustinianum* 6 (1966), 5–17.

Review of *Ausgehendes Mittelalter: Gesammelte Aufsätze zur Geistesgeschichte des 14. Jahrhunderts*, by Anneliese Maier, Edizioni di Storia e Letteratura, vol. 1 (Roma, 1964), in *Augustinianum* 6 (1966) 165.

Review of D. Durandi Magistri a Sancto Porciano, O.P., *Quolibeta Avenionensia tria additis Correctionibus Hervaei Natalis ...*, ed. P.T. Stella (Roma: Libreria Anteneo Salesiano, 1965), in *Augustinianum* 6 (1966), 119–120.

Review of *Der Augustiner-Eremitenorden u. der Beginn der humanistischen Bewegung*, by Rudolph Arbesmann OSA, Cassiciacum 20 (Würzburg: Augustinus-Verlag, 1965), in *Augustinianum* 6 (1966), 164–165.

Review of *Der Herbst der mittelalterlichen Theologie*, by Heiko A. Oberman, trans. M. Rumscheid und H. Kampen, Spätscholastik und Reformation 1 (Zurich: EVZ Verlag, 1965), in *Augustinianum* 6 (1966), 126–127.

Review of Gabrielis Biel, *Canonis Misse Expositio*, Pars Prima, eds. Heiko A. Oberman et William J. Courtenay, (1963); Pars Secunda, eds. Heiko A. Oberman et William J. Courtenay, (1965); Pars Tertia, eds. Heiko A. Oberman et William J. Courtenay cooperante Daniel E. Zerfoss, (1966); Veröffentlichungen des Instituts f. Europ. Gesch. Mainz, Abt. abendl. Religionsgesch. 31–33 (Wiesbaden: F. Steiner, 1963–1966), in *Augustinianum* 6 (1966), 561–562.

Review of Guilelmi Ockham, *Expositionis in LL. Log, Prooem. et Expositio in L. Porphyrii De Praedicabilibus*, ed. E.A. Moody, Franciscan Institute Publications (New York: St. Bonaventure, 1965), in *Augustinianum* 6 (1966), 161–162.

Review of *Il Tractatus de Gratia di Guglielmo d'Auvergne*, ed. Guglielmo Cordi, Corona Lateranensis 7 (Roma, 1966), in *Augustinianum* 6 (1966), 562–563.

Review of *Katalog der abendländischen Handschriften der Österreichischen Nationalbibliothek Neuerwerbungen*, by O. Mazal und F. Unterkircher, Teil 1 (Wien, 1964), in *Augustinianum* 6 (1966), 165.

Review of *La unión hipostática segum Egidio Romano*, by J.M. Ozaeta OSA (Real Monasterio de El Escorial, 1965), in *Augustinianum* 6 (1966), 326–327.

Review of Paul of Pergola, *Logica* and *Tractatus De sensu composito et diviso*, ed. Mary Anthony Brown, OSF, Franciscan Institute Publications, Text Series no. 13 (New York, 1961) in *Augustinianum* 6 (1966), 171–173.

1967

"J. Langs 'Christologie bei H. von Langenstein': eine dogmengeschichtliche Untersuchung?" *Augustinianum* 7 (1967), 525–532.

Review of *Die Einheit der Kirchen auf den spätmittelalterlichen Konzilien von Konstanz bis Florenz*, by August Leidl, Konfessionskundliche und kontroverstheologische Studien 17 (Paderborn: Verlag Bonifacius-Druckerei, 1966), in *Augustinianum* 7 (1967), 399–400.

Review of *Peter Martyr Vermigli: An Anatomy of Apostasy*, by Philip McNair (Oxford: University Press, 1967), in *Augustinianum* 7 (1967), 398–399.

1968

Documentazione Ritiana Antiqua, ed. A. Damasus Trapp, vol. I: *Il Processo del 1626 e la sua letteratura*, Edizione anastatica con introductuzioni e indici, (1968); vol. II: *Il Volto veritiero di Santa Rita*,

(1968); vol. III: *Gli Statuti di Cascia Stampati a Cascia nel 1545.* Edizione anastatica con introduzione e letteratura anastatica, (1968); vol. IV: *L'Archivio notarile di Santa Rita (L'ambiente agostiniano),* (1970), (Cascia: Monasterio di Santa Rita, 1968–70).

Giuseppe Bartolomeo Menocchio OSA, Prefetto del Sacrario Apostolico, Confessore di Pio VII (1741–1823): Diari e Lettere, eds. Damasus Trapp and G.L. Masetti-Zannini, 6 vols. (Roma, 1968–1970).

Review of Aeneas Sylvius Piccolominus (Pius II), *De gestis concilli Basiliensis commentariorum libri II,* eds. and trans. Denys Hay and W.K. Smith (Oxford: University Press, 1967), in *Augustinianum* 8 (1968), 183–184.

1969

Album Santa Rita, (Cascia: Monasterio di Santa Rita, 1969).

1974

"Dreistufiger Editionsprozess und dreiartige Zitationsweise bei den Augustinertheologen des 14. Jahrhunderts" *Cor Unam* 32 (1974), 100–107. (cf. *Augustiniana* 25 (1975), 283–292).

"Rapporto sul SFB 8 di Tübingen," *Analecta Augustiniana* 37 (1974), 415–417.

1975

"Dreistufiger Editionsprozess und dreiartige Zitationsweise bei den Augustinertheologen des 14. Jahrhunderts", *Augustiniana* 25 (1975), 283–292. (cf. *Cor Unam* 32 (1974), 100–107).

1977

"Der Anselmische Gottesbeweis in der Wertung Gregors von Rimini," *Analecta Augustiniana* 40 (1977), 47–60.

1979

Gregorii Ariminensis OESA Lectura Super Primum et Secundum Sententiarum, ed. A. Damasus Trapp and Venicio Marcolino, vol. I: Super Primum Dist. 1–6 (1981); vol. II: Super Primum Dist. 7–17 (1982); vol. III: Super Primum Dist. 19–48 (1984); vol. IV: Super Secundum Dist. 1–5 (1979); vol. V: Super Secundum Dist. 6–18 (1979); vol. VI: Super Secundum Dist. 24–44 (1980); vol. VII: Indices (1987), Spätmittelalter und Reformation Texte und Untersuchungen 6–12, (Berlin: Walter de Gruyter, 1979–1987).

"Notes on the Tübingen Edition of Gregory of Rimini," *Augustiniana* 29 (1979), 238–241.

"Notes on the Tübingen Edition of Gregory of Rimini II," *Augustiniana* 30 (1980), 46–57.

"Notes on the Tübingen Edition of Gregory of Rimini III: The Critical Edition of Gregory (d. 1358) promoted by the SFB 8 of the University of Tubingen advances steadily," *Augustiniana* 30 (1980), 251–253.

1981

Rita of Cascia, Augustinian Publications 66 (New York and Marylake, 1981).

1984

"A Round-Table Discussion of a Parisian OCist-Team and OESA-Team about Ad 1350," *Recherches de Théologie ancienne et médiévale* 51 (1984), 206–222.

1985

"Gregor v. Rimini (c. 1300–1358)," *Theologische Realenzyklopädie*, eds. Gerhard Krause und Gerhard Muller (Berlin: Walter de Gruyter, 1985), XIV, 181–184.

LIST OF CONTRIBUTORS

Prof. Dr. William J. Courtenay
University of Wisconsin-Madison
Department of History
4102 Humanities
Madison, Wisconsin 53706

Prof. Dr. Lothar Graf zu Dohna
Institut für Geschichte
Technische Hochschule Darmstadt
Im Schloss
6100 Darmstadt
Bundesrepublik Deutschland

Dr. Frank A. James, III
#35 Alan Bullock Close
Caroline Street
St. Clements
Oxford OX 4 1AU
United Kingdom

Prof. Dr. Heiko A. Oberman
Division for Late Medieval and Reformation Studies
The University of Arizona
Department of History
Tucson, Arizona 85721

Mr. Eric Leland Saak
Division for Late Medieval and Reformation Studies
The University of Arizona
Department of History
Tucson, Arizona 85721

Priv. Doz. Dr. Manfred Schulze
Tannenweg 4
7400 Tübingen
Bundesrepublik Deutschland

Dr. Walter Simon
Institut für Spätmittelalter

und Reformation
Universität Tübingen
Hölderlinstrasse 17
7400 Tübingen
Bundesrepublik Deutschland

Prof. Dr. David C. Steinmetz
The Divinity School
Duke University
Durham, North Carolina 27706

Dr. Richard Wetzel
Unterer Fauler Pelz 4
6900 Heidelberg
Bundesrepublik Deutschland

D. Dr. Adolar Zumkeller, O.S.A.
Steinbachtal 2a
Augustinus-Institut
8700 Würzburg
Bundesrepublik Deutschland

LIST OF TRANSLATORS

Caron Cadle: Manfred Schulze, "*Contra rectam rationem*: Gabriel Biel's Reading of Gregory of Rimini versus Gregory".

Robert L. Hiller and Timothy J. Wengert: Lothar Graf zu Dohna, "Staupitz and Luther: Continuity and Breakthrough at the Beginning of the Reformation".

Tracisius Rattler, O.S.A.: Adolar Zumkeller, O.S.A., "The Augustinian Theologian Konrad Treger (ca. 1480–1542) and his Disputation Theses of May 5, 1521".

Ruth Wenzel-Whittle and Anne E. Lincoln: Richard Wetzel, "*Staupitz Augustinianus*: An Account of the Reception of Augustine in his Tübingen Sermons".

INDEX OF NAMES AND PLACES

INDEX OF MODERN AUTHORS

INDEX OF LATIN TERMS

STUDIES IN MEDIEVAL
AND REFORMATION THOUGHT

EDITED BY HEIKO A. OBERMAN